CHURCH, KINGSHIP, AND LAY INVESTITURE

IN ENGLAND, 1089-1135

PRINCETON STUDIES IN HISTORY

VOLUME 10

CHURCH, KINGSHIP, AND LAY INVESTITURE IN ENGLAND 1089·1135

BY NORMAN F. CANTOR

1969
OCTAGON BOOKS
New York

Reprinted 1969
by special arrangement with Norman F. Cantor

OCTAGON BOOKS
A DIVISION OF FARRAR, STRAUS & GIROUX, INC.
19 Union Square West
New York, N. Y. 10003

LIBRARY OF CONGRESS CATALOG CARD NUMBER: 74-96174

Printed in U.S.A. by
TAYLOR PUBLISHING COMPANY
DALLAS, TEXAS

To Mindy

PREFACE

THIS book is intended as the first of three related studies in the history of church-state relations during the period of the Gregorian reforms and investiture controversies. The subsequent studies will be concerned with Lanfranc and Paschal II. The special justification for the present history of church-state relations in England from 1089 to 1135 is given in Chapter I, part 3.

The controversies of this period in England can be regarded as the consequence of the contrary and conflicting views on church-state relations held, on the one hand, by Archbishop Lanfranc and, on the other, by Pope Paschal II. Lanfranc played a great part in the creation of the Anglo-Norman church-state system; he is representative of the defenders of royal authority over the church, which the Gregorian reformers attacked. Paschal II made the most vigorous attempt at the complete overthrow of Lanfranc's system; he is representative of the most radical group among the Gregorian reformers. Archbishop Anselm of Canterbury, with whose troubled pontificate this work is largely concerned, in general stood somewhere between these two extremes. His episcopal career reveals the enormous tension produced by the conflict between the two opposing conceptions of church-state relations in the late eleventh and twelfth centuries.

This work was originally accepted by the Department of History, Princeton University, in April 1957, as a dissertation in partial fulfillment of the requirements for the degree of Doctor of Philosophy in history. Some changes have been made in preparing my dissertation for publication. I wish to thank the supervisor of my dissertation, Professor J. R. Strayer, for many helpful suggestions and criticisms and, in general, for his encouragement and assistance. I am also very

Preface

grateful to Professor T. E. Mommsen of Cornell University for his continued interest in my researches and his valuable advice on difficult problems, and to Mr. R. W. Southern of Balliol College, Oxford, who generously provided me with important information drawn from his thorough knowledge of the period. I regret that I have not been able to use Mr. Southern's forthcoming edition of the *Vita Anselmi*, which will be a valuable contribution to Anselm's biography. Professor E. H. Kantorowicz of the Institute for Advanced Study and Professor K. Weitzmann of Princeton University have also assisted me on some particular questions. I am, of course, alone responsible for any errors or shortcomings of any kind in this book.

I am grateful to the keepers of the manuscripts in the following libraries for allowing me to consult manuscripts in their collections and/or for their assistance in obtaining photographic reproductions of manuscripts: the British Museum; the Bodleian Library, Oxford; and the Rouen Public Library. The staff of the Princeton University Library has rendered me valuable assistance in obtaining printed books.

The greater part of the research for this book was accomplished while I was a Porter Ogden Jacobus Fellow in the Princeton Graduate School and a Rhodes Scholar at Oxford. I wish to thank the Princeton Graduate School and the Rhodes Trustees for this financial assistance.

Finally, I would like to express my gratitude to my parents for their encouragement and support. Without their assistance, I would not have been able to undertake the long preparatory training necessary for an academic career at the present time.

N.F.C.

Princeton, New Jersey
January 1958

CONTENTS

Contents

ILLUSTRATIONS

(following page 146)

Fig. 1. The Coronation of Henry I. Rubric (*Coronatio Hen. primi Regis*) and illumination preceding the earliest text of the "Anselm" coronation *ordo* in *Cotton Claudius A.III*, a twelfth-century manuscript.

British Museum, *MS. Cotton Claudius A.III*, fol. 19r. Reproduction courtesy the Trustees of the British Museum.

Fig. 2. The Coronation of St. Edmund the Martyr. Illumination from a twelfth-century manuscript in the Morgan Library.

Morgan Library, *M.736*, fol. 8v. Reproduced with permission of the Director of the Pierpont Morgan Library. Morgan Library, *Holford Collection* (1924), pl. III.

Fig. 3. The Anointing of Edward the Confessor. Coronation scene from a thirteenth-century manuscript of the *Vita Aedwardi Regis*.

Cambridge University Library, *MS. Ee 3.59*. Reproduced with permission of the Librarian, Cambridge University Library. M. R. James, *St. Edward* (1920), pl. 13.

Fig. 4. The Coronation of Henry I.

Fig. 5. The Coronation of Stephen.

Fig. 6. The Coronation of Edward II.

Figs. 4, 5, and 6 are three of the ten English coronation scenes in the thirteenth- and fourteenth-century St. Albans manuscript of the *Flores Historiarum*. Figs. 4 and 5 are thirteenth-century illuminations; Fig. 6 was added to the manuscript in the fourteenth century. The manuscript is now in Chetham's Library, Manchester.

A. Hollaender, "The Pictorial Work in the *Flores Historiarum*," *Bulletin of the John Rylands Library*, 28 (1944), 361ff., pls. IVa, IVb, VIb. Reproduced with permission from the *Bulletin of the John Rylands Library* with the approval of the Librarian of Chetham's Library, Manchester.

Illustrations

Fig. 7. The Coronation of Otto III. Ottonian illumination from the manuscript commonly known as the *Bamberg Apocalypse*.

Bamberg Staatliche Bibliothek, *MS. 140*, fol. 59v. Reproduced with permission of the Librarian, Bamberg Staatliche Bibliothek. H. Wölfflin, *Die Bamberger Apokalypse* (1921), pl. 51.

Fig. 8. The Coronation of Henry I. Scene from a fourteenth-century illustrated chronicle in the Beatty Collection.

E. G. Millar, *The Library of A. Chester Beatty, A Descriptive Catalogue of the Western Manuscripts*, II (1930), pl. CLIIb. Reproduced with permission of the Librarian, Chester Beatty Library, Dublin.

AO   F. S. Schmitt, ed., *S. Anselmi Opera Omnia*, 5 vols. (1946-1951)

A-S Chron. E.   Recension E (Peterborough) of the Anglo-Saxon Chronicle. Text in C. Plummer and J. Earle, eds., *Two of the Saxon Chronicles Parallel*, 2 vols. (1892, 1899). Translation in D. C. Douglas, *English Historical Documents*, II (1953), 110ff.

Davis, *Reg.*   H.W.C. Davis, *Regesta Regum Anglo-Normannorum*, I (1913)

Farrer, "Itinerary"   W. Farrer, "An Outline Itinerary of King Henry the First," *EHR*, xxxiv (1919), 303-382, 505-579

Florence of Worcester, *Chronicle*   B. Thorpe, ed., *Florentii Wigorniensis Monachi Chronicon*, 2 vols. (1848-1849)

GP   N.E.S.A. Hamilton, ed., *Willelmi Malmsesbiriensis Monachi de Gestis Pontificum Anglorum Libri Quinque* (RS, 1870)

GR   W. Stubbs, ed., *Willelmi Malmesbiriensis Monachi De Gestis Regum Anglorum* (RS, 1889)

HC   Hugh the Cantor's *History of the Four Archbishops of York*, in J. Raine, ed., *Historians of the Church of York*, II (RS, 1886)

Henry of Huntingdon, *Hist. Angl.* and *De Contemptu*   T. Arnold, ed., *Historia Anglorum* and *De Contemptu Mundi* (RS, 1879)

HF   M. Bouquet, ed., *Recueil des Historiens des Gaules et de la France*, 24 vols. (1840-1904)

HN   M. Rule, ed., *Eadmeri Historia Novorum in Anglia* (RS, 1884)

J-L   P. Jaffe, S. Lowenfeld, et al., eds., *Regesta Pontificum Romanorum*, I (1885)

Abbreviations

Johnson, *Reg.*   C. Johnson and H. Cronne, *Regesta Regum Anglo-Normannorum*, II (1956)

JW   J.R.H. Weaver, ed., *The Chronicle of John of Worcester* (1908)

Lib. de Lite   MGH, *Libelli de Lite Imperatorum et Pontificum*, 3 vols. (1892-1897)

Liebermann, *Gesetze*   F. Liebermann, ed., *Die Gesetze der Angelsachsen*, 3 vols. (1903-1916)

OV   A. le Prevost, ed., *Orderici Vitalis Historiae Ecclesiasticae Libri Tredecim*, 5 vols. (1840-1855)

PU   W. Holtzmann, ed., *Papsturkunden in England*, in *Abh. d. Ges. d. Wiss. zu Göttingen, Phil.-Hist. Kl.*, I: 1930-1931; II: 1935; III: 1952

Raine, *Docts.*   Documents relating to the Church of York, in J. Raine, *Historians of the Church of York*, III

Robertson, *Becket*   J. C. Robertson, ed., *Materials for the History of Thomas Becket*, 5 vols. (*RS*, 1875-1885)

Round, *CDF*   J. H. Round, ed., *Calendar of Documents Preserved in France*, I (1889)

RS   Rolls Series (*Rerum Britannicarum Medii Aevi Scriptores.* London: 1858-1896)

Sym. Durham, *HDE*   Symeon of Durham, *Historia Dunelmensis Ecclesiae*, in T. Arnold, ed., *Symeonis Monachi Opera Omnia*, 2 vols. (RS, 1882)

Tillmann, *Legaten*   H. Tillmann, *Die päpstlichen Legaten in England* (1926)

CHURCH, KINGSHIP, AND LAY INVESTITURE

IN ENGLAND, 1089-1135

CHAPTER I

INTRODUCTION: THE GREGORIAN REFORMS AND THE NORMAN CHURCH-STATE SYSTEM

I. HISTORIOGRAPHY OF THE GREGORIAN REFORMS

VERY few periods of medieval history have been studied as intensively and by such a large group of eminent scholars as the age of the Gregorian reforms and the investiture controversy—the last three or four decades of the eleventh century and the first two or three decades of the twelfth century. It has long been recognized that the investiture controversy was the fundamental turning-point in medieval German history, and the exhaustive history of the reigns of Henry IV and Henry V by G. Meyer von Knonau, completed in 1909,[1] provide a very firm foundation for the study of the investiture controversy in Germany. But it is only in this century and actually within the last thirty years that the significance of the investiture controversy in the history of medieval civilization has begun to be perceived.

The general interpretation of the Gregorian reform movement a half century ago was still very inadequate and was based upon a very poor understanding of the fundamental issues involved in the investiture controversy. The Gregorian reform movement was still regarded as a product of the Cluniac attempt to reform the monastic order and no clear distinction was drawn between the ideals of the Cluniac and Gregorian reformers.[2] In the last decade of the nineteenth

[1] G. Meyer von Knonau, *Jahrbücher des Deutschen Reiches unter Heinrich IV und Heinrich V*, 7 vols. (1890-1909).
[2] See, for example, Thatcher and McNeal, *A Source Book of Medieval History* (1914), 133-14. The account of the investiture controversy in this American textbook reflects the general state of scholarship on the subject a half-century ago.

I. Introduction

century, however, the leading authority on the history of Cluny, E. Sackur, sharply distinguished the aims of the monastic order from the program of the Gregorian reformers.[3] His conclusion indicated that the prevailing interpretation of the investiture controversy was inadequate and that a new investigation of the Gregorian reformers was needed. The publication of the theoretical literature of the investiture controversy by the *Monumenta Germaniae* made this possible.[4]

The fundamental study of the Gregorian reformers, to which all subsequent research must be related, was published by A. Fliche in 1924.[5] His three-volume study of the Gregorian reforms placed our knowledge of the investiture controversy on a sound scholarly basis for the first time. Fliche rejected the naive view that the Gregorians were simply the successors of the Cluniacs. On the other hand, he insisted that Gregory VII was not an originator of new ideas. Hildebrand was rather an ecclesiastical statesman who attempted to put into practice doctrines well known in the early Middle Ages. Gelasius, Gregory I, and Nicholas I were the sources of the Gregorian view of church-state relations. The Cluniacs prepared the way by arousing concern for the moral reform of the church. Even in his own circle Gregory VII was not the leading theorist; he derived all his doctrines from Cardinal Humbert. In Fliche's opinion, Gregory VII wanted to achieve the moral reform of the clergy, but he had no intention of starting a war between the German emperor and the papacy. He was driven to this by the intransigence of Henry IV.

As soon as Fliche's work appeared, it was attacked by E. Caspar, the great historian of the papacy in the early Middle

[3] E. Sackur, *Die Cluniacenser*, II (1894), 445, 464-65.

[4] *MGH, Libelli de Lite Imperatorum et Pontificum*, 3 vols. (1892-1897). Several of the tracts published in this collection have not as yet been carefully studied.

[5] A. Fliche, *La Réforme Grégorienne* (1924), 3 vols., esp. I, 59-60, 366-68, 383-88; II, 108, 309-16, 409-13.

4

Ages.[6] Caspar contended that the doctrines of the Gregorian reformers were revolutionary in their implication. As for Gregory VII, his doctrines were not derivative; rather he was "the great originator who stood quite alone." The debate between these two interpretations, first presented by Fliche and Caspar, continues to the present day.

The most eloquent presentation of the view that the Gregorians were revolutionaries is contained in the study of Gregorian ideas published by G. Tellenbach in 1935.[7] Tellenbach's work is an excellent example of the modern German school of *Ideengeschichte*, a tendency to adopt highly dialectical interpretation and to study ideas in and for themselves, apart from their immediate practical consequences. Tellenbach sharply distinguished the Cluniacs and the Gregorians, pointing out that the former were not interested in the condition of the church outside the monastery. He regarded the investiture controversy as the great turning-point in medieval civilization. The Gregorians were revolutionaries who consciously set out to destroy the early medieval system of church-state relations and to set up a new "right order in the world."

The interpretation of the Gregorians as revolutionaries was carried to rather extreme lengths by the English historian Z. N. Brooke.[8] He argued that even the term investiture controversy was not adequate as a definition of the real issues involved in the dispute between Gregory VII and the German emperor. The abolition of lay investiture was the only issue upon which compromise could be reached. There could be no compromise on the fundamental conflicts between opposed conceptions of church-state relations.

Such extreme positions have led to a rebuttal against the

[6] E. Caspar, "Gregor VII in seinen Briefen," *Historische Zeitschrift*, 130 (1924), 11-12, 22-30.
[7] G. Tellenbach, *Libertas* (1935), trans. R. F. Bennett, *Church, State, and Christian Society at the Time of the Investiture Contest* (1940), esp. 81-85, 95-97, 137-38, 147-48, 161-68.
[8] Z. N. Brooke, "Lay Investiture and Its Relation to the Conflict of Empire and Papacy," *Proc. Br. Acad.*, XXV (1939), 217-19, 225-28, 239-44.

I. Introduction

view of the Gregorians as revolutionaries. This rebuttal has followed two lines. In the first place, the history of canon law in the eleventh century by P. Fournier and G. le Bras[9] has revealed that the Gregorian reformers were inspired by, and were dependent on, doctrines found in the early medieval law of the church. This canon law was being collected, edited, and studied intensively in the eleventh century. Gregory VII encouraged the work of the canon lawyers. Secondly, a recent and very technical survey of early medieval political thought by W. Ullmann appears to return to Fliche's interpretation.[10] The Gregorian doctrines were not revolutionary and not a departure from early medieval political tradition. Rather Gregorian doctrine is derived from the hierocratic tradition, a commonplace of western political thought for several centuries before the investiture controversy.

2. THE INVESTITURE CONTROVERSY AS A WORLD-REVOLUTION

My own interpretation of the investiture controversy is very much indebted to the work of Tellenbach, but it gives even more universal significance to the intellectual conflicts of the period.

It has been characteristic of the history of the West that its destiny has been shaped by four world-revolutions in which previous tendencies culminated and from which new ideas and systems emerged. By a world-revolution I mean a widespread and thoroughgoing revolution in world-view, the emergence of a new ideology which rejects the results of several centuries of development, organized into the prevailing system, and calls for a new right order in the world. In modern history these world-revolutions are well known—the Protestant Revolution of the sixteenth century, the liberal

[9] P. Fournier and G. le Bras, *Histoire des Collections canoniques en Occident* (1931), II, 4-15.
[10] W. Ullmann, *Growth of Papal Government in the Middle Ages* (1955), 262-63, 271, 299-309.

6

2. The Controversy as World-Revolution

revolution of the eighteenth century, the Communist revolution of the twentieth. The investiture controversy constitutes the first of the great world-revolutions of western history, and its course follows the same pattern as the well-known revolutions of modern times.

Each of the world-revolutions has begun with some just complaint about moral wrongs in the prevailing political, social, or religious system. In the case of the investiture controversy the leaders of the revolution, who have been called the Gregorian reformers, complained about the domination of the church by laymen and the involvement of the church in feudal obligations. This system had led to severe abuses, especially that of simony, which came to be defined in its most general sense as the interference of laymen with the right ordering of church offices and sacraments. In their condemnation of simony as heresy, the Gregorians had a perfectly valid complaint.

It has been characteristic of all the world-revolutions, however, that while each has begun by complaining about abuses in the prevailing world order, the ultimate aim of the revolutionary ideologists has been not the reform of the prevailing system, but rather its abolition and replacement by a new order. In the case of the investiture controversy, complete freedom of the church from control by the state, the negation of the sacramental character of kingship, and the domination of the papacy over secular rulers, constituted the ideal new order.

As in the case of all other world-revolutions, the ideology of the Gregorians called forth violent opposition on the part of both vested interests and sincere theoretical defenders of the old order. After many acrimonious disputes and a flood of propaganda literature, bitter and protracted warfare resulted. The polarization of educated society into revolutionary and conservative left a large group of uncommitted moderates, including some of the best minds of the age, who could see right and wrong on both sides.

7

I. Introduction

As in the case of all other world-revolutions, the ideologists of the investiture controversy were only partially successful in creating the new order. They succeeded in destroying the old system, but the new world was not the revolutionary utopia. Rather it was a reconstruction of the political and religious system which took into account both old and new elements and left room for the human limitations of greed and power. The church gained a large measure of freedom from secular control, and there was a noticeable improvement in the moral and intellectual level of the clergy. But the church itself, from the time of the investiture controversy, became more and more interested in secular affairs, and the papacy of the high Middle Ages competed successfully for wealth and power with kings and emperors. The church itself became a great super-state governed by the papal administration.

As in the case of all other world-revolutions, the ideologists during the investiture controversy were themselves united only upon the most immediate and more limited aims of the revolution. As the revolution proceeded, the Gregorians divided into a moderate and a radical wing, each led by eminent cardinals. The radicals were headed by Humbert and Hildebrand, the moderates by Peter Damiani. As in the modern world-revolutions, the radicals were for a short period in control of the Gregorian reform movement, a period which was long enough to destroy the old order. But as the conservatives and moderates of various complexions perceived at last the real aim of the radicals and their reckless disregard for consequences, the radicals lost their leadership and were unable to realize their utopian ideals.

As in the modern world-revolutions, the radicals lost their leadership not to the moderates of their own group, whom they had earlier swept aside, but rather to the politicians, the practical statesmen, who called a halt to revolution and tried to reconstruct from the shattered pieces of the old system and the achievements of the revolution a new and workable synthesis which would again make progress possible. This tend-

8

ency is already evident during the pontificate of Urban II in the last decade of the eleventh century, and it became dominant in the papacy during the 1120's.

Like all world-revolutions, the investiture controversy never reached a final and complete solution. New ideas in a new generation made former issues less meaningful and the men of the new generation turned to other interests and new problems. Just as Voltaire and Hume could not understand why the men of the sixteenth and seventeenth centuries should have fought over abstruse theological principles, so already in the 1130's a canon of York Cathedral could not understand why Anselm and Henry I should have quarrelled over lay investiture two decades before.[11]

The age of the investiture controversy may rightly be regarded as the turning-point in medieval civilization. It was the fulfillment of the early Middle Ages because in it the acceptance of the Christian religion by the Germanic peoples reached its final and decisive stage. On the other hand, the greater part of the religious and political system of the high Middle Ages emerged out of the events and ideas of the investiture controversy.

3. THE STUDY OF THE GREGORIAN REFORMS IN ENGLAND

THE history of the Gregorian reform movement and of the investiture controversy in England has not yet found its historian. The lack of interest which historians in England have shown towards this subject is indicated by the noticeable absence of any English contribution to the *Studi Gregoriani* series which has now reached four large volumes. It is this lacuna in our knowledge of the Gregorian reforms and the investiture controversy in England which justifies this book.

After a half century, the study of church-state relations in Anglo-Norman England and in Normandy by H. Böhmer

[11] *HC*, 110-11.

9

I. Introduction

remains the only substantial work in the field.[12] Z. N. Brooke has added to our knowledge of canon law of the period,[13] D. Knowles has written the definitive history of the monastic order,[14] and R. W. Southern and C.N.L. Brooke have contributed some important articles on the English church in the period.[15] Otherwise, our knowledge of church-state relations in Anglo-Norman England has not been enhanced since Böhmer's work.

Little can be added to Böhmer's study of church and state in Normandy, because the paucity of sources on the Norman secular clergy has not been altered in the last fifty years. As regards England, however, we have new material, such as the *Regesta* of the Anglo-Norman kings and W. Holtzmann's *Papsturkunden*, and better editions of sources available than in Böhmer's day, such as F. Schmitt's edition of Anselm's letters. Even more important, the historian of the investiture controversy in England can now draw on a much more extensive knowledge of the political history and institutions of the period and upon a much deeper understanding of the Gregorian reforms. Böhmer's work will always be very useful, although it has a fundamental weakness. It covers the period from 1066 to 1154 in too short a space, with the result that his book provides an account of church-state relations which is excessively condensed and which lacks a detailed and coherent narrative. He tried to give us a general picture of the English and Norman Churches at various times between 1066 and 1154. While these analyses are very valuable, the investiture controversy itself is dismissed in five pages.

This book is not an attempt at a new edition of Böhmer. Rather it aims to provide a comprehensive history of the controversies over church-state relations in England during the

---

[12] H. Böhmer, *Kirche und Staat in England und in der Normandie im XI. und XII. Jahrhundert* (1899).

[13] Z. N. Brooke, *The English Church and the Papacy* (1931), esp. appendices.

[14] D. Knowles, *The Monastic Order in England* (1940).

[15] See below, Select Bibliography, *s.n.*

3. Study of the Reforms in England

crucial period from the death of Lanfranc in 1089 to the end of the reign of Henry I in 1135. It is based upon an exhaustive study of the sources, including manuscripts where necessary, and employs modern works only in a supplementary way or in order to relate events in England to the history of the Gregorian reforms and the investiture controversy on the Continent.

The proper perspective for the history of church-state relations after the death of Lanfranc can perhaps only be gained fully when we have a definitive study of the Anglo-Norman church during the reign of William the Conqueror. I have gathered part of the material necessary for such a study. An account of the origins of the Norman dukes' ecclesiastical policy, which was carried to England after 1066, is given below in the following section of this chapter.

A definitive study of the Anglo-Norman church under William I would have to focus on the work and thought of the Italian-Norman theologian and canonist, Archbishop Lanfranc, who still remains for us a shadowy though central figure in the life of northern Europe in the eleventh century. In studying Lanfranc's ecclesiastical policy we are at the present time hampered by a very inadequate edition of his letters and other writings. As a preface to the history of church-state relations in England during Anselm's episcopate, the following surveys of the establishment of ducal authority over the Norman Church and the consequent church-state system created in England by William I and Lanfranc, will suffice.[16]

[16] There is no study of the ecclesiastical policy of the Norman dukes but there are valuable discussions of it in the more general works of H. Prentout, C. H. Haskins, J. Steenstrup and D. C. Douglas. The following are important for this subject: W. Schultze, "Gerhard von Brogn," *Forsch. z. deutsch. Gesch.*, XXV (1885); J. Laporte, "Les origines du monachisme dans la province du Rouen," *Revue Mabillon*, XXXI (1941); W. Williams, "William of Dijon," *Downside Review*, 52 (1934); G. Mollat, "Le droit de patronage en Normandie," *Rev. d'hist. eccles.*, XXXIII (1937); F. Soudet, "Les seigneurs patrons des églises normandes au moyen âge," *Travaux de la semaine du droit normand tenue à . . . 1923* (1925); H. Prentout, "La trève de Dieu en Normandie," *Mémoires de l'Académie na-*

I. Introduction

4. THE ORIGINS OF THE NORMAN CHURCH-STATE SYSTEM

THE Scandinavian people who settled in Neustria early in the tenth century and accepted the Christian faith retained into the twelfth century the fierce and turbulent characteristics of their race. In a memorable passage, Orderic Vital described the Normans of his day as still bearing the impress of their fierce Scandinavian heritage.[17] The bringing of these Scandinavians in Neustria under the impress of Latin Christianity was accomplished only against the resistance of an alien heathen culture. The Scandinavian affinities of the Normans remained at first very strong and their heathen attachments for long lingered just below the surface.[18]

In relations between church and state, the Duke Rollo and his successors adopted the same view that their northern kinsmen were to take when they were converted to Christianity in the following century. The Christian Norwegian kings of the eleventh century maintained complete control over the church in their territory. Only in the middle of the twelfth century, with the coming of the reforming papal legate Cardinal Nicholas Brekespear to Norway, did there appear an effective threat to this control.[19]

This attitude towards the church, common to the Scandinavian world, was strongly influenced by the position of the heathen Scandinavian kings. These kings were regarded as the descendants of divine ancestors, "the brand of Woden's own race."[20] Hence the king was superior to all religious authori-

---

tionale . . . de Caen, VI (1931); E. Porée, Histoire de l'Abbaye de Bec (1901); J. F. Lemarignier, Étude sur les privilèges d'exemption et de juridiction ecclésiastique des abbayes normandes depuis les origines jusqu'en 1140 (1937).

[17] OV, III, 474.

[18] Cf. D. C. Douglas, "The Rise of Normandy," PBA, 33 (1947), 111.

[19] A. O. Johnsen, "Nicolaus Brekespear and the Norwegian Church Province, 1153," The Norseman, XI, no. 4 (1953), 1ff., a summary of the author's detailed study of Brekespear's legateship in Norway (Oslo, 1945).

[20] G. Vigfusson and F. York Powell, eds., Corpus Poeticum Boreale (1883), II, 479.

ties. He was the high priest and the mediator between the gods and men, "the warden of the holy altar, the prophet of the hallowed twigs of divination."[21] This heathen Scandinavian conception of monarchy as superior to the priesthood was carried over into the system of church-state relations in Christian Norway and Normandy.

It frequently occurred in the Middle Ages that the best theoretical defense of a political system was expounded when that system had become archaic and was under attack from novel conceptions and changed attitudes. It will be seen that the best exposition of the early medieval idea of theocratic monarchy occurs in the Anonymous of York tracts, when this idea of kingship was already on the wane. Similarly, the clearest exposition of the Scandinavian view of church-state relations, applicable to both Normandy and Norway, is to be found in the *Address against the Bishops*, published in 1199 by King Sverre as a defense of the old order against the reforming party in the Norwegian episcopate.[22]

Although the author of the *Address*, who was probably a royal clerk, frequently appeals for support to Gratian's *Decretum*, the principles and practices advocated in the tractate come from an earlier age.[23] The right and duty of a divinely-appointed king to govern the holy church is the cardinal doctrine advocated in the *Address*:

. . . The salvation of a man's soul is at stake when he does not observe complete loyalty, kingly worship, and a right obedience; for kingly rule is created by God's command, and not after man's ordinance, and no man obtains kingly rule except by divine dispensation. . . . Duty binds a King to answer to God himself, and to render an account of his protection and care of Holy Church

---

[21] *Ibid.*, 477, 479.

[22] *En Tale mod Biskopperne*, ed. G. Storm (1885). English transl. by J. Shepton under the title *Anecdota Sverreri*, in *The Saga of King Sverri of Norway* (1899), 241ff. For King Sverre's conflict with the reform party in the Norwegian Church, see G. M. Gathorne-Hardy, *A Royal Impostor. King Sverre of Norway* (1956), ch. 19.

[23] L. M. Larson, *The King's Mirror* (1917), 39, 43.

I. Introduction

. . . and duty binds a minister of Holy Church to be obedient to the King, to afford him hearty worship and guileless loyalty.[24]

The author of the *Address* then goes on to defend lay control over the church on a lower level, the right of "knights and guardsmen, and even yeomen, [to] have oversight in Holy Church if they are the patrons of churches."[25] He concludes with the theme that the king's word is final in ecclesiastical appointments:

We are well informed touching the custom existing of old times in this land, when kings appointed to churches of their own will whomsoever they thought good to appoint. So also in choosing bishops and abbots they chose whomsoever they thought fit, and appointed them to what diocese they would, without any guidance from the clergy. . . . This custom existed from the introduction of Christianity.[26]

These views on church and kingship presented in the *Address* reflect the actual relations between the king and higher clergy not only in Norway but also in Denmark and Sweden during the earlier period of Scandinavian Christianity.[27] As might be expected, the *Address* also serves as an excellent summary of the ecclesiastical policy of the Norman dukes as it was developed in the tenth and early eleventh centuries.

The life of Rollo and the reigns of other tenth-century Norman dukes are obscure in many aspects. This obscurity is in part caused by the lack of a comprehensive and definitive edition of tenth-century ducal charters. An intensive study of archaeological and place-name evidence may also yet throw light on the history of tenth-century Normandy. But the study of the period is hampered by the unreliability of the chief narrative source, which consists of a long panegyric on Rollo and his successors to the death of Richard I (996).[28] This

---

[24] *Address*, Shepton transl., 251. [25] *Loc.cit.* [26] *Ibid.*, 254-55.
[27] See the summary of recent Scandinavian scholarship in I. Nylander, *Das kirchliche Benefizialwesen Schwedens während des Mittelalters* (1953), 40, 45, 46, for church-state relations in Denmark and Sweden.
[28] *De Moribus et Actis Primorum Normanniae Ducum*, ed. J. Lair (1865). The best critical study is by H. Prentout, *Études Critiques sur Dudo* (1916).

work was produced at the Norman court, at the request of Duke Richard II[29] in the second or third decade of the eleventh century by Dudo, formerly dean of St. Quentin in Vermandois. While genuine oral tradition was undoubtedly available to him, Dudo's main concern was to gain the gratitude of his patron by proclaiming the glory of the ducal dynasty.[30] As a result, on several points, it is very difficult and perhaps impossible to separate fact from fiction in his narrative.

If Dudo's work thus offers immense difficulties, it nevertheless allows as clear, although less detailed, an insight into the Norman mind of the tenth and early eleventh centuries as Gregory of Tours' history into Merovingian thought. Dudo's *De Moribus et Actis Primorum Normanniae Ducum* reveals the theoretical assumption and historical myths which guided the policy of the Norman dukes towards the church down to and including the reign of Richard II, which ended in 1026.

Dudo makes Rollo into a new Clovis. His work belongs to the same genre of Christian apologetics for rulers newly converted to Christianity as Gregory Tours' *History of the Franks* and the prototype of this kind of literary work, Eusebius' *Life of Constantine*.[31] Since the eleventh-century Norman dukes believed that they had been destined from the first to rule the church in their land, Dudo related that Rollo was divinely inspired from the beginning of his transmarine conquests. He described a dream which came to Rollo while he was still in Denmark (*Dacis*) in which it was prophesied that the as yet heathen Rollo would be the protector of the French church. Rollo was supposedly a friend of Alsten (Athelstan?) the very Christian King of the English, and on very good terms with Archbishop Franco of Rouen, who served as the intermediary between the leader of the Normans and Charles the Simple. From the very beginning of his

---

[29] *De Moribus,* 119.

[30] See, e.g., *De Moribus,* 122, 165, 169, 180, 210, 215, 221, 234, 238, 242, 245.

[31] Cf. L. Halphen, "Grégoire de Tours, historien de Clovis," *Mélanges Ferdinand Lot* (1925), 235-44.

conquest, Rollo was thus the friend of the metropolitan of Neustria. His depredations and ruinations of churches were explained away by Dudo as the result of irritation caused by misfortune and the deaths of his soldiers. In Dudo's account, Rollo was soon baptised by Archbishop Franco and emerges immediately as a model Christian prince. He became the patron of many churches and repaired the Christian places of worship which the heathens, that is his own army, had destroyed. He governed his land in the peace which God had given him and died as a pious Christian.[32]

Dudo's account of Rollo's life was undoubtedly conditioned by a desire to glorify the founder of his patron's dynasty. Even William of Jumièges, another Norman court historian writing a half-century later, was conscious of Dudo's shortcomings as an historian.[33] But it does seem probable that after his baptism Rollo, like Clovis, became a firm supporter of the church.[34]

The acceptance of Latin Christianity by the Scandinavian conquerors of Neustria was, of course, only superficial, and, after the murder of Duke William Long-Sword in 942, there was a reaction to heathenism.[35] It was not until the Treaty of Gisors of 965 between Lothar and Richard I finally brought an end to a half-century of confused conflicts in Neustria and inaugurated thirty years of peace, which Dudo in his grandiose manner compared to the best years of the Roman Empire,[36] that an attempt at re-establishment of the church in Normandy could be made.[37] In these three decades, Richard I put into

[32] *De Moribus*, chs. 5, 8, 17, 18, 19, 20, 22.

[33] *Gesta Normannorum Ducum*, ed. J. Marx (*Soc. Hist. Norm.*, 1914), bk. II, in which Rollo is depicted simply as a Viking chief and Dudo's account is, by implication, criticized.

[34] Douglas, *op.cit.*, 111; cf., for a different view, J.C.H.R. Steenstrup, *Normandiets Historie under de syv fyrste Hertuger 911-1066* (1925), § 24.

[35] Flodard, *Annales*, ed. P. Lauer (1905), 63.

[36] *De Moribus*, 128.

[37] Douglas, *op.cit.*, 112; Prentout, *Dudo*, 389; Steenstrup, *Hertuger*, 148.

practice the view of church-state relations which is adumbrated in Dudo's history.

The flourishing centers of monastic life which had been established in the province of Rouen between the end of the fourth and the end of the ninth centuries[38] had suffered severely, and perhaps had been totally obliterated, by the Scandinavian invasions of the tenth century.[39] The episcopate had also felt the effects of the invasions. There are many gaps in the list of tenth-century bishops in the province of Rouen, and five successive bishops of Coutances were forced to absent themselves from their sees and to take up residence in Rouen.[40]

The monastic life revived first, and it always remained the foundation of religious fervor and church reform in Normandy. The reasons for this development are not hard to perceive. In the reformed monasteries of Lorraine and Flanders and in the eremetic tendencies of north Italian religious life lay the whole reforming zeal of the period, while the rest of the church, including the papacy, remained under the domination of various lay authorities.[41] The history of Norman monasticism in the tenth and eleventh centuries represents, from one point of view, the effect on a peripheral but remarkably receptive outpost of Latin Christian civilization, of influences emanating from the religious and cultural center of the civilization in Lorraine, Burgundy, and especially in northern Italy.[42]

The success of the Norman monastic revival must, however, be primarily attributed to the support accorded the mon-

[38] See the excellent study by J. Laporte, "Les origines du monachisme dans la province du Rouen," *Revue Mabillon*, 31 (1941), pts. 1 & 2.

[39] H. Prentout, *Essai sur les origines et la fondation du Duché de Normandie* (1911), 197-98; Laporte, "Origines," pt. 3.

[40] *Gallia Christiana*, XI, coll. 474, 679, 765; instr. col. 217.

[41] The best survey of the church in the tenth century is E. Ammann and A. Dumas, *L'Église au pouvoir des laïques (888-1057)* (1940).

[42] On the cultural relations between northern Italy and northern France, F. Novati, "Les rapports de l'Italie et de la France au XIᵉ siècle," *Comptes rendus . . . 1910, Académie des Inscriptions et Belles-Lettres*, 169ff., is of some value for the eleventh century, but no study has been made for the tenth century.

I. Introduction

asteries by ducal authority. It is probable that confirmation of the possessions of St. Ouen de Rouen and St. Denis were obtained from Rollo on the occasion of his baptism.[43] William Long-Sword assisted in the restoration of monastic life at Jumièges. To some of the original community who returned to their monasteries after the ending of the Scandinavian invasion, he added a dozen others from the Abbey of St. Cyprian in Poitou.[44] But it was during the last three decades of the reign of Richard I—that is, c.960-996—that the monastic revival in Normandy really began and, at the same time, that the pattern of church-state relations in Normandy came to be established.

During the minority of Richard I the Carolingian King Louis IV d'Outremer attempted to intervene in the affairs of the duchy. In retaliation the Normans found it expedient to align themselves with the Capetian family. In 987 Richard I energetically supported the election of Hugh Capet. During the same reign, the Normans became involved in the complex of feudal relations existing between the Seine and Loire and came to play an important part in the political development of northern France. Richard had already intervened in Flanders in 966.[45] The Norman Duke's participation in affairs outside the duchy undoubtedly abetted the establishment of relations between the Norman Church and French and Flemish centers of church reform.

During the last two decades of the tenth century Normandy was also shaken out of its economic isolation. From 980 to about 1030 Rouen was a prosperous international port, a cosmopolitan city where Greek, Italian, English, Scandinavian, and French merchants engaged in trade.[46] Normandy's re-

[43] Douglas, *op.cit.*, 111.

[44] *De Moribus*, 200-01; *Hist. Invent. S. Wulfranni*, ed. d'Achery, *Spicilegium* (1723), II, 285. The *Lament* for Duke William (ed. J. Lair, 1893, 61-2) represents the Duke wishing to enter the Jumièges community. See further Prentout, *Dudo*, 330-33; Laporte, "Origines," 50.

[45] Prentout, *Dudo*, 367-71, 392-95; Steenstrup, *Hertuger*, §§36, 40, 41, 43, 45, 48, 49.

[46] L. Musset, in *RHDFE*, 4th ser., XXXI (1953), 321.

ligious isolation ended in the same period as these important political and economic changes occurred.

The first external impact on the moribund Norman Church came from Flanders. St. Gerard of Broigne was one of the leading church reformers of the tenth century. He belonged to a prominent Lorraine family, was educated at St. Denis and was in the forefront of the monastic revival, first in Lorraine and later in Flanders.[47] It is probable that he came to Normandy early in Richard I's reign in an attempt to recover the relics of St. Wandrille, and that he established contact with the ducal court which opened the way for later developments.[48] From Ghent in 960, Gerard's disciple Mainard, who was perhaps a Norman by birth, entered Normandy and with ducal support succeeded in reestablishing a community at Fontanelle.[49] Richard I seems to have desired a widespread monastic revival in his duchy.[50] At the same time, he saw how Mainard could be used to advance Norman influence in Brittany.[51] Hence in 961 he sent Mainard to replace the canons at Mont St. Michel.[52]

Within the duchy Richard concentrated his reform efforts on Fécamp, where he had been born and brought up.[53] Like William Long-Sword, he regarded Fécamp as a favorite place of residence and wished to make it a great religious center for Normandy.[54] The consecration in 990 of a new church

[47] On St. Gerard, see W. Schultze, "Gerhard von Brogn," *Forsch. z. deutsch. Gesch.*, xxv (1885); K. Hauck, *Kirchengeschichte Deutschlands*, 4th ed. (1906), III, 346-52.

[48] *Inv. S. Wulfranni*, 285. The reliability of this mid-eleventh-century source is rejected by Sackur, *Cluniacenser*, I, 135, and F. Lot, *Études Critiques sur . . . St. Wandrille* (1913), xliii, but is accepted by Laporte, "Origines," 51. The author of the *Inv. S. Wulfranni* could have relied on an earlier account, and there appears to be no reason for rejecting this source.

[49] *Inv. S. Wulfranni*, 285-87; Lot, *St. Wandrille*, xliii-xliv; Laporte, "Origines," 51.

[50] Sackur, *Cluniacenser*, II, 44.   [51] Prentout, *Dudo*, 403.

[52] *Inv. S. Wulfranni*, ch. VI.

[53] *De Moribus*, 218.

[54] J. F. Lemarignier, *Étude sur les privileges d'exemption* . . . (1937), 30.

at the Fécamp Abbey, which had been built at the Duke's direction,[55] symbolized the close association of the Norman monastic revival with the ducal family. Fécamp became the St. Denis of the Norman dukes. Richard I had established the pattern of church-state relations for his successor. The Duke's word had become supreme even in the inner life of the Norman Church.[56] With sincere piety, all the Norman dukes founded and patronized great monastic houses which assured for them earthly glory and eternal salvation and at the same time secured for themselves control over the most vital part of the Norman Church, the regular clergy.

Because of his admiration for Cluny and because lay patronage of great religious foundations was perfectly acceptable in the Cluniac view of church-state relations, Richard I appealed to Abbot St. Majolus of Cluny for monks to replace the canons at Fécamp. But because Duke and Abbot could not agree on the concession of pannage to Fécamp and perhaps also because Normandy was still regarded as too distant and too backward for Cluniac endeavors, St. Majolus refused the Duke's request.[57]

The court historian William of Jumièges celebrated the piety of Richard II (996-1026),[58] and with good reason. His benefactions to monasteries within and outside the duchy were numerous[59] and there is even a contemporary story that the monasteries of Mount Sinai sent monks to Rouen to appeal to the Duke's generosity.[60] As in the reign of Richard I, the po-

---

[55] *De Moribus*, 291; Lemarignier, *Étude*, 52, n. 30.

[56] *De Moribus*, 262: ". . . Gubernacula ecclesiasticae dispensationis, corde serenissimo, licet laicali ordine adornabat. *Ibid.*, 295: Sustinuit namque maledictiones pro fide catholica, pro regni tutela, pro paganorum attritione severissima, pro monachorum negligentium regulam contritione sanctissima, pro canonicorum intea se dissidentium concordia, pro laicorum pace intermissa."

[57] *Anon. Fiscan.*, MPL 151, coll. 718-19; *Vita S. Maoli, Acta Sanct.*, v, 776.

[58] *Gesta Ducum*, 73.

[59] H. Prentout, *Richard II*[e] (1929), 88; Laporte, "Origines," 53-54.

[60] *Analecta Bolland*, XXII, 423ff.; pointed out by Steenstrup, *Hertuger*, 174, n. 3.

4. The Norman Church-State System

litical ambitions of the Normans brought them outside their duchy and into regions where they could know at first hand the work of the new reformed monastic centers. The alliance of the Norman dukes with the Capetian family continued under Richard II. The Duke and a large contingent of Normans supported Robert the Pious in the French King's campaign in Burgundy in 1003-1005.[61] Richard was with the King at the sieges of Auxerre and Avellon, in the very heart of the Cluny country.[62] It is even possible that Richard at this time met Odilo, the great Abbot of Cluny.

But even before his adventures in Burgundy, Richard II continued his father's efforts for a monastic revival and succeeded in bringing Normandy within the scope of the Cluniac movement. What was even more important, he brought the Norman Church into contact with north Italian culture. His reign marks both a religious and cultural renaissance in Normandy.

In 1008 Duke Richard appointed a French monk as Abbot of Fontanelle.[63] But his most successful endeavor to reform the Norman Church occurred about 1000 when he invited William of Volpiano, a prominent disciple of St. Majolus, to rule and reform the Abbey of Holy Trinity at Fécamp.[64] The background and early life of Abbot William, who was one of the leading monastic reformers of his age, were typically Cluniac. He was the scion of an aristocratic Piedmontese family of Swabian origin; on his mother's side he was a member of the princely house of Ivrea. William was well educated in the schools of Vercelli and Pavia and was acquainted with St. Romuald, the leader of the eremitic movement in northern Italy and the friend of Otto III. William was thus

[61] R. Pfister, *Études sur le règne de Robert le Pieux* (1885), 257-59.
[62] *Ibid.*, 257.
[63] *Inv. S. Wulfranni*, ch. 19.
[64] The principal sources for the career of William of Volpiano as a monastic reformer are the *Vita* by Ralph Glaber, *MPL* 142, col. 697ff., and *Liber de revelatione . . . Fiscannensis*, *Acta Sanct.*, VI, i, 353ff. There is a careful study by W. Williams in *Downside Review*, 42 (1934), 520-44.

I. Introduction

a product of both the north Italian monastic movement and the Ottonian Renaissance. His learning and aristocratic background fitted him well for entering Cluny in 985. Like many other Cluniacs, William, according to his biographer Ralph Glaber, was on intimate terms with both princes and popes. Before he came to Normandy he had governed several reformed Cluniac houses including St. Benigne-de-Dijon.

After first refusing Duke Richard's invitation because of the reputed "barbarous" nature of the Norman dukes,[65] William came to Fécamp with a dozen Burgundian monks in 1001 and ruled there as Abbot until shortly before his death in 1031. Not only did William establish a great reformed monastery at Fécamp; his influence and through him, the impress of Cluny, were also felt at St. Ouen de Rouen, Jumièges, Mont St. Michel, and perhaps St. Taurin d'Evrey.[66] He also founded Bernay in 1024.[67] The extensive founding and reforming of monasteries under ducal auspices encouraged the principal Norman baronial families to imitate the work of Richard II. In the third decade of the eleventh century, Norman lay barons appear as the founders and patrons of religious houses for the first time.[68]

The scope of Abbot William's work went further than monastic reform. His most important achievement was the creation of a school at Fécamp for regular and secular clergy, the first of the great Norman monastic schools.[69] Some of the leading Norman and Anglo-Norman ecclesiastics of the next two generations were educated at Fécamp.[70] The details of Abbot William's cultural work are obscure, but he did make available to the Norman Church the products of the Ottonian Renaissance. It is at least known that he brought into Nor-

---

[65] *Liber de revelatione*, 353.
[66] Laporte, "Origines," 53.
[67] *Gallia Christiana*, XI, 830.   [68] *OV*, II, 12.
[69] Ralph Glaber, *Vita*, ch. 14; Williams, *op.cit.*, 59.
[70] L. Maître, *Les Écoles Épiscopales*, 80-81. Among these Fécamp students were Archbishop Maurice of Rouen, Bishop Remi of Lincoln, and Bishop Herbert Losinga of Norwich.

mandy the mass *ordo* of Rhenish origin which became known as the "Séez mass."[71]

William of Volpiano was not the only Italian who came into Normandy in Richard II's reign. A certain philosopher Bernard from "Etruria" was reported also to have come to the ducal court.[72] Another Italian, Suppo, became Abbot of Mont St. Michel.[73] But it is primarily to William that the origins of the extensive cultural relations between Italy and Normandy in the late tenth century should be attributed. It is at the monasteries of Fécamp, Bernay, and Mont St. Michel that Romanesque art makes its first appearance in Normandy.[74] It is significant that, of the three great Italian monks who were the intellectual leaders of the Norman Church in the eleventh century—John of Ravenna at Fécamp, and Lanfranc and Anselm at Bec—one of them, John, was William's disciple and succeeded him as Abbot in 1029 and another, Anselm, came from Piedmont which was William's birthplace.

Although the great monasteries were originally founded as places of religion and education, they were brought within the scope of Norman feudalism well before the reign of William the Bastard. The exact period in which the monasteries assumed military obligations is not known, but a St. Wandrille charter of about 1024, at the end of the reign of Richard II, already refers to the *homines* of the monks.[75] Perhaps by this time, and certainly by the end of the reign of Robert the Magnificent in 1035, the older Norman monasteries had been erected into baronies owing the definite quotas of knight service peculiar to Norman feudalism, such as were set down in

[71] M. Andrieu, *Les Ordines Romani*, I, ch. 6, esp. 510.

[72] *Gesta Ducum*, 89.

[73] Prentout, *Richard IIe*, 90-91.

[74] *Ibid.*, 87, 91.

[75] Lot, ed., *St. Wandrille*, no. 9, p. 40. Admittedly the term *homines* here is rather ambiguous, but it may refer to the knights of the monastery: ". . . Monachi e contra ad quodcunque vellent quartam accipient, et de reditibus ipsarum siluarum similiter facerent et tam ipsi quam homines ipsorum in siluis, in pascuis sine ulla coustuma communionem per omnia haberent."

the famous returns of 1172.[76] By the beginning of the reign
of William the Bastard, the Norman dukes were not only
the founders and patrons of the great monasteries, but also the
feudal overlords of the abbots. This feudal dependence of
great ecclesiastics on the crown was to become the greatest
obstacle to the introduction of the Gregorian reforms into
Normandy and the Anglo-Norman kingdom.

The revivification of monastic life was followed, at the end
of the tenth century, by the slow restoration of diocesan administration and improvement in the life of the secular clergy.
Most of the interruptions in the list of bishops in Normandy
cease after the founding of Fécamp in 990, the most important
act of monastic reform under ducal aegis.[77] But the secular
clergy in Normandy remained unaffected by any outside reform center. The way in which the early dukes dealt with the
secular clergy was not to bring in outside reformers, but on the
contrary to make appointments to vacant sees from the lay
aristocracy and, in many cases, from their own family. The
metropolitan see of Rouen itself was held from 990 to 1054
by sons of the dukes.[78] Similar dynastic appointments were
occasionally made at Avranches and Bayeux.[79] By the beginning of the reign of William the Bastard, the secular clergy
in Normandy had not been affected by any reforming movement from outside the duchy.

Two reasons can be given for the marked difference in the
condition of the monastic and secular clergy in Normandy.

[76] *HF*, XXIII, 693-99. For detailed studies of the feudal obligations of
the Norman ecclesiastics, see Haskins, *Norman Institutions*, chs. 1-3, and
S. E. Gleason, *An Ecclesiastical Barony of the Middle Ages; the Bishopric
of Bayeux*, 1066-1204 (1936).

[77] M. de Bouard, "De la Neustrie Carolingienne à la Normandie féodale,"
BIHR, 28 (1955), 8.

[78] Douglas, *op.cit.*, 113-14; Prentout, *Richard IIe*, 75-77. The chief
source for the history of the archbishops of Rouen in this period is the
Acta Archiepiscoporum Rothomagensium (*HF*, XI, 70ff.). This work,
written in the seventh or eighth decade of the eleventh century, is unfortunately very meagre, and provides little information on church-state
relations.

[79] Bouard, *op.cit.*, 8.

4. The Norman Church-State System

In the first place, the situation in Normandy was similar to the general condition of the secular clergy throughout the Western Church before the Gregorian reforms. Throughout France the bishops and cathedral canons were under the domination of the lay authorities. Dynastic appointments to the episcopate were common, and the principle of canonical election was ignored.[80]

Furthermore, a special cause can be given for the domination of the dukes over the secular clergy in Normandy. It is possible that Rollo was endowed with authority over the church by Charles the Simple in 911. Rollo's legal relationship to the Carolingian King is obscure and constitutes a disputed question in early Norman history. But it is at least certain that Rollo and his successors were vassals of the crown.[81] While the terms of the Treaty of St. Claire-sur-Epte of 911 are not known by any surviving text, L. Musset's thesis that the treaty with Rollo was modelled on the agreement of 867 ceding the Cotentin to the Bretons is plausible.[82] The power exercised around Rouen by Rollo and his immediate successors indeed indicates that by the Treaty of 911, as in the case of the cession of 867, the Carolingian King transferred his judicial authority to another ruler. It appears that Rollo received the *comitatus* with the royal domain, involving authority over the bishoprics (*episcopium*).[83] It is possible, then, that a legal grant of authority followed the Scandinavian conquest and provided a theoretical basis for the establishment of ducal authority over the episcopate in the province of Rouen.

Additional legal sanction for the dominant ducal position in Norman church-state relations came from the papacy. The

[80] Cf. P. Imbart de la Tour, *Les Élections Épiscopales dans l'Église de France du IXe au XIIe Siècle* (1890), chs. 1-3.

[81] J. Dhondt, *Étude sur la naissance des principautés territoriales en France* (1948), 117; F. Lot, *Fidèles ou Vassaux?* (1904), 177ff.

[82] L. Musset in *RHDFE*, 4th ser., xxx (1952), 275. This is a summary of Musset's detailed study, "Ruine et reconstitution d'une administration; de la Neustrie franque à la Normandie ducale," *Compte rendu des Jours d'histoire de Droit et des Inst. des Pays de l'Ouest de la France*, June 1951, 4ff.

[83] Bouard, *op.cit.*, 3.

I. Introduction

complete subjection of the Norman episcopate to ducal control was never challenged by the papal curia, which was itself at the mercy of various lay authorities, especially the Roman nobility. The assumption of ducal authority over the regular clergy received special papal confirmation.

Although Pope John X in about 914 rejoiced in the conversion of the *Northmanni*,[84] through most of the tenth century and in fact until the reign of William the Bastard, Normandy was virtually outside the sphere of papal activity. Given the reputed barbarity of the Normans and the precarious position and limited aims of the tenth-century papacy, the meagre condition of Norman-papal relations during the period is not surprising. In the last decade of the tenth century, Abbot Leo, of St. Boniface and St. Alexius in Rome, was sent to Rheims as a papal legate to deal with the dispute over the legality of Gerbert's election as Archbishop.[85] In 995 Abbot Leo summoned all the bishops of France to a great council at Rheims,[86] but there is no indication that any Norman prelate attended.

Nevertheless, there are a few isolated but significant instances of Norman-papal relations before 1035 which established precedents for the later conciliatory policy of the reformed papacy towards the Norman dukes. In 991 a papal legate, Bishop Leo of Trevi, negotiated a peace between King Aethelred of England and Richard I of Normandy,[87] establishing a precedent for Hildebrand's interference in the dispute between Duke William and King Harold in 1066 over the English throne. Shortly afterwards the dukes obtained papal sanction for the system of church-state relations which they had established. Richard I in 966 had already obtained the blessing of Pope John XIII for his monastic reforms, at least in the case of Mont St. Michel.[88] Richard II was even

[84] J-L, 3553.
[85] T. Schieffer, *Die päpstliche Legaten in Frankreich* (1935), 37-44.
[86] J-L, 3855. Cf. Mansi, *Concilia*, XIX, 193.
[87] J-L, 3840; *GR*, II, 191ff.
[88] L. Halphen, ed., *Rec. d. Actes de Lothaire et de Louis V* (1908), XXIV, 53.

more successful; he obtained papal endorsation for his general authority over the Norman Church.

In 995 William of Volpiano had obtained a papal *privilegium* from John XV for his abbey in Dijon.[89] He was probably also "the faithful envoy" whom Richard II sent to Rome in 1016 to obtain from Benedict VIII confirmation of the privileges and possessions he had granted to Fécamp.[90] The papal privilege was directed not to the Abbot but to the Duke himself as the "beloved son" of the Pope. Benedict further recognized the proprietary nature of the Duke's control over Fécamp. The monastery is referred to in the papal privilege as "your church." Benedict, after confirming the ducal grants to Fécamp and according the monastery general apostolic protection, prohibited any bishop from exercising any power of excommunication not only over the exempted house but also over the Duke as well.[91] The establishment of ducal power in the ecclesiastical sphere thereby received papal approval, and the Norman Duke came under the special protection of the papacy.

By the beginning of the reign of William the Bastard the Norman episcopate was completely in the Duke's hand, while the papacy had given its express approval to patronage and control exercised by the dukes over the great monasteries, the vital force in the Norman Church. These monasteries had been founded by the dukes themselves, and hence, by 1035, a tradition had been established in Normandy that the reform of the church was to be conducted under ducal leadership, and it was inevitable that the reform councils of the Norman Church in the reign of William the Bastard would be held under ducal supervision.

[89] J. v. Pflugk-Harttung, ed., *Acta Pontificum Romanorum Inedita* (1881), I, no. 12, p. 10.

[90] *Ibid.*, no. 13, p. 11. Cf. *Liber de revelatione*, 354-55.

[91] *Acta Pontificum*, p. 11: "Hoc etiam decernimus, constituimus, iubemus, ut nullus episcoporum audeat, excommunicationis iaculo te, vel ecclesiam tuam, vel aliquem ex his, de quibus iusticiam facere volueris, impetere, nisi ante sedem apostolicam iusta et legalis cenveniensque discussio hinc facta fuerit."

I. Introduction

The Conqueror's special contributions to the development of the Norman church-state system were his support of reforming councils in Normandy designed to improve the moral and intellectual level of the clergy, his eager participation in the Peace of God movement, and his conquest of England under the papal banner. None of these innovations can be regarded as a relaxation of ducal authority over the church; on the contrary, they were intended to assist in the general increase of ducal power. A better educated clergy provided more efficient clerks for William's administration; the peace movement helped William to control the unruly Norman nobility; the acceptance of the papal banner for his invading army was little more than a subterfuge on William's part. Undoubtedly the Conqueror was pious, at least according to the rather simple and superstitious standards of his class and age, but in his dealings with the church he exhibited that same combination of guile and force and that same unyielding desire for power which he exhibited in other aspects of his long and remarkably successful reign. In every possible way he continued and strengthened the ducal authority over the Norman Church which his predecessors had established. This was the system of church-state relations carried to England by the Conqueror and Lanfranc.

In the final analysis, the Norman church-state system was founded on the principle of lay domination over the church which was common to all of Western Europe in the early Middle Ages, especially after the disintegration of the Carolingian Empire in the ninth and tenth centuries. The Ottonian-Salian *Reichskirchensystem* reveals marked affinities to the situation in Normandy, and only the lack of feudal institutions in Germany before the investiture controversy prevented the development in the Salian Empire of virtually identical institutions in church-state relations.

It is clear that the Norman church-state system was not modelled upon Ottonian-Salian institutions. Some of the monastic scholars, however, who were brought from the east by the dukes in the late tenth and early eleventh centuries, could possibly have reinforced ducal authority by spreading German ideas of church and kingship in Normandy. William of Volpiano, it has been noted, was a typical Cluniac and he was certainly prepared to accept, perhaps even to encourage, ducal patronage and control over the Norman monasteries. Furthermore, in the writings of Dudo of St. Quentin there are reflections of the traditional early medieval veneration of the Christian ruler, hearkening back to Eusebius and Gregory of Tours and indicating that the thought-world of the early medieval West influenced ducal policy by the beginning of the eleventh century.

Aside from these possibilities, it is evident that the Norman church-state system arose out of attitudes to the church and to kingship common to the Scandinavian world, out of the peculiar conditions of the Norman conquest of Neustria, and out of the strenuous and remarkably successful efforts made by the dukes from Rollo to William the Conqueror to assert their authority over the bishoprics and abbeys of the Province of Rouen.

5. THE ECCLESIASTICAL POLICY OF WILLIAM I AND LANFRANC

IN accordance with the traditional policy of the Norman dukes in ecclesiastical matters, the Conqueror assumed the role of both reformer and actual supreme ruler of the church in England. His leave was required to recognize a pope or to receive a papal letter, to propose legislation in a council of the English Church and to implead or excommunicate any of his barons or ministers.[92] Royal supremacy over the church in England during the reigns of William I and his sons, as will be shown fully in the next chapter, was founded upon William's rapid feudalization of church lands and the bring-

[92] *HN*, 9-10. I am here following the paraphrase of Eadmer's account by F. M. Stenton, *Anglo-Saxon England* (2nd ed. 1947), 665.

I. Introduction

ing of the episcopate and abbots within the feudal order which he established in England. The Conqueror, however, was not loth to strengthen his position by making use of the traditions of theocratic monarchy, ultimately derived from Byzantine and Carolingian sources, which had dominated political thought in the late Old English period. He took over the Anglo-Saxon coronation order and anointment, by which kings were thought to assume priestly powers and a sacred right to interfere in the life of the church. Contemporary *laudes* refer to him as *Basileus.*[93]

In imposing the Norman church-state system upon England, William found a perfect partner in his long-time friend, Archbishop Lanfranc of Canterbury.[94] This learned Italian, while Prior of Bec, had been renowned as an eminent theologian and canonist. During his career at Canterbury, he demonstrated that he was an ecclesiastical leader given to moderation and caution who remained, on the whole, unmoved by the stirring events of Gregory VII's pontificate.

Lanfranc is an outstanding example, perhaps the classic case, of the eleventh-century reforming ecclesiastic whose outlook remained non-Gregorian. Although the Archbishop journeyed to Rome to receive the pallium from Alexander II, a former pupil, he refused to allow papal interference in the affairs of the English Church. The learned Archbishop worked assiduously to advance Norman monasticism in Eng-

---

[93] See P. E. Schramm, *A History of the English Coronation* (1937), 29-31, and the sources there cited. On the theocratic nature of late Anglo-Saxon kingship, see also H. R. Loyn, "The King in Late Anglo-Saxon England," *History,* XLII (1957), 92-93.

[94] Lanfranc's theology has been far more carefully studied (by R. W. Southern, "Lanfranc and Berengar of Tours," *Studies presented to F. M. Powicke,* 1948; and by G. Ladner in his *Theologie und Politik vor dem Investiturstreit,* 1935) than has his career as archbishop. The most detailed work is A. J. Macdonald, *Lanfranc* (1926) but the most perceptive, in spite of its brevity, is Stenton, *A-S Engl.,* 654-658. Brooke, *The English Church and the Papacy,* chs. 5 and 8, is valuable for Lanfranc as a canonist and for his relations with Rome. For Lanfranc's attempt to assert the primacy of Canterbury over York, see H. Böhmer, *Die Fälschungen Erzbischof Lanfranks von Canterbury* (1902).

5. Policy of William I and Lanfranc

land, to improve the intellectual and moral level of the secular clergy, to establish the supremacy of Canterbury over the whole British episcopate, and to introduce canon law collections, of the more conservative, pre-Gregorian type, into England. These endeavors constituted the limit of his reforming aims. Like the Cluniacs, he was reluctant to raise fundamental controversial issues on the nature of church-state relations. An appraisal of his career and writings from the available evidence indicates that when pressed by Gregory VII, Lanfranc became more and more hostile to the zealots in the papal curia and their revolutionary doctrines. The skill and firmness which he demonstrated in implementation and defense of William's ecclesiastical policy reveal a more than passive acceptance of the principles of the Norman *Landeskirche*. From a cautious pre-Gregorian position Lanfranc was advancing, in the closing years of his pontificate, towards an openly anti-Gregorian stand.

While Lanfranc opened the way for later developments by establishing separate ecclesiastical courts and by introducing continental canon law collections into England, as long as he lived there was no papal interference in the Anglo-Norman Church. The Archbishop believed that the crown should exercise jurisdiction even over excommunications.[95] William I completely refused the Pope's demand for fealty,[96] and Lanfranc not only rejected Gregory's repeated summonses to Rome,[97] but even wavered in his allegiance to that Pope.[98]

[95] J. A. Giles, ed., *Lanfranci Opera* (1844), I, 65.

[96] *Ibid.*, I, 32; Brooke, *op.cit.*, and in *EHR*, XXVI (1911). The question of Gregory VII's demand for fealty from the Conqueror should perhaps be seen within the scope of general papal policy. See K. Jordan, "Das Eindringen des Lehnswesens in das Rechtsleben der römischen Kurie," *Archiv f. Urkundenforschung*, XII (1931-2); P. Kehr, "Belehnungen der süditalienischen Normannenfürsten durch die Päpste (1059-1192)," *Abh. d. Preuss. Ak. d. Wiss.*, 1934, Phil.-Hist. Kl., no. 1; P. Scheffer-Boichorst, "Die Ansprüche Gregors VII auf Gallien als zinspflichtigen Land und auf Sachsen als Eigentum der Kirche," *Ges. Schriften* (1903), I, 107ff.

[97] *Lanfranci opera*, I, 32-33.

[98] *Ibid.*, 79. See also P. Kehr in *Sitzungsberichte d. Preuss. Ak. d. Wiss.*, 1921, 355-68, and F. Lieberman, "Lanfranc and the Antipope," *EHR*, XVI (1901).

I. Introduction

As of 1089, between the two rival claimants for the papal throne, no successor to Gregory VII had been recognized in England.[99] By the death of Lanfranc, therefore, the Gregorian reform movement had made no penetration among the Anglo-Norman clergy,[100] and the English bishops were accustomed to look to the king as the source of all advancement and for most of their guidance in church affairs as well.

The careers of many of the English bishops had begun in the royal chancery. At least since the reign of Canute, it had been a commonly accepted policy in England that the king should recruit for his administration ambitious and well-educated clerks, sometimes of rather humble origins, and reward them for faithful service with lucrative ecclesiastical appointments. With the expansion of the royal administration in the Conqueror's reign, this practice increased. Early in the 1090's perhaps half the bishops and more important abbots had formerly been royal chaplains,[101] and in the period from 1089

[99] *HN*, 52.

[100] If the *de injusta vexatione Willelmi episcopi primi* were in fact contemporary with the events it purports to describe, then this statement would need much qualification. For in this work William of St. Calais, the Bishop of Durham, is represented as taking the same view of papal authority as Anselm did seven years later at Rockingham: "Apostolicam sedem, Romanam sanctam ecclesiam, et beatum Petrum eiusque vicarium appello. . . . Et ego praesto cum judicia mihi facta in Romana ecclesia contradicere, de qua pendet et pependit ab apostolorum tempore et infra ordinis mei diffinitivia sententia." (T. Arnold, ed., *Symeonis Monachi Opera Omnia*, R.S., 1882, I, 184 and 186). But H. S. Offler in *EHR*, LVI (1951) has shown that the *de vexatione*, in its present form at least, is not a contemporary record but dates from the second quarter of the twelfth century. It would seem to be *a priori* improbable that bishop William should hold these doctrines on papal supremacy in 1088 and yet condemn Anselm a few years later for holding the same opinions.

[101] This identification has been made by R. W. Southern, "Ranulf Flambard and Early Anglo-Norman Administration," *TRHS*, 4th ser. XVI (1933), 116, of the witnesses to the charter of William II of January, 1091, confirming to Bishop John of Bath the abbey of Bath. See Davis, *Reg.*, no. 315. It appears that in Normandy from 1035 to 1065 the episcopate was recruited from the lay aristocracy, and there was nothing comparable in the duchy to the late Anglo-Saxon practice of appointing royal chaplains to bishoprics. (See D. C. Douglas, "The Norman Episcopate before the Norman Conquest," *Cambridge Hist. Jrnl.*, XIII [1957], 102-03.) In appointing royal clerks to the episcopate, William the Conqueror was

5. Policy of William I and Lanfranc

to 1109 only two bishops among sixteen appointed had not served in the royal administration in some capacity.[102] It was already the custom for chancellors to be rewarded with bishoprics as a matter of course, although as yet the two offices were not held concurrently.[103] This repeated transmutation of royal administrators into eminent ecclesiastics meant that in the period under discussion the majority of the English episcopate had spent their early careers in close contact with the person of royal majesty and in advancing his powers. It was only to be expected that Gregorian reform ideas would be coldly received and even strongly opposed by them.

Nor could these reforms expect much support even from the bishops who had previously been monks or canons. Bishop William of Durham had at one time been a monk of St. Calais in Normandy. He was renowned for his kindness to his monks at Durham and his benefactions to his see.[104] Yet in

---

therefore adopting an Anglo-Saxon procedure, not bringing over an innovation from Normandy.

[102] The bishops appointed in the period 1089-1109 who for certain had previously served the king are as follows: Hervey [Bangor 1092, Ely 1109] (*DNB*, XXVI, 276), royal clerk; Robert Bloett [Lincoln 1094], chancellor (Davis, *Reg.*, xviii; *EHR*, XXVI, 84); Gerard [Hereford 1094 and York 1101] chancellor (V. H. Galbraith, *EHR*, XLVI [1931] 77-79); Samson [Worcester 1096], royal chaplain (Davis, *Reg.*, xxi); Ranulf Flambard [Durham 1099], "publicanorum princeps infamissimus," *AO* ep. 214: for precise nature of Ranulf's financial offices see Southern, *op.cit.*, in n. 101; William Warelwast [Exeter 1107], royal chaplain (*HN*, 68); Roger the royal larderer, appointed to Hereford, 1107, but died before consecration (*GP*, 303); Regenhelm [Hereford 1107], reginae cancellarius (*GP*, 303); William Giffard [Winchester 1107], chancellor (Davis, *Reg.*, xviii); Richard de Beaumes [London 1108], sheriff of Shropshire (*DNB*, IV, 199); Thomas [York 1109], royal chaplain (*HC*, 111). Of the four remaining bishops consecrated in this period, Herbert Losinga (Thetford-Norwich 1091) may have possibly been a chaplain of William I (Davis, *Reg.*, xix) and Ralph Luffa (Chichester 1091) was a justiciar in Rufus' administration (Davis, *Reg.*, no. 424). Aside from Anselm, only Ralph d'Escures (Rochester 1108) did not serve in the royal administration, of the bishops appointed in this period. Ralph was a former abbot of Séez in Normandy, who became a disciple of Anselm (see R. W. Southern, "St. Anselm and his English pupils," *Med. and Ren. Studies*, I, 1941).

[103] G. H. White, "The Household of the Norman Kings," *TRHS*, 4th ser., XXX (1941), 131, 135.

[104] On William of St. Calais, see Sym. Durham, *HDE*, I, 119-134;

the dispute between William II and Anselm he was the Archbishop's most vigorous opponent among the episcopate.[105] An
ambitious monk like Herbert Losinga, who bought his way
from being Prior of Fécamp to Abbot of Ramsey to Bishop of
Norwich, could disregard canonical practices as much as any
royal clerk. William of Malmesbury called Herbert "the
kindling of simony."[106] Herbert's bad conscience about his
early career, which led him to seek absolution from the pope,
did not prevent him from acting as a royal envoy to Rome
during the English investiture controversy.[107] The prohibition
of simony at Lanfranc's London Council of 1075[108] did not
have any effect, whatever the provenance of the bishop.

When a reformer like Anselm became Archbishop of Canterbury after Lanfranc's death it was inevitable that he would
quarrel not only with the king but also with the great majority
of his episcopal colleagues.

6. ANSELM AND HIS EPISCOPAL COLLEAGUES

IN SPITE of their general hostility to the Gregorian reform
program, the bishops of English sees in 1089 were a remarkably able group. Their origin was not homogeneous and their
interests and talents were varied. They had been brought over
from the Continent by William I and Lanfranc to serve in
the royal administration and reform the church in England.[109]

R. B. Mynors, *Durham Cathedral Manuscripts*, introduction; H. S. Offler,
"William of St. Calais," *Trans. of Architect. and Archeol. Soc. of Durham
and Northumberland*, x (1950), 258ff.

[105] *HN*, 69.

[106] *GP*, 151: "fomes simoniae." Herbert's biography is attempted in
E. M. Goulburn and H. Symonds, *The Life, Letters and Sermons of Bishop
Herbert de Losinga* (1878), 2 vols. For a contemporary poem attacking
Herbert as a simoniac see *GR*, II, 386.

[107] *HN*, 132-33.   [108] Wilkins, *Concilia*, I, 363.

[109] The view of the English Church on the eve of the Norman Conquest
as decadent, corrupt, out of touch with the reform movement on the Continent, and completely dominated by the king and laymen, given in *Böhmer,
Kirche und Staat*, ch. 2, was dependent on William of Malmesbury in *GP*
and his other works, written in the second and third decades of the twelfth

6. Anselm and his Episcopal Colleagues

Only one Anglo-Saxon bishop, Wulfstan of Worcester (1062-1095), still held his episcopal office at the time of Lanfranc's death. The other Anglo-Saxon bishops had either died by this time or had been deposed by Lanfranc. It was in fact only Wulfstan's great reputation for sanctity which had saved him from the harsh treatment which Lanfranc had meted out to other Anglo-Saxon ecclesiastics. Wulfstan had no vested interest in preserving the ecclesiastical system of continental origin, and he carried no weight in decisions affecting the life of the church.[110]

Gundulf of Rochester (1077-1108) had been brought from Bec by Lanfranc to serve as the diocesan ordinary of Canterbury. He was a friend and disciple of Anselm and he was more or less required by reason of his office to be loyal to the Archbishop in all cases.[111] Only Wulfstan and Gundulf gave Anselm any support in the Archbishop's dispute with William Rufus.

---

century. A vigorous attack on this view was made by R. R. Darlington, "Ecclesiastical Reform in the Late Old English Period," *EHR*, LI (1936), 385ff. I am inclined to believe, however, that the view of William of Malmesbury was, on the whole, correct. William's account of the Anglo-Saxon church cannot be simply dismissed as Norman prejudice. He admired St. Wulfstan of Worcester and wrote the saint's *vita*, which would indicate that William's view of the Anglo-Saxon church was not based simply on uncritical hostility, as Darlington maintains. Furthermore, William's view of the decadence of the late Anglo-Saxon church is confirmed by the *Vita Aedwardi Regis*, ed. Luard (RS), ll.1438-1546, which is now known to have been written between 1067 and 1075 for a member of Godwin's house. (R. W. Southern, "The First Life of Edward the Confessor," *EHR*, LVIII [1943], 385ff.; E. K. Henningham, "The Genuineness of the *Vita Aedwardi Regis*," *Speculum*, XXI [1946], 419ff.) The evidence from this source certainly cannot be dismissed as Norman prejudice. For a recent discussion of the lack of distinction between the jurisdictions of church and crown in the late Anglo-Saxon period, see T. J. Oleson, *The Witanegemot in the Reign of Edward the Confessor* (1955), 3, 4, 15, 77, Appendix R. Lanfranc's expressed intention to reform the church in England by bringing over ecclesiastics from the Continent must, therefore, be accepted as sincere and based on good reasons.

[110] On St. Wulfstan, see William of Malmesbury, *Vita Wulfstani*, ed. R. R. Darlington (Camden Soc. 3d ser., vol. 40, 1928), with a valuable introduction by the editor.

[111] *Vita Gundulfi*, MPL 159, col. 813ff.; R.A.L. Smith, "The Place of Gundulph in the Anglo-Norman Church," *EHR*, 58 (1943), 257ff.

I. Introduction

Anselm's metropolitan colleague, Thomas I of York (1070-1100) had been a canon of Bayeux. He devoted himself to the defense of the independent position of his province against Canterbury's claim to the primacy in Britain, and took no part whatsoever in the controversy over church-state relations.[112] At the death of Lanfranc there was only one other see in the Province of York; Carlisle was not created until 1133. At Durham, William of St. Calais imposed the Benedictine rule on his canons and devoted most of his efforts to the building of the great Romanesque Cathedral of Durham.[113]

At least three of the bishops at the beginning of Anselm's pontificate were typical curialists whose major interest was service in the royal administration, although they were also renowned for other things. Walkelin of Winchester (1070-1098) devoted the resources of his see to cathedral building.[114] John of Bath and Wells (1088-1122), a native of Tours, was famous as a physician.[115] Maurice of London (1086-1107) had an unenviable reputation as a woman-chaser.[116] In the category of strictly-curialist bishops was probably also Robert de Limesey, Bishop of Lichfield (1086-1117), and Ralph Luffa, Bishop of Chichester (1091-1123).

Two of the bishops in 1089 had a reputation for learning. Robert of Hereford (1079-1095) was a product of the Lorraine schools and was known as a mathematician and astronomer.[117] Robert's friend was Osmund of Salisbury, who was canonized in the fifteenth century. Within a century of his

---

[112] *HC*, 99ff.; M. Dueball, *Der Suprematstreit zwischen den Erzdiözesen Canterbury und York, 1070-1126* (Ebering's Hist. Stud., Heft 184, 1929).

[113] On William's monastic and artistic interests, in addition to the works cited in n. 104 above, see C. H. Turner in *J. Theol. Studies*, XIX (1918), 124-32; O. Pächt, "Hugo Pictor," *The Bodleian Library Record*, III, no. 30 (1950), 96-103.

[114] *DNB*, LIX, 40-41.

[115] J. Hunter, ed., "A Brief History of the Bishoprick of Somerset from its Foundations to the year 1174," in *Ecclesiastical Documents* (Camden Soc., vol. 8, 1840), 21-22; R.A.L. Smith, "John of Bath and Wells," *Downside Review*, LXX, 1942.

[116] *GP*, 145; *DNB*, XXXVII, 94-95.

[117] *GP*, 300-301; *DNB*, XXXIV, 146-67. There was a vacancy at Lincoln in 1093.

6. Anselm and his Episcopal Colleagues

death Osmund was renowned as a great liturgist, but scholars have not yet succeeded in establishing the extent of his authorship of Sarum liturgical works.[118]

The learning of Osmund and Robert did not induce them to support Anselm in his dispute with William II. They were merely less intransigent than the strictly-curialist bishops. Since even the best scholars among Anselm's episcopal colleagues showed no enthusiasm for Gregorian reforms, it would be wrong to attribute the hostility of the Anglo-Norman episcopate towards Anselm's reforming·endeavors simply to ignorance and selfishness. The case of the Anglo-Norman bishops presented a particularly frustrating problem to the Gregorian reformers: a bishop could be a learned and sincere churchman and yet not be a supporter of the doctrines emanating from Rome.

It would be wrong, for instance, to dismiss Herbert of Norwich (1091-1119) as unsuited for his office, in spite of his reputation for simony. Many of his letters and sermons survive, and they reveal not the uncouth and unworthy bishop we might expect but rather a conscientious, learned, and humane churchman.[119] Herbert had been a monk at Fécamp when John of Ravenna, one of the greatest scholars of the eleventh century, had been its abbot.[120] Herbert's writings reveal that he learned a great deal from his Italian teacher

[118] On Osmund and the Sarum Liturgy, see W. H. Rich Jones, *Register of St. Osmund* (RS, 1883), 2 vols., esp. II, xxiff.; W. H. Frere, "Use of Sarum," *Selected Essays*, Alcuin Club Coll., vol. 35; E. H. Kantorowicz in *Harvard Theol. Rev.*, 34 (1942); J. W. Legg, *The Sarum Missal* (1916); J. A. Jungman, *The Mass of the Roman Rite* (1951), I, 102. Frere has identified *MS.B.M. Cotton Tiberius C.I.*, fol. 43ff. as a Roman *ordines* with pontifical offices probably compiled by Osmund. For Osmund's canonization in 1457 see *Archaelogia*, IX (1789), 39-44.

[119] Herbert's sermons are published in Goulburn and Symonds, *op.cit.*, II. His letters, which survive only in a seventeenth-century transcript, were published by R. Anstruther, ed., *Epistolae Herberti de Losinga, Osberti de Clare, et Edmeri* (1846). The edition is not altogether reliable. The Ramsey pontifical in *MS.B.M.Add.28.188* was probably compiled by Herbert. (W. H. Frere, *English Pontificals in Manuscript*, 96-97).

[120] On John of Fécamp, see J. Leclercq and J. P. Bonnes, *Un maître de la vie spirituelle au XIe siècle, Jean de Fécamp* (1946).

and he continued to regard himself as a disciple and son of Fécamp for the rest of his life.[121]

For Herbert the authority of a bishop was a weighty thing.[122] Although he was fully aware of the evils at work among his contemporaries[123] and of his own sins,[124] he was convinced that the rulers of the church had miraculous powers to overcome the forces of evil.[125] For Herbert, as for many thinkers in the eleventh century, the world and the church were synonymous and identical.[126]

Although his letters reveal Herbert attending the *curia regis*,[127] they also show him tenderly caring for his monks at Norwich Cathedral Priory[128] and taking infinite pains to set up a school there for the benefit of the monastic community.[129] He wanted to spread Norman learning into England. Nevertheless he was careful to insist that the study of classical literature be limited to prevent harm to the dogma of the faith.[130] His own writings reveal the profound penetration of the patristic-Biblical tradition into the mind of a quite obscure bishop in a minor English see. The Augustinian influence as expressed in the doctrine of the six ages, the elect, and the heavenly city, was very pronounced in Herbert's sermons.[131] The mind of Herbert Losinga—revealed to us by a lucky accident while bishops of the same background and status are mere names known only from their appearance in the witness list of a royal charter or in one of William of Malmesbury's droll stories—is a remarkable revelation of the educational achievement of the Norman monastic schools.

---

[121] Herbert, *Epistolae*, epp. 5 and 24.

[122] Sermon 7, Goulburn and Symonds, II, 106.

[123] Ser. 10, p. 280.   [124] Ser. 8, p. 228.   [125] Ser. 8, p. 220.

[126] Ser. 11, p. 320; Ser. 14, p. 413; Ser. 4, p. 101.

[127] Epp. 11, 57.   [128] Epp. 13, 48.

[129] Epp. 17, 20, 39, 47, 49. Herbert also encouraged the establishment of a monastic school at Ramsey, while he was Abbot from 1087 to 1091. (See *MPL* 155, col. 81).

[130] Ep. 28: Herbert describes a dream similar to St. Jerome's, in which he is warned against the dangers of heathen literature.

[131] Ser. 2, pp. 60, 62-4; Ser. 14, pp. 397, 429.

6. Anselm and his Episcopal Colleagues

These monastic schools were primarily the creation of Italians of whom William of Volpiano and John of Ravenna at Fécamp, and Lanfranc and Anselm at Bec were the most influential.[132] Anselm, who was of aristocratic lineage, had come from Aosta to Normandy about 1060, attracted by the great scholarly reputation of the Prior of Bec, Lanfranc. Eventually Anselm became the head of the monastic school, Prior, and finally in 1078, Abbot of Bec.[133] Both before and after

[132] It is remarkable that no study of the migration of several learned Italians from northern Italy to Normandy in the late tenth and early eleventh centuries has been made. Their effect on Norman religious life was very profound, and it is not inconceivable that the Norman dukes may have received suggestions for administrative reform from these Italian scholars. Lanfranc was reputed to have taught Roman law before coming to Normandy.

[133] There is no modern biography of Anselm which meets scholarly standards. Several were written in the nineteenth century but they are, without exception, of no value. The more recent biographies by J. Clayton (1933) and A. Levati (1929) are no better. The following are the only valuable contributions to Anselm's biography: F. G. Fruatz, "Sainte Anselme et la Vallée d'Aoste," in *Revista Storica Benedettina*, anno 4, fasc. 15 (1909), 67-89; E. Porée, *Histoire de l'Abbaye de Bec* (1901), II; F. Liebermann, "Anselm von Canterbury u. Hugo von Lyons," *Historische Aufsätze . . . G. Waitz Gewidmet* (1886), 156-203; R. W. Southern's studies of Anselm's relations with his monastic disciples in *Med. and Ren. Studies*, I (1941), 3-34 and III (1954) 78-99. Among contemporary lives the most important is the *Historia Novorum* by Eadmer, Anselm's secretary. It aims to give an account of Anselm's pontificate. Completed in the decade after Anselm's death, it is the first major Latin historical work in England since Bede (cf. R. R. Darlington, *Some Anglo-Norman Historians* [1950], 6-7) and is one of the greatest achievements of Anglo-Norman historiography. Eadmer was perhaps too clever, since he suppressed any facts which put Anselm, the reform party in England, or the papacy in a bad light. There are two manuscripts: *B.M. Cotton Titus A.IX* (MS.A) and *C.C.C. 452* (MS.B.). MS.A was published by J. Selden in 1623, MS.B. by M. Rule in the Rolls Series in 1884. The variants are few and insignificant. In addition to HN, Eadmer wrote a complete *Vita Anselmi* (also published in Rule's edition of *HN*) which is valuable for Anselm's early life. The best critical study of Eadmer's historical work is by F. Liebermann in his *Ungedruckte Anglo-Normannische Geschichtsquellen* (1879), 284-302. M. Rule in *Cambridge Antiq. Soc. Proc.*, VI (1888), 195-304, makes a few valuable observations but unfortunately also several bordering on the fantastic. There are two other lives of Anselm, independent of Eadmer's work. An anonymous life incorporated in Ralph de Diceto's chronicle (ed. Stubbs, *RS*, I, 223-229) supplies a small amount of information not given by Eadmer, and, as Stubbs suggests, has the character of an independent work. Rule's suggestion that the author was Baldwin of Tournay,

I. Introduction

his election as Archbishop of Canterbury, Anselm devoted himself to the philosophical and theological works which have gained him the title of first of the scholastics.[134] His ontological proof of the existence of God, rejected by Thomas Aquinas, was revived by Descartes and Leibniz. It constitutes an enduring contribution to theology.

Anselm's whole attitude towards life was that of a typical Benedictine monk. Submission to God's will, absolute obedience to the abbot, brotherly love for other religious, ascetic rejection of the world—these are the themes which recur constantly in his writings.[135]

In spite of Anselm's great admiration and love for Lanfranc, he differed from his master in his attitude to the Gregorian reforms. Gregory VII was probably aware of this, for in 1079 he praised Anselm's learning as advantageous to the whole church of God.[136] Gregory was not inclined to praise Lanfranc in such extravagant terms. At the very time that

---

a member of Anselm's Canterbury household (*Cam. Proc.* VI, 292) is very plausible. William of Malmesbury, *GP*, 173-225, makes use of Eadmer, but appears to have had access to other accounts, perhaps oral. The life of Anselm by John of Salisbury (*MPL* 199, col. 1009ff.) is based entirely on Eadmer's works. Eadmer's *Miraculi S. Anselmi* in Liebermann, ed. *Ung. A-N Gesch.*, 282ff., are valuable as a reminder that the primary purpose of Eadmer's historical work was to portray Anselm as a saint, and to remove any doubts on this score that may have arisen during Anselm's disputes with William II, Henry I, and the papacy. Hence the historian must at all times compare Eadmer's account with whatever evidence is available from other sources. In some instances Anselm's own letters, to which Eadmer had free access and probably helped to edit, contradict Eadmer's account.

[134] In the last three decades a revival of interest in Anselm's theology has occurred. Among many other studies, see M. Grabmann, *Gesch. d. scholastischen Methode* (1909), I, ch. V, which is still the best introduction to Anselm's thought; K. Barth, *Fides quaerens Intellectum* (1931), a critique of Anselm's proof of the existence of God; E. Gilson, "Sens et Nature de l'Argument de St. Anselme," *Archives*, IX (1934); and a summary of recent literature in J. McIntyre, *St. Anselm and his Critics* (1954).

[135] *AO*, epp. 2, 4, 5, 6, 9, 13, 41, 51; Oratio 17, *AO*, II, 68ff.

[136] *AO*, ep. 102, ll. 3-7: "Quoniam fructum tuorum bonus odor ad nos usque redoluit, quam dignas grates deo referimus, et te in Christi dilectione ex corde amplectimur; credentes pro certo tuorum studiorum exemplis ecclesiam dei in melius promoveri, et tuis similiumque tibi precibus etiam ab instantibus periculis, Christi subveniente misericordia posse eripi."

40

6. Anselm and his Episcopal Colleagues

Lanfranc was refusing to recognize Urban II in 1088, and was in fact wavering towards the anti-Pope Wibert, Anselm wrote Urban to tell him that he "did not cease to pray assiduously for you and the tribulation of the Roman Church."[137] In the same letter Anselm revealed that he was well aware of the condition of the church outside his monastery—canons and priests were depraved; laymen were oppressing the church.[138] The leader of the high Gregorians in France, Archbishop Hugh of Lyons, was the Abbot of Bec's close friend.[139] Unlike his teacher Lanfranc, Anselm was an advocate of at least the more moderate Gregorian reform doctrines and his election as Archbishop of Canterbury in 1093 was destined to be a decisive moment in the history of church-state relations in Anglo-Norman England.

[137] *AO*, ep. 126, ll. 6-7: "Pro vestra et Romanae ecclesiae tribulatione, quae nostra et omnium vere fidelium est, non cessamus orare deum assidue. . . ." In this letter Anselm referred to himself as "servus servorum dei Becci commanentium" (l. 2). After he became Archbishop of Canterbury, he also used the papal title "servant of the servants of God" to indicate his sympathy for the reforming papacy. See below, Ch. II, p. 74 and n. 155.

[138] *AO*, ep. 126, ll. 35-40: "Canonici quidem et presbyteri hoc illi faciunt, quia eos a pravis consuetudinibus, et maxime e mulierum reproba conversatione vult prohibere, et filios eorum sive quos sibi secundum placitum haeredes eligunt, a praebendarum haereditaria successione atque a sacrorum ordinum promotione conatur arcere. Laici vero idcirco, quia invasionibus rerum ecclesiae inordinate factis non vult favere."

[139] *AO*, epp. 100 and 109.

CHAPTER II

THE BEGINNINGS OF THE CONTROVERSY OVER
CHURCH-STATE RELATIONS, 1089-1097

I. THE ECCLESIASTICAL POLICY OF WILLIAM II

LANFRANC's death in 1089 marked a turning-point in the relations between church and state in the Anglo-Norman kingdom. Anselm at one time aptly described the English Church under the harmonious rule of William I and Lanfranc as a plough drawn by two well-matched oxen.[1] Soon after Lanfranc's death this harmony gave way to a long and confused series of disputes which did not end completely until the third decade of the twelfth century.

Contemporaries were well aware of the significance of Lanfranc's passing, but royal curialists and ecclesiastical reformers differed as to where the onus of blame for bringing on the new conditions in church-state relations ought to be placed. William II and Henry I claimed that they were only trying to defend the ecclesiastical rights which their father had possessed against the radical innovations of church reformers who had no regard for the custom of England.[2] Anselm charged that Rufus, with all "the ferocity of an untamable bull,"[3] willfully destroyed the harmonious relationship between church and state which his father and Lanfranc had built up. In similar vein, Eadmer's *Historia Novorum*, the official history of the reform party completed in the third decade of the twelfth

---

[1] *HN*, 36 (Anselm in 1092): "Aratrum ecclesiam perpendite juxta apostolum dicentem, 'Dei agricultura estis, Dei aedificatio estis' [I Corinthians 3:9]. Hoc aratrum in Anglia duo boves caeteris praecellentes regendo trahunt et trahendo regunt, rex vidilicet et archiepiscopus Cantuariensis."

[2] See below, pp. 76, 80 and Ch. IV, pp. 155, 201.

[3] Continuation of Anselm's speech quoted in n. 1 above: "Horum bovum unus, scilicet Lanfrancus archiepiscopus, mortuus est, et alius ferocitatem indomabilis tauri obtinens iam juvenis aratro praelatus. . . ."

century, accused Rufus of introducing severe and unjust innovations in church-state relations. As long as Lanfranc lived, Eadmer said, Rufus preserved moderation out of respect for the great archbishop. But "how grievous a calamity befell the churches as a consequence of Lanfranc's death."[4]

Eadmer's accusations against William II consist substantially of the charge that during the vacancy at Canterbury, from 1089 to 1093, the King "put up the church of Christ for sale," that he brought "baleful oppression against the churches of God."[5] The greater part of Eadmer's catalogue of William II's "wrongdoing" involves acts of financial oppression by Rufus' administration against the church. The official history of the reformers stated that in the period 1089-1093 the King's officials assessed annually all that belonged to the Church of Canterbury. After fixing an allowance for the monks, Rufus reckoned the rest of the Canterbury temporalities as part of his demesne. Each year the King farmed the Canterbury temporalities to the highest bidder. The royal officials, "the most impious of men engaged in extortion of royal money," virtually ruled the Church of Canterbury, lording it over everyone and "manifesting their power to the utmost." Some monks of Christ Church were dispersed to other monastic houses and the tenants of the abbey "were ground down with misery and devastation." The same practices were carried out by royal officials in other widowed churches. Eadmer concluded that Rufus was the first English king to treat the church in this way; he inherited no such tradition from his father. He alone held widowed churches in his *dominium*. For he would not appoint successors to vacant sees and abbacies "so long as he could exact from them, through his officials, whatever price he calculated."[6]

[4] *HN*, 26: ". . . quam gravis calamitas ex obitu illius ecclesias Angliae devastaverit."

[5] *HN*, 26-7.

[6] *HN*, 27: ". . . nullatenus eam [oppressionem] ex paterna traditione accipiens. Destitutas ergo ecclesias solus in dominio suo tenebat. Nam alium neminem praeter se substituere volebat quamdiu per suos ministros

43

II. Beginnings of the Controversy, 1089-1097

Many of Eadmer's accusations are founded upon facts which can be confirmed from other sources.[7] During Rufus' reign there were four long vacancies in episcopal sees.[8] Vacant sees were quickly filled with new bishops only in return for a simoniacal payment, as at Thetford-Norwich in 1091, or with the intention of rewarding one of the royal clerks, as at Durham in 1099.[9] Since abbacies did not constitute such lucrative rewards as bishoprics for royal officials, several abbeys remained without pastors in Rufus' reign. Their revenues were farmed by the royal treasury. According to the Anglo-Saxon Chronicle, there were eleven abbeys "let out for rent" in 1100.[10]

The royal policy towards the vacant see of Canterbury is revealed in a writ of William II to Haimo the sheriff and all the barons of Kent, which referred to the *dominium archiepiscopi* held by the King *in manu mea*.[11] As the richest see, Canterbury must have been the special object of the financial exactions of Rufus' administration from the church. Eadmer spoke for the monks of Christ Church. The chronicler of St. Augustine's, Canterbury, also complained that the King put up churches throughout England for sale, and that he intended to keep the pastoral staffs in his own hand and dispose of them according to his own will.[12] Such sweeping con-

---

aliquid quod cuiusvis pretii duceret ab eis extrahere poterat." The reading *destitutas* (MS.A) for the first word in the second sentence quoted seems better than *destructas* (MS.B) given by Rule.

[7] For some other chroniclers and contemporary historians see *OV*, bk. VIII, ch. 8 and bk. x, ch. 8 and *GR*, II, 36-70 who depended upon Eadmer's work, and *A-S Chron. E*, *s.a.* 1100 and *Ann. Winton.*, *s.a.* 1092, which are independent sources.

[8] Canterbury, 1089-93; Chichester, 1088-91; Lincoln, 1092-94; Worcester, January 1095 to June 1096.

[9] On Herbert Losinga who became bishop of Norwich in 1091, see above, Ch. I, pp. 37-38. On Ranulf Flambard, appointed to Durham, in 1099, see the study of his career by R. W. Southern, "Ranulf Flambard and Early Anglo-Norman Administration," *TRHS*, 4th ser., XVI (1933), 95-128.

[10] *A-S Chron. E*, *s.a.* 1100; cf. *Ann. Winton.*, *s.a.* 1088.

[11] Davis, *Reg.*, no. 458.

[12] Thorne's chronicle, in Twysden, *SS*, col. 1794. For the sources of Thorne's chronicle of St. Augustine's, see below, Ch. V, n. 65.

demnations may be exaggerated. But it is at least certain that in 1095-96, during the vacancy of the see of Worcester, the King used the same methods which Eadmer said were applied at Canterbury in 1089-93. A royal writ to the tenants of the see of Worcester informed them that since Bishop Wulfstan was dead, the honor of Worcester was being taken into the King's hand. The tenants of the see were to pay reliefs to the royal treasury on pain of forfeiture of their property.[13] Eadmer's account of the repeated assessment of Canterbury lands by royal officials may be related to Orderic Vital's description of the general remeasurement of England by Ranulf Flambard, Rufus' chief financial agent.[14]

No doubt the royal administration saw that payments to the royal treasury for appointment to bishoprics and abbacies could be made a steady source of income for the King. Turstin, Abbot of Glastonbury, had been expelled from his abbey in 1083 after a violent quarrel with the monks. At the beginning of Rufus' reign, according to William of Malmesbury, Turstin was able to redeem the Abbey from the King for 500 pounds of silver.[15] In 1091 Herbert Losinga, Abbot of Ramsey, bought the see of Thetford-Norwich for himself and the Abbey of Winchester for his father for the sum of £1,000.[16] Remi, Bishop of Lincoln, paid the King a considerable sum in 1092 for summoning his episcopal colleagues to participate in the consecration of a new cathedral at Lincoln.[17]

[13] *Heming's chartulary*, ed. Hearne, I, 79. Davis, *Reg.* no. 387: "Et qui hoc facere noluerit Urso et Bernardus saisiant et terras et pecunias in manu mea." Also Davis, *Reg.* no. 388. Poole, *Domesday Book to Magna Charta*, 171, says that this was a malpractice "which no feudal theory could justify." But was feudal theory yet so well-developed and specific?

[14] *OV*, bk. VIII, ch. 8 (vol. III, pp. 311-12): "Flambardus . . . inquietavit regem, incitans ut totius Angliae reviseret descriptionem, Anglicaeque telluris comprobans iteraret partitionem. . . ." For a full discussion, see Southern, *op.cit.*, 106ff.

[15] *A-S Chron.* E, *s.a.* 1083 and Will. of Malmesbury, *de antiq. Glaston*, ch. 65.

[16] Bartholomew Cotton, *Hist. Angl.*, ed. Luard (*R.S.*), 390. Cf. Goulburn and Symonds, *Herb. Los.*, I, 78-79.

[17] Florence of Worcester, *Chronicle*, *s.a.* 1092.

II. Beginnings of the Controversy, 1089-1097

In 1094 his successor Robert Bloet is said to have paid the King the vast sum of £3,000 for settling his dispute with the Archbishop of York.[18] Two monks of Hyde Abbey tried to outbid each other for royal appointment as abbot.[19]

In Eadmer's history such acts were attributed simply to Rufus' wicked character; Eadmer assumed they were to be expected from a man who was renowned as a homosexual, a skeptic, and whose favor could be bought by the Jews.[20] The background of the ecclesiastical administration of Rufus' reign is more complex than this, however. In the first place, William II did not violently break with his father's tradition in church-state relations, as Eadmer claimed. The Conqueror had asserted his complete authority over the English Church and Lanfranc had helped him implement this authority.[21] Orderic Vital implicitly recognized that Rufus' ecclesiastical policy was not a marked departure from the Conqueror's relations with the church. For he compared Rufus' so-called malpractices not with the Conqueror's administration but rather with the relations between church and state in the supposed golden age of the "old English kings."[22] In keeping sees vacant and in fostering the purchase of ecclesiastical offices, the Conqueror and Lanfranc had already established precedents for Rufus. In the reign of William I there had been one long episcopal vacancy lasting for five years.[23] Lanfranc himself was accused by the monks of St. Augustine's of using "the

[18] HC, 106.

[19] Liber Monasterii de Hyda, 299.

[20] The monastic chroniclers' opinions on Rufus' character are collected by Freeman, William Rufus, II, 490-504. Rufus' relations with the Jews are discussed below, Ch. III, p. 126f. It might be said here that I believe that there is no evidence to support the thesis put forth by the anthropologist Margaret Murray (The God of the Witches, pp. 160-62), that Rufus was one of Sir James Fraser's "dying gods" and "divine kings."

[21] See above, Ch. I, pt. 5.

[22] OV, VIII, 8: vol. III, 312: "Princeps itaque, nimia cupiditate flagrans, suo infert aerario largas opes, quas ecclesiae Dei gratanter et devote dederunt antiqui Anglorum reges."

[23] At Lichfield-Chester-Coventry from 1067 to 1072.

impudent prudence of Simon Magus" in the abbatial election of 1087.[24]

Rufus' financial measures against the church can only be fully understood when seen in a broad perspective. The Conqueror and his sons required huge sums to conduct their many wars.[25] But the period from the Conquest to the early twelfth century was one of economic slump and a low volume of production and exchange,[26] a poor economic basis for protracted wars. Hence, to pay for their wars, William I and his two sons who succeeded him on the English throne had to take full advantage of the opportunities for taxation provided by the kind of feudal relationships the Conqueror had established in England. Among these relationships was the assessment of church fiefs with definite *servicia debita*.[27] The church was thenceforth part of the feudal order and subject to feudal taxation.

William I's heavy taxation for war purposes gained for him a great reputation for avarice.[28] For his campaigns in Normandy, William II also poured out huge sums for mercenaries and other war expenditures.[29] Suger refers to Rufus as "that rich man, a squanderer of English treasure and a marvellous buyer and collector of knights."[30] Rufus' extravagant expenditure on his knights dates from the very outset of his reign.[31] Already in his reign the alienation of the royal

[24] Thorne's chronicle, in Twysden, *SS*, coll. 1792-3.

[25] See, in general, J. O. Prestwich, "War and Finance in the Anglo-Norman State," *TRHS*, 5th ser., IV (1954), a very valuable study, on which I have relied extensively in this and the following paragraph.

[26] M. M. Postan, "Rise of a Money Economy," *Ec. Hist. Rev.*, XIV (1944), 129, 133.

[27] H. M. Chew, *Ecclesiastical Tenants-in-Chief* (1932), 3-4.

[28] *GR*, II, 335-36. Cf. Prestwich, *op.cit.*, p. 24.

[29] Prestwich, *op.cit.*, 26-28.

[30] *Vie de Louis VI le Gros*, ed. H. Waquet, p. 8: ". . . ille opulentus et Anglorum thesaurorum profusor mirabilisque militum mercator et soli-. dator. . . ."

[31] *GR*, II, 368: "Namque cum primis initiis regni metu turbarum milites congregasset, nihil illis denegandum putabat, majora in futurum pollicitus."

demense, the old *terra regis*, had begun.[32] Consequently, to increase or at least maintain the income of the Conqueror, Rufus and his officials had to resort to exploiting the judicial and feudal possibilities of the monarchy.

Henry I's coronation charter indicates that Rufus' administrators, of whom the chief was Ranulf Flambard, regarded wardships and reliefs as the most lucrative source of revenue for the crown.[33] From William I's time, the great ecclesiastics had held most of their lands from the king by military tenure. Consequently, the royal administration under Rufus proceeded to treat bishoprics and abbeys as lay fiefs held in wardship by the king. Their revenues were enjoyed by the king while they were *in manu regis*, and they could only be redeemed for a large relief. If an ecclesiastic did not hold his lands in exchange for knight-service, the royal officials attempted to change his frank-almoign tenure into a military one.[34] It was this feudal taxation of the property of vacant bishoprics and abbacies which the official history of the reformers later condemned so vehemently. Ranulf Flambard was hated so much by the reformers because he was, in Anselm's words, that "most infamous chief of tax-gatherers."[35]

As far as we can get to know Rufus personally, he seems not to have been a man of exceptionally bad character, but

[32] R. S. Hoyt, *The Royal Demense in English Constitutional History* (1951), 86.

[33] F. Liebermann, "The Text of Henry I's Coronation Charter," *TRHS*, VIII (1894), 41: "Si quis baronum meorum, comitum sive aliorum qui de me tenent, mortuus fuerit, haeres suus non redimet terram suam, sicut faciebat tempore fratris mei, sed legitima et iusta relevatione relevabit eam." For the importance of wardship as a source of revenue for the crown, see S. Painter, *Studies in the History of the English Feudal Barony*, 64-5. For Ranulf Flambard as the chief royal financial agent, see Southern, *op.cit.*

[34] In 1092 Odo, Abbott of Chertsey, resigned his office "nolens eam [abbatiam] de rege more saecularium tenere." *Ann. Winton.*, *s.a.* 1092. The effects of abbatial vacancies were lessened after c.1100 by separating the lands and income of the abbot from those of the community. See Knowles, *Monastic Order*, 404-6.

[35] *AO*, ep. 214, ll. 35-6: "non solum publicanus, sed et publicanorum princeps infamissimus."

simply that kind of bold and grasping lord "who feared God but little and man not at all,"[36] generous to his knights and ruthless to everyone else. Feudal Europe produced such men in abundance. In spite of Eadmer's complaints, Rufus was not without some consideration for the monks. He set aside part of the revenues of Canterbury in 1089-93 and of Worcester in 1095-6 for the support of the monks of those vacant sees.[37] One of his writs directed his officials to reseise the Abbot of Ramsey with some lands of which a royal official had disseised the Abbot, "for the King does not desire the Abbot to lose anything that pertains to the food and raiment of the monks."[38] Rufus could not have been universally hated by the regular clergy since in 1095 Abbot Roger of St. Evroult requested his aid against the depredations of Robert of Bellême.[39] It is nevertheless true that the monks of vacant English sees seem to have been the worst sufferers from the financial policy of William II's administration.

On the other hand, with the Anglo-Norman bishops who were, like himself, great feudatories, Rufus was on excellent terms in the period of the vacancy of Canterbury. They had supported Rufus in 1088 at the time of Duke Robert's invasion. At that time they had set before him the example of King David. This indicates that the bishops may have attributed to Rufus some powers of theocratic monarchy.[40] After the revolt of 1088, amity between the King and Wil-

---

[36] *GR*, II, 367: "parum Deum reverebatur, nihil homines."

[37] *HN*, 26; Davis, *Reg.*, no. 388.

[38] Davis, *Reg.*, no. 413. For Rufus' grants to Norman churches, see Round, *CDF*, nos. 1150, 1234, 1376. Cf. Freeman, *Rufus*, II, 504-8.

[39] *OV*, III, 421.

[40] The bishops asked Rufus to be as merciful as David (*OV*, III, 275). But David was the archetype of the anointed king in early medieval thought; the association of Rufus with David may have extended to the sphere of theories of kingship. Rufus accepted David as his example. See *OV*, III, 276: "Unde reor omnino esse justum, ut David magni regis, quem mihi propuistis imitandum, irrefragabiliter teneamus judicium." In this passage Rufus is viewed as an Augustinian *rex iustus*. On the influence of Augustine on *OV* see the excellent historiographical study by H. Wolters, *Ordericus Vitalis* (1955), 93-4, 131-2.

liam of St. Calais was rapidly restored; William had been the only bishop with whom the King had quarrelled early in his reign. The Bishop of Durham and his men in 1088 gained the king's peace, and royal grants to the see of Durham followed in 1091.[41] The royal clerk, John, appointed to the see of Bath in 1088 was well rewarded for his administrative services to the King by several royal grants to his see.[42] The firm adherence of the older curialist bishops Osmund of Salisbury and Remi of Lincoln was also gained with royal grants of lands and privileges.[43]

Rufus took care that his chaplains and clerks filled up the vacant bishoprics at Bath (1088), Lincoln (1094), Worcester (1096), and Durham (1099). He appointed the great ecclesiastics not for their religion but for the extent of their services in secular affairs.[44] The bishops attended so frequently at the *curia regis* in the period 1089-93 that the witness lists of several royal charters could easily be lists of general councils of the episcopate.[45]

With the support of the episcopate Rufus was able to act virtually as the head of the English Church. In spite of Eadmer's complaints, the English Church managed to conduct its affairs successfully without a primate. Gundulf of Rochester, the diocesan ordinary, conducted the internal affairs of the see of Canterbury[46] and Thomas of York performed the service of consecration of bishops when required.[47] The King could

---

[41] Davis, *Reg.*, nos. 298 and 318; *Liber Vitae* (Surtees Soc.), p. 77.

[42] Davis, *Reg.*, nos. 314, 315, 326.   [43] Davis, *Reg.*, nos. 319, 328.

[44] *OV*, IV, 11: "nec in illis tantum religionem, quantum favorem servitiumque sibi gratum ritu saeculari attendebat."

[45] See the witness lists in Davis, *Reg.*, nos. 315, 318, 319, 328, 338, which are royal charters from the period 1091-3.

[46] Goscelin, *Hist. S. Aug.*, bk. I, ch. 8; *MPL* 155, col. 17: ". . . venerabilis pontifex ecclesiae Roffensis Gundulfus, qui tunc archpraesulis defunct auctorali vice pollebat." The *Vita Gundulfi* also says that the Bishop of Rochester administered the see of Canterbury during the vacancy (*MPL* 159, cols. 825-6). On Gundulf as diocesan ordinary see R. L. Smith, "The Place of Gundulf in the Anglo-Norman Church," *EHR*, LVII (1943), 257-72.

[47] Thomas consecrated the bishops of Norwich, Chichester, and Bangor. *HC*, 104.

deal with any other ecclesiastical questions that arose, such as enforcing obedience of the monks of the Abbey of Stowe to their new abbot.[48] In fact, the King's position as feudal suzerain gave him a hold over the English Church greater than an Archbishop of Canterbury could exercise. For Rufus could command the Abbot of Ramsey not to alienate any part of his demesne without the King's license and counsel.[49]

The papacy did not intervene to condemn this system of church-state relations or even to urge the ending of the Canterbury vacancy. Early in the 1090's Urban II was concerning himself with the reform of the French Church. He sent a letter to the French bishops reproaching them for their culpable negligence in the matter of Philip I's adulterous marriage,[50] and towards the end of 1093, in order to bring about the reform of the French Church, he reappointed Archbishop Hugh of Lyons as the papal legate in France.[51] But Rufus had not yet recognized either Urban or the anti-pope, although he was reputed to be favorable to the claims of Wibert.[52] Therefore Urban could not afford to antagonize the powerful English King. The Pope concerned himself with the affairs of the English Church only in minor matters. In 1089 he sent a letter to Rufus asking the King to restore William of St. Calais to his bishopric.[53] Four years later a papal letter to Thomas of York demanded to know why Thomas had made his profession of obedience to Lanfranc.[54] Herbert Lo-

---

[48] Davis, *Reg.*, no. 334.
[49] Davis, *Reg.*, no. 329.
[50] *HF*, XIV, 702.
[51] A. Rorey, "La Légation d'Hugues, Archevêque de Lyon, sous le Pontificat d'Urbain II," *Rev. des Questions Historiques*, 112 (1929), 126, 129.
[52] *GP*, 86: "Consensu dubio fluctuabat Anglia, in Guibertum tamen pro metu regis inclinatior." Eadmer (*HN*, 52) says only that no pope had been recognized in England: ". . . per plures annos ecclesiam Angliae in tantum occupavit, ut, ex quo venerandae memoriae Gregorius qui antea vocatur Hildebrandus defunctus fuit, nulli loco papae usque ad hoc tempus subdi vel oboedire voluerit." Lanfranc, in the last years of his life, had tended to be sympathetic to Wibert (see above, Ch. I, pt. 5) and this probably gave rise to a rumor that Rufus favored the anti-pope. Cf. Liebermann, *EHR*, XVI (1901), 329.
[53] J-L, no. 5397.
[54] *HC*, 103-4.

singa, Bishop of Norwich, visited Rome in 1093. Upon his return to England near the end of that year, he was appointed a papal legate and commissioned to concern himself with the case of Thomas' profession.[55] Probably he also brought the papal letter to Thomas. But Herbert appears to have had no other duties assigned him. Urban ignored the most vital problem of the English Church, the Canterbury vacancy.

2. THE ELECTION OF ANSELM AS ARCHBISHOP OF CANTERBURY

AFTER the election of Anselm as Archbishop of Canterbury in 1093, however, Rufus' supreme authority over the English Church was challenged by a renowned and venerated ecclesiastic who, as time went on, became more and more the champion of the ideas of the Gregorian reformers. According to the principles of these reformers the relations between church and state in England stood condemned as simoniacal heresy. Why and how did this election which was to usher in fourteen years of bitter controversy take place?

From St. Ambrose to Gregory the Great to Hildebrand it was traditional for a nominated bishop to proclaim his unworthiness for episcopal office and to have the dignity thrust upon him by clergy and people. In Eadmer's highly dramatic account of Anselm's election as archbishop in 1093 and in Anselm's letters of that year, Anselm expressed surprise that the choice had fallen upon him and vigorously protested his unworthiness for episcopal office.[56] But this expression of surprise and protest of unworthiness, while no doubt sincere, ought not to obscure the fact that Anselm's succession to his teacher Lanfranc and the perpetuation of the preeminent Bec

---

[55] Herbert was back in England by December 25 (Davis, *Reg.*, no. 338). He and the Cardinal Deacon Roger were appointed joint legates for both England and Normandy (*HC*, 103-4; *Gall. Christ.* XI, Instr. XIV, 19) but there is no evidence that Roger ever came to England. Cf. Tillmann, *Legaten*, 19.

[56] *HN*, 32-7; *AO*, epp. 148, 156, 159, 176.

school in the Anglo-Norman episcopate were only natural and almost inevitable.

In the *Historia Novorum*, the series of events leading up to Anselm's election began when Rufus fell dangerously sick shortly after the Christmas court of 1092. The illness was thought to be fatal and the King feared that he would perish in soul and body if he ended his life with the archbishopric in his possession. Anselm had come to England, according to Eadmer's official history, five months previously at the request of Hugh of Avranches, Earl of Chester, an old friend of the Abbot of Bec, who was ill and needed Anselm's spiritual comfort. The King had refused to allow Anselm to leave the country. Now that Rufus thought he was dying, he begged Anselm to accept the primacy.[57]

E. A. Freeman was bothered by the apparent incongruity in this account that William II's leave was required for Anselm, the subject of the Duke of Normandy, to return to his own country.[58] Nevertheless, Freeman followed the account of Anselm's election given in the *Historia Novorum*. If all the sources for Anselm's election are taken into account, however, a somewhat different order of events appeared. Eadmer wanted to hide the fact, which was later unpalatable to the reformers, that Anselm came to England in 1092 partly at the invitation of the King and the magnates.

According to the *Historia Novorum*, it was only at the Christmas court of 1092 that the magnates began to urge the King to end the vacancy at Canterbury.[59] But it appears that already in May of 1092, the King and the lay and ecclesiastical magnates were expecting the end of the vacancy at Canterbury in the near future. A charter of that date confirming the grants of previous donors to the church of Lincoln leaves a blank in the witness list for the name of the next archbishop of Canterbury.[60] It is unlikely that the royal clerk would have

---

[57] *HN*, 28-32.   [58] Freeman, *Rufus*, I, 388, n. 1.
[59] *HN*, 29-30.
[60] *Monasticon*, VIII, col. 271 = Davis, *Reg.*, no. 328. See also Davis's note.

drawn up the witness list in this way if the election of a new archbishop were not expected soon.

By the summer of 1092 the choice of many of the magnates, and perhaps even of the King, had fallen on Anselm. In the *Vita Anselmi* Eadmer revealed an important fact which he had suppressed in his official history. Hugh's final successful invitation to Anselm was supported "by many other magnates of the realm of the English who had chosen Anselm as the physician and advocate of their souls."[61] Already in the summer of 1092, then, many of the magnates had recognized Anselm as their spiritual leader and therefore they must have advocated his election as archbishop. This fact clarifies a statement in the *Historia Novorum*. Early in 1092 Anselm refused to come to England at the request of the Earl of Chester, who wanted the Abbot of Bec to establish the Benedictine rule at St. Werburgh, which was under the Earl's patronage. Anselm knew at that time that he was already being talked about as the successor to Lanfranc.[62]

Although the account of Anselm's election given in the "Diceto life" is confused in its chronology, it does add one important fact to the story. It implies that Anselm was summoned to England by the King and the magnates after the magnates counselled the King on the ending of the vacancy at Canterbury.[63] Anselm's letters provide evidence which con-

[61] *Vita Anselmi*, II, 1 (ed. Rule, p. 359): "Anselmus invitatus . . . ab Hugone Cestrensi comite multisque aliis Anglorum regni principibus, qui eum animarum suarum medicum et advocatum elegerant. . . ."

[62] *HN*, 27: ". . . nonnulli adinvicem loquebantur, eum, si Angliam iret, archiepiscopum Cantuariensem fore." On Hugh of Avranches, Earl of Chester, and his plans for transforming the old college of canons at St. Werburgh into a monastic community, see J. Tait, ed., *The Chartulary or Register of St. Werburgh, Chester* (Chetham Soc., n.s., vol. 79, 1920), introd., pp. xxii-xxiv.

[63] Ralph de Diceto, *Abbreviationes Chronicorum*, ed. Stubbs, I, 224: "Postremo rex Anglorum secundus Willelmus, ad extrema fere perductus, sed ad tempus fervore caritatis accensus, anno iiii post decessum Lanfranci, de consilio Cantuariensis ecclesiae tractatum coepit habere cum suis. Consilio quorum, sed maxime procerum, abbatem Anselmum e Normmannia celerius evocatum, procuravit in archiepiscopum sulimari." On the "Diceto Life" see above, Ch. I, n. 133.

firms this interpretation of his election given in the "Diceto life." After his election, the new Archbishop was accused by several Norman ecclesiastics of obtaining the English primacy through vicious "covetousness."[64] They could only have suspected the motives of a man of such estimable life and character because he had been invited to England by the King and magnates, or at least by the magnates alone. The *curia regis* must have known that Anselm would be reluctant to accept the see of Canterbury. Therefore they arranged that Anselm's friend, the Earl of Chester, should invite the Abbot of Bec to England, perhaps on a pretext of requesting Anselm's spiritual comfort during illness. Hugh of Chester was present at the *curia regis* in May 1092, when a decision to appoint a new archbishop may have been made.[65]

Anselm had a pretext for going to England in the summer of 1092 even without Hugh's invitation. The Abbot of Bec found it necessary to attend to affairs of his monastery in England. The Bec community asked their Abbot to secure from William II a reduction of the royal taxation on their English lands.[66] Anselm arrived at Canterbury on September 7th and then hastened to Chester. On the way he had an interview with the King, who had recently returned from his expedition in the north. When he arrived at Chester, he found

---

[64] See *AO*, ep. 156, ll. 22-25: "Quamvis sint quidam, ut audio—qui autem sint, Deus scit—qui aut fingunt malitia aut suspicantur errore aut coguntur dicere indiscreto dolore, quod magis trahar ad archiepiscopatum vitiosa cupiditate, quam cogar religiosa necessitate." Cf. *AO*, ep. 159, ll. 33-35.

[65] Davis, *Reg.*, no. 328, witness list.

[66] *AO*, ep. 198, ll. 10-13: ". . . cum in Normannia Beccensis monasterii abbas extitissem . . . occulto dei iudicio pro utilitatibus ecclesiasticis in Angliam veni." *GP*, 79: "Ut prediorum suorum vectigalia lenito intercessionibus suis rege levigaret." *Vita Anselmi*, II, i, p. 359: ". . . prece atque praecepto pro communi utilitate coactus, Angliam ingressus est." On the English lands and alien priories of Bec, see M. Morgan, *The English Lands of the Abbey of Bec* (1946), ch. 1; Freeman, *Rufus*, I, 375-6. In Domesday, Bec held four manors, one *in capite* from the king (*DB*, I, 34b, 69b, 159b). There was at least one alien priory of Bec in England in 1092 (*Monasticon*, VII, col. 1052).

that Earl Hugh had recovered.[67] Probably the report of the Earl's illness was a ruse to get Anselm to come to England.

Anselm stayed at Chester long enough to witness the foundation charter of the new monastic community at St. Werburgh.[68] Then he must have gone to the *curia regis* to transact the business of his monastery, for at Christmas he was in the vicinity of the royal court.[69] In Eadmer's account in the *Historia Novorum*, Anselm wanted to leave England at this time but the King refused to give him permission to do so.[70] But a letter which Anselm wrote to the monks of Bec about Christmas time, 1092, indicates that Eadmer's account was specious. Anselm informed the Bec community that the King had put off consideration of his petition on the subject of taxation of Bec lands in England. The Abbot added, however, that the King and magnates had shown him love and honor beyond his due. He did not expect to be back at Bec before Lent.[71] It is clear from this letter that the King kept Anselm in England not by prohibiting the Abbot from leaving the country, which would have been virtually impossible since Anselm was not his subject, but by postponing consideration of Bec affairs at the *curia regis*. Meanwhile, Rufus and the magnates would consider electing Anselm the new Archbishop of Canterbury.

At the Christmas court of 1092, Anselm was requested by the bishops to arrange the form and the substance of the pray-

---

[67] *Vita Anselmi,* 359-60; *HN,* 29-31. Cf. R. W. Southern, "Anselm and Gilbert Crispin," *Med. and Ren. Studies,* III (1954), 87.

[68] Tait, *Chartulary of St. Werburgh,* intro., p. xxiv.

[69] *HN,* 29.

[70] *HN,* 29: "Post haec in Normanniam regredi volens, negate a rege licentia, copiam id agendi habere non potuit."

[71] *AO,* ep. 147, ll. 4-7, 10: "Nondum vobis possum aliquid mandare de utilitate nostri itineris in Angliam, quantum pertinet ad nostram ecclesiam. Differt enim adhuc rex respondere petitioni nostrae, quamvis ipse et alii principes Angliae mihi nimis ultra mensuram meam amorem et honorem exhibeant. . . . Reditum nostrum ante Quadragesimam non spero futurum." Anselm said nothing in this letter about having been refused a royal license to leave the country. Eadmer tried to hide the fact that Anselm remained in England of his own volition.

2. Election of Anselm

ers to be offered in all the churches of England that God would move the King to appoint a new Archbishop of Canterbury.[72] Before the King's illness, therefore, Anselm was already recognized by the English bishops as their spiritual leader. But royal approval was still needed, and this was obtained from Rufus on the first Sunday in Lent (March 6) of 1093, after the King had taken ill:

> . . . All good men advised the King to release the common mother of the whole kingdom from her recent widowhood by the appointment of a shepherd for her. He willingly acquiesced and granted that he would attend to this. Accordingly they began to seek for a man worthy of the honor. But since everything depended on the King's will he himself proclaimed Abbot Anselm to be the man most worthy of such an honor. With one voice all acclaimed his decision.[73]

Eadmer does not specify who were these "good men." Probably Gundulf, Bishop of Rochester and the diocesan ordinary of Canterbury, was one. The tenants-in-chief of Canterbury, who included some of the greatest magnates in the kingdom,[74] and who had especially suffered from the retention of the metropolitan see in the king's hand,[75] were undoubtedly also among the "good men." Two of the leading tenants of Canterbury, Hugh de Montfort and Haimo, sheriff

[72] *HN*, 29.

[73] *HN*, 32: "Interea a bonis quibusque suadetur, quatinus communem totius regni matrem instituendo ille pastorem solvat a pristina viduitate. Consentit libens, ac in hoc animum suum versari fatetur. Quaeritur itaque, quis hoc honore fungi dignius posset. Sed, cunctis ad nutum regis pendentibus, praenunciavit ipse, et concordi voce subsequitur acclamatio omnium, abbatem Anselmum tali honore dignissimum."

[74] See the list of Canterbury tenants-in-chief and the knight service they owed to the archbishop in D. C. Douglas, ed., *The Domesday Monachorum of Christ Church Canterbury* (1944), p. 105; De Militibus Archiepiscopi. At the head of the list, after the Bishop of Rochester who owed the service of ten knights, are Haimo, sheriff of Kent, with a *servicium debitum* to the archbishop of six knights, and Hugh de Montfort, who owed the service of four knights. From *DB*, 1, 4, 4b, it is apparent that the Count of Eu was also a tenant of the archbishop.

[75] *HN*, 26: "Quid de hominibus ecclesiae dicam, qui tam vasta miseria miseraque vastatione sunt attriti, ut dubitarem, si sequentia mala non essent, an salva vita illorum possent miserium atteri?"

of Kent, were at the *curia regis* in May 1092 when Rufus and the magnates were probably already thinking of appointing a new primate.[76]

The choice of the king and magnates fell upon Anselm because, first of all, he was the disciple of Lanfranc and a friend of the Conqueror. In depicting Rufus' request that Anselm accept the primacy, Eadmer made Rufus say to the Abbot of Bec: "Please remember the faithful friendship which my father and mother had for you and which you had for them. . . ."[77] In 1093 Anselm was sixty years old, an advanced age for those times. This fact also may have influenced Rufus' decision to accept Anselm as archbishop. In 1088 the King had spared the older barons among those who had unsuccessfully revolted against him, for he shrewdly thought that senility and death would soon prevent their giving him any trouble.[78] Similarly Rufus might have expected that Anselm would die soon after his election and that the see of Canterbury would again fall *in manu regis*. Certainly the King did not expect any trouble from a primate who appeared to be in his declining years.

Anselm was well known in England. He had made two previous visits and several of his Bec disciples were now members of the Christ Church community.[79] The Anglo-Norman bishops knew him as a saintly man and scholar and acknowledged him as their religious master. His election was especially acceptable to them because they did not expect him to interest himself in those affairs of this world in which most of them readily participated. They anticipated that Anselm would pray to God for them and that they would take charge of his secular

---

[76] Davis, *Reg.*, no. 328, witness list.

[77] *HN*, 33-4: "Recordare, quaeso, fidelis amicitiae quam pater meus et mater mea erga te, et tu semper habuisti erga eos." Cf. *HN*, 23: ". . . Regi praefato [Willemlmo primo] necne Lanfranco archiepiscopo sacratissima familiaritate [Anselmus] copulabatur."

[78] *OV*, III, 280.

[79] R. W. Southern, "Anselm and his English Pupils," *Med. and Ren. Studies*, I (1941), 3ff.

business.[80] Anselm's protestation of his unsuitability for the secular affairs of episcopal office encouraged the bishops to regard him in this way. "Give me leave to remain in peace," he told the bishops before his election, "and do not entangle me in public affairs which I have never loved and for which I am not fitted."[81] Similarly in his letters written in 1093 Anselm described himself as a "despiser of the world."[82]

Besides Anselm's sense of personal inadequacy and his contempt for the world, there may have been another reason which made him refuse the primacy for several months. While at Bec, Anselm had come under the influence of the great Archbishop of Lyons, the papal legate Hugh.[83] It is significant that the accounts of Anselm's election as archbishop as given by Eadmer and in Anselm's letter to Hugh of Lyons in 1094, closely parallel the circumstances of Hugh's first election to the episcopate to the see of Die in 1073.[84] The account of Hugh's election as Bishop of Die by Hugh of Flavigny was written thirty or forty years after the event, but the actual event was probably well known to Anselm. Hugh, at that time a cathedral dignitary of Lyons, happened to be passing through Die at the time of an episcopal election. He was acclaimed by the people, but only after a miraculous sign did he accept his elevation to the episcopate. Perhaps Anselm in 1093 felt that he had to emulate the stages of Hugh's election as Bishop of Die twenty years before.

[80] *HN*, 33: (The bishops urge Anselm to accept the archbishopric:) "Tu Deo pro nobis intende, et nos saecularia tua disponemus pro te."

[81] *HN*, 33: "Quare sinite me pacem habere, et negotio quod nunquam amavi, ne non expediat, implicare nolite."

[82] *AO*, ep. 159, ll. 45-49: ". . . Non mentem meam trahit aut alligat ad archiepiscopatum terrenae rei alicuius, quam servus Dei, contemptor mundi, contemnere debeat, cupiditas, sed timoris Dei cogit, quam adhuc non video quomodo rumpere possim sine peccato, necessitas." Cf. *AO*, ep. 156, ll. 48-65.

[83] See above, Ch. I, p. 41 and F. Liebermann, "Anselm von Canterbury und Hugo von Lyon," *Hist. Aufsätze Waitz Gewidmet* (1886), 157.

[84] Hugh of Flavigny, *Chronicon, MPL* 154, col. 274; cf. H. L. Lühe, *Hugo von Die und Lyon* (1889), ch. 1, and A. Rorey, Hugues de Romans," *Rev. des Questions Historiques*, vol. 107 (1927), 293-4.

II. Beginnings of the Controversy, 1089-1097

As a monk Anselm's cardinal principle of ethics was obedience.[85] He saw in his acclamation as archbishop by clergy and people the will of God, which he finally had to accept after six months' resistance. "By the decision of God," he wrote to his beloved monks at Bec, "things have undoubtedly come to this pass."[86] Monastic obedience furthermore meant that he ought to obey the commands of his superiors Duke Robert and Archbishop William of Rouen who, at the request of Rufus ordered Anselm to accept the see of Canterbury.[87] Consequently, after holding out for six months after his acclamation by the King and lay and ecclesiastical magnates, on March 6, 1093, Anselm finally consented to become Archbishop of Canterbury and was enthroned on September 25.[88]

The King and the bishops might have concluded from Anselm's words and actions during these six months that their previous estimation of the Abbot of Bec was partly in error. They could have perceived that he would take an active interest in the affairs of the English Church and that while he called himself a despiser of the world, he nevertheless had a considerable knowledge of secular affairs. They might even have concluded from his words and acts that Anselm tended to be sympathetic to the more moderate doctrines of the Gregorian reformers. Although the King, after recovering from his illness, was reluctant to fulfill his promise to accept Anselm as the new Archbishop,[89] there is no indication that either he or the bishops were aware of Anselm's attitude on questions of church-state relations.

The Abbot of Bec accepted the Gregorian doctrine of canonical election. He was greatly encouraged by the fact, as he wrote to his mentor, the Gregorian reformer Hugh of

[85] See above, Ch. I, n. 135.
[86] *AO*, ep. 148, ll. 59-62: "Ad hoc enim res ista indubitabiliter iudicio Dei perducitur, ut aut necesse sit me—si quid boni Deus dignatur per me operari—servire et prodesse vobis et multis aliis, aut omnino nec mihi nec vobis nec aliis, non deficiente voluntate sed potestate."
[87] *AO*, epp. 153, 154; *HN*, 37.
[88] *HN*, 41.   [89] *HN*, 38-9, 41.

60

2. Election of Anselm

Lyons, that he had been elected by "the whole of England," that is, by clergy and people.[90] Anselm furthermore realized that his acceptance of such Gregorian principles could bring him into conflict with the King and the curialist bishops. In Eadmer's official history, Anselm made a remarkable speech to the bishops in which he foretold, before his election, his disputes with William II. Anselm warned that he would become worn out by injuries inflicted by the King's hand, and that he would be unable to come to an understanding with his episcopal colleagues.[91]

Even if this reported speech is based mainly upon Eadmer's hindsight, there is no doubt that Anselm in 1093 made demands upon Rufus before accepting the archbishopric, which indicated the course Anselm's pontificate might take. Although Rufus later feigned ignorance of Anselm's allegiance to Urban II, it is quite certain that Anselm, before his election, had informed the King that he had already accepted Urban as the lawful pope.[92]

Anselm claimed in 1093, in a letter which could have been written by Gregory I, that he preferred the life of a simple monk even to that of abbot, and above all, that he had no desire to reign as a secular prince in the world and possess landed wealth.[93] Nevertheless, it was apparent even before his consecration that he considered it his duty to defend firmly

[90] *AO*, ep. 176, ll. 11-13: "Tandem timore Dei ob multas rationes coactus, subdidi me dolens praecepto archiepiscopi mei et electioni totius Angliae, et sacratus sum."

[91] *HN*, 36-7: ". . . Praedico vobis quia me, de quo lanam and lac verbi Dei et agnos in servitium eius nonnulli possent habere, extra quam modo putetis regia feritas, diversis a se fatigatum injuriis, opprimet, et gaudium, quod nunc de me quasi pro relevationis vestrae spe vos tenet, multos, cum nil consueti consilii aut sperati auxilii per me habere potuerint, versum in moestitiam dolentes efficiet."

[92] *AO*, ep. 176, ll. 9-11; *HN*, 40.

[93] *AO*, ep. 160, ll. 50-55: "Potius et libentius eligerem sub abbate et sub regulari disciplina in monachica paupere et humilitate esse et oboedire et servire, quam regnare in hoc mundo saeculariter, aut dominari, aut archiepiscopatum sive episcopatum possidere vel abbatiam, aut hominibus quibuslibet praeesse ad animarum gubernationem sive ad corporum sustentationem, in magna terrarum et rerum terrenarum possessione et opulentia."

the temporal possessions of his see against the incursions of the royal power. His hesitation to accept the archbishopric was partly due to a reluctance to rule the see with temporalities reduced from those which Lanfranc had held.[94] Before accepting the archbishopric, Anselm consequently demanded from the King all the lands which Canterbury had possessed under Lanfranc.[95] Rufus seems to have required a final payment of the annual rent which the royal treasury had been receiving from Canterbury since Lanfranc's death.[96] But in September 1093 Rufus finally acceded to Anselm's demand and a royal writ returned the Canterbury temporalities to the new Archbishop.[97] After taking the advice of his counsellors, of whom William of St. Calais and Robert of Meulan already appear as the most prominent, the King refused to make any agreement with Anselm "covering the possessions which were not held under the late archbishop."[98] This provided Rufus with a legal loophole in the matter of the Canterbury lands.

But for the moment Anselm was satisfied with the concessions he had gained from Rufus. Early in September 1093 he was invested "after the manner and example of his predecessors and he became the King's liegeman in accordance with the custom of the land."[99] The influence of Hugh of Lyons upon Anselm was not yet strong enough to make him refuse investiture from the King. But Anselm had indicated to Rufus earlier in 1093 that he reserved the right to raise later important issues on relations between church and state. For he had said to the King: "I desire that in matters pertaining to

[94] Cf. D. C. Douglas, *Domesday Monachorum*, intro., 64: ". . . His reluctance to assume office as archbishop was caused not only by his character nor even solely by his devotion to the general principles of the reforming party in the church. He was also concerned with a specific question of feudal practice: the feudal arrangements on the lands of the archbishopric."

[95] *HN*, 39.   [96] Florence of Worcester, *Chronicle*, s.a. 1093.

[97] Davis, *Reg.*, no. 336.

[98] *HN*, 40: ". . . Sed de illis, quas sub ipso non habebat, in praesenti nullum tecum conventionem instituo. . . ."

[99] *HN*, 41: "Illi igitur, more et exemplo praedecessoris sui inductus, pro usu terrae homo regis factus est. . . ."

God and Christianity you will listen to my advice in preference to that of others; and inasmuch as I wish to have you
as my earthly lord and protector, so also you on your part
ought to have me as your spiritual father and counsellor of
your soul."[100] This right of advising the King in ecclesiastical
affairs remained one of Anselm's primary demands on secular
rulers.[101]

3. ANSELM'S INITIAL DISPUTES WITH RUFUS
AND THE BISHOPS

ANSELM was enthroned at Canterbury on September 25, 1093,
with great solemnity amidst the enthusiasm of "monks, the
clergy, and the whole people."[102] His difficulties began on
the very day of his enthronement when Rufus asserted in the
most drastic fashion the royal authority over the church which
had appeared to be weakening in the previous six months. On
the day of Anselm's enthronement, Ranulf Flambard, "the
principal agent of the royal will"[103] brought a suit against
Anselm pertaining to a matter of ecclesiastical jurisdiction,
which in the Archbishop's opinion was outside the province
of royal justice. The following year Rufus also took steps to
strengthen his hold over the episcopate by appointing Robert
Bloet, the royal chancellor, to the wealthy bishopric of Lincoln.[104]

On the day of his consecration on December 4th, 1093,

[100] *HN*, 40: ". . . Volo ut in iis quae ad Deum et Christianitatem pertinent te meo prae caeteris consilio credas, ac, sicut ergo te volo terrenum
habere dominum et defensorem, ita et tu me spiritualem habeas patrem et
animae tuae provisorem."

[101] See below, Ch. V, n. 172: Anselm rejoices that Henry I will take the
counsel of religious persons.

[102] *HN*, 41.

[103] *HN*, 41: "regiae voluntatis maximus executor."

[104] Robert was consecrated by Anselm in February 1094 (*HN*, 47). It is
interesting that Florence of Worcester mentioned the appointments of Anselm and Robert Bloet in the same sentence (*s.a.* 1093). Florence implied
that Rufus "gave" the archbishopric to Anselm and at the same time
counterbalanced this appointment by giving the wealthy bishopric of Lincoln to a royal clerk, Robert Bloet.

II. Beginnings of the Controversy, 1089-1097

Anselm also found himself in a dispute with the Archbishop of York. Anselm wanted to be consecrated as primate of all England by Thomas of York. Thomas, however, insisted that he had professed obedience to Lanfranc during his lifetime but not to Lanfranc's successors. Only when Anselm's title was changed from primate of all England to metropolitan of Canterbury would Thomas proceed with the consecration.[105] Thus Anselm lost Lanfranc's advantage over York. Henceforth, one of the new Archbishop's chief ambitions became the restoration of the jurisdictional power of Canterbury as it had been under Lanfranc.

Not until almost the end of his pontificate, however, was Anselm free to turn to this matter. But from the time of this episode at Anselm's consecration, the relations between the Archbishop of Canterbury and his leading colleague were strained. At first Thomas tried to prevent Anselm from consecrating Robert Bloet on the grounds that Lincoln was part of the Province of York. The Archbishop of York's claim was unsuccessful.[106] After his consecration, Robert Bloet attempted to complete the removal of the seat of his diocese to Lincoln, which his predecessor Remi had begun. Thomas of York then opposed this move. He and the Bishop of Lincoln also quarreled about the jurisdiction over several vills and abbeys near the border dividing their dioceses.[107] Although Anselm must have known about these disputes, he did not intervene, and it was left for the King to mediate.[108] Apparently Anselm felt that an increase in the wealth and power of the see of Lincoln would help to decrease the influence of his rival, the Archbishop of York. It was inevitable that after these differences between Anselm and Thomas that the Archbishop of

[105] *HN*, 42-3: *HC*, 104-5. Cf. W. H. Dixon and J. Raine, *Fasti Eboracenses*, 152-3.
[106] *HC*, 105-6.   [107] *HC*, 106.
[108] See also the royal document stating the terms of the settlement: Raine, *Docts.*, no. 7 (*Historians of the Church of York*, III, p. 21). Like many of the documents pertaining to the Province of York in this period, this one is not free from suspicion of interpolation.

York would be reluctant to take Anselm's side in any dispute he might have with the King.

In the two years following his consecration Anselm also antagonised several of the royal curialist bishops and isolated himself from this, the largest and most powerful group among his episcopal colleagues. Although many of these curialist bishops had begun their careers as monks in Normandy, they had come to identify their interests with their sees, and the royal administration.[109] With Lanfranc who had worked so harmoniously with the Conqueror and who was not influenced by the reformed papacy, the curialist bishops were of one mind. The curialists came into conflict with Anselm for several reasons. He was sympathetic to the views of reformers like Hugh of Lyons and Urban II; he quarreled with Rufus; he defended the monastic against the regular clergy and sought to build up the power of Canterbury against all other churches. To these ends he interfered in the administration of their sees. Finally, because of his temperament and perhaps also because of his advanced age, Anselm took no part in the royal administration, to whose interests the curialist bishops were devoted.

The initial cause of Anselm's alienation from his episcopal colleagues in the two years following his consecration was his exclusive loyalty to the interest of the two ecclesiastical bodies with which he was associated—the Church of Canterbury and the English and Norman regular clergy. Late in 1093 or in January of 1094, Anselm and Maurice of London disputed the jurisdiction over a *propria ecclesia*. Each bishop claimed the parish church of Harrow for his own diocese.[110] Anselm

[109] See above, Ch. I, p. 32ff.

[110] According to *HN*, 45, while Anselm was consecrating the parish church which Lanfranc had built in his *villa* called *Herga*, he was interrupted by two canons of St. Paul's. They gave the Archbishop a letter from the Bishop of London which claimed that Harrow was in the diocese of London. Anselm (*AO*, ep. 170, l. 15) refers to the object of dispute as *villa et ecclesia*. Wulfstan clarifies the issue as one involving jurisdiction over a proprietary church by referring in his judgement to *"dedicationem*

appealed to the decision of his most venerable episcopal colleague, Wulfstan of Worcester, who decided in favor of Canterbury's claim.[111]

Anselm's special desire to maintain jurisdiction over the church of Harrow is readily explained. At the beginning of the Canterbury manuscript known as the *Domesday Monachorum* of Christ Church, there is a list of Kentish churches owing chrism-money to Canterbury for the holy oil to be used in baptism, which the parochial clergy received from the mother church in Holy Week.[112] Harrow is not mentioned in this list of parish churches owing chrism-money to Canterbury, only because the list dates from Lanfranc's time.[113] Payment of chrism-money to a mother church was an attribute of a proprietary church in England,[114] and Harrow undoubtedly owed this payment as did other Kentish churches. Anselm would not want to lose it. Furthermore, a fragment of the original Kentish Domesday returns giving the respective rights of the King and Archbishop in Kent,[115] which is incorporated in the *Domesday Monachorum*, reveals that the manor of Harrow provided a very profitable return for the Archbishop.[116] Anselm did not want the jurisdiction of the Bishop of London to penetrate here and eventually to interfere with the archiepiscopal rights and income. Anselm was not influenced by the Gregorian reformers' suspicion of proprietary churches. In fact this institution was never to be questioned in England. But Anselm was determined to establish the rights of the mother Church of Canterbury over its own proprietary churches and this brought him into dispute with Maurice of London.

. . . *propriarum ecclesiarum*" (*AO*, ep. 171, ll. 16-17). Cf. H. Böhmer, "Die Eigenkirchentum in England," *Liebermann Festschrift* (1921), 302-3.

[111] *AO*, epp. 170, 171.   [112] *Domesday Monachorum*, 77-78.

[113] See Douglas' excellent discussion of the chrism-money list: *ibid.*, intro., 5ff.

[114] Böhmer, *op.cit.*, 303.

[115] Douglas, *Domesday Monachorum*, intro., 27 n. 1.

[116] *Domesday Monachorum*, 99.

3. Initial Disputes

After his consecration, Anselm continued to regard himself as the leader of the Norman regular clergy. He advised the monks not only at Bec but also at the Abbey of Séez on the affairs of their communities.[117] Even after his election to the English episcopate, Anselm continued to believe in the primary value of monastic life over the life of the secular clergy. He castigated the Bishop of Paris for not allowing a Paris cathedral official to become a monk, and went so far as to urge this cathedral dignitary to assume the monastic habit even over the opposition of his bishop.[118] Thereby Anselm violated his own principle of obedience to ecclesiastical superiors at all times.

Finally Anselm used his episcopal authority in order to favor the English monks, and this produced friction between him and his episcopal colleagues. His injunctions to monks and nuns who had forsaken their vows to return to their communities could not annoy his bishops.[119] But Anselm went so far as to command his episcopal colleagues to assume the same role as himself, that of defender and supporter of the monks. Osmund of Salisbury was ordered to make the nun Edith, the daughter of King Malcolm Canmore, return to the Abbey of Wilton, which was located in Osmund's diocese.[120] Osbern, Bishop of Exeter, was ordered by Anselm to defend the monks of Battle Abbey against the attacks of the clerks of Exeter cathedral.[121] This last letter of Anselm's is especially significant. It indicates that the aura of special sanctity which

---

[117] *AO*, epp. 173, 175, 178.   [118] *AO*, epp. 161, 162.

[119] *AO*, epp. 168, 169.

[120] *AO*, ep. 177, ll. 12-15: "Unde hortor, moneo ac diligenter rogo beatitudinem vestram, quatenus eam auctoritate pastorali ad ordinem, quem superbe contempsit, per humilitatis viam redire compellatis, ne salutem eius contemnere videamini. . . ." On Anselm and Edith (Mathilda) see Ch. IV, p. 148.

[121] *AO*, ep. 172, ll. 5-11: "Hac igitur fiducia reverentiam vestram obsecro, ut monachos de monasterio quod vulgo dicitur de Batailla, in vestra civitate morantes, propter Deum et propter nostrum—si quid ad hoc valere potest—amorem, paterna et episcopali pietate adiuvetis et ab omnibus adversariis pro possibilitate vestra—sicut vos decet—defendatis. . . . Audivi enim quod quidam de clericis vestris fecerunt illis quaedam quae fieri non oportuit."

the monastic life had assumed in England under Lanfranc's special favor[122] was beginning to fade, and that the secular clergy were beginning to launch those attacks on the monks which were to become more and more vociferous through the course of the twelfth century.[123] From the beginning of these controversies between the regular and secular clergy Anselm assumed the role of the defender of the monks. But he also became the leader of the Gregorian reformation in England. Consequently, the two movements which he headed became confused with one another and the Gregorian reform party within the English church, at least until 1104, gained support only from the regular clergy, and at that only from the small group of Anselm's monastic disciples. By his vehement partiality to the monks in the two years following his consecration, Anselm must have so antagonised the proud and wealthy curialist bishops that, if for no other reason, they would have been reluctant to accept the reform principles which he was to advocate at Rockingham in 1095.

The desertion of Anselm by his episcopal colleagues at Rockingham was mainly caused, however, by his bitter quarrels with the King, from whom the bishops gained their wealth and power. It was apparent from very early in Anselm's pontificate that the new Archbishop did not accord to kingship the special sanctity with which the Anglo-Saxon kings had been surrounded, and which had also influenced ideas of church-state relations in the Conqueror's reign.[124] For he wrote in 1093 to Gunnilda, daughter of Harold Godwinson, who had forsaken her religious vows: "What is the glory of the world which you love? You were the daughter of a king and queen. Where are they? They are worms and dust."[125] Gregory VII might have written these lines. Anselm

[122] D. Knowles, *The Monastic Order in England* (1940), 107ff.
[123] See below, Ch. VI, pp. 294-96.
[124] See above, Ch. I, pt. 5.
[125] *AO*, ep. 169, ll. 18-19: "Quid est gloria mundi, quid est quod amas? Filia regis et reginae fuisti. Ubi sunt? Vermes et pulvis sunt."

deprived kings of any special dignity; he regarded them as ordinary mortals. Secular rulers, he maintained, must govern with justice and mercy in order to obtain the kingdom of heaven.[126]

The quarrels between Rufus and Anselm were eventually resolved, at Rockingham, into a conflict between conflicting principles of church-state relations. But it was not upon this highly theoretical level that the first disputes between the King and Archbishop occurred. In the two years before Rockingham, William and Anselm disputed the obligations of the Archbishop to the crown arising out of his position as a royal tenant-in-chief.

The see of Canterbury was itself the greatest ecclesiastical barony in England. By 1100 nearly one hundred knights' fees had been created out of the Archbishop's lands.[127] Anselm was undoubtedly conscious of his eminent feudal position. Shortly after his consecration, or at least between December 1093 and October 1096, he caused to be drawn up in the Canterbury *scriptorium* a list of knight service owed to the Archbishop by Canterbury tenants.[128] In fulfillment of his duty as a great baron, Anselm went to the Christmas court of 1093 to give counsel to the King. Although the new Archbishop was at first joyfully received by the King and magnates, Rufus and Anselm eventually quarreled.[129] As Anselm wrote later to Hugh of Lyons, this was the beginning of his strife with Rufus: "From that time he has appeared to seek opportunities

---

[126] *AO*, ep. 180 (Anselm to Robert, Count of Flanders), ll. 17-23: "Semper igitur in actibus suis servet iustitiam vestra prudentia, et in offensionibus quae sibi fiunt, indulcet eam sua misericordia. . . . Breviter monui quod cor meum assidue desiderat, sed omnipotentem Deum precor, ut sic ipse vobis terrenum principatum gubernare tribuat, quatenus in futura vita regnum caeleste vobis retribuat." There is no extant correspondence between Anselm and Rufus. Perhaps these letters were suppressed by Eadmer, Anselm's secretary, because they did not altogether agree with his version of Anselm's dispute with the King.

[127] Douglas, *Domesday Monachorum*, intro., 70-1.

[128] *Domesday Monachorum*, 105. Cf. Douglas, intro., 64.

[129] *HN*, 43-5.

against me."[130] After the Christmas court of 1093, Anselm never again attested any of William II's charters.[131]

It is important, therefore, to determine the cause of this quarrel at the Christmas court of 1093. According to Eadmer and Anselm, the King was about to set out for Normandy on an expedition against his brother. The Archbishop "on the advice of his friends" offered the King a feudal aid of five hundred pounds which Rufus at first accepted. But "certain men of malignant mind" gave their opinion that this sum was not sufficient. They suggested that Anselm should give two thousand or at least one thousand pounds as a feudal aid. Rufus then rejected Anselm's aid and demanded a larger sum. A bootless interchange between the King and the Archbishop followed.[132]

Undoubtedly this was the course of events in outline. But Eadmer and Anselm have tried to hide a significant fact which is, however, hinted at in Anselm's letter to Hugh of Lyons:

He rejected it as too little, that I might give more; but I would not. Thanks be to God, who pitying the simplicity of my heart, caused it to happen thus, lest if I had promised nothing or little, there might have seemed a just cause for anger; or if he had accepted it, it might have turned into an accusation against me and a suspicion of nefarious purchase.[133]

The payment of a feudal aid was not simony. Yet Anselm feared that this aid might bring upon him the charge of "nefarious purchase" of his see. The reason for his fear was that everyone at the Christmas court of 1093 must have regarded his aid as a substitute for the usual simoniacal payment to the

---

[130] *AO*, ep. 176, l. 22: "Ex illa hora visus est quaerere occasiones adversum me."

[131] Davis, *Reg.*, no. 338 (December 25, 1093) is the last royal charter which Anselm attested in Rufus' reign.

[132] *HN*, 43-4; *AO*, ep. 176, ll. 15-17.

[133] *AO*, ep. 176, ll. 17-21: "Sprevit quasi modicam, ut plus darem; sed nolui. Gratias Deo, quo miserante simplicitatem cordis mei hoc factum est, ne, si nihil aut parum promisissem, iustam videretur habere causam irascendi; aut si accepisset, verteretur mihi in gravamen et in suspicionem nefandae emptionis."

royal treasury by a new bishop. Nearly all of Anselm's episcopal colleagues were present at the Christmas court of
1093.[134] They must have been the "friends" who advised him
to give the feudal aid to the King. The bishops had respect
for Anselm's tender conscience. Since they knew he would not
commit an act of simony, they advised their primate to give
a feudal aid to the King.

Who then were "those malignant men"[135] who ruined this
plan? It has already been seen that earlier in 1093 William II
had taken the counsel of the Bishop of Durham and Count
Robert of Meulan on the question of returning the temporalities of Canterbury to Anselm.[136] Probably they also counselled
the King on Anselm's offer of a feudal aid. From November
of 1088, when William of St. Calais and his men were given
the king's peace, this astute and powerful magnate had been
a powerful member of the *curia regis*.[137] While the Bishop of
Durham was certainly present at the Christmas court of
1093,[138] there is no definite evidence that Count Robert of
Meulan was present. The charter which dates from the Christmas court of 1093 was witnessed only by bishops and abbots.
H.W.C. Davis, following Orderic Vital, believed that Robert
was in Normandy from 1090 to 1096, nominally in the service
of Duke Robert.[139] But Davis seems to have overlooked Eadmer's reference to Robert's presence at the *curia regis* in the
latter part of 1093.[140] One of the royal writs which Robert
witnessed could possibly date from December 1093.[141]

Robert of Meulan was by now a leading counsellor of the
King. He was the elder son of Roger de Beaumont to whose
great fiefs of Beaumont and Pont Audemer he succeeded in

[134] Davis, *Reg.*, no. 338, witness list.
[135] *HN*, 43.
[136] *HN*, 40.
[137] Davis, *Reg.*, nos. 298, 304, 305, 306, 308, 310, 318, 327, 330, 332,
336, 337. Cf. Ch. I, n. 104.
[138] Davis, *Reg.*, no. 338, witness list.
[139] Davis, *Reg.*, no. 384 note; *OV*, III, 337, 475.
[140] *HN*, 40.
[141] Davis, *Reg.*, no. 395 (dated generally by Davis 1087-97).

the middle of the 1090's when his father entered the family abbey of St. Peter of Preaux.[142] Robert thus became a powerful vassal in both Normandy and England. On the death of the Conqueror, Robert of Meulan and his brother Henry had espoused the cause of Rufus and thenceforth remained high in the royal favor.[143] Robert had previously witnessed several of the Conqueror's charters and he was to become a very prominent member of the *curia regis* in the reigns of Rufus and Henry I.[144] In the controversies over church-state relations in the reigns of William I's two sons, Count Robert was to play an increasingly conspicuous part.[145] If he was in England in December of 1093, as seems quite possible, Robert of Meulan, along with William of St. Calais and perhaps some other curialist bishops such as Walkelin of Winchester and a few prominent magnates, were the "malignant men" who advised Rufus not to accept Anselm's feudal aid.

In 1097 Anselm's feudal obligations to the crown were again a matter of dispute between him and the King. At that time Rufus complained that the quality of the contingent of Canterbury knights which Anselm had sent to the King's Welsh expedition of 1097 was highly unsatisfactory.[146] Professor Stenton investigated this quarrel and made the suggestion that these inferior Canterbury knights could be identified with the famous "drengs" of Lanfranc, who are mentioned in a letter from the sub-prior of Christ Church to Henry II. William I in a great emergency could not obtain sufficient knight service from his tenants-in-chief for the defense of England against northern invaders; hence, he ordered Lanfranc to convert pre-Conquest drengs (the Scandinavian word

---

[142] *OV*, III, 426-28.

[143] J. H. Round, *DNB*, IV, 65.

[144] See Davis, *Reg.*, index, *s.n.*, and Johnson, *Reg.*, index, *s.n.*, for Robert's frequent attestation of royal charters.

[145] See below, p. 85; Ch. IV, 167; Ch. V, pt. 4; Ch. VI, 281, 300-01.

[146] *HN*, 78: ". . . Litteras rex a Gualis reversus archiepiscopo destinat, mandans in illis se pro militibus quos in expeditionem suam miserat nullas ei nisi malas gratias habere, eo quod nec convenienter, sicut aiebat, instructi, nec ad bella fuerant pro negotii qualitate idonei." Cf. *Vita Anselmi*, 377.

for *cniht*), into knights. Professor Stenton suggested that Rufus complained about the quality of the Canterbury knights because Anselm had sent Lanfranc's converted drengs to the feudal host in 1097.[147]

A passage in Anselm's letter to Hugh of Lyons in 1094, which Professor Stenton apparently overlooked, confirms his hypothesis. The letter further indicates that three years before the Welsh expedition of 1097 the King and Archbishop were engaged in a quarrel arising out of the status of these drengs. Anselm complained that, as English knights (*milites Angli*) who had lands from before the conquest under the Archbishop of Canterbury died without heirs, Rufus maintained that he could constitute as their heirs whom he wanted.[148] In other words, as these English knights died off, Rufus wished to enfief his own knights with their lands. Anselm also complained that this process of enfiefment of royal knights on what were really Canterbury lands had already begun in 1094.[149] These English knights mentioned by Anselm must be Lanfranc's drengs. The dispute between the King and the Archbishop over their status had already begun in 1094.

When Rufus had promised Anselm, before his consecration, to return the Canterbury lands, he added the saving clause that he would not return those estates which Lanfranc had not really possessed.[150] He must have had in mind the fees held by English knights. Anselm, however, refused to accept

---

[147] F. M. Stenton, *The First Century of English Feudalism* (1932), 147-8. Drengage was essentially a ministerial tenure (*ibid.*, 146, n. 4).

[148] *AO*, ep. 176, ll. 45-8: "Quoniam terras easdem, antequam Normanni Angliam invaderent, milites Angli ab archiespiscopo Cantuariae tenuisse dicuntur et mortui sunt sine haeredibus, vult asserere se posse iuste quos vult eorum haeredes constituere." In *DB*, II, 372, there is a reference to *milites Anglicos* in the service of the Norman abbot of Bury St. Edmunds. (Cf. D. C. Douglas, *Feudal Documents from Bury St. Edmunds* (1932), cvi-cvii). The English knights at Canterbury are therefore not entirely an isolated instance.

[149] *AO*, ep. 176, ll. 39-41: ". . . Quasdam terras non parvas, quas archiepiscopus Lanfrancus tempore patris eius et tempore eius quiete usque in diem sui obitus tenuit, militibus partim daret, partim dare disponat. . . ."

[150] *HN*, 40.

73

this specious argument. He feared that "if until my death I shall have held the archbishopric impaired, in this way the church would lose through me."[151] Consequently, he demanded from the King in 1094 that Rufus fulfill his promise to give the archbishopric as Lanfranc had held it until the end of his life.[152] Rufus refused to comply, and throughout his reign he and the Archbishop quarreled about the Canterbury lands.[153]

The disputes arising out of Anselm's position as tenant-in-chief were the initial causes of Rufus' hostility to the new Archbishop. But this would not have caused the King to try to drive the Archbishop into exile. In 1094 and 1095, however, Anselm revealed his intention to institute ecclesiastical reforms which threatened Rufus' supreme authority over the English Church. The King's firm opposition to these reforms led to a fundamental controversy over principles of church-state relations.

From the beginning of his pontificate Anselm set out to reform the English Church. He wanted to use the authority of his office "to recall whatever was irregular to due order."[154] Shortly after his consecration he used intermittently the title by which popes since Gregory I had referred to themselves, *servus servorum Dei.*[155] By this remarkable usurpation of the

[151] *AO*, ep. 176, ll. 51-58: "Rex mihi dedit archiepiscopatum, sicut eum Lanfrancus usque in finem suae vitae tenuit. . . . Si ergo ita tenuero archiepiscopatum imminutum usque ad obitum meum, hoc modo perdet ecclesia per me."

[152] *AO*, ep. 176, ll. 42-44.

[153] See Anselm's letter to Urban II in 1098: *AO*, ep. 206, ll. 35-39.

[154] *AO*, ep. 198, ll. 23-26: "Proinde infulatus sedule quid Christo, quid eius ecclesiae pro loco, pro officio deberem cogitare coepi, et pastorali regimine vitia resecare, preaesumptores coercere, et quaeque inordinata, ut mea intereat, ad ordinem debitum volui revocare."

[155] *AO*, epp. 165, 167. Cf. ep. 170: "servus servorum Christi." Lanfranc used only the title *Dei gratia Cantuariensis archiepiscopus* (*Epistolae* in *Opera Omnia*, ed. Giles, vol. 1, *passim*). Anselm's use of the title *servus servorum Dei* was therefore a distinct innovation, as far as Canterbury was concerned. Although it is true that in the early Middle Ages the *servus servorum* title was sometimes used by other ecclesiastics than Gregory I's successors (cf. L. Levillain, "Servus Servorum Dei," *Le Moyen Age*, 3d.

papal title, Anselm apparently intended to signify his sympathy with the aims of the reformed papacy. At first, however, the new Primate was content to follow the methods of his teacher Lanfranc, by which the King played the leading part in church reform. Early in 1094, Anselm requested Rufus to summon a reform council of bishops "according to ancient usage."[156]

Although the King refused to summon a reform council,[157] Anselm soon went much further in his demands upon the King. There were still vacant abbacies held in the King's hand. In requesting the King to appoint new abbots for these monastic communities, Anselm argued that, in any case, abbeys were meant to sustain God's ministers and not to provide the King with revenues for the support of his military expeditions.[158] The Gregorian doctrine of freedom of the church from secular control was reflected in this argument; it was revolutionary in its implications. The great English abbots were among the leading tenants-in-chief. The *servicium debitum* of Peterborough in 1166 was sixty knights, equal to the amount of knight service owed by Canterbury. The knight service of other great abbeys like Glastonbury and Bury St. Edmunds were also

---

ser., vol. 40 [1930], 5-7), by the eleventh century it was distinctively the papal title and its use by Anselm is remarkable. In a letter to Anselm, Bishop Wulfstan of Worcester referred to himself as "servorum dei minimus" (*AO*, ep. 171, l. 2), but this peculiar imitation of the papal title appears in fact to be an imitation of Anselm's servus servorum Christi title (*AO*, ep. 170) in the Archbishop's letter to Wulfstan to which the Bishop of Worcester is replying. Perhaps also Wulfstan wanted to indicate his sympathies with Anselm's reform attempts through use of an imitation of the papal title, for he was certainly sympathetic to the reformers as the body of the letter indicates (see below, n. 189). It would appear that C. R. Cheney's view that the use of the papal title by Anselm and Wulfstan (*From Becket to Langton* [1956], 19) is not unusual and very significant is erroneous.

[156] *HN*, 48: "Jube . . . si placet, concilia ex antiquo usu renovari. . . . Generale . . . concilium episcoporum. . . ." Cf. *AO*, ep. 176, ll. 27-29.

[157] *HN*, 48-9.

[158] *HN*, 50: "Dei scimus eas esse, ut sui ministri inde vivant, non quo expeditiones et bella tua inde fiant. Denique villas et quamplures redditus habes, unde pleniter adminstrare tua potes. Ecclesiis si placet sua dimitte."

indispensable to the feudal host.[159] No more in England than in Germany could the King afford to lose control of the military fiefs he had granted to the great ecclesiastics.

Anselm's argument seemed to refer specifically to the holding of vacant abbacies in the King's hand. But as long as this practice was not carried to excess, it was part of the legitimate rights of a feudal suzerain. Anselm's doctrine, if carried to its logical conclusion, however, threatened not only this practice but the whole scheme of feudal relationships which William I had established between the King and the greater abbots. Rufus may not have perceived the Gregorian overtone of Anselm's statement, but he at least realized that the Archbishop was advocating a new and dangerous departure from Lanfranc's view of church-state relations. "Your predecessor," he complained angrily to Anselm, "would never have dared to speak in this way to my father."[160] He deprived the Archbishop of the royal friendship.[161]

To the curialist bishops the absence of the King's favor meant the loss of their eagerly-sought-after positions of great feudal magnates. Therefore they advised their Primate to do what they themselves would have done in such case, to buy himself back into the King's friendship.[162] Although Anselm wanted to regain the King's favor,[163] he refused to follow the advice of his colleagues, lest he should "seem to be acknowledging a fault which did not exist."[164] He persisted in his criticism of Rufus' policy in ecclesiastical affairs.[165] The final break between the King and the Archbishop came late

[159] H. M. Chew, *Ecclesiastical Tenants-in-Chief*, 4-5. For a study of a great abbey's obligations to the crown during this period, see D. C. Douglas, *Feudal Documents from Bury St. Edmund*, introduction.

[160] *HN*, 50: "Nec enim antecessor tuus auderet ullatenus patri meo talia dicere."

[161] *HN*, 50.

[162] *HN*, 50-51.

[163] *AO*, ep. 176, l. 35: ". . . Rogavi ut amorem suum mihi redderet." Cf. *HN*, 50.

[164] *AO*, ep. 176, ll. 37-8: "Visus est mihi velle pecuniam. Quam dare nolui, ne culpam, quae non erat, viderer fateri."

[165] *HN*, 51.

in 1094 when the King announced that he would no longer regard Anselm as his spiritual father and Archbishop.[166]

From his attack on the relations between church and state which the Conqueror had established in England, Anselm proceeded late in 1094 and early in 1095 to a condemnation of the relations between England and the papacy which William I had decreed. The Conqueror had prohibited any English ecclesiastics to recognize a pope or to go to Rome without royal permission.[167] In 1093 Herbert Losinga, Bishop of Norwich, went to Rome to secure papal absolution from the sin incurred by his simoniacal purchase of his see. Apparently Herbert left England without royal permission, for after his return, Rufus temporarily took away his pastoral staff.[168] This episode must have brought home to Anselm the existence of William's decrees on Anglo-papal relations, if he was not aware of them previously.[169] Anselm felt strongly that if a metropolitan bishop like himself did not obtain his pallium from the reigning pope within a year of his consecration, he ought to be removed from his archbishopric.[170] But his determination in 1095 to go to Rome to obtain his pallium[171] was made especially difficult by the fact that Urban had not yet been recognized in England as the lawful pope.

The King now saw clearly that Anselm intended to bring about important changes in the relations between the church and state in England. He undoubtedly knew full well that Anselm, while still Abbot of Bec, had given his allegiance to Urban.[172] But the King decided to make an issue of this allegiance in the hope of driving his troublesome primate into

---

[166] *HN*, 52.   [167] See above, Ch. I, pt. 5.

[168] *A-S Chron. E*, s.a. 1094.

[169] Anselm must have known about the King's treatment of the Bishop of Norwich because he was at Hastings when Rufus met Herbert Losinga there and took away his pastoral staff. (*A-S Chron. E*, s.a. 1094; *HN*, 41).

[170] *AO*, ep. 176, ll. 68-70: "Si metropolitanus sacratus episcopus per totum primum annum nec papam viventem nec pallium requiro, cum possum: iuste ab ipso honore removendus sum."

[171] *HN*, 52.

[172] *HN*, 52; *AO*, ep. 176, ll. 9-11.

exile. He charged that Anselm's recognition of Urban as the rightful pope was not in accordance with his custom and that of his father, that no man should be recognized as pope in the realm of England without royal approval. If Anselm persisted in his desire to go to Rome, he would be infringing the royal prerogative and "depriving the king of his crown."[173]

Anselm accepted Rufus' challenge on the issue of papal supremacy. He felt that it would be better that he should "give up the archbishopric than be false to the apostolic see."[174] He appealed to an assembly of bishops, abbots, and magnates of the whole realm to determine whether or not he could maintain his allegiance to his earthly sovereign while preserving the reverence and obedience he owed to the apostolic see.[175] If this assembly decided that this could not be done, Anselm said that he would recognize papal authority as superior to royal power. "I confess," he told Rufus, "that I would rather go into exile until such time as you acknowledge the pope, than deny obedience to blessed Peter and his vicar for a single moment."[176]

By royal decree almost all the magnates of the kingdom were summoned to meet at the royal castle of Rockingham on February 25, 1095 for the purpose of deciding on Anselm's proposition.[177] Within fifteen months of his consecration, Anselm had thus succeeded in bringing before the lay and ecclesiastical magnates a fundamental aspect of Gregorian reform doctrine—the ultimate superiority of the pope to all secular rulers.

---

[173] *HN*, 53: "Quo rex audito dixit illum pro apostolico se nondum recepisse nec suae vel paternae consuetudinis eatenus extitisse, ut praeter suam licentiam aut electionem aliquis in regno Angliae papam nominaret, et quicunque sibi huius dignitatis potestatem vellet praeripere, unum foret ac si coronam suam sibi conaretur auferre."

[174] *AO*, ep. 176, l. 52: ". . . Immo melius est ut ego archiepiscopatum reiciam, quam apostolicum abnegem."

[175] *HN*, 53.

[176] *HN*, 53: ". . . Fateor malo terram tuam donec apostolicum suscipias exeundo devitare, quam Beati Petri eiusque vicarii oboedientiam vel ad horam abnegare."

[177] *HN*, 53.

4. THE ROCKINGHAM ASSEMBLY AND
DEBATE OF 1095

UNDER the conditions of Anglo-Norman feudalism, the dividing line between church and state in England, if it existed at all in the minds of most contemporaries, was at best irregular and doubtful. In decisions affecting the church, such as the election of a primate in 1093, the voice of the King and lay magnates as well as the decision of bishops and abbots was necessary. The assembly at Rockingham was at no time called a council by Eadmer. It was a meeting of the "nobility of the whole kingdom"[178] of the *curia regis* in its fullest aspect, called together to decide on the validity of Anselm's proposition that he could give allegiance at the same time to the Pope and the King.[179] At Rockingham the King, Primate, bishops, and lay magnates including the Canterbury knights all expressed their opinions during a four-day debate.

Rufus' intention was to defend the authority over the church which his father had established. The King and the royal officials perceived that this ecclesiastical authority gave Rufus greater authority than that enjoyed by other kings.[180] But the King feared that he was not in complete possession of royal dignity so long as anyone in the land was said "to have or to be able to do anything, even in matters pertaining to God, except through himself."[181] Since Anselm threatened

---

[178] *HN*, 53.

[179] G. B. Adams, *Council and Courts in Anglo-Norman England* (1926), 65, called the assembly at Rockingham a trial of Anselm for "lese-majeste," and complained that Eadmer's account was "untechnical." As is not uncommon in Adams' works, this view of Rockingham is anachronistic. Not Eadmer's account but the *curia regis* was "untechnical," that is, its functions and procedures were not yet specific and differentiated. The meeting at Rockingham began as a debate on an ecclesiastical issue and ended as a royal *placitum* against Anselm. (See below, n. 187)

[180] William of St. Calais speaking for Rufus to the Primate, *HN*, 60: "Quod enim dominus tuus et noster, in omni dominatione sua praecipuum habebat, et quo illum cunctis regibus praestare certum erat. . . ."

[181] *HN*, 60: "Nec enim regia dignitate integre se potitum suspicabatur, quamdiu aliquis in tota terra sua, vel etiam secundum Deum, nisi per eum quicquam habere, nota dico, vel posse dicebatur."

his ecclesiastical authority, the King was determined either to force the Archbishop to renounce his allegiance to the Pope, or to secure his banishment from the realm.[182]

The royal spokesman and protagonist at Rockingham was William of St. Calais, one of the King's chief counselors. In the latter part of the reign of Henry I, Roman law manuscripts are known to have been disseminated in England. An interest in Roman history is also evident in this period.[183] It is impossible to say whether these texts were yet available in England in 1095. But the Bishop of Durham's charges against Anselm were sufficiently technical in form to be under the influence of Roman legal ideas. By resorting to overriding papal authority, by claiming that obedience to the Pope was ultimately superior to fealty to the King, Anselm had violated the *"consuetudines regiae dignitatis."*[184] And this meant that he aimed to deprive Rufus of his *corona* and *imperium*. The Bishop of Durham demanded that Anselm return to William II the *"dignitas sui imperii"* by renouncing his allegiance to Urban.[185] Rufus again announced that he would no longer hold Anselm as Archbishop and his spiritual father and demanded that the bishops and lay magnates do the same.[186] He transformed the Rockingham meeting into a royal plea against the Primate.[187]

Anselm's alienation of the sympathy of his episcopal col-

---

[182] *HN*, 60.

[183] See extracts from the Theodosian code and Orosius and other Roman histories in *MS. Bodl. Arch. Selden B.16*. See also below, Ch. V, 280.

[184] The bishops bring a message from the King to Anselm, *HN*, 58: "Quicunque enim regiae dignitatis ei consuetudines tollit, coronam simul et regnum tollit."

[185] *HN*, 60: "Revesti eum primo, si placet, debita imperii sui dignitate, et tunc demum de induciis age."

[186] *HN*, 63.

[187] *HN*, 62 (the King to the bishops on the third day of the proceedings at Rockingham) : "Et sic sciebatis eum [Anselmum] tanto in causa sua robore fultum, quare permisistis me incipere placitum istud contra eum?" But Rufus' remark was, in part, a subterfuge. The magnates had not been summoned to a royal *placitum* against Anselm. Because of the indefinite nature of the functions of the *curia regis* the King was able, after two days of debate, to turn the meeting into a trial of the Archbishop.

4. The Rockingham Assembly

leagues in the two years following his consecration placed him in a very weak position at Rockingham. Of the whole English episcopate only Gundulf, the Bishop of Rochester, and therefore Anselm's vicar and diocesan ordinary, and perhaps also Ralph Luffa, Bishop of Chichester, supported their Primate.[188] Had Wulfstan of Worcester lived beyond the beginning of 1095, he too might have sided with Anselm against the King. For this last of the Anglo-Saxon episcopal saints seems to have been a man from an earlier, non-feudal world where the meaning of Gelasius' *duo quippe sunt* was still understood. He had written to Anselm in 1094 begging the new Archbishop to defend the holy mother church against the oppressions of the secular power.[189]

The curialist bishops had been well informed of the King's point of view before the start of the debate at Rockingham, and they looked to William during the proceedings for advice on the stand they should take.[190] Anselm began by asking the counsel of his episcopal colleagues whether or not he could maintain his obedience to the apostolic see in keeping with his allegiance to the king.[191] The bishops could only advise him to do what they had learnt to be advantageous to themselves, that is, to rely upon the will of the lord King.[192] Accustomed

[188] For Gundulf's support of Anselm at Rockingham, see *Vita Gundulfi*, *MPL*, 159, col. 827 and *Vita Anselmi*, 376. Cf. *AO*, ep. 330, which makes clear Gundulf's general support of the Archbishop in controversies over church-state relations. Ralph Luffa's position at Rockingham is mentioned only by *GP*, 205. William of Malmesbury states that the Bishop of Chichester also sided with Anselm at Rockingham.

[189] *AO*, ep. 171, ll. 5-11: "Novit prudentia vestra cotidianos labores et oppressiones sanctae ecclesiae, malignis eam opprimentibus, et ipsis quos oportuerat eam tueri auctoribus existentibus. Ad hos repellendos et contra tales sanctam ecclesiam defendere, sanctitas vestra locata est in summa arce. Ne igitur dubitet, non eam saecularis potentiae timor humiliet, non favor inclinet, sed fortiter incipiat, incepta cum Dei adiutorio perficiat, insurgentibus obsistat, opprimentes reprimat, sanctamque matrem nostram contra tales defendat." On Wulfstan's relations with Anselm, cf. Darlington, *Vita Wulfstani*, xliv.

[190] *HN*, 53-4.   [191] *HN*, 55.

[192] *HN*, 56: ". . . Si pure ad voluntatem domini regis consilii tui summam transferre volueris, promptum et quod in nobis ipsis utile didicimus a nobis consilium certum habebis."

as the bishops were to regard an anointed king as the possessor of some sacerdotal powers,[193] they were dismayed and very angry when Anselm merely enunciated the Gelasian view of church-state relations. He would render obedience to the vicar of the blessed Peter in divine matters and give counsel and service to the King in matters pertaining to his earthly dignity.[194] To the bishops this doctrine came as a radical and disturbing novelty. Never before in their lives did Anselm's episcopal colleagues have to make the agonising choice between king and pope which the Archbishop now placed before them. Those of the bishops who, in conformity with Rufus' demands, renounced their allegiance and submission to their Primate unconditionally, the King treated as his faithful friends and liegemen, the desired status of a feudal baron. But those who finally acknowledged the validity of Anselm's resort to the supreme authority of the Roman pope—apparently only Gundulf of Rochester and Ralph Luffa of Chichester—the King branded as traitors and enemies of his will. In this novel dilemma, it is no wonder that the bishops remained confused and terror-stricken.[195]

The Bishop of Durham finally concluded that Anselm restate his whole case "on the word of God and the authority of St. Peter."[196] This made it very difficult for the King to win his plea against Anselm. For the Archbishop appealed not to the custom of England but to another law. At the beginning

[193] This seems to be the only explanation for the violent reaction of the bishops to Anselm's quite commonplace statement (*HN*, 57): "Omnes igitur assidentes oppido turbati cum festinatione et magno tumultu surrexerunt, turbationem suam confusis vocibus exprimentes, ut eos illum esse reum mortis una clamare putares."

[194] *HN*, 57: ". . . 'Reddite quae sunt Caesaris Caesari, et quae sunt Dei Deo.' Haec verba, haec consilia Dei sunt. Haec approbo, haec suscipio, haec nulla ratione exibo. Quare cuncti noveritis in commune, quia in iis quae Dei sunt vicario Beati Petri oboedientiam, et in iis quae terrenae domini mei regis dignitati jure competunt ei fidele consilium et auxiliam pro sensus mei capacitate impendam."

[195] *HN*, 64-5.

[196] *HN*, 62: ". . . Ratio eius innitatur verbis Dei et auctoritate Beati Petri."

of the Rockingham debate, Anselm believed that the Gelasian doctrine on the relative powers and jurisdiction of church and state would be acceptable to the *curia regis*. For in 1093 he had said that this doctrine was fully operative in England in the Conqueror's reign—the king's jurisdiction was over the things of this world, the archbishop's over the things of God.[197] Therefore, in claiming that his allegiance to Urban was compatible with his fealty to the King, Anselm thought he was appealing to precedent and not violating the laws of England. The violent reaction of the bishops to this commonplace doctrine led Anselm to adopt a more radical position. He fell back on a canon law principle much favored by the Gregorian reformers in their attempts to establish the effective universal jurisdiction of the papacy over the church: "The Archbishop of Canterbury can neither be judged nor condemned by any man except the Pope alone; nor can he be compelled by any man, except the Pope, to answer any accusation against his will."[198]

This doctrine is founded partly on the historical fact that the archbishopric of Canterbury was the special foundation of the papacy but it also is directly influenced by the principles of church-state relations contained in four key clauses of the *Dictatus Papae*: the pope alone can depose or reinstate bishops; no one shall dare to condemn anyone appealing to the apostolic see; the more important cases of every church should be referred to the apostolic see; without the assembly of a synod, the pope alone can depose and reinstate bishops.[199]

---

[197] *HN*, 36: "Iste saeculari justitia et imperio, ille divina doctrina et magisterio." This is, of course, the moderate aspect of the Gelasian theory.

[198] *HN*, 61: "Protinus enim [episcopi] intellexerunt, quod prius non animadverterunt nec ipsum [Anselmum] advertere posse putaverunt, videlicet archiepiscopum Cantuariensem a nullo hominum, nisi a solo papa, judicari posse vel damnari, nec ab aliquo cogi pro quavis calumnia cuiquam, eo excepto, contra suum velle respondere." Although Eadmer does not directly quote Anselm's enunciation of the principle that the Archbishop of Canterbury can be judged by the Pope alone, this passage makes clear that this principle was Anselm's final position at Rockingham.

[199] *Dictatus Papae*, 3, 20, 21, 25 (E. Caspar, ed., *Register Gregors VII*, *MGH Epistolae* tom. II, fasc. I [1920], pp. 202, 206-7).

II. Beginnings of the Controversy, 1089-1097

Since Anselm, while Abbot of Bec, had been in correspondence with Gregory VII, he could have become familiar with the text of the *Dictatus Papae* which was a product of Gregory VII's circle.[200]

The doctrine of papal supremacy which Anselm finally proposed at Rockingham, however, may be founded on Anselm's familiarity with the text of the so-called *Dictatus* of Avranches.[201] This is a twelfth-century manuscript now at Avranches which consists of a collection of theses on papal power drawn from Deusdedit and other eleventh century canon law collections.[202] The Avranches canons on *Auctoritates Apostolicae Sedis*, as they are called in the manuscript, are therefore similar in principle, although separate in text, from the *Dictatus Papae* of Gregory VII. There is a distinct possibility that the *Dictatus* of Avranches was drawn up in Normandy in the late eleventh century; hence, it might have been the source for Anselm's doctrine on papal authority advocated at Rockingham.[203] The existence of the Avranches *Dictatus*

[200] One letter of Gregory VII to Anselm is extant (*AO*, ep. 102). The exact nature of the document known as the *Dictatus Papae* is not certain. It seems, however, to have been an unofficial collection of canon law principles on papal power made early in Gregory VII's pontificate by the pope or one of his intimates and intended to serve as a statement of the ideals of the reformed papacy. See K. Hoffman, *Der "Dictatus Papae" Gregors VII* (1933) and the same author in *Stud. Gregor.* (1947) I, 530-7; R. Koebner, "Der *Dictatus Papae*" in *Festschrift für Robert Holtzmann* (1933), 64-92.

[201] Avranches Municipal Library MS 146, fol. 146r, under the rubric: "Hec sunt proprie auctoritates apostolice sedis"; published by S. Lowenfeld in *Neues Archiv*, 16 (1891), 198-200, and by B. Jacqueline in *RHDFE*, 4th ser., vol. 34 (1956), 573-74.

[202] E. Sackur, *Neues Archiv*, 18 (1893), 150-53; Caspar, *Reg. Greg. VII*, 201, n. 1.

[203] The recent study by B. Jacqueline (*op.cit.*, 569-73) establishes a French provenance for the manuscript containing the *Dictatus*. (The rest of the text consists of extracts from pseudo-Isidore and papal and conciliar decrees of the late eleventh and early twelfth centuries.) There is also some evidence for a more specific origin, either at Rouen or in Flanders. See chs. 3, 7, and 9 of the Avranches *Dictatus* as possible sources for Anselm's statement on papal authority at Rockingham: "Nullus episcopus deponi debet vel potest sine illius [papae] assensu. . . . Solus papa quoslibet episcopos etiam patriarchas deponere potest. . . . Solus papa in omnes partes mundi mittit predicatores et episcopos consecat vel disponit."

at least indicates the dissemination of Gregorian ideas on papal authority in Normandy, where Anselm had presumably encountered them before his election to the see of Canterbury. Finally, Anselm might have been familiar with the canon law collections, especially those of Deusdedit and Burchard of Worms, upon which both the *Dictatus Papae* and the Avranches *Dictatus* were based.[204]

A privilege which Urban II had granted to the Archbishop of Rheims in 1089 may also have encouraged Anselm to propound the doctrine that the Archbishop of Canterbury can be judged by the pope alone. Urban had been a canon of Rheims cathedral. Among the privileges he granted to his former church in 1089 was the submission of cases involving the archbishop to the decision of the pope alone.[205] Anselm undoubtedly knew that this privilege had been granted to the metropolitan of Rheims. He wanted this Gregorian principle applied to Canterbury as well. The position he finally adopted at Rockingham, while radical from the point of view of the recent history of the English church, was thus well founded upon canon law doctrines, and the precedent of the privilege granted to the Archbishop of Rheims.

The King and the bishops perceived the radical significance of Anselm's arguments at Rockingham. The lay magnates, however, refused to support their attacks on the Archbishop. William of St. Calais wanted to deprive Anselm of his ring and staff and to drive him from the kingdom. But this proposal was not acceptable to the lay magnates. Their spokesman seems to have been none other than Count Robert of Meulan.[206] Finally Rufus asked the barons to join the bishops in refusing Anselm all faith and friendship. Again the lay magnates refused to support the King: "He is our archbishop. He governs Christianity in this land and on that account we who are Christians are not able to deny his authority while

---

[204] See Caspar's analysis of the canon law sources of *Dictatus Papae*, 3, 20, 21, 25.
[205] *HF*, XIV, 695.   [206] *HN*, 62.

we live here, especially as the stain of no offense is attached to him, which compels us to act otherwise concerning him."[207]

The lay magnates had no quarrel with Anselm. For the two years following his consecration, the Archbishop of Canterbury had antagonised the King and his episcopal colleagues, but there is no evidence that he engaged in any dispute with a powerful lay lord. The magnates still regarded him as their venerated spiritual father, as the leader of Norman monasticism which Robert of Meulan and other great lords admired and supported.[208] Anselm's reform doctrine was not yet sufficiently specific to worry Count Robert and the lay magnates. On the other hand, they must have sympathised with Anselm's resistance to the demands of the royal administration. The lay magnates looked with apprehension on the financial measures of the royal government. They did not want to remove an archbishop who shared their hatred of the royal tax-gatherers. The lay magnates at Rockingham were the pioneers of a favorite baronial policy of the twelfth and thirteenth centuries, that of attempting to rebuff the advancing power of the royal administration by discomfiting the king in ecclesiastical affairs. Furthermore, the tenants of Canterbury among the magnates feared the effect of another prolonged vacancy which might follow Anselm's expulsion from his see. The knight who stepped from the crowd at Rockingham to comfort the Archbishop while he was under bitter attack from his episcopal colleagues[209] must have been a Canterbury tenant.

Since the lay magnates refused to participate in the expulsion of the Archbishop or even to deny him their allegiance, the Rockingham debate ended in a deadlock. Anselm on his

---

[207] *HN*, 64: "Archiepiscopus noster est, Christianitatem in hac terra gubernare habet, et ea re nos qui Christiani sumus eius magisterium dum hic vivimus declinare non possumus, praesertim cum nullius offensae macula illum respiciat, quae nos secus de illo agere compellat."

[208] For Robert of Meulan's gifts to St. Peter of Preaux, see Round, *CDF*, nos. 325, 326, 329.

[209] *HN*, 61: "miles unus de multitudine."

own accord, however, perceived that he had been deprived of
the King's protection and wanted to leave England. He asked
Rufus for a safe-conduct to a port for himself and his companions. This request placed Rufus in a dilemma. He wanted
to be rid of the troublesome reforming Primate, but on the
other hand he did not wish him to leave England while he
was still in possession of his archbishopric. Nor could he find
a way "to disseise Anselm of his pontificate." The King
blamed the bishops for having brought him to this impasse.[210]

Finally at the King's request, the lay magnates and some
of the bishops arranged a truce with the Archbishop until the
octave of Pentecost (20 May 1095). During this time neither
party was to molest the other. It was hoped that something
could be done during the truce to bring the King and Primate
to their former friendship. Anselm agreed to accept "what
the King and you think fit to establish, under God, for the
preservation of peace." To this promise, however, the Archbishop added the clause: "saving the reverence and obedience
I owe to the lord Urban, pontiff of the apostolic see."[211]
Thus four days of bitter attack from the King and bishops
had failed to force Anselm to make any retreat whatsoever
from his original doctrine.

5. URBAN II AND THE CONTROVERSY

IN THE MIDST of this controversy with the King and the English episcopate over his recognition of Urban, Anselm looked
for support and aid to the Pope to whom he had given his
allegiance. But Urban II proved to be a weak reed to the
English Primate in his time of trouble. Urban was a French-
man, Odo of Lagey, who had begun his career as a canon and
archdeacon of Rheims. Later he became a monk and Prior
of Cluny and, on the recommendation of Abbot Hugh, Greg-

[210] *HN*, 65-66.
[211] *HN*, 66: ". . . Concedo suscipere quod domino regi et vobis placet
pro pacis custodia secundum Deum statuere, salva semper apud me debita
reverentia et oboedientia domini Urbani sedis apostolicae praesulis."

ory VII took him into his service and made him Cardinal Bishop of Ostia. Odo became pope in March 1088, probably on the recommendation of the dying Victor III. The more intransigent episcopal reformers, led by Hugh of Lyons and Ivo of Chartres, had strongly criticized Pope Victor because of his evident lack of enthusiasm for the Gregorian reform program. They hoped that Urban would revive Gregory VII's policies.[212]

Although Urban fully supported the Gregorian doctrines in theory[213] and secured renewed prohibitions of simony and lay investiture at his councils of Piacenza and Clermont in 1095,[214] he tended towards compromise with secular rulers in practice. The high Gregorians, and even less radical church reformers, regarded him as too moderate in his relations with the French king and the German emperor. Ivo of Chartres complained that the Church of Christ had a "weak head."[215] Hugh of Lyons protested against Urban's leniency towards Philip I on the question of the French king's adulterous marriage.[216] Pope Urban, on the other hand, felt himself hardpressed by Hugh's intransigent attitude. At the beginning of his pontificate Urban had to contend with an imperial antipope and Henry IV's army at Rome and he felt that it would be prudent to relax the severity of the reform program in some cases. He took away from his legate Hugh the direction of the papal process against Philip.[217] When Hugh, apparently

[212] On Urban II's career see A. Fliche, *La Réforme grégorienne et la Reconquête chrétienne* (1940), ch. 8; F. Duncalf, "The Councils of Piacenza and Clermont" in Setton and Baldwin, *A History of the Crusades* I, (1955), 25ff; J. Sydow, "Untersuchungen zur kurialen Verwaltungsgeschichte im Zeitalter des Reformpapsttums," *Deutsches Archiv*, 11 (1954), 39-55.

[213] See Urban's letter to the German bishops written the day after his election on March 12, 1088: "De me porro ita credite, sicut de beatissimo Gregorio; cuius ex toto sequi vestigia cupiens, omnia quae respuit respuo, quae damnavit damno, quae dilexit prorsus amplector." (J-L, 5348)

[214] *Hefele-Leclercq*, vol. 5, pt. 1, pp. 389-395, 400-403.

[215] *MPL*, 162, col. 35.

[216] On Urban's relations with Hugh of Lyons see A. Rorey in *Rev. d. Quest. Hist.* 112 (1937), 133-45.

[217] A. Fliche, *Le Règne de Phillippe Ier* (1912), 54.

in protest, absented himself from the Council of Piacenza, the Pope temporarily suspended him from his office of legate.[218] Urban's attitude towards Hugh's friend and admirer, the English Primate, was initially not more sympathetic.

Because of his difficult position in Italy, Urban in any case would not have dared to arouse the opposition of the English King, who still had not recognized any pope. But during the course of his pontificate Urban acquired other interests besides the revival of the Gregorian reform program. He developed the administration of the papal curia and papal taxation.[219] To achieve this elaboration of the international administrative techniques of the papal curia, it was necessary for him to compromise with secular rulers. Early in 1095, the Pope began to devote his attention and great organizing ability to his new project for a crusade against Islam. At Piacenza in March 1095 the Pope, in response to an embassy from Constantinople, urged Western warriors to go to the aid of the emperor Alexius.[220] The idea of a crusade was probably already forming in his mind in the early months of 1095.[221] He was especially eager, therefore, not to antagonise one of the most powerful European kings whose English knights could eventually form an important part of a crusading army. These circumstances induced Urban, much to Anselm's surprise and disappointment, to adopt a very moderate and conciliatory policy towards the English King.

Late in 1094 or early in 1095 Urban issued his call for a reform council to be held at Piacenza on March 1. It is improbable that he even attempted to summon bishops from England. He recognised that his authority had not penetrated

---

[218] J-L, 5541. But cf. Rorey, *op.cit.*, 145, for a different view.

[219] Sydow, *op.cit.*, 55: "Diese Papst ist . . . der Schöpfer der neuen Organisation der Kurie. . . ."

[220] *Bernoldi Chronicon*, MGH, SS, v, 462; Munro, *AHR*, 27 (1922), 731-3.

[221] Urban's intentions at Piacenza are a matter of dispute. Cf. Duncalf, *op.cit.*, 229-30; A. Fliche in *Rev. de l'histoire de l'église de France*, XIII (1927), 289-93.

there.[222] But early in 1095, at the initiative of William II, an opportunity was provided Urban for obtaining his recognition as lawful pope in England. At this time, there appeared at the papal curia a delegation from Rufus consisting of two royal clerks, Gerard and William. Rufus had sent them secretly to Rome when it became apparent that he would be unable to force Anselm to retreat from his Gregorian views.[223]

Rufus wanted Urban to hand over to his envoys the pallium for the Archbishop of Canterbury. The King could then give it to whomever he pleased when he had expelled Anselm from his see and the country.[224] In other words, what the royal envoys actually sought from the Pope was permission for Rufus to deprive Anselm of his archbishopric. In view of the later negotiations between Rufus and Urban's legate,[225] it is likely that the King now offered, through his envoys, to strike

[222] Bernold (*Chronicon, MGH, SS*, v, 461) states that Urban summoned bishops from Italy, Burgundy, France, Allemania, Bavaria, and other countries to Piacenza. There is no surviving document or chronicle reference to indicate that England was among "the other countries."

[223] *HN*, 68: "Siquidem ipse rex ubi sensit Anselmum suae voluntati nolle in praescriptio negotio obtemperare, clam et Anselmo ignorante eosdem clericos Romam miserat. . . ." Gerard was the later Bishop of Hereford and Archbishop of York; William was William Warelwast, the later Bishop of Exeter. The dating of the mission of the two royal clerks is not certain. If they actually saw the Pope at Rome, it must have been before September 12, 1094, for from this date Urban was on a tour of various north Italian cities (J-L, I, 675-7). But the word Rome is used in a broad sense by Eadmer. He says that "there were two popes in Rome in those days" (*HN*, 68); Rome is here used in a generic sense. Therefore, Gerard or William could have had their interview with the Pope in one of the north Italian cities where the Pope was staying from the early part of September 1094. Since the royal envoys and the papal legate arrived in England early in May 1095 (*HN*, 68) and since it took about two months to travel from northern Italy to England at this time (or to be specific, at least seven weeks in the middle of the twelfth century. See R. L. Poole, *Historia Pontificalis of John of Salisbury*, intro., p. liii, n. 1), the interview between the royal envoys and the Pope could not have taken place later than the second week of January 1095.

[224] *HN*, 68. Tillmann, *Legaten*, 20, n. 44, regards Eadmer's account of negotiations between Urban and the royal envoys as "unglaubwürdig." But in view of the later relations between Urban and Rufus, it is entirely possible. Eadmer's account is confirmed by *GP*, 89, which is here an independent source.

[225] See below, p. 92f.

a bargain with the Pope. He would recognize Urban as lawful pope in return for papal approval of Anselm's expulsion. Urban could not agree to such a project which would have scandalised Christendom and weakened his moral position as leader of the crusade. But he saw his great opportunity to secure the allegiance of England for himself at a crucial moment in his pontificate. At about the same time that Anselm was resisting the King and the bishops at Rockingham in order to maintain his allegiance to Urban, the Pope was dispatching his legate to England with instructions, as it later appeared, to obtain Rufus' allegiance in exchange for any price short of Anselm's expulsion.

The papal legate was Walter, Cardinal Bishop of Albano. He had been appointed to the college of cardinals by Urban himself and therefore must have been one of Urban's firmest adherents.[226] He landed at Dover early in May of 1095, about three weeks before the truce between the King and Anselm was to expire. The royal envoys Gerard and William accompanied the papal legate. Walter told no one that he had brought with him the archbishop's pallium. He passed silently through Canterbury, avoided Anselm, and hurried to meet the King.[227] Anselm and his *familia* at Christ Church must have heard of the arrival of the papal legate only when Walter made his appearance at the *curia regis* on Pentecost (May 13, 1095). The Archbishop and his monastic supporters expected that Walter would at first concern himself with Anselm's troubles, and that on Anselm's behalf he would arrange peace between the King and the Archbishop. But Walter followed the instructions given him by Urban and ignored Anselm's affairs.[228] The reformers began to complain that gold

[226] Walter's provenance is unknown. His first subscription to a papal document was on March 20, 1091, and his last on November 20, 1100. (H. W. Klewitz, "Die Entstehung des Kardinalcollegiums," *ZRG, KA*, 25 [1936], 208.)

[227] *HN*, 68.

[228] *HN*, 69: ". . . Nil penitus ipsi pro Anselmo locutus est quod pacem inter eos conciliaret. . . ."

and silver were apparently more important than justice at the papal curia.[229]

In the subsequent negotiations between the King and the papal legate, Rufus was represented by the Bishop of Durham.[230] The King again offered to recognise Urban in exchange for Anselm's deposition. Walter refused to concede this,[231] but he granted Rufus important privileges in return for this acknowledgment of Urban as the lawful pope. No papal legate was to be sent to England except on Rufus' invitation, and no English ecclesiastic was to receive or to obey a papal letter without royal permission.[232] The King is also reported to have been granted the privilege of papal confirmation for his acts.[233] Rufus accepted these concessions. He not only recognized Urban but transmitted Peter's Pence to Rome through the legate.[234]

While Rufus had again been unable to secure papal approval for Anselm's expulsion, he had a plan for reassertion of his authority over the Archbishop. The curialist bishops informed Anselm that Walter had brought the archbishop's pall to England, and Rufus restored Anselm to royal favor so that the Primate would come to the *curia regis* to receive it. Rufus then proposed that "in order to honor the royal majes-

---

[229] *HN*, 69.

[230] *GP*, 89. The *Historia Novorum* omits many of the details of these negotiations and the later disputes between Walter and Anselm. Eadmer was reluctant to make clear how little Urban did to help Anselm in his struggle to reform the English church and the extent of the concessions granted to the King by the papal legate. The details of Walter's legateship can be determined from *GP*, 89, Anselm's letters and Hugh of Flavigny, *Chronicon*, *MGH*, *SS*, VIII, 475. Hugh was in England in the following year as the secretary of the papal legate Abbot Gerento, and could have easily obtained accurate information on Walter's legateship.

[231] *HN*, 69-70 says that Rufus first recognized Urban as the lawful pope and then requested the legate to depose Anselm; Walter refused to do this. It seems unlikely, however, that such shrewd and able men as William II and the Bishop of Durham could have been fooled so easily by the papal legate.

[232] Hugh of Flavigny, *Chronicon*, 475.

[233] *GP*, 89: "Si Urbanus in Anglia reciperetur ad papam, fore ut quaecunque rex petenda estimasset, ille privilegio sedis apostolicae roboraret."

[234] *A-S Chron E*, s.a. 1095.

ty" the Primate should take his pallium from the royal hand.[235] Implicit in this proposal was that theocratic view of the King which the doctrine of the Gregorian reformers vehemently refused to accept. The Archbishop maintained that the gift of his pallium derived not from the royal dignity but from the singular authority of St. Peter. He refused to accept the pall from the King's hand. Instead, Anselm proposed that the legate should place the pall on the altar at Canterbury and he would take it from there "as if from the hand of St. Peter." The legate agreed to this procedure and on May 27, 1095, Anselm finally assumed his pallium at Canterbury.[236]

Now that Anselm had officially regained the King's friendship, the way was open for the Archbishop and papal legate to work together for the reform of the English Church. Walter wanted to meet with Anselm after the Archbishop had assumed the pallium for the purpose of discussing "the cause of the churches of God."[237] Had the legate and Anselm achieved an agreement on a program of reforming the English Church, the controversy over lay investiture in England might have begun in 1095. But instead Walter and Anselm quarrelled, and nothing was achieved in the way of reform.

Anselm did not forgive the legate for the rather unscrupulous secrecy of his arrival in England and his unseemly haste to engage in negotiations with Rufus. In June of 1095 the King was expecting an invasion of England by Duke Robert[238] and he placed Anselm in charge of the defense of Canterbury.[239] Anselm gave these military obligations as the reason why he could not at that time discuss church reform with the legate.[240] It was a rather flimsy subterfuge because Duke Robert never set foot in England in the summer of 1095. Anselm's

---

[235] *HN*, 70-1.   [236] *HN*, 72.

[237] *AO*, ep. 191, ll. 4-6 (Anselm to Walter): "Quod mandat mihi prudens vestra sollicitudo, ut aliquo in loco conveniamus de causis ecclesiarum Dei fraterno ac caritativo ad invicem consilio acturi et quae corrigenda sunt correcturi."

[238] Freeman, *Rufus*, II, 43-5.   [239] *AO*, ep. 191, ll. 13-19.

[240] *Ibid.*, ll. 10-13, 18-19.

real reason for avoiding the legate was undoubtedly his suspicion of Walter's intentions. The legate had already shown that he was willing to make almost any concession to the English King if it served Urban's interests. Anselm undoubtedly felt that church reform was not Walter's primary aim. In any reforming council of the English church, the cardinal legate would take precedence over the Archbishop of Canterbury. But how could Walter be trusted in view of his previous conduct in England? Anselm believed that the papal legate could not be trusted with leadership of the reform movement in the English Church.

The quarrel between Anselm and Walter was also induced by the legate's assumption of the role of judge in the controversy between the Archbishop and the curialist bishops. Instead of denouncing the bishops for their disloyalty to their primate, Walter seriously considered accusations which the bishops brought against Anselm. Probably William of St. Calais took a leading part in bringing these charges. Since Rufus and the curialists had failed to expel Anselm themselves, they tried to get him suspended by the papal legate on the grounds that his investiture and consecration as archbishop had been uncanonical. The bishops pointed out to the papal legate that Anselm had accepted investiture from a schismatic king and consecration from schismatic bishops. Walter confronted Anselm with these accusations.[241] Furthermore, he went so far as to ask the Primate why he had lost the loyalty of his bishops.[242] Anselm replied angrily that the legate should have raised these "calumnies" before granting him the pallium. In any case, he maintained, the King and bishops had not been schismatics. And if Walter wanted to know why the bishops had deserted him, let the legate ask them.[243]

As the result of these differences between the legate and the Archbishop nothing was achieved in the way of church

---

[241] *AO*, ep. 192, ll. 38-43.
[242] *Ibid.*, ll. 33-34.
[243] *Ibid.*, ll. 43-60, 35-37.

5. Urban II and the Controversy

reform during Walter's stay in England. He and Anselm were partly reconciled before he left England in the summer or autumn of 1095,[244] but Anselm was probably not sorry to see him leave. Walter's negotiations with Rufus and his leniency towards the bishops were a severe shock and deep disappointment to Anselm. In general, the legate had been very slow to support the Primate's attempt to introduce the Gregorian reform program into England. Nevertheless, Anselm did not yet doubt that Urban would support and assist him. He sent back with Walter a gift and a letter for the pope.[245] In this letter he thanked Urban for sending the pallium, explained that he had not been able to go to the papal curia because of the King's opposition, and asked for papal aid in his struggle with Rufus and the bishops.[246]

Although Walter had been concerned that Anselm had lost the allegiance of the suffragan bishops, the legate did not succeed in effecting a general reconciliation between the Primate and the English bishops. After Rockingham, Anselm achieved a formal reconciliation with three of his episcopal colleagues. Two of the most learned among them, Osmund of Salisbury and Robert of Hereford, begged Anselm's forgiveness for their desertion at Rockingham. They did penance and were absolved.[247] Maurice of London promised obedience to Anselm in matters pertaining to his diocese.[248] But with the innermost group of curialist bishops, especially William of St. Calais and Walkelin of Winchester, there was not even a formal reconciliation. Anselm and his episcopal colleagues could come to no understanding on principles of church-state relations. In the spring of 1095, most of the bishops were still urging their primate to buy his way back into the King's friend-

[244] This reconciliation is apparent from *AO*, ep. 194. It is not known exactly when Walter left England.

[245] *AO*, ep. 193, ll. 54-55; ep. 194, l. 14.

[246] *AO*, ep. 193, ll. 4-7, 18-20, 48-53.

[247] *HN*, 72. Anselm's partial reconciliation with Osmund is also indicated by *AO*, epp. 185, 190, 195 .

[248] *AO*, ep. 200, ll. 4-6.

ship.[249] Anselm, on the other hand, would not retreat from his support of the Gregorian reform program. He insisted that ecclesiastical doctrine must be enforced "with canonical severity."[250]

Nevertheless, the aged Archbishop began to regret his almost complete isolation from his episcopal colleagues and his apparent failure to reform the English Church. Already at Rockingham he reminded the bishops that he had never wanted "to take up every man's burden"[251] as Primate of the English church. After Cardinal Walter made him aware of the deviations of papal politics, Anselm became more and more nostalgic for the old happy days at Bec where his duties had been much simpler. He wrote with longing to the monks of his former community.[252] Deep feelings of regret and a sense of failure are reflected in one of his letters of this period:

. . . Those whom I ought to have as helpers in the cause of God have been greatly offended and do me harm; the cause of God which ought to advance through me, goes to ruin when I am present. Whence . . . very bitter distress overcomes me when I remember the fruitful peace I have lost and when I reflect that I have incurred this fruitless danger.[253]

While Anselm was beginning to regret his acceptance of the archbishopric, Rufus, in the latter half of 1095, was reestablishing his complete control over the church, which had been temporarily threatened at Rockingham. It was necessary

---

[249] HN, 70.

[250] AO, ep. 198, ll. 38-41 (Anselm to the Irish bishops): "Praeterea, quamquam recte viventem recteque sapientem, pastorali sollicitudine fraternitatem vestram monere compellor, quatenus viriliter ac vigilantius agat in doctrina Dei, canonica severitate, si quid contra ecclesiasticam doctrinam in provinciis suis inventum fuerit, compescens et secundum Dei voluntatem cuncta disponens."

[251] HN, 55: "Rapuistis me, et coegistis onus omnium suscipere. . . ."

[252] AO, ep. 205.

[253] AO, ep. 198, ll. 26-31: "Qua causa quos adiutores me oportuerat habere in causa Dei, terribiliter offensos patior; et quae per me crescere debuerat, me presente deperit causa Dei. Unde . . . invenerunt me amarissimae tribulationes, dum et quietem fructuosam me reminiscor perdidisse et infructuosum periculum me considero incurrisse."

first to reward the curialist bishops who had been the protago-
nists of the royal cause. The reformers later claimed that
William of St. Calais had taken the lead in attacking Anselm's
views at Rockingham, because the Bishop of Durham coveted
the archbishopric of Canterbury for himself.[254] This interpretation seems to be specious, for William of Calais undoubtedly knew that his succession to the metropolitan see in the
event of Anselm's expulsion would be uncanonical. The Bishop of Durham was sufficiently rewarded for his role as Anselm's chief opponent by valuable grants of royal privileges
and confirmations. The King continued to favor the see of
Durham even after William of St. Calais' death in January,
1096.[255] The two remaining great curialist bishops, Walkelin
of Winchester and Robert of Lincoln, were similarly rewarded.[256] Herbert Losinga, to whom Urban II had granted
a legatine commission in 1093, concerned himself only with
building up the wealth and power of his see of Norwich, and
took no part in the controversy over church-state relations.
Herbert was also a recipient of royal favor.[257]

In order to weaken Anselm's resistance to the royal will
the King decided to isolate him as much as possible, by depriving him of the support of his chief disciples in the Christ
Church *familia*. The Archbishop's confidant, and head of his
household, Baldwin, and two other clerks upon whom Anselm
relied were expelled from England.[258] The tenants of Canterbury again suffered so much from the depredations of the
royal administration that they began to complain that the
Church of Canterbury had formerly been better off without
a pastor than it was now under a pastor of this kind.[259] Even

---

[254] *HN*, 59.

[255] Davis, *Reg.*, nos. 363-5 (spurious?), 412, 463. Privileges to monks
of Durham after death of St. Calais: *Ibid.*, nos. 396, 426, 478, 480, 481.

[256] *Ibid.*, nos. 377 (Walkelin); 374, 406-7 (?) (Robert).

[257] *Ibid.*, no. 385. [258] *HN*, 67.

[259] *HN*, 67: "Passa est igitur ea tempestate ecclesia Cantuariensis in
omnibus hominibus suis tam saevam tempestatem, ut fere universi concla-
marent melius sibi absque pastore iam olim fuisse quam nunc sub huiusmodi pastore esse."

the lay magnates—almost Anselm's sole supporters at Rockingham—were becoming weary of the effects of his prolonged controversy with the King.

The Primate could now depend for support, in his struggle to reform the English Church, only upon Rome. But in the latter part of 1095 and in the following year, Urban II slowly dispelled this last hope. After Piacenza Urban decided to call a similar reform council in France.[260] As he crossed the Alpine passes in the late summer of 1095, he was probably already contemplating his great scheme for a holy war.[261] From Le Puy, in the middle of August he issued letters summoning a great convocation of bishops for Clermont on November 18. The Pope was certainly by now envisaging a crusading army since the bishops were told to bring lay magnates as well as abbots with them.[262] The revival of Gregory VII's universal reforming policy was taking second place in his mind to plans for the holy war.

Historians of the first crusade have assumed that the English bishops were invited to the Council of Clermont.[263] Runciman observed that "Urban sent letters to the bishops of France and neighboring lands," presumably including England. Duncalf concluded that "William II did forbid his clergy to go" to Clermont, assuming that Urban had previously invited the English clergy to attend the Council. Neither historian cites evidence for this assumption.[264] Chalandon argued that a circular letter "must have been addressed to the metropolitans obedient to Urban," calling them to the council and commanding them to invite their suffragans.[265] While this is a plausible thesis, no such circular letter is extant. The evidence cited by Chalandon, consisting of a letter from the

[260] Duncalf, op.cit., 230.

[261] S. Runciman, A History of the Crusades (1951), I, 105.

[262] J-L, 5570, 5571. Cf. R. Crozet, "Le Voyage d'Urban," Rev. Hist., 179 (1937), 276.

[263] This question was not discussed at all by Freeman, Rufus, and A. L. Poole, From Domesday Book to Magna Carta.

[264] Runciman, I, 106; Duncalf, 236.

[265] F. Chalandon, Histoire de la première Croisade (1925), 19-20.

5. Urban II and the Controversy

Archbishop of Rheims to one of his suffragans, proves only that Urban wrote to this metropolitan and ordered him to summon his suffragan bishops to Clermont.[266] It does not necessarily follow, without corroborative evidence, that the Pope sent such a letter to the metropolitan of Canterbury.

Although Anselm's extant correspondence is voluminous, it does not contain any letter which passed between him and the Pope on the subject of Clermont. Nor does Anselm ever mention the Council of Clermont in his correspondence. Eadmer's official history omitted any reference to Clermont, which would be strange if the Primate received an invitation and had been prevented from attending the Council because of Rufus' opposition. Eadmer never failed to enumerate any of the King's alleged malpractices; and he certainly would not have overlooked this one.

There is, on the other hand, some positive evidence to suggest that neither Anselm nor any English bishop was invited to Clermont. Orderic Vital stated that the bishops of France and Spain were summoned to the Council by the Pope, but he does not mention England in this regard.[267] He was in a position to know whether or not the English clergy were summoned. The Anglo-Saxon Chronicle did not mention the Council of Clermont under its entry for 1095. By the end of this year the author of the chronicle would have heard that the English episcopate had been invited by the Pope to attend a Council at Clermont. The Peterborough chronicler only mentioned under 1096 the reaction in western Europe to Urban's call for the crusade.[268] If any English bishops were sum-

---

[266] Mansi, *Concila*, xx, coll. 693-4: "Dilectissimam nobis fraternitatem vestram ignorare nolumus, quoniam domini papae Urbani epistolam nuperrime suscepimus, quod nos ut ad concilium quod in octavio S. Martini, quartodecimo videlicet Calendas Decembris, apud Arvernensem, quae et Clarimontis dicitur, ecclesiam celebraturus est, accederemus praesentialiter, praemonuit, et ut omnes nostrae metropolis suffraganeos convocatis tam abbatibus quam caeteris ecclesiarum primoribus, sed et excellentioribus principibus ad ipsum concilium invitaremus praecepit."

[267] *OV*, III, 463.

[268] *A-S Chron E*, s.a. 1096.

moned to Clermont, the author of the Anglo-Saxon Chronicle obviously did not hear of it. The only account of Anselm's connection with Clermont, which is to be found in the life of Abbot Boso of Beç, stated simply that Anselm "heard that Urban had summoned a general council at Clermont."[269] If Anselm had actually been invited to Clermont, it seems likely that the author would have said so specifically. Finally, if Rufus had prevented English ecclesiastics from obeying a papal summons to Clermont, Urban would undoubtedly have condemned this prohibition at the Council. But while the Pope concerned himself with several matters pertaining to the church in France, including the excommunication of Philip I, the affairs of the English Church were not discussed at all at Clermont.[270]

While it is possible, therefore, that Anselm and the English bishops were summoned to the Council, the existing evidence actually points to the opposite conclusion. This is why Eadmer completely ignored the Council in his detailed history of Anselm's pontificate. The reformers did not want their official history to reveal the disturbing fact that the metropolitan of Canterbury, the leader of the Gregorian reformers in England, had not been summoned to the great reform Council of Clermont. Urban could not issue such a letter of summons because by the terms of the agreement made between William II and the papal legate earlier in the year, the English Church had been completely cut off from free and independent communication with the papacy.[271] The Pope must have also believed that he was bound by this agreement not to preach the crusade in England. For there is no indication that an attempt was made to promote the crusade in Wil-

---

[269] *Vita Bosonis*, in J. A. Giles, ed., *Lanfranci Opera* (1845) I, 328: "Eodem tempore audiens Anselmus Urbanum papam convocasse concilium generale apud Clarummontem. . . ." All historians of the Council of Clermont appear to have overlooked this source.

[270] Crozet, *op.cit.*, 287ff.; Hefele-Leclercq, v, pt. 1, 404-6; Fliche, *La Réforme Grég.*, 279-83.

[271] See above, p. 92.

liam II's kingdom, and only two English barons are known to have joined Robert Curthose's crusading contingent.[272]

Although it appears that Anselm did not receive a summons to Clermont, he sent an observer there. For only the Pope and the continental reformers who assembled at Clermont in November of 1095 remained to assist him in his controversy with the King and his episcopal colleagues. Rufus would not let the Primate leave England, but Anselm succeeded in despatching to Clermont his monastic disciple Boso, whom he had brought over from Bec to Christ Church.[273] While the Norman Church's delegation at the Council consisted of three bishops and an abbot, lead by Odo of Bayeux, the Conqueror's half-brother,[274] the whole English Church was represented among the three hundred ecclesiastics present by a solitary monk.

The long and arduous journey proved too much for Boso. He fell ill and had to convalesce at Bec on his way back to England from Clermont.[275] Not until the first or second month of 1096, therefore, could Anselm have learned the details of the proceedings at the Council. Anselm's envoy must have consulted with Hugh of Lyons, who was present at Clermont,[276] about the English Primate's difficult situation. Boso probably brought back with him to Canterbury one or more copies of the Clermont conciliar decrees, for two of the best recensions of canons of the Council are to be found in early twelfth-century English manuscripts.[277]

[272] C. W. David, *De Expurgatione Lyxbonensi* (1936), intro., p. 5.
[273] *Vita Bosonis*, 328-9: ". . . Qui ipse [Anselmus] non potuit ire misit praedictum Bosonem ad idem concilium. . . ."
[274] *OV*, III, 470.   [275] *Vita Bosonis*, 329.
[276] Crozet, *op.cit.*, 283.
[277] One recension of the Clermont decrees is in *GR*, II, 391-3. *GR*, II, 393-8 is also one of the most important versions of Urban's speech at Clermont. Another and slightly different recension of the Clermont decrees is to be found in an early twelfth-century papal history which ends with the decrees of the council of 1119. (*Cambridge U. Lib. MS. KL. IV.6* [2021] fol. 224-80). See W. Levison, *Neues Archiv*, 35 (1910) 393-4, on this recension. One of the two recensions, and perhaps both, could have been brought back to Canterbury by Boso for Anselm's perusal.

II. Beginnings of the Controversy, 1089-1097

In Normandy, Archbishop William of Rouen quickly summoned a council of his suffragans to ratify the Clermont decrees.[278] No such subsidiary council was summoned in England. Since Anselm did not attend the Clermont Council, he did not feel himself obligated to enforce its decrees. He already had enough causes of dispute with the King without attempting to implement the Clermont Council's prohibition of lay investiture. Only after he had attended the reforming Council of Bari in 1098, where lay investiture was again condemned, did he feel himself obligated to advocate this radical measure in England.[279]

In taking this attitude towards the efficacy of conciliar decrees, Anselm was following the accepted view of the period. No study has been made of what the publication of conciliar decrees really entailed at this time. But it appears that ecclesiastics did not feel themselves bound to obey a conciliar decree merely because they heard of its existence. They believed that the canons of reform councils had binding force only when they themselves had some actual connection with the decrees, either by participating in the council that promulgated them, or by receiving a direct papal command to obey them.

There is no evidence that Urban informed Anselm of the decrees of the Council of Clermont and ordered the Primate to enforce them in England. Nevertheless, Anselm must have been encouraged by Boso's report of the Pope's vigorous reforming endeavors in France to hope for a similar papal policy in England. The arrival of another papal legate in England in April of 1096 gave Anselm real cause to expect that at long last he would receive papal support in his controversy with the King and the English bishops.

Abbot Gerento of Saint-Benigne of Dijon was the legate whom Urban sent to England in the spring of 1096.[280] He

---

[278] *OV*, III, 473ff.; Bessin, *Concilia*, 77.

[279] See below, Ch. III, pt. 4.

[280] The only source for Gerento's legateship in England is Hugh of Flavigny, *Chronicon*, *MGH*, *SS*, VIII, 474-5. Hugh was Gerento's secretary and accompanied the abbot to England.

5. Urban II and the Controversy

acted as a papal representative in controversies over the Gregorian reforms on the continent[281] and he had recently been at the Clermont Council.[282] Although Abbot Gerento's legatine commission is not extant, he must have received it in February or March of 1096 while the Pope was laying plans in western France for his crusade.[283] Urban commissioned the legate to arrange a peace between the King of England and Robert Curthose so that the feckless Duke of Normandy could embark on the holy war. Gerento was with Rufus at Easter (April 13) of 1096. He accomplished successfully the task assigned him by the Pope.[284]

The legate then proceeded to attack Rufus' authority over the English Church. He complained about the retention of vacant bishoprics and abbacies in the King's hand, simony, and sexual immorality among the clergy.[285] In concerning himself with church reform, it would appear that Gerento exceeded the limits of his commission. His attempt to assist Anselm came to nothing. By the terms of Walter of Albano's agreement with William II of the previous years, it would have been necessary for Urban to obtain the King's permisison before sending his legate to England. Rufus, therefore, had ample warning of Gerento's coming and he cleverly forestalled the legate. In advance of the legate's arrival in England, the King had sent an envoy to the papal curia equipped with ten gold marks. Rufus postponed consideration of Gerento's demands on church reform until the royal envoy returned from his interview with the Pope. When the royal envoy came back to England, he was accompanied by one of Urban's relatives, a layman, who offered further postponement until Christmas of 1096, in return for payment of Peter's Pence.[286] Gerento now considered that his legatine com-

---

[281] Lühe, *Hugo von Die u. Lyon,* 102, 104.
[282] Crozet, 283.   [283] J-L, I, 681-5.
[284] Hugh of Flavigny, 475; cf. C. W. David, *Robert Curthose* (1920), 90-1.
[285] Hugh of Flavigny, 474-5.
[286] *Ibid.,* 475. Tillmann, *Legaten,* 21-22 and W. Lunt, *The Financial*

mission in England had been abrogated. Before the end of May the legate crossed over to Normandy to conduct his negotiations with Duke Robert.[287] Urban had been prevented from supporting his legate's attempt to reform the English Church by the terms of Walter of Albano's agreement with Rufus.

Abbot Gerento's failure made perfectly clear Anselm's impossible position. He had not been able to diminish at all the King's control over the church, and in fact, in the latter half of 1096 Rufus' power continued to increase. He appointed two of his clerks, Samson and Gerard, to the vacant sees of Worcester and Hereford.[288] With papal approval, William II gained Normandy in pledge from his brother in return for a loan of 10,000 marks of silver to the Duke.[289]

In order to raise this huge sum, the royal treasury had to resort to heavy and extraordinary taxation. The barons, of course, were required to pay an aid. By placing his demesne vill of Peckham in *vif gage* for seven years as security, Anselm was able to borrow two hundred marks from the cathedral treasury as his share of the aid.[290] Because he was a great baron and because the loan was in aid of a crusader, Anselm could not protest against contributing this sum. It was the King's extraordinary methods of taxing the church, however, which the Archbishop must have regarded as obnoxious. The royal treasury levied a danegeld at the heavy rate of four shillings to the hide. Although the clergy had previously been exempt from paying this tax, the church was now subjected to the geld "not on account of law but because of necessity."[291] Anselm

---

Relations of the Papacy with England to 1327 (1939), 34-35, are suspicious of the accuracy of Hugh of Flavigny's account. But in view of the agreement between Urban's legate and Rufus in the previous year and because of the fact that Hugh was an eye-witness to these events, there is no reason to doubt his account of Gerento's legateship.

[287] David, *Robert Curthose*, 91; Haskins, *Norman Institutions*, 67.

[288] They were consecrated by Anselm at St. Paul's on June 8, 1096. *HN*, 74.

[289] David, *Robert Curthose*, 91.

[290] *HN*, 75. Cf. David, 92, n. 19.

[291] *Leges Edwardi Confessori*, Liebermann, *Gesetze*, I, 637, col. 2 (re-

must have taken the lead in protesting against this infringe-
ment of the "liberty" of the church.[292] The King also demanded that bishops, abbots, and abbesses should break up
the gold and silver ornaments of their churches and surrender
them to the royal treasury. His authority was so great that
the ecclesiastics readily complied.[293] Crucifixes were despoiled
and chalices melted down for the use of the royal fisc.[294] At
the Abbey of Malmesbury alone, twelve copies of the Gospels,
eight crosses, and eight shrines were stripped of their gold
and silver.[295]

The success of these new kinds of taxation of the church
must have been a hard blow to Anselm. Probably he was not
among the more enthusiastic supporters of the crusade. At
least he ordered his suffragan bishops to prevent monks in
their dioceses from setting out for Jerusalem.[296] He believed
that the certain way to salvation was by the contemplative
path. In his eyes, the unprecedented means of taxing the
church, even for the purpose of a loan to a crusader, would
not have been justified.

At the beginning of 1097, the Primate again fell out of
favor with the King, after their dispute about the quality of
Canterbury knights sent to Rufus' Welsh expedition.[297] The
leaders of church and state had come to a complete impasse.
Alarmed at the ever-increasing royal control over the church,
and chagrined by his failure to reach any agreement with his
episcopal colleagues, Anselm decided to appeal in person to
"the authority and decision of the apostolic see."[298] Anselm
had become involved in his controversy with the King and

---

census of c.1140-59): ". . . Concessit ei [regi] non lege statutum tamen
neque firmatum, sed hac necessitatis causa, ex unaquaque hida sibi dari
quator solidos, ecclesia non excepta."

[292] *Ibid.*, I, 637, col. 1 (recension of c.1130-35); "Quorum dum fieret
collectio, clamabat ecclesia, libertatem suam respocens; sed nihil sibi pro-
fuit."

[293] Florence of Worcester, *Chronicle*, s.a. 1096; *GR*, II, 371-2.

[294] *GR*, II, 372.   [295] *GP*, 432.   [296] *AO*, ep. 195, ll. 20-2.

[297] *HN*, 77-8. See above, pp. 72-73.   [298] *HN*, 79.

bishops over church-state relations because he had obeyed and tried to enforce decrees emanating from Rome. Consequently, he looked to the Pope for support in his struggle to reform the English Church. Although Urban had already given sufficient indication that he was reluctant to intervene in the affairs of the English Church, Anselm must have hoped that his personal appeal at the curia would influence the Pope. Probably he also planned to consult at Lyons with the leader of the high Gregorians, Archbishop Hugh.

Three times in 1097 Anselm requested, and failed to obtain royal permission to leave England.[299] Finally, in October he came to the *curia regis* and asked the counsel of the curialist bishops, Walkelin of Winchester, Robert of Lincoln, and John of Bath. He made a last appeal to these bishops to support the Gregorian reform program rather than serve the King. He reminded them that as bishops their first task was to set in order and preserve the things of God before all other things. "You are bishops," he said, "prelates in the church of God; you are sons of God."[300] This description of the bishops as sons of God was an allusion to a doctrine which the advocates of sacerdotal supremacy had been proposing since the fifth century. Priests possess divine attributes; they can judge all men, including kings, and can be judged by God alone. The sacerdotal power is therefore superior to lay authority. This doctrine had been delineated by Rufinus in his ecclesiastical history, when he made Constantine address the bishops at Nicea: *dii estis*.[301] It was advocated again, in the same terms, by Gregory I, in the reign of Louis the Pious by the French bishops, and repeated by the Gregorian theorists.[302]

[299] *HN*, 79-80.
[300] *HN*, 82: "Fratres, ideo feci vos venire ad me, quia vestri officii est ea quae Dei sunt prae caeteris tractare, disponere, servare. Episcopi enim estis, praelati in ecclesia Dei estis, filii Dei estis."
[301] Rufinus, *Hist. Eccles.*, I. 2. (*MPL*, 21, col. 468-9): "Vos etenim nobis a Deo dati estis dii, et conveniens non est ut homo judicet deos. . . ."
[302] Gregory I, *Reg.* v, 36; *MGH, Leg.* sect. II, vol. II, no. 196; Gregory VII, *Reg.* IV, 2, VIII, 21, IX, 27: Deusdedit, *Lib. contra invasores, Lib. de*

5. Urban II and the Controversy

Although Anselm's appeal to the curialist bishops was founded upon this important tradition in medieval thought, it was to no avail. After consulting with the King, the four bishops returned and replied to the Primate. Their speech, as given by Eadmer, is perhaps the most interesting passage in the whole of the *Historia Novorum*:

"Lord father, we know that you are a religious and holy man, and that your manner of life is heavenly. We admit, however, that having been burdened by our kinsmen whom we support and by many worldly things which we love, we cannot rise to the sublimity of your life, nor along with you, can we scoff at this world. . . . The fealty which we owe to the king, we will not withdraw." Then Anselm said, "You have spoken well. Go then to your lord and I will hold fast to God." They did as he had said, and Anselm remained almost alone.[303]

By October of 1097 Rufus was confident that his authority over the English Church was secure. He had become reconciled with Robert of Meulan with whom he had differed at Rockingham.[304] The bishops consistently refused to support their Primate. The Pope had repeatedly refused to intervene in England. In 1096 or 1097 Rufus obtained from the abbey of St. Stephen's at Caen his father's crown and regalia.[305] He now possessed the symbols as well as the substance of his father's power. Only Anselm remained to condemn the existing system of church-state relations. The King would be well rid of the troublesome Archbishop. On October 15, 1097, he

---

Lite, II, 350, l. 25ff.; Gerhoh of Reichberg, *Oposculum, Lib. de Lite*, III, 150, l. 37ff.

[303] *HN*, 82-3: " 'Domine pater, scimus te virum religiosum esse et santum, et in caelis conversationem tuam. Nos autem, impediti consanguineis nostris quos sustentamus, et multiplicibus saeculi rebus quos amamus, fatemur, ad sublimitatem vitae tuae surgere nequimus, nec huic mundo tecum illudere. . . . Nos fidelitatem quam regis debemus, non excedemus.' At ille ait, 'Bene dixistis. Ite ergo ad dominum vestrum, ego me tenebo ad Deum.' Fecerunt ut dixerat, et remansit Anselmus quasi solus."

[304] *HN*, 86.

[305] Davis, *Reg.*, no. 397. In his study of royal symbols in Anglo-Norman England, P. E. Schramm has overlooked this incident. Cf. *Herrschaftzeichen u. Staatsymbolik* (1956), III, 755ff.

finally gave Anselm permission to leave England.[306] But he gave the Archbishop one last demonstration of his authority. The royal clerk William detained Anselm for two weeks at Dover while his baggage was inspected "as if he were a common fugitive."[307] Only after this final humiliation could Anselm at last set sail for the Continent to enlist the aid of Urban II and Hugh of Lyons in his struggle to reform the English Church.

[306] *HN*, 86-7.   [307] *HN*, 88; *Diceto* life, 226.

CHAPTER III

ANSELM AND THE PAPACY, 1097-1100

I. ANSELM'S EXILE AT CLUNY AND LYONS

WHEN ANSELM left England in October of 1097 there were four ecclesiastical groups on the Continent to which he could appeal for support in his struggle to reform the English Church. These four groups were the papacy, the Cluniac order, the newer and more rigorous monastic orders, and the radical reformers of whom Hugh of Lyons was the acknowledged leader. There was a considerable difference in attitude towards the Gregorian doctrines among these four groups. It is impossible to establish many of the details of Archbishop Anselm's first exile on the Continent, from 1097 to 1100. But it is clear that he was so determined to reform the English Church and he felt that his position in England had become so desperate, that he sought the sympathy and aid of all the four prominent groups in the Western Church at this time.

When Anselm left England, he concluded that it was not prudent to head for Normandy which was now under William II's rule. In the latter part of October 1097, accompanied by his secretary Eadmer, he landed at Wissant near Boulogne and then visited the monastery of St. Bertin which was near the coast, for two weeks.[1] St. Bertin belonged to a group of Flemish monasteries under Bec influence,[2] and it was natural for the venerated former Abbot of Bec to visit there.

Eadmer gives no detail of Anselm's stay at St. Bertin but other sources reveal that it was significant in two ways. When Anselm was at St. Bertin he dispatched a letter to Urban II

[1] HN, 89.
[2] K. Hallinger, Gorze-Kluny (1950, Studi Anselmiani, fasc. XXII-XXIII), I, 476.

taking the side of the Flemish abbots and the Countess of Flanders in a disputed episcopal election in the see of Messines.[3] Hugh of Lyons intervened in this dispute on the same side as Anselm.[4] Their candidate, whom Urban eventually accepted, was a canon of Messines renowned for his learning. The other candidate, although chosen by a majority of the cathedral canons, had inferior qualifications.[5] Anselm was continuing to take an active interest in reform of the church wherever he happened to be, whether in England or on the Continent. He was also continuing to cooperate with Hugh of Lyons in church reform.

It is also significant that two years after Anselm's visit to St. Bertin, its abbot, Lambert (1095-1125), placed his monastery under the jurisdiction of Cluny. It is probable that Anselm influenced Abbot Lambert to make this move, for Anselm greatly admired the Cluniacs.[6] During Anselm's abbacy. and even earlier, Bec had been loosely affiliated with Cluny,[7] and in this sense, it is no exaggeration to say that Anselm was a "Cluniac at heart."[8] He may well have encouraged Abbot Lambert to accept Cluniac jurisdiction. At any rate, having left England as a result of a controversy with the King, Anselm first turned for support to the great community which was the spiritual head of the whole Benedictine order.

[3] B. Guérard, ed., *Cartulaire de L'Abbaye de Saint-Bertin* (1840), ch. 57, p. 266. Since this source was overlooked by J-L and Anselm's biographers, it deserves extensive quotation: "Pars vero utraque Romam pervenit. Abbates itaque causam suam in curia explicantes, citius sunt auditi et exauditi, quia litteris prefate comitisse [Flandrarum] roborati . . . et predicti Hugonis [Archbishop of Lyons] auctoritate animati, domnique Anselmi, archipresulis Cantuariensis, viri per cuncta laudabilis, quem Anglia expulsum a Willelmo Rufo ibique exulantem offenderant, auxilio confortati, citius impetravere ad quod venerant. Nec mora, pars adversa capud flexit, nostrisque consensit. Quibus in idipsum consentientibus cum apostolicis munimentis."

[4] *Ibid.* See quotation in n. 3.

[5] *Ibid.*, ch. 56, p. 266.

[6] H. Sproemberg, *Alvisus, Abt von Anchin (1111-1131)*, Hist. Stud. Ebering, fasc. 202 (1931), 48; Hallinger, I, 476.

[7] Hallinger, I, 475, n. 8.

[8] B. Schmitz, *Gesch. d. Benediktinerordens* (1947), I, 156.

1. Exile at Cluny and Lyons

Anselm expressly announced that, having left England "for the cause of the Christian religion," his intention was to go to Rome.[9] But, as the result of his previous disappointment with Urban's policies, it is apparent that he deemed it prudent first to enlist the aid and seek the advice of friends and colleagues in Burgundy and France before proceeding to the papal curia. After leaving St. Bertin and delivering a sermon at St. Omer in November 1097,[10] he crossed France to Burgundy where he had a brief interview with Duke Odo of Burgundy, the nephew of Abbot Hugh of Cluny. Anselm's saintly nature made a very favorable impression on the Duke. The Archbishop arrived at Cluny in time to celebrate Christmas there.[11]

At Cluny the renowned theologian and religious was received with the highest veneration.[12] But nothing transpired there to affect Anselm's relations with William II and the Pope. In his official history, Eadmer intentionally passes over the events of Anselm's visit to Cluny in a few words[13] and does not even mention it in his hagiographical life of Anselm.

While Cluny had only just passed the apogée of its influence on the popes and secular rulers of Europe, Anselm could count on no real support from Abbot Hugh in the controversy over church-state relations in England. Abbot Hugh was a fervent admirer of the former Abbot of Bec and a personal friend of Anselm.[14] In the purity of their personal lives and devotion to the religious life, Anselm and Hugh were men of similar disposition.[15] Notwithstanding their personal friendship and Hugh's undoubted sympathy for Anselm's difficulties, however, there is no evidence that he offered any constructive assistance to Anselm in his quarrel with William II.

[9] See Anselm's statement to Duke Odo of Burgundy, whom he encountered on his way to Cluny (*HN*, 90) : "Causa religionis Christianae, vir venerande, Angliam exivi; et, miserante Deo, Romam ire disposui."
[10] *HN*, 89; *AO*, ep. 207, note.
[11] *HN*, 89-90; A. L'Huillier, *Vie de Saint Hughes* (1888), 443.
[12] *HN*, 90. [13] *HN*, 90: ut paucis dicam.
[14] See Abbot Hugh's letter to Anselm in 1101: *AO*, ep. 259.
[15] L'Huillier, *Saint Hughes*, 443.

III. Anselm and the Papacy, 1097-1100

Abbot Hugh was unwilling to help Anselm because the Cluniac attitude to church-state relations was fundamentally pre-Gregorian. Cluny took no sides in the great church-state controversies of the age. The great Burgundian monastery had always been reluctant to support Gregorian doctrine and become embroiled in disputes with secular rulers even when battlelines were clearly drawn during the pontificate of Gregory VII.[16] Now that the situation had become more complex and when even the Pope tended to pursue a cautious and in fact prevaricating policy on the question of the freedom of the church, the Abbot of Cluny, no matter how much he admired Anselm personally, would not actively take Anselm's side in the Archbishop's struggle against Rufus and in his differences with the Pope. Abbot Hugh had another reason for refusing to intercede with Urban II on Anselm's behalf. Earlier in 1097, Cluny had received extensive privileges from the Pope, who had begun his ecclesiastical career as a member of the great monastery.[17] Now Abbot Hugh would be reluctant to annoy Cluny's papal benefactor.

Eadmer gives some hint of Anselm's frustrations at Cluny by emphasizing the Primate's joy at receiving an invitation to come to Lyons from Archbishop Hugh, upon whose judgement and advice Anselm so greatly depended.[18] He set out for Lyons immediately and arrived there at the end of January 1098. Throughout his stay on the Continent, Anselm was warmly greeted by the ecclesiastical and lay magnates through whose lands he passed,[19] and Lyons was no exception. The famous religious was received with ceremony

---

[16] Sackur, *Cluniacenzer*, II, 453ff.; L. M. Smith, *Cluny in the Eleventh and Twelfth Centuries* (1930), 56ff.; K. Hallinger, "Zur geistigen Welt der Anfänge Klunys," *DA*, 10 (1954), 417ff.

[17] J-L, no. 5682; *MPL*, 151, ep. 214; Smith, *Cluny*, 95-96.

[18] *HN*, 90-91: "Mittit interea nuncium, qui suum venerabili Hugoni archiepiscopo Lugdunensi notificet adventum. Erat quippe idem vir Anselmo iam ex multis praecedentibus annis notus, et, sanctae dilectionis illius igne succensus, magno videndi eum desiderio fatigabatur. Quem etiam Anselmus in tantum diligebat, eiusque prudentiam atque consilii auctoritatem tanti pendebat. . . ."

[19] At least according to Anselm: *AO*, ep. 208, ll. 14-17.

and the Archbishop of Lyons rejoiced at the presence of his friend and honored him greatly.[20]

Hugh of Lyons especially could sympathize with Anselm's troubles because, following his elevation to the episcopal order as Bishop of Die in 1073, he had himself become involved in a situation similar to Anselm's in 1097.[21] Following his election as Bishop of Die, Hugh had suffered oppression from the lay power in the person of a local count. Furthermore, Hugh had refused to accept consecration as bishop from the incumbent Archbishop of Lyons because the latter was reputed to be a simoniac. Hugh went to Rome to obtain the support of Gregory VII, just as Anselm was now intending to go to Rome to seek the aid of Urban II in his own controversy with William II.

By the time of Anselm's arrival at Lyons early in 1098, Hugh had achieved a *rapprochement* with Urban II and was again designated as papal vicar in France.[22] Nevertheless, the dispute between the Archbishop of Lyons and Urban in 1095 over church reforms in France, which had resulted in Hugh's temporary suspension from his office of papal legate,[23] had undoubtedly made Hugh aware that Urban's pontificate marked the abandonment of Gregory VII's uncompromising struggle for the freedom of the church.

This disagreement between the Archbishop of Lyons and the Pope was ultimately responsible for Anselm's decision not to go to Rome as he had originally intended, but instead to dispatch a letter to Urban. In his official history, Eadmer related that Anselm gave up his plans to go to Rome at this time because of ill health and because he believed that the road was beset by agents of Henry IV and the anti-pope Wibert.[24] The bearer of Anselm's letter to Urban must have excused the Archbishop's absence at Rome with the same rea-

---

[20] *HN*, 91; *AO*, ep. 208, ll. 18-19.
[21] A. Rorey in *Rev. Quest. Hist.*, 107 (1937), 294-95.
[22] J-L, nos. 5685 and 5690.
[23] See above, Ch. II, nn. 216-218.
[24] *HN*, 91, 94.

sons.[25] While these excuses are plausible, Anselm was also dissuaded from continuing to Rome by a warning from Hugh that Urban would do little or nothing to intervene in the dispute with William II. In a letter to the Archdeacon of Canterbury written shortly after he arrived at Lyons, Anselm in fact hinted that the Archbishop of Lyons had given him this kind of advice. Anselm said that Hugh had insisted that he remain at Lyons "as long as I am in exile from our Church."[26] Apparently Hugh could see no purpose in the continuance of Anselm's journey to Rome. Disappointment at his failure to receive assistance from Cluny may also have played a part in Anselm's decision not to request help personally from a Cluniac pope.

That Anselm abandoned his plan to go to Rome for a reason other than the one officially given, is also revealed by the letter he dispatched to Urban from Lyons. In this letter Anselm stated that the motive for his voyage to Rome had been to seek papal absolution from the burdens of his episcopal office.[27] He pleaded that his nature, age, ill health, and ignorance made him unfit to be a bishop and that his continuance in the office would endanger the salvation of his soul.[28] There is no indication, however, that Anselm had actually left England with the intention of going to Rome to resign as Archbishop of Canterbury, as he now stated in his letter to Urban. On the contrary, he had always maintained that he wanted to obtain Urban's advice and assistance in the controversy over church-state relations in England.[29]

Anselm's desire to resign his office after he reached Lyons was a radical change in attitude on his part. It may have been

[25] *AO*, ep. 206, ll. 11-12: "Cur autem non possim [venire], per praesentium latorem cognoscetis."

[26] *AO*, ep. 208, ll. 19-20: ". . . Et desiderat me semper secum, quamdiu exsul ero ab ecclesia nostra, manere."

[27] *AO*, ep. 206, ll. 58-61: ". . . Haec est summa supplicationis meae, propter quam ad vos ire volebam, ut . . . animam meam de vinculo tantae servitutis absolvatis. . . ."

[28] *Ibid.*, ll. 22-27, 55-57.

[29] See e.g., above n. 9 and *HN*, 79-80.

in part due to ill health. But primarily it was induced by a
renewed awareness, as a result of his experiences at Cluny
and the advice given him by Hugh of Lyons, that he could
expect no effective support from Urban II. It was now fully
apparent to him, if it had not been before, that Walter of
Albano's agreement with Rufus had been made at Urban's
behest. Anselm now saw that his position had become untenable, and that if he was to remain faithful to his reform
principles, he had no alternative than resignation from his
episcopal office.

Anselm's intention was now to accept the hospitality of his
friend, the Archbishop of Lyons, and to retire from the world.
With his illness to remind him that many years could not be
left to him, Anselm aimed to set down in writing the theological speculation which had been his greatest delight since
his days at Bec. At Lyons in the early months of 1097 he
completed his work on the incarnation, the *Cur Deus Homo*.[30]
He continued his correspondence with his disciples at Bec,
although he was afraid that the King would intercept his letters.[31] It might be thought that as a devout religious, Anselm
would be inclined to forgive William II in a spirit of Christian
charity and leave him to the judgement of heaven. On the
contrary, Anselm continued to feel animosity towards Rufus
"who hates everything belonging to me and those who love
me."[32]

In view of the Archbishop's inability to forget his controversy with William II, it must have been with considerable
satisfaction that he received the letter from Rome which a
papal nuncio brought him about the beginning of March 1098.
Urban ignored Anselm's letter of resignation and instead summoned him to Rome.[33] Along with Baldwin, the former head
of his household, who had now joined him, and with Eadmer,

[30] *AO*, ep. 209, ll. 17-20.
[31] *Ibid.*, l. 16.
[32] *Ibid.*, l. 15: "[Rex] . . . qui omnia quae a me sunt et quae me dili-
gunt odit. . . ."
[33] *HN*, 94. Urban's letter has not survived.

III. Anselm and the Papacy, 1097-1100

the Primate left Lyons on March 16, 1098 for Rome. It appeared that his stand on church-state relations in England would receive effective papal support at last.

2. ANSELM, URBAN II, AND ROGER I

IN SPITE OF the great moral prestige which the papacy had gained from launching the First Crusade, Urban's position was not yet secure even at Rome. Partisans of the anti-pope were to be found even in the Eternal City.[34] Urban could not afford to precipitate a scandal which might have resulted in Anselm's resignation. In summoning Anselm to Rome Urban intended to make use of the prestige of the venerable theologian in a council which he was planning to assemble.

Disguised as simple monks to avoid capture by the supporters of Henry IV, Anselm and his two companions arrived in Rome at Easter 1098.[35] The Pope invited Anselm to the Lateran but refused to consider the possibility of the Archbishop's resignation. Instead the Pope dispatched a letter to Rufus, demanding that the English King restore to Anselm whatever belonged to him. Anselm sent an accompanying letter to Rufus in the same vein.[36] The letters were of no avail. Rufus did not restore Anselm to his see, and it was not until the following year that he even deigned to give this negative reply.[37]

Anselm was now caught up in the maelstrom of international papal politics. Urban would neither let Anselm resign his see nor would he give the exiled Archbishop any real assistance in his dispute with the English king. He wanted Anselm to remain in Italy, however, in order to bolster some of the current papal projects with the aura of Anselm's great prestige throughout Christendom.

After remaining at the Lateran for ten days, Anselm accepted the invitation from a former student, Abbot John, to

[34] Fulcher of Chartres, *Historia Hierosolymitana*, ed. Hagenmeyer (1913), 167.
[35] *HN*, 94-96.   [36] *HN*, 96.   [37] *HN*, 98, 110.

visit him at his abbey of San Salvatore which was south of Naples. Abbot John took his venerable master to a nearby village in the mountains, where Anselm regained his health.[38]

Count Roger of Apulia, who was besieging Capua at this time, invited Anselm to meet him at the camp of the Norman army. Roger and Anselm were joined at Capua by the Pope. From Capua, Anselm and Urban journeyed to Aversa where in June 1098, according to Eadmer's account, Anselm again requested Urban to release him from his archbishopric. The Pope again refused and instead summoned Anselm to the council which he had called for Bari on October 1. Urban promised that Anselm's case would be considered at the council. Anselm returned to his mountain retreat provided by Abbot John to await the beginning of the council.[39]

In this account of the meeting of Urban, Anselm, and Count Roger under the walls of Capua, and Anselm's second attempt to resign his episcopal office, Eadmer again suppressed the salient facts which illuminate the real issues dividing Anselm and the Pope. As Meyer von Knonau noted, Eadmer only mentioned Urban's presence at Capua in passing, nor did he give any reason for it.[40] Another account of the events outside the walls of Capua, which is to be found in Geoffrey Malaterra's history, gives priority to the meeting of the Pope and Count Roger.[41]

Urban was present at Capua for two reasons. In the first place he attempted, unsuccessfully, to make peace between Capua and the Normans.[42] Secondly, and of much greater importance, Urban and Roger engaged in a cordial discussion

---

[38] HN, 96-97.

[39] HN, 97-98, 103-04.

[40] Jahrbücher . . . Heinrich V, v (1904), 42, n. 29; cf. HN, 97.

[41] Gaufredus Malaterra, De Rebus Gestis Rogerii Comitis, ch. 26, Muratori, Rer. Scrip. Ital., new ed., v, 106: "Cum ista aguntur, papa Urbanus, colloquium ducis et comitis desiderans, a Roma progreditur et apud Capuam, ubi in obsessione manebant, venit; comesque, sex tentoria illi deliberans ad hospitandum, sumptus necessarios abundantissime ministravit."

[42] See Urban's own statement of his peace-making endeavors in Privileg. de libertate Messanens. eccles. in Meyer von Knonau, op.cit., 43, n. 31.

on the disputed issue of papal jurisdiction in Sicily.[43] This dispute had threatened, since the beginning of 1097, to disrupt the papal-Norman entente.[44] The discussion at Capua was preparatory to the famous concordat on Norman-papal relations, embodied in the privilege which Urban granted to Roger at Salerno on July 5, 1098. By this remarkable privilege, the foundation of the "Sicilian monarchy," Count Roger and his hereditary successors received extensive legatory powers over the Sicilian church.[45] This privilege resembled the agreement which the papal legate, Walter of Albano, had made with William II in 1096. It involved even greater concessions to a secular ruler and represented the antithesis of the Gregorian doctrine of the freedom of the church.

The real cause of Anselm's second attempt to resign his episcopal office, which Eadmer omitted from his official history, was Urban's negotiations with Count Roger. According to Eadmer, Anselm attempted to resign because he had come to enjoy his recent freedom from worldly affairs and looked with foreboding upon the prospect of returning to the burdens of his troubled see.[46] But something more than Anselm's personal inclination was involved in his second attempt to secure release from his office. Urban's grant of jurisdiction over the Sicilian church, *legati vice*, to Roger was a flagrant contradiction of the policy of the reforming papacy from the beginning of the pontificate of Gregory VII. Anselm was present at Capua during the negotiations which resulted in the famous privilege of the following month and he must have known the terms of the concession which Urban was about to make to the Norman-Sicilian ruler. Anselm wanted to resign his see because once again he had been made to realize that he could expect no assistance from a pope who was willing to

[43] E. Jordan, "La Politique Ecclésiastique de Roger I," *Le Moyen Age* 34 (1923), 48-49.

[44] Jordan, 45ff.

[45] J-L, no. 5706; Geoffrey Malaterra, *op.cit.*, v, ch. 29, p. 107. For an analysis of the papal privilege to Count Roger see Jordan, *op.cit.*, 61-64.

[46] *HN*, 99.

abandon the fundamental doctrines of the Gregorian reformers for the sake of immediate tactical advantage and military security. Only Urban's promise to bring the Archbishop's case before the Council of Bari in October 1098 could have induced Anselm to refrain from renouncing his office.

3. THE COUNCILS OF BARI AND ROME

In 1098 and 1099 Urban II attempted to strengthen his position in his struggle with the anti-pope Wibert by calling councils of bishops loyal to himself. The first of these councils met early in October of 1098 at Bari. In the following year Urban finally managed to gain control of Rome and summoned another council for the Vatican in April. The attendance of bishops at these two councils was impressive, indicating the great prestige which the launching of the First Crusade had given Urban. It is reported that one hundred and eighty-five bishops were present at Bari in 1098, and that one hundred and fifty attended the Roman Council at the Vatican in 1099.[47] Anselm attended both councils and played an important part in the proceedings of the Council of Bari. The *Historia Novorum* of Eadmer is the major source for the Council of Bari, and also provides an important account of the Council of 1099.

There is, however, a peculiar contradiction in Eadmer's account of the relations between Anselm and Urban at the two councils. This contradiction has already been noted by Baronius and Hefele-Leclercq, but they did not subject Eadmer's account to careful scrutiny.[48] In the official history of the Anglo-Norman reformers, Anselm emerges as the leading figure, next to the Pope, at the Council of Bari. The Archbishop of Canterbury was called upon by the Pope to defend

---

[47] Hefele-Leclercq, *Conciles*, V, Pt. 1 (1912), 459, 468. F. Duncalf in Setton and Baldwin, eds., *History of the Crusades*, I (1955), 227, has confused the councils of Bari of 1089 and 1098, with the result that Anselm "of Canterbury" is present at the Council of 1089 five years before he became Archbishop!

[48] Baronius, *Annales*, s.a. 1098, n. 2; Hefele-Leclercq, 462.

the Roman doctrine of the procession of the Holy Spirit from the Son against the South Italian and Sicilian Greek ecclesiastics who were present at the Council. In this work of apologetics, the learned theologian acquitted himself well. The Pope then informed the Council of William II's unjust treatment of Anselm and asked the judgement of the assembled bishops, who called for the excommunication of the English King. But Anselm threw himself at Urban's feet, Eadmer's account continues, and successfully implored the Pope to avert the sentence. The Archbishop's generosity gained him the universal admiration of the bishops.[49]

After Anselm had accepted the Pope's invitation to proceed to Rome for Christmas, a reply finally arrived from William II to the letters sent by Urban and Anselm in the previous year. According to Eadmer's official history, the royal clerk William Warelwast informed the Pope that Anselm had forfeited his episcopal office by his departure from England. Urban at first replied that if the King did not restore Anselm to his archbishopric, he would suffer excommunication. But the English royal envoy obtained a secret meeting with Urban. By conciliatory promises to the Pope and a judicious distribution of gifts in the papal curia, he obtained a postponement of William II's case, which in fact became an indefinite suspension of the proceedings against Rufus. Eadmer concluded his account of this episode by relating that Anselm now believed that his own case at Rome was lost, and that the Archbishop asked leave to return to Lyons. The Pope, however, retained the venerable theologian at Rome until the conclusion of the Council of the Vatican, which was held three weeks after Easter of 1099.[50]

The conduct of both Urban and Anselm in this account provided by Eadmer appears ambiguous and inconsistent. Anselm first prevented Urban from excommunicating Wil-

---

[49] *HN*, 105-7. On Anselm's defense of the western doctrine of the Trinity, see S. Runciman, *The Eastern Schism* (1955), 76-77.
[50] *HN*, 110-112.

3. The Councils of Bari and Rome

liam II, but three months later the Archbishop was very disappointed because the Pope did not excommunicate the King. Urban, on the other hand, was willing to excommunicate Rufus at Bari, but not three months later at Rome. Eadmer's account is therefore highly improbable, and it is furthermore contradicted by one of Anselm's own letters.

After the accession of Paschal II in August of 1099 Anselm wrote to the new Pope, setting forth the history of his troubled pontificate. After reviewing William II's injustices, Anselm informed Paschal that he had not excommunicated the King for two reasons. In the first place, Anselm had not deemed it right to be both plaintiff and judge in the same case. Secondly, Rufus would have ignored excommunication by the Archbishop of Canterbury and thereby have made a mockery of Anselm's episcopal jurisdiction.[51] The implication is strong in this statement that Anselm had wanted the Pope to excommunicate Rufus and that Urban had never agreed to do this. Anselm implied that the Pope as judge of all Christendom should have excommunicated the English King, and that furthermore, papal excommunication would have been effective in England. But Urban had refused to assist Anselm and hence the Archbishop had been defeated by the King. Before his election, Paschal had been a cardinal and a supporter of Urban. He was in an excellent position to have known the subtleties of papal politics at first hand.[51a] Anselm would not have written to the new Pope implying that his predecessor had never offered to excommunicate Rufus, if this had not been the truth which Paschal now had to acknowledge. Eadmer's history, in its account of the councils of 1098 and 1099, again contains a perversion of the truth

---

[51] *AO*, ep. 210, ll. 49-54: "Quaerent quidem minus intelligentes cur ego regem non excommunico; sed sapientiores et rectum habentes consilium consulunt ne hoc faciam, quia non pertintet ad me utrumque, et querimoniam scilicet et vindictam facere. Denique ab amicis nostris, qui sub eodem rege sunt, mandatum mihi est quia mea excommunicatio, si fieret, ab illo contemneretur et in derisium converteretur."

[51a] Paschal had been present at the Council of Bari in 1098 (*AO*, ep. 282, l. 8).

designed to hide the deep conflict between Anselm and Urban.

Although Urban had forced Anselm to remain in Rome in order to use his prestige at the Vatican Council, the Pope suffered a sharp rebuke for his harsh treatment of the leader of the Anglo-Norman reformers. At the conclusion of the Council while Bishop Ranger of Lucca, a zealous reformer and an eminent scholar and poet, was reading the conciliar decrees to the bishops, he paused and severely criticized the Pope for his failure to help the Archbishop of Canterbury.[52] But Urban interrupted Ranger's remarks and demanded that the high Gregorian Bishop of Lucca resume his reading of the canons. Urban's forceful personality and great prestige easily withstood this single instance of criticism and Anselm received no effective support from the Council of 1099.[53] In May of that year, after the conclusion of the Council, he left Rome to resume his refuge with Archbishop Hugh of Lyons.[54]

The Archbishop of Canterbury could hardly have reached Lyons when Urban II died on July 22, 1099. The election of a new pope by the Sacred College followed almost immediately. On August 13 the cardinals chose as pope Rainier, Cardinal-Priest of St. Clement, and Abbot of St. Lawrence-outside-the-Walls. He took the name of Paschal II.[55]

Among the Gregorian popes, Paschal II is perhaps second in importance only to Hildebrand himself, but he has been

---

[52] *HN*, 113: "Sed, vae, quid faciemus? Praeceptis subditos oneramus, et iniquis tyrannorum saevitiis non obviamus. Oppressiones namque quas ipsi sua tyrannide ecclesiis inferunt, et exspoliationes personarum quae tuendis illis institutae sunt quotidie ad hanc sedem referuntur. . . . Iam annus secundus est quo huc venit; sed, vae, quid hucusque subventionis invenit? Si de quo dico non omnes agnoscitis, ipse est Anselmus archiepiscopus Anglicae regionis." On Ranger (called Reinger by Eadmer) see A. Overmann in *Neues Archiv*, 21 (1896), 405ff.; B. Schmeidler, *Neues Archiv*, 43 (1922) 515-549, *passim*; P. Guidi in *Miscellanea Lucchese . . . in Memoria di Salvatore Bongi* (1931), 13ff.

[53] *HN*, 113-114.

[54] *HN*, 114-115.

[55] J-L, 1, p. 703; B. Monod, *Essai sur les Rapports de Paschal II avec Philippe I* (1907, *Bib. de l'École des Hautes Études*, fasc. 104), p. 1.

relatively the least studied.[56] It is usually stated that Paschal, who was born in northern Italy, became a monk at Cluny.[57] But the best evidence indicates that he was a monk of Vallambrosa, near Florence.[58] He attracted the attention of Gregory VII, who made Rainier his protégé and appointed him to the Sacred College. Before his election, Paschal had served as Urban's legate in Spain.[59]

Only this bare outline of Paschal's early life is known. Many aspects of his papal policy are also obscure as yet. Not even the most dramatic event of Paschal's pontificate, the famous Concordat of Sutri of 1111, in which the Pope promised to give back the temporal possessions of the Church to their lay patrons, if Henry V would surrender imperial interference in ecclesiastical affairs, has been definitively studied. Fliche's acceptance of Paschal's revolutionary concordat with the German emperor, as the result of the Pope's sincere beliefs, is an improvement over the older view that Paschal was simply acting under *force majeure*. But Fliche's explanation of the ideas which motivated Paschal to make the revolutionary concordat is vague and unsatisfactory.[60] In my view, the full significance of the Concordat of Sutri will only be perceived when it is understood that Paschal was a product of north-Italian monasticism, which for over a century had been exhibiting pronounced eremitic, extremely ascetic, and perhaps even heretical tendencies. As will be seen in the following chapter, Paschal II was a fanatical high Gregorian, who violently opposed any interference by laymen in the Church. The mystical view of the Church as the *sponsa Christi* appears to have dominated his thinking.[61] When it is re-

[56] The most important contributions are Monod's monograph cited in n. 55; vols. 5 and 6 of Meyer von Knonau, *passim*; A. Fliche, *La Réforme Grégorienne et La Reconquête Chrétienne* (1940), ch. XII; H. K. Mann, *Lives of the Popes*, VIII (1910), chs. I-VII; J. L. Cate, "The Crusade of 1101," Setton and Baldwin, eds., *Crusades*, I, 343ff.

[57] Fliche, *op.cit.*, 339.

[58] Mann, *Popes*, VIII, p. 7, esp. n. 4.

[59] *Ibid.*, 7-8.   [60] Fliche, *op.cit.*, 359-60.

[61] See below, Ch. IV, n. 67.

membered that Gregory VII's doctrines and reforming zeal led him temporarily to espouse the Donatist heresy, it is by no means inconceivable that Paschal II's intransigence induced him to conclude that the apostolic poverty of the Church was the solution to the investiture controversy.

In any case, the dour old monk who became Pope in 1099 had a much more doctrinaire attitude toward church-state relations than his immediate predecessor, Urban II. In the last months of 1099 when the election of Paschal was known at Lyons, Anselm sent his initial letter to the new Pope, setting forth the lugubrious details of his pontificate. The Archbishop begged Paschal not to order his return to England unless the King would support the laws of the Church and return to Anselm the temporalities of his see.[62] It was not until the following year, when Anselm had returned to England, that a reply was received from the Pope.[63] Until that time the policy of Paschal towards the controversy over church-state relations in England remained unknown.

4. EMERGENCE OF THE INVESTITURE ISSUE

In 1099 and 1100 Anselm was again a wanderer on the Continent. He at first found a happy and quiet haven of refuge with his friend and advisor Archbishop Hugh of Lyons.[64] But in 1099 Hugh was allowed to resign from his office of papal legate in France in order to take the Cross.[65] As Hugh began to make plans to set out for the Holy Land in the following year, Anselm turned to other leading churchmen for refuge and support. In a letter written to the Archdeacon of Canterbury at this time, Anselm related how warmly he had been received on the Continent by both laymen and ecclesiastics of

---

[62] *AO*, ep. 210, ll. 40-43: "Precor igitur et obsecro quanto possum affectu, ut nullo modo me in Angliam redire iubeatis, nisi ita ut legem et voluntatem dei et decreta apostolica voluntati hominis liceat mihi praeferre, et nisi rex mihi terras ecclesiae reddiderit. . . ."

[63] See below, Ch. IV, n. 65.

[64] *AO*, ep. 211, ll. 4-5: ". . . Sanus et laetus est mecum apud Lugdunum. . . ."

[65] Merlet, ed., *Saint Yves, évêque de Chartres. Lettres* (1886), 217, n. 1.

all kinds.[66] No doubt his great reputation as a religious gained for him admiration from all sides. But it was actually to the religious orders that Anselm appealed for assistance, now that the papacy had disappointed him and his powerful friend the Archbishop of Lyons was about to set out for the East. Anselm again visited the most universally respected leader of the Western Church at the end of the eleventh century, Abbot Hugh the Great of Cluny. But again Hugh declined to interfere in the affairs of the English Church. The only comfort which he could give Anselm was to prophesy the early death of William II on the basis of a dream.[67]

Finally Anselm turned for support to the new reformed and more vigorous monastic orders which were beginning to emerge on the Continent, and which would eventually result in the formation of the Cistercian order within three or four decades. The Archbishop of Canterbury was staying at one of these reformed monasteries, Chaise Dieu (*Casa Dei*) near Lyons in the summer of 1100. Here, about the middle of August, he was found by a monk sent from Bec and by one of his monastic *familia* at Canterbury.[68] They informed Anselm that his antagonist William Rufus had been killed in a hunting accident in the New Forest. After taking counsel with Hugh of Lyons, Anselm immediately set out for England.[69]

---

[66] *AO*, ep. 208, ll. 14-17.

[67] *Vita Hugonis*, ed. L'Huillier, *Saint Hughes*, 588-89. This visit is not mentioned in *HN*.

[68] *HN*, 118. Chaise Dieu was founded in 1043 by a former Cluniac monk. It became the center of a reforming movement which comprised several houses in France and Germany, and which imposed a more ascetic life than was to be found at Cluny. Cf. M. Heimbücher, *Orden u. Kongregationen* (1933), I, 202.

[69] *HN*, 118. J. H. Round, *Feudal England*, 472, pointed out that the wife of Walter Tirel, who discharged the fatal arrow, was of the Clare family, and that Henry I treated the Clares with obvious favor. On the basis of this evidence, and Henry's presence in the ill-fated hunting party, A. L. Poole suspects premeditated murder. (*From Domesday Book to Magna Carta* [1951], 113-14). More conclusive evidence than this would be necessary to prove that William II was murdered, for the assassination of kings was a crime virtually unknown among Christians in the early Middle Ages.

III. Anselm and the Papacy, 1097-1100

The tasks facing the reforming Archbishop on his return to England would be arduous. William II had strengthened royal authority over the English Church during Anselm's exile. The abuses condemned by the Gregorian reformers had never been more rife in the Anglo-Norman Church: absence of canonical election, royal appointment of unworthy bishops, clerical marriage. In 1099 the monks of St. Augustine's, Canterbury, attempted to bribe the King in order to obtain permission to make their own choice of a new abbot. The King refused, appointed one of his own kinsmen to the vacant abbacy, and in order to demonstrate the church's dependence on the crown, he had the new abbot consecrated in the royal chapel.[70] In the same year the King installed his favorite minister, Ranulf Flambard, as Bishop of Durham, an appointment specially scandalous to the reformers. The widespread existence of priests' wives and concubines still troubled the Anglo-Norman Church in spite of prohibitions during Lanfranc's pontificate.[71] The treasury continued to exploit the feudal position of the greater ecclesiastics. In 1100 the King held in his hand not only several abbeys but also the bishoprics of Canterbury, Winchester, and Salisbury.[72]

In addition to these usual abuses in church-state relations, the Anglo-Norman reformers were incensed at William II's friendly attitude towards the Jewish merchants whom William the Conqueror had brought over from Rouen.[73] To

[70] *Thorne's Chronicle*, in Twysden, *SS*, col. 1795.

[71] The continued existence of priests' wives in the see of Durham, c.1096, is vividly described in a dream of a certain Boso, a knight of St. Cuthbert, which is reported in Sym. Durham, *HDE*, I, 131. He describes a multitude of women, priests' temptresses, who are destined for hellfire. For an excellent discussion of this curious literary dream, which provides an interesting picture of England at the time as seen by a Norman knight, cf. R. L. Graeme Ritchie, *The Normans in Scotland* (1954), 88-91.

[72] *A-S Chron E, s.a.* 1100; Florence of Worcester, *Chronicle, s.a.* 1100.

[73] Eadmer described William II's friendly relations with the Jews at great length: *HN*, 99-102 (cf. *GR*, II, 320-21). It should be noticed that Eadmer was here working within a well-defined literary tradition stemming from St. Ambrose, the defender of the freedom of the church against a powerful secular ruler who was also (at least in one instance) sympathetic towards the Jews.

discredit the King, the reform party in the English Church availed themselves of the great wave of anti-semitism unleashed by the First Crusade.[74] Abbot Gilbert Crispin of Westminster, a disciple of Anselm, produced a tract which upheld the superiority of Christianity over the Hebrew religion,[75] and the reformers violently attacked Rufus as a friend of the Jews and betrayer of Christ.[76]

What was most disturbing to the reformers was William II's great prestige in Western Europe, even among leading churchmen on the Continent. The eminent canonist Bishop Ivo of Chartres, in a letter written during Anselm's exile, called Rufus a generous and wise man.[77] The famous troubador Duke of Aquitaine, William IX, wanted to pledge his Duchy to Rufus in order to obtain crusading money from the wealthy English King.[78] Since William II had already obtained Normandy from his brother on the same conditions, only the King's death prevented the establishment of an empire such as Henry II was to create a half-century later, stretching from England to the Pyrenees. It was, therefore, with great joy and relief that the reformers heard of Rufus' death and regarded it as a special act of providence. The sud-

[74] There was a great massacre of Rouen Jews by crusading knights in 1096. (C. Roth, *History of the Jews in England* [1941], p. 6). The massacres of·Jews in Rhenish cities by the knights of the First Crusade are well-known.

[75] *Disputatio Judaei cum Christiano, MPL* 159, col. 1005ff.: Gilbert's tract, which is dedicated to Anselm, supposedly based on a real dispute between Gilbert and a Jewish merchant who had been educated at the great Talmudic school in Mainz; Gilbert claimed that he succeeded in converting him. For detailed discussion on Gilbert's tract see Roth, *op.cit.*, 5-6; and especially A. Lukyn Williams, *Adversus Judaeos* (1935), 375-80.

[76] See e.g., Eadmer's story that Rufus forced a Jew who had been converted to Christianity, to deny Christ and return to his old errors (*HN*, 99). The role of the Gregorian reformers in the upsurge of anti-semitism at the·end of the eleventh century has not been studied. Yet it is remarkable that the earliest two, of the many anti-Jewish tracts produced during the eleventh and twelfth centuries, were written by Peter Damiani (*MPL* 145, coll. 41ff., 57ff.). It would be worth considering to what extent Damiani's treatises served as the models for the many that followed.

[77] Merlet, *op.cit.*, 148.

[78] Freeman, *Rufus,* II, 313-14.

den and mysterious manner of his demise encouraged this view.[79]

William II's younger brother and successor, Henry I, was a man different in every way from Rufus. If the reform program which Anselm was now bringing back with him from the Continent had been the same as the one which Anselm had attempted to introduce during the previous reign, a period of continued harmony and peace between the leaders of church and state would have been inaugurated. But Anselm now believed that he had to make a demand of Henry I which he had never requested from William II—the abolition of lay investiture in England. The Archbishop of Canterbury had been present at the councils at Bari and Rome, where the investing of ecclesiastics with the symbols of their offices by laymen had been condemned on pain of excommunication.[80] Since he had participated in these councils, Anselm felt that he was particularly bound to their decrees.[81]

Lay investiture, or to use the contemporary phrase "investiture of churches,"[82] would now have to be prohibited in Eng-

[79] Various accounts of William II's death, contemporary or written somewhat later, are collected by Freeman, *Rufus*, II, 657ff. They reveal the fear which Rufus aroused by his harshness and eccentricity, and reflect widespread relief on the part of churchmen at his death. Some of the accounts tell the story that Rufus was warned to mend his ways, shortly before his death, by Gundulf of Rochester, Anselm's disciple and diocesan ordinary.

[80] On the prohibition of lay investiture at the Council of Bari, see Paschal's letter to Anselm in 1102 (*AO*, ep. 282, ll. 5-10): "Reverendae in Christo memoriae praedecessoris nostri domni Urbani tempore, apud Barim collecto venerabilium episcoporum et abbatum ex diversis partibus concilio, in quo tua religio et nos ipsi interfuimus, sicut fratres qui nobiscum aderant reminiscuntur, in eandem pestem [i.e. lay investiture] excommunicationis est prolata sententia." On Council of Rome, *HN*, 114: "Qua sententia [excommunicationis] omnes quoque laicos investituras ecclesiarum dantes, et omnes easdem investituras de manibus illorum accipientes, necne omnes in officium sic dati honoris hiusmodi consecrantes, pari modo involvit."

[81] See below, Ch. IV, pt. 3.

[82] *investitura (e) ecclesiarum.* This is the term used by all parties and persons involved in the English investiture controversy, including Paschal II, to refer to the investiture of ecclesiastics with ring and staff by laymen. The term was also frequently used on the Continent. Cf. *MGH, Lib. de Lite*, III, 752, *s.n.* investitura. The history of the term has not been studied. It strongly reflects the origin of lay investiture in the association of church office and church feudal property.

land, where the issue had never risen before. Embroiled in his bitter dispute with William II over other and relatively secondary issues, Anselm had found it impossible to raise the investiture question. Nor did he feel compelled to do so. He had not been invited to the Council of Clermont or any other papal council condemning investiture, nor had he received any communication from Urban II on this subject. Hence the Archbishop did not regard himself as bound to demand the prohibition of lay investiture in the Anglo-Norman kingdom. In 1093 Anselm had accepted investiture from William II.[83] In 1096 the papal legate Cardinal Walter of Albano accused Anselm of accepting investiture from a schismatic king, but he did not hold the Archbishop culpable simply for the act of lay investiture.[84] As part of Urban II's very conciliatory attitude, the papacy had not opposed lay investiture in England during the reign of William II. Even Gregory VII had never raised the issue with William I and Lanfranc.

When the investiture issue was raised in England, it could only result in a bitter and protracted controversy, for the institution of lay investiture had become deeply ingrained in Norman church-state relations. The importance of lay investiture in Normandy and Anglo-Norman England was the inevitable consequence of the feudalization of the church and the lay domination over the church in those countries. In Normandy the receipt of the pastoral staff from the ducal hand was considered so necessary, that in 1091 the newly elected Abbot of St. Evroult crossed the Channel to England in order to receive the symbol of his office from the hand of Duke Robert, who was visiting at his brother's court.[85] In Normandy it was necessary for a bishop to receive special authorization from the Duke before investing an abbot in his own diocese.[86]

[83] See above, Ch. II, n. 99.
[84] *AO*, ep. 192, ll. 38-43.
[85] *OV*, III, 380-81.
[86] Davis, *Reg.*, no. 310: Duke Robert grants to Bishop Odo of Bayeux the right of investing the abbots of St. Vigor, a monastery in his diocese,

III. Anselm and the Papacy, 1097-1100

As a consequence of the feudalization of the Anglo-Norman Church under William I, lay investiture and the simultaneous homage of ecclesiastics to the king also became a central institution in English church-state relations. With the exception of the Bishop of Rochester, who received investiture from his lord the Archbishop of Canterbury, no one could be made a bishop or abbot if he did not become the king's man and receive the investiture of the pastoral staff from the royal hand.[87] By 1100, lay investiture was "ancient custom" in England.[88] Anselm's acceptance of the papal prohibition of lay investiture, and the accession of a doctrinaire high Gregorian to the throne of Peter, opened the way for a new and crucial issue in the controversy over church-state relations in England.

with the pastoral staff. For another example of lay investiture in Normandy, during the reign of William the Conqueror, see Round, *CDF*, no. 1044.

[87] *HN*, 1-2: "Ipsa denique causa nova res huic nostro saeculo esse videtur, et a tempore quo in Anglia Normanni regnare coeperunt, non dico prius, Anglis inaudita. Ex eo quippe qo Willelmus Normanniae comes terram illam debellando sibi subegit, nemo in ea episcopus vel abbas ante Anselmum factus est, qui non primo fuerit homo regis, ac de manu illius episcopatus vel abbatiae investituram per dationem virgae pastoralis susceperit, exceptis duobus episcopis, Ernosto scilicet atque Gundulfo. Hi namque, unus post unum Rofensi ecclesiae praesidentes, ex more a venerandae memoriae Lanfranco archiepiscopo Cantuariensi in capitulo fratrum Cantuariae ipso episcopatu investiti fuerunt."

[88] During the English investiture controversy, the reformers never questioned the King's claim that lay investiture was the custom of his predecessors. They argued only that it was bad custom (cf. below, Ch. IV, pt. 3, and *GR*, II, 493, where lay investiture is also described as *antiqua consuetudo*). Eadmer states explicitly that in 1093 Anselm did homage to William II "pro usu terrae" (*HN*, 41). He also mentions that when the King and bishops were urging Anselm to accept the archbishopric of Canterbury, Rufus extended to Anselm the "virgam pastoralem" or "baculum" (*HN*, 35) at the bishops' urging. Obviously lay investiture was the regular practice in England by 1093.

CHAPTER IV

THE INVESTITURE CONTROVERSY, 1100-1104

I. THE ACCESSION OF HENRY I

WILLIAM RUFUS had maintained complete control over the English Church during the last three years of his reign, while the reforming Archbishop of Canterbury was in exile. The circumstances of the accession to the throne of Henry I, however, gave Anselm and the reformers cause to hope that a change in church-state relations in England was imminent.[1]

---

[1] It is necessary to reject interpretations of the English investiture controversy propounded by A. Fliche and F. Liebermann. Fliche contended that the English investiture controversy was only an outgrowth and an aspect of the dispute over the Archbishop of Lyons' claims for primatial authority. ("Y-a-t-il eu en France et en Angleterre une querelle des investitures?", *Rev. Bénédictine*, 46 [1934], 283ff.) The only valid evidence to support this thesis is Anselm's friendship with Hugh of Lyons, which was the result of their common sympathy for Gregorian doctrines. There is no evidence that Anselm actively supported Hugh's claim to the primacy in France. Even if this were true, it is impossible to establish any relationship between the dispute over Lyons' authority and the English investiture controversy. The following chapter will show that the investiture controversy in England, as in Germany, was the result of fundamental disagreements on the nature of church-state relations (cf. below, n. 80). Liebermann's thesis ("Anselm u. Hugo," *Waitz Festschrift*, 156) is rather similar to Fliche's, although stated more delicately. He says that "unter den Söhnen Wilhelm des Erobers kämpfte der Patriarch Britanniens fast allein gegen Krone, Adel, und Clerus für das canonische Recht: daher bildet der Englische Investiturstreit nur einen Theil der Geschichte Anselms von Canterbury." Liebermann then goes on to say that Anselm found his inspiration not in the Papacy "sondern im Zwiespalt der Pflichten handelte er nach der Entscheidung der Gallicanischen Kirche, deren Geist er verkörpert sah in heiligen Erzabt von Cluny und besonders in ihrem Primas, der Erzbischof Hugo von Lyon." Apart from the mistake about Hugh of Cluny's involvement in controversies over church-state relations, Liebermann's thesis fails to appreciate the decisive role of Paschal II in the English investiture controversy. It will be seen in this and the following chapter that Paschal emerged as the chief protagonist of Gregorian doctrines in the English investiture controversy. Anselm's role is secondary to the Pope's. Finally, Liebermann failed to appreciate that the investiture controversy constitutes a chapter in the history of the Anglo-Norman episcopate. By 1105, several bishops had

IV. The Investiture Controversy, 1100-1104

As the youngest son of William I, Henry had received only a lucrative money payment at the time of his father's death in 1087. In 1088 he purchased the Cotentin and Avaranchin from his brother Duke Robert, but lost these lands three years later when his brothers united against him. At the same time, Robert and William II made an agreement to exclude Henry from succession to the throne of either Normandy or England. Although Rufus subsequently attempted to pacify Henry with some lands in England, his life up to his accession in 1100 had been mainly that of a high-born but landless knight, eagerly searching for a patrimony. He saw his opportunity when Rufus died suddenly and Robert was still on his way home from the First Crusade. Henry seized the royal treasury at Winchester by force and in great haste had himself crowned at Westminster.[2] Although Henry's reputation for learning was greatly exaggerated in the twelfth century—the well-known epithet Beauclerc was not contemporary—he could read and was a man of considerable intelligence.[3]

Because his claim to the throne was weak and was threatened by his brother, Henry had to turn to the church for support. In this endeavor he was very successful. In 1101, during

---

come to support Anselm in his dispute with the King (see below, Ch. V, pt. 4). Two nineteenth-century German dissertations on the English investiture controversy (by T. Klemm in 1880 and M. Schmitz in 1884) are no longer of any value. The accounts of the English investiture controversy provided by H. Böhmer (*Kirche und Staat*, 158-62) and A. L. Poole (*From Domesday Book to Magna Carta*, 177-82) are very brief and constitute very limited contributions to the subject.

[2] On Henry's early life and accession to the throne, see *GR*, II, 467-70; Freeman, *Rufus*, I, 279ff., II, 510ff.; Poole, *op.cit.*, 99, 104.

[3] Henry I's reputation for learning was severely criticized by C. W. David, "The Claim of Henry I to be Called Learned," *Haskins Anniversary Essays* (1929), 45ff. While David succeeded in proving that Henry's reputation for learning was virtually groundless, this kind of historical skepticism should not be carried too far. Contemporaries like William of Malmesbury and Orderic Vital regarded Henry as a literate and highly intelligent man, and there appears to be no reason why their testimonies cannot be accepted at face value. Cf. the judicious remarks on this subject by V. H. Galbraith, "The Literacy of Medieval English Kings," *PBA*, XXI (1935), 13-14, and the sources there cited.

the invasion of Duke Robert, Anselm saved the throne for Henry. By removing canonical obstacles to Henry's marriage with a descendant of Edward the Confessor, Anselm again strengthened Henry's hold on the English crown. It will be seen that Anselm was so sympathetic towards the new King that he was even reluctant to demand from him the prohibition of lay investiture, as required by Paschal II.[4] This support which the King gained from Anselm and the reform party in the English Church was the direct result of the concessions made by Henry at the beginning of his reign. Henry's success in winning Anselm's sympathy and loyalty stems from the drastic actions taken by the King at the time of his coronation.

Henry was crowned at Westminster on August 5, 1100.[5] Very soon afterwards he issued his famous coronation charter and distributed more than thirty copies throughout England.[6] The first clause of the charter promised to abandon William II's ecclesiastical policy and made concessions to the church in order to gain the support of the Archbishop of Canterbury and the reform party:

And since the kingdom has been oppressed by unjust exactions, I, through fear of God and through the love that I have for you all, in the first place make the Holy Church of God free, so that I will neither sell nor put at farm nor, on the death of an archbishop, bishop, or abbot, take anything from the demesne of a church, or from its men, until a successor enters upon it.[7]

Immediately after his coronation, Henry also sent a friendly letter to Anselm, begging the Primate to return to England. This letter reveals Henry's conviction that Anselm's support was necessary for the strengthening of his weak hold

---

[4] See below, pts. 3 and 4.

[5] Johnson, *Reg.*, no. 488.

[6] F. Liebermann in *THRS*, n.s., VIII (1894), 29.

[7] Liebermann, *Gesetze*, I, 521: "Et quia regnum oppressum erat iniustis exactionibus, ego, respectu Dei et amore quem erga vos omnes habeo, sanctam Dei ecclesiam imprimus liberam facio; ita quod nec vendam nec ad firmam ponam nec, mortuo archiepiscopo sive episcopo sive abbate, aliquid accipiam de dominio aecclesiae vel de hominibus eius, donec successor in eam ingrediatur."

on the English throne. It also discloses the King's intention to go a long way towards compliance with the demands of the reform party in order to gain their allegiance. The letter was extremely deferential and apologetic in tone. In it, Henry attempted to justify his seizure of the throne by the assertion that he had been chosen as king according to the principle of canonical election, by the clergy and people:

Henry, by the grace of God, King of the English, to his most reverend spiritual father, Anselm, Bishop [sic] of Canterbury, greeting and token of all friendship. Be it known to you, dearest father, that my brother King William, is dead and that with God's approval, I have been elected by the clergy and people of England and, albeit unwillingly, already crowned king in your absence. In concert with the people of the whole realm of England, I entreat you as a father to come as quickly as possible and to give counsel to me, your son, and this same people, whose souls have been committed to your care. I commend myself and all the people of this realm to your counsel and that of those who ought to advise me, together with yourself. I beg you not to be displeased that I have accepted the royal title without your blessing, for had it been possible, I would sooner have received it from you than from any other.[8]

In order to demonstrate the sincerity of his avowal to abandon his predecessor's attitude towards church-state relations, Henry committed Ranulf Flambard, Bishop of Durham and the chief minister of Rufus, to the Tower on August 15.[9] An additional concession made by the King to the reformers

[8] *AO*, ep. 212, ll. 8-12: "Scias, pater carissime, quod frater meus, rex Willelmus, mortuus est, et ego, nutu dei a clero et a populo Angliae electus et, quamvis invitus propter absentiam tui, rex iam consecratus, requiro te sicut patrem cum omni populo Angliae, quatenus mihi, filio tuo, et eidem populo, cuius tibi animarum cura commissa est, quam citius poteris, venias ad consulendum. Me ipsum quidem ac totius regni Angliae populum tuo eorumque consilio, qui tecum mihi consulere debent, committo. Et precor, ne tibi displiceat quod regiam benedictionem absque te suscepi, de quo, si fieri posset, libentius eam acciperem quam de alio aliquo." The full significance of Henry's statement that he had been elected "by clergy and people" will be discussed below, pt. 2, p. 139.

[9] Sym. Durham, *HDE*, I, 138; *A-S Chron E, s.a.* 1100; Farrer, "Itinerary," no. 3a.

2. The Coronation of Henry I

in 1100 will become evident from a careful analysis of the circumstances of Henry's coronation.

2. THE CORONATION OF HENRY I

AT THE TIME of his coronation, Henry had only a small group of supporters among the lay and ecclesiastical magnates. Among the lay barons his leading supporters were the two leaders of the Norman house of Beaumont, Earl Henry of Warwick, and his brother, Count Robert of Meulan. They had been bitter enemies of Robert Curthose since he had disseized them of some of their Norman lands in the previous decade. It was the Earl of Warwick who silenced the supporters of Duke Robert among the Anglo-Norman barons.[10]

Henry gained the support of William II's chancellor, William Giffard, by giving him the vacant wealthy bishopric of Winchester.[11] The only consecrated bishops present at Henry's coronation were Maurice of London and Gerard of Hereford.[12] Henry's supporters among the lay and ecclesiastical magnates were powerful men, but they were very few in number. Their support was reinforced, however, by the presence of Abbot Gilbert Crispin of Westminster at the coronation, which took place in his abbey. Gilbert was a disciple of Anselm and the leader of the reformers in England in the absence of the Archbishop. His name appears in the witness list of several copies of the coronation charter.[13]

The identity of the bishop or bishops who crowned Henry is a matter of dispute. W. Farrer, in his itinerary of Henry I, citing Florence of Worcester, the Peterborough Chronicle, and Symeon of Durham, concluded that Henry was consecrated by Maurice of London and crowned by Thomas of

[10] *GR*, II, 470; *OV*, III, 338. Henry of Warwick attested the coronation charter: Johnson, *Reg.*, no. 488a, witness list.

[11] *A-S Chron E*, *s.a.* 1100; Johnson, *Reg.*, no. 488a, witness list.

[12] Johnson, *Reg.*, no. 488a, witness list.

[13] Johnson, *Reg.*, no. 488f. On Gilbert as Anselm's disciple, see R. W. Southern, "St. Anslem and Gilbert, Abbot of Westminster," *Med. and Ren. Studies*, III (1954), 78ff.

York.[14] With the Archbishop of Canterbury out of the country it would fall to the Archbishop of York and the Bishop of London, as the next ranking members of the episcopate, to perform the coronation. But a critical examination of the sources excludes the presence of Thomas of York. Hugh the Cantor, in his authoritative history of the archbishops of York, revealed that Thomas arrived at Westminster too late for the coronation.[15] Thomas appears in no witness list of Henry's coronation charter, and Hugh's testimony must be accepted.

The only bishop aside from Maurice of London present at Henry's coronation was Gerard of Hereford.[16] William Giffard was only a bishop-elect and could not perform episcopal acts. A writer in the reign of Henry II, the court satirist Walter Map, stated that Gerard crowned Henry I who, as a reward for the Bishop's services, promised him the first vacant archbishopric.[17] Walter's story has been neglected by historians. It would indeed be remarkable that Henry should let himself be crowned by a bishop of the second rank, from the frontier see of Hereford. But the weight of evidence indicates that Gerard did indeed join Maurice of London in crowning Henry I, as Walter and one of his contemporaries stated.[17a]

Gerard was certainly present at Henry's coronation since he attested the coronation charter. His name also appears in the witness list of Henry's letter to Anselm, which no other bishop attested.[18] It is thus apparent that at this time Gerard was already a leading adviser of the King. Walter Map's story of the bargain between Gerard and Henry is given plausibility by the fact that Gerard was indeed given the first vacant archbishopric by the King, when Thomas of York died at the end of 1100. The participation of a second bishop, who could only

---

[14] Farrer, "Itinerary," p. 4.   [15] *HC*, 107.

[16] Johnson, *Reg.*, no. 488a, witness list.

[17] Walter Map, *De Nugis Curialium*, ed. M. R. James (1914), 234: "Girardus autem Herefordensis ignominiosus episcopatus, pacto sibi sub iuramento archiepiscopatu priore uacante, coronauit eum [Henricum]."

[17a] William Fitzstephen's life of Becket (Robertson, *Becket*, III, 110) also mentions that Gerard crowned Henry I.

[18] *AO*, ep. 212, witness list.

be Gerard, in the coronation ceremony of 1100 also tends to be corroborated by iconographic evidence. This will appear from analysis of the kind of coronation order used at Westminster in 1100.[19]

The history of the English coronation in the first half of the twelfth century is at present in a fragmentary and confused state. The leading authority on medieval coronations, P. E. Schramm, concluded that some time between 1100 and 1154, the old Anglo-Saxon "Edgar" coronation *ordo* of 973 was replaced by a new coronation order. This order bears the impact of reform ideas and hence was termed the "Anselm" order by Schramm. The Anselm order is derived from an *ordo* originating in a tenth-century German version; it had become the "Roman" coronation order by general use. The Anselm order placed less emphasis than the Edgar version on theocratic monarchy and therefore was more acceptable to the Gregorian reformers. Schramm argued that the new order did not use chrism in the anointment of the king, with its implications of the idea of king-priest. It used instead only the less significant "holy oil," probably catechumen oil. The limitation of the king's power in the Anselm order is also implied through the questioning of the people and clergy on their acceptance of the king.[20] Schramm was not able to determine if the Anselm order was used at the coronation of Henry I or Stephen. He concluded, however, that Henry II was certainly crowned according to the new order. Thomas Becket recalled in a letter that Henry II was anointed on the head, breast, and arms, which is in accordance with the Anselm rather than the Anglo-Saxon order.[21]

[19] See below, p. 143.

[20] P. E. Schramm, "Ordines-Studien III: Die Krönung in England," *Arch. f. Urkundenforschung* 15 (1938), 321-4. Cf. Schramm, *A History of the English Coronation* (1937), 36-37.

[21] Schramm, "Krönung," 324; *MPL* 190, col. 651a. But Schramm appears to have overlooked Gilbert Foliot's statement that Henry II was anointed with chrism: Robertson, *Becket*, v, 532. It would appear that the coronation of Henry II was conducted according to recension A of the Anselm *ordo*, which is discussed in the next paragraph.

IV. The Investiture Controversy, 1100-1104

Unfortunately, Schramm's study failed to take into account the careful analysis of the leading manuscripts of the Anselm *ordo*, which had previously been undertaken by H. A. Wilson.[22] The problem has been most recently investigated by P. L. Ward, whose conclusions substantiate Wilson's work and indicate that Schramm's study was oversimplified and not altogether satisfactory.[23] Wilson and Ward have pointed out that there are two recensions among the manuscripts of the Anselm *ordo*. One of them (recension A) requires that in the anointment of the king, a cross should be made on his head with both holy oil and chrism; the other (recension B) omits both the chrism and cross-making.[24] While Schramm's conclusions were based only on recension B, Wilson and Ward have shown that recension A was probably the earlier and original version.[25] On the basis of this evidence, Ward negated Schramm's association of the new coronation *ordo* with Anselm and the reform party.[26]

This conclusion is, however, unwarranted. For Schramm had associated the new *ordo* with the reform party not only because of the exclusion of chrism, but also because the new *ordo* contained a section in which the clergy and people had to approve the new king before his anointment. Even the

[22] H. A. Wilson, ed., *The Pontifical of Magdalen College* (1910), xiii-xxix.

[23] P. L. Ward, "The Coronation Ceremony in Medieval England," *Speculum* 14 (1939), 173-76.

[24] Wilson listed four MSS of recension A and two of recension B (*op.cit.*, xxix), and Ward has discovered a few others (*op.cit.*, 174, n. 6 and n. 7). Recension A has been published by Wilson from the Magdalen pontifical (*op.cit.*, 87ff.) and recension B from a Cotton MS by L. G. Wickham Legg in his *English Coronation Records* (1901), 30ff. The following are the anointing rubrics. Recension A: "Postea vero pectus et scapule ambeque compages brachiorum ipsius unguantur de supradicto oleo et de eodem crux fiat super caput eius et postea de crismate et dicantur sequentes orationes" (Wilson, *op.cit.*, 92; cf., for another MS of the same recension, *B.M. MS. Cotton Claudius A.III*, fol. 23r). Recension B: "Postea vero caput pectus et scapulas ambasque compages brachiorum ipsius unguat metropolitanus ita dicens: Unguatur caput istud pectus scapulae et compages brachiorum de oleo sanctificato. . . ." (Legg, *op.cit.*, 33).

[25] Wilson, *op.cit.*, xxix, 275; Ward, *op.cit.*, 174.

[26] Ward, *op.cit.*, 176.

2. The Coronation of Henry I

more conservative recension A, of which the earliest manuscript appears to be in *MS. Cottón Claudius A.III*, retains this approving section.[27] Hence the new *ordo* can still be associated with the ideals of Anselm and the reform party within the English Church.

Although Schramm rejected Böhmer's view that Henry I was certainly crowned according to the old Edgar *ordo*,[28] he was unable to prove that the new reform order was used in 1100. He concluded that the *"Bearbeitung"* of the new order began about 1100, but was not fully developed until after Henry's coronation.[29] There is, however, evidence which indicates that recension A of the Anselm *ordo*, as found in *Claudius A.III*, was used for Henry's coronation.

In the first place, it is necessary to recall the peculiar statement made by Henry in his letter to Anselm written immediately after coronation. Henry claimed that he had been elected king by clergy and people.[30] This statement is explained by the approval clause of the Anselm *ordo*, in which the king is indeed officially elected by clergy and people. In claiming election by the clergy and people, Henry implied that he had been crowned according to the new *ordo* sponsored by Anselm and the reform party.

Further evidence for the use of the Anselm *ordo* is supplied by a rubric and an illumination preceding the earliest text of the Anselm order, in *Claudius A.III*. Both Wilson and Schramm were aware that at the top of the folio in which the text of the *ordo* begins, there is the rubric: *Coronatio Hen. primi Regis* (Fig. 1).[31] But they rejected the historical value

---

[27] Recension A (Wilson, *op.cit.*, 89; *Claudius A.III*, fol. 20v): "His expletis unus episcoporum alloquatur populum si tali principi ac rectori se subicere ac iussionibus eius obtemperare velint. Tunc a circumstante clero et populo respondeatur: Volumus et concedimus." Recension B (Legg, *op.cit.*, 31) is identical. On the *Claudius* MS as the earliest text of Recension A, see Ward, *op.cit.*, 176, n. 1; Wilson, *op.cit.*, xxix.

[28] Schramm, "Krönung," 323, n. 2; Böhmer, *Kirche und Staat*, 327.

[29] Schramm, "Krönung," 319, 321.

[30] See above, n. 8. Cf. *ordo* text in n. 27.

[31] *Claudius A.III*, fol. 19r. Reproduction courtesy Trustees of the British Museum.

of this rubric on the grounds that it was in a seventeenth-century hand.[32] A careful observation of the manuscript, however, leads to a different conclusion.

The first and second words of the rubric are separated by an illumination of a coronation scene which is certainly truncated (Fig. 1). It is highly improbable that the illuminator would not have given himself enough room at the top of the folio to complete the picture. Hence the top of the folio, bearing the rubric and the upper part of the illumination, must have been cut off when the manuscripts now comprising *Claudius A.III* were bound into a codex for Sir Robert Cotton's library in the seventeenth century.[33] The present rubric was then added by Cotton's librarian to replace a rubric in the original twelfth- or thirteenth-century hand, which had been removed from the top of the folio in the course of binding. It can be assumed that the original rubric was the same as the one now found at the top of the folio, ascribing the illumination and therefore the text of the *ordo* to the coronation of Henry I.

This hypothesis is supported by an investigation of the iconography in the coronation scene of the *Claudius A.III* illumination. It must be remembered that medieval manuscript illuminators copied a prototype whenever they could, rather than invent an entirely new scene. Changes from the prototype were employed for some special purpose, which is usually quite obvious. The Anglo-Norman artist, required to produce an illumination of a coronation scene, copied from Ottonian prototypes. In Anglo-Norman as well as Ottonian coronation scenes, the seated king is flanked on either side by ecclesiastics,

---

[32] Schramm, "Krönung," 320, n. 1; Wilson, *op.cit.*, 273.

[33] *Claudius A.III* comprises a miscellany of MSS from the tenth to the twelfth century. For the contents of this codex see *A Catalogue of Manuscripts in the Cotton Library* (1802), 188-89. The codex assumed its present form in the seventeenth century. Cf. T. Smith, *Catalogus . . . Bibliothecae Cottonianae* (1696), 37, which lists the contents of *Claudius A.III* as they are at present. The binding appears to be from the seventeenth century. G. Ellard, *Ordination Anointings in the Western Church* (1933), 80, has also noticed that the *Claudius* codex is a "composite volume."

one or more of whom perform the crowning or anointing. Laymen are sometimes also present in these scenes, flanking the throne.[34] The Ottonian coronation prototype is evident in an illumination of the crowning of St. Edmund the Martyr (Fig. 2)[35] in a twelfth-century *Vita*, and also in a thirteenth-century manuscript of the *Vita Aedwardi Regis* (Fig. 3),[36] which is probably a direct copy from a twelfth-century illumination. The same coronation iconography is found in the ten English coronation scenes in a thirteenth- and fourteenth-century manuscript of the *Flores Historiarum* (Figs. 4, 5, 6).[36a]

The illumination of Henry I's coronation in *Claudius A.III* (Fig. 1), which precedes the Anselm *ordo*, is certainly in a style much later than the twelfth-century hand of the text. The general artistic style and the ermine robes worn by the King in the picture indicate a date not earlier than 1400, while the architectural style of the surrounding building may be as late as the seventeenth century. At first sight, it might appear that the illumination has no relevance to the text, that a much later artist capriciously filled in a space in the twelfth-century manuscript where room had been left for a picture which was not executed. But the iconography of this scene is such that only the coronation of Henry I could be depicted in it. It appears that an original twelfth-century rubric (*Coronatio Hen. primi Regis*), which had been intended as a guide for the twelfth-century illuminator, had directed the later artist to attempt to depict the coronation of Henry I, and that he had based his picture on a twelfth-century prototype which has not survived. What is the evidence for this conclusion? Why must the iconography of the *Claudius A.III*

[34] For Ottonian coronation scenes, cf. P. E. Schramm, *Die deutschen Kaiser und Könige in Bildern ihrer Zeit* (1928), figs. 72b, 73, 74a & b, 75 and below, fig. 4.

[35] Morgan Library, *Holford Coll.* (1924), pl. III.

[36a] A. Hollaender, "The Pictorial Work in the 'Flores Historiarum,'" *Bulletin of the John Rylands Library* 28 (1944), 361ff., pls. IVa, IVb, VIb. Hollaender has published all ten illuminations in this valuable study.

coronation scene be associated exclusively with the coronation of Henry I?

It will be noticed immediately that the coronation iconography in the *Claudius A.III* illumination differs radically from the Edmund and Edward scenes (Figs. 2, 3), which are the earliest examples of English coronation iconography following the Ottonian model. While Edward is anointed and Edmund crowned by one bishop, with the other bishops only assisting, in the *Claudius A.III* scene two mitred bishops, flanking the seated and robed King, together place the crown on his head. There appears to be no exact Ottonian model for this English coronation scene. In the *Bamberg Apocalypse* illumination (Fig. 7)[37] of Otto III's coronation, whose iconography is the most similar, the crowning bishops are not mitred and are not robed in their ecclesiastical vestments, as they are in the *Claudius A.III* scene. How then did the novel coronation iconography, as found in the *Claudius A.III* illumination, come to be developed? In the two known pictures of Henry I's coronation in medieval manuscripts, the iconography is indeed radically different from the *Claudius A.III* scene. In a thirteenth-century St. Albans illumination in the *Flores Historiarum* (Fig. 4) and in a fourteenth-century illustrated chronicle scene (Fig. 8),[38] which belong to the same iconographical tradition, the two flanking robed and mitred bishops acclaim King Henry but do not place the crown on his head, as they do in the *Claudius A.III* version. Among the ten *Flores Historiarum* coronation illuminations, however, there are two instances in which two flanking robed and mitred bishops place the crown on the head of a seated king: the coronation of Stephen (Fig. 5) and the coronation of Edward II (Fig. 6). But these scenes are historically false; each of these kings was crowned in a traditional and legal way by an Archbishop of Canterbury.[38a] The medieval manuscript il-

---

[37] H. Wölfflin, *Bamberg Apoc.* (1921), pl. 51.

[38] Beatty Collection, *Cat. Western MSS*, II (1930), pl. CLII b.

[38a] Edward II was actually crowned by the Bishop of Winchester, acting as the appointed deputy of the Archbishop of Canterbury who was ill (J. H. Ramsay, *The Genesis of Lancaster*, I [1913], 10).

2. The Coronation of Henry I

luminator, in deviating from a traditional prototype, would only do so with some definite purpose in mind. But in the case of Stephen and Edward II, there would be no need, and in fact it would be historically false to alter the English coronation iconography found in its original form in the Edmund and Edward the Confessor scenes, in which only one bishop crowns (Fig. 2) or anoints (Fig. 3) with the other bishops merely assisting or acclaiming. Thus the iconography of the two bishops crowning a seated king could not have originated in an illumination of the coronations of Stephen and Edward II, even though the illuminators of the *Flores Historiarum* erroneously adapted this prototype for their illustrations of these coronations.

The only medieval English king who was actually crowned by two bishops, in view of the absence of the Archbishop of Canterbury, was Henry I in 1100. Although the *Claudius A.III* scene is much later than the text which it accompanies, this coronation picture is a legitimate copy of a prototype, probably originating in the twelfth century, which depicted the coronation of Henry I according to the same iconography. The artist who created this prototype by deviating from the Ottonian, Edmund, and Edward models employed the iconographic details of two mitred bishops crowning the king in order to make clear that this was an illustration of Henry I's coronation. The documentary and literary sources indicate that Henry was in fact crowned by two bishops, Gerard of Hereford and Maurice of London[39] and the *Claudius A.III* illumination provides artistic corroboration of the other evidence. Bishop William of Winchester was also present at the coronation, but he was only a bishop-elect. He was not mitred and could not participate in the coronation ceremony. The coronation scene in *Claudius A.III*, therefore, could be only an illustration of the coronation of Henry I and the illuminator intended that the iconographic details of his scene should make this identification clear.

[39] See above, pt. 1, p. 136.

Henry's reference to his election by clergy and people, as well as the rubric and the illumination preceding the text of the Anselm *ordo* in *Claudius A.III*, indicate that this order was the one used at Henry's coronation. The use of the reform order was another aspect of Henry's concerted attempt to gain the support of Anselm and the reform party in England, and hence the papacy, for his weak claim to the English throne. The other aspects of this policy were the first clause of Henry's coronation charter, his letter begging Anselm to return to England, and the imprisonment of Ranulf Flambard. Taken in conjunction with these acts, Henry's willingness to use the new coronation order in 1100 explains Anselm's sympathy for the King after his return to England, and the Archbishop's reluctance to engage in a dispute over lay investiture with Henry.

The text of the Anselm order certainly would not have been produced at Westminster by the curialist bishops Maurice of London and Gerard of Hereford. Maurice was not a scholar, while Gerard was a particularly vehement supporter of the old Anglo-Saxon order and the ideas of theocratic monarchy emphasized in it. It will be seen that when Anselm felt constrained to demand the prohibition of lay investiture, Gerard attempted to counteract the influence of Gregorian doctrines by resurrecting the old Edgar *ordo*.[40] It is possible, however, that Gerard took the lead in demanding the retention of anointment with chrism in the coronation ceremony of 1100.

Among those present at Henry's coronation, only Abbot Gilbert Crispin could have produced the text of the Anselm *ordo*, since he was in an ideal position to serve as mediator between King and Primate. Although Westminster was the royal abbey of England, Gilbert was the close friend and disciple of Anselm and a firm advocate of the doctrines of the more moderate Gregorian reformers.[41]

[40] See below, pt. 5.
[41] On Gilbert's attitude towards Gregorian doctrines, see below, p. 170ff.

2. The Coronation of Henry I

The provenance of the oldest manuscript of the Anselm *ordo*, in *Claudius A.III*, supports the hypothesis that it was Gilbert who produced the text of the new order at the time of Henry's coronation. The *Claudius A.III* text is part of a pontifical which Schramm, following the earlier work of W. G. Henderson, attributed to Osmund of Salisbury.[42] It is a priori improbable that a curialist bishop like Osmund would have taken the trouble to bring over a reform *ordo* from the Continent, and scholarly consensus confirms this assumption. The leading authority on eleventh- and twelfth-century English pontificals, W. H. Frere, rejected the assigning of the *Claudius A.III* pontifical to Osmund.[43] More recently, N. R. Ker has designated that part of *Claudius A.III*, which contains the reform coronation *ordo*, as a Christ Church, Canterbury, manuscript.[43a] In view of Anselm's leadership of the reform party in England, the production of the manuscript containing the reform *ordo* at Christ Church is entirely logical and to be expected.

All of the evidence points to the conclusion that the new coronation order used in 1100 at Henry I's coronation was produced in that reform group in the English Church of which Anselm was the leader and Gilbert Crispin a leading member. As in other Anglo-Norman liturgical works, the new coronation order was modelled on a continental version. It is known that the liturgy of the Anglo-Norman mass found in the Sarum Missal was strongly under the influence of the Norman mass developed at Séez.[44] Similarly, the new coronation order forced upon Henry I during the throne crisis of

[42] Schramm, "Krönung," 320; W. G. Henderson, *Liber Pontificalis Chr. Bainridge* (1875, Surtees Soc. 61), 268.

[43] W. H. Frere, *English Pontificals in Manuscript*, 95. B.M. MS. Cotton *Tiberius C.I*, which Frere attributes to Osmund (*op.cit.*, 97) contains no coronation *ordo*.

[43a] N. R. Ker, *The Medieval Libraries of Great Britain* (1941), 22.

[44] M. Andrieu, *Les Ordines Romani du haut Moyen-Age* (1931; *Spicilegium Sacrum Lovaniense*, fasc. 11), I, ch. 6, esp. p. 510; J. A. Jungman, *Missarum Sollemnia*, Engl. transl. (1949), I, 92-3, 96, 103, and ch. 10, *passim*.

1100 must have been brought over from the Continent by the Anglo-Norman reformers, probably at the beginning of Anselm's pontificate in 1093.

3. DEVELOPMENT OF THE INVESTITURE
CONTROVERSY, 1100-1103

In RETURN for Henry's acceptance of the reform program as it had stood in the reign of William II, Anselm established the King firmly on the English throne in the year following his coronation. The Archbishop made possible Henry's marriage with a descendent of Edward the Confessor and rallied the English Church and lay magnates to the King when Duke Robert invaded England.

Anselm had already left Chaise-Dieu for England and had reached Cluny when he received Henry's letter. He landed at Dover on September 23, 1100 and almost immediately went to see the King, who received him with rejoicing.[45] It was probably at this time, and at Anselm's request, that the coronation charter was reaffirmed and reissued.[46]

Henry, as a matter of course, then asked Anselm to do him homage and to receive the Archbishopric of Canterbury from the royal hands. But Anselm felt he could not comply with this request. He believed that he was bound by the prohibition of lay investiture at the papal councils which he had attended in the previous two years, and he threatened to leave the kingdom again rather than disobey the Pope.[47] Henry was shocked and greatly disturbed. His carefully laid plans

[45] HN, 118-19.
[46] L. Reiss, "The Reissue of Henry I's Coronation Charter," EHR, 41 (1926), 321ff., esp. 324.
[47] HN, 120: ". . . Postulatus est pro consuetudine antecessorum suorum regi hominium facere, et archiepiscopatum de manu eius recipere. Quibus cum ille nequaquam se aut velle aut posse assensum praebere responderet, interrogantibus quare, statim quid super his et quibusdam aliis in Romano concilio acceperit manifesta relatione innotuit, itaque subinferens ait; 'Si dominus rex ista suscipere et suscepta servare voluerit, bene inter nos et firma pax erit. Sin autem, non video remanere meum in Anglia utile fore vel honestum. . . .' "

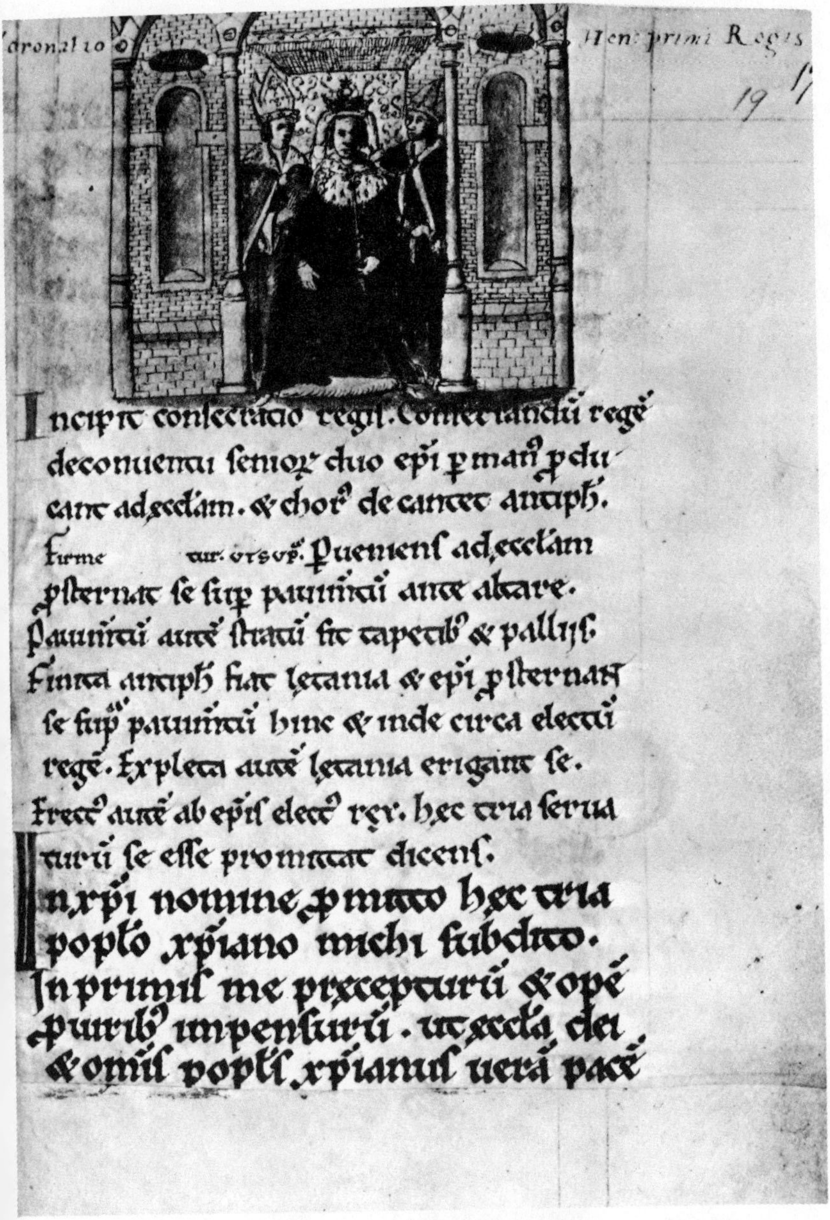

ncipit consecracio regis. Consec iandū regē
deconuentu senior duo epi p man p du
cant adecclam. & chor' de cancet antiph.

firme   cur. ors os. Pueniens adecclam
psternat se sup pauimtcu ante altare.
pauimtcu autē stratū sic tapetib' & pallijs.
finita antiph fiat letania & epi psternant
se sup pauimtcu hinc & inde circa electū
regē. Explecta autē letania erigant se.
Frecc' autē ab epis elect' rgr. hec tria seruia
turū se esse promittat dicens.

n xpi nomine p mitto hec tria
poplo xpiano michi subdito.
In primis me pracepturū & ope
puntib' impensurū. ut eccla dei
& omis popls xpianus uerā pace

Fig. 1. The Coronation of Henry I.
(British Museum, *MS. Cotton Claudius A.III*, fol. 19r)

Fig. 2. The Coronation of St. Edmund the Martyr.
(Morgan Library, *M.736*, fol. 8v)

Fig. 3. The Anointing of Edward the Confessor.
(Cambridge University Library, *MS. Ee* 3.59)

Fig. 4. The Coronation of Henry I.
(St. Albans MS of the *Flores Historiarum* in
Chetham's Library, Manchester)

Fig. 5. The Coronation of Stephen.
(St. Albans MS of the *Flores Historiarum*)

Fig. 6. The Coronation of Edward II.
(St. Albans MS of the *Flores Historiarum*)

Fig. 7. The Coronation of Otto III.
(Bamberg Staatliche Bibliothek, *MS. 140*, fol. 59v)

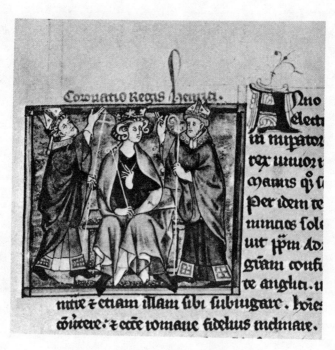

Fig. 8. The Coronation of Henry I.
(from a fourteenth-century MS chronicle in the
Chester Beatty Library, Dublin)

for securing the support of Anselm and Paschal II and bolstering his shaky throne were in danger of immediate failure. He faced a dilemma. To give up lay investiture would mean "the loss of half his kingdom." On the other hand, if he refused to abandon lay investiture, the Archbishop and the Pope would probably shift their allegiance to Duke Robert, who was returning from the First Crusade to Normandy.[48]

From this dilemma Anselm rescued the King, at least for the moment. The Archbishop was a sick and weary old man who was in no mood for another protracted dispute and exile, especially when Henry appeared to be sincere in his promise to remedy the abuses of William II's ecclesiastical policy. Anselm offered to request Paschal II to mitigate the apostolic decrees on lay investiture in favor of the ancient usage of the kingdom. In the meantime a truce on lay investiture was to be maintained until Easter of 1101, when the Pope's decision on Anselm's request would be known. Henry gladly accepted Anselm's offer and returned the temporalities of Canterbury to the Archbishop without investiture and homage.[49]

The postponement of the decision on lay investiture would allow the implementation of a policy which was much favored by both the King and Archbishop. This policy was the marriage of Henry to Mathilda (Maud), the daughter of King Malcolm of the Scots and his Queen, the Anglo-Saxon Princess Margaret, the grandniece of Edward the Confessor.[50] According to William of Malmesbury, Henry was persuaded

[48] *HN*, 120: "His rex auditis graviter conturbatus est. Grave quippe sibi visum est investituras ecclesiarum et hominia praelatorum perdere, grave nihilominus Anselmum a regno ipse nondum in regno plene confirmatus pati discedere. In uno siquidem videbatur sibi quasi dimidium regni perderet, in alio verebatur ne fratrem suum Robertum, qui tunc de Ierusalem Normanniam redierat, Anselmus adiret, et eum in apostolicae sedis subjectionem deductum, quod facillimum factu sciebat, regem Angliae faceret." A few months later (February 1101) Paschal revealed to Anselm that Robert had indeed complained to the papal court that Henry had seized the English throne while the Duke was on the crusade (*AO*, ep. 213, ll. 14-18).

[49] *HN*, 120-21.

[50] Cf. Ritchie, *The Normans in Scotland*, 99ff., for a detailed account of the arranging of this marriage.

to marry Mathilda "by the advice of his friends, chiefly the bishops," undoubtedly led by Anselm.[51] The prospect of a marriage which would ally him with the Anglo-Saxon royal house, and thereby give him a stronger claim to the throne, appealed to Henry.

Anselm and the reformers favored this marriage for two reasons. In the first place, Anselm was well acquainted with Mathilda, who was receiving her education at the nunnery of Wilton. It is probable that Mathilda, even before her marriage to Henry, regarded Anselm as her spiritual father.[52] A queen who looked to Anselm for advice could be a great help to the reform cause. The reformers also favored this marriage because they were enthusiastic that a descendant of Edward the Confessor would gain the English throne.

Attempting to find some intellectual roots in England, where the quite cosmopolitan Norman bishops and abbots had been hostile to reform ideas, Anselm and his disciples fastened upon the Anglo-Saxon saints and assiduously associated themselves with Old English religiosity. Eadmer produced several Anglo-Saxon saints' lives, including a *vita* of St. Dunstan, the reformer of the English Church in the tenth century.[53] Another of Anselm's disciples, Gosselin of St. Augustine's, Canterbury,[54] also worked at Anglo-Saxon hagiography.[55] Above all, the reformers attempted to foster the tradition that Mathilda's great-grand-uncle Edward was a saint. In 1102 Gilbert Crispin, with the help of Anselm's diocesan ordinary, Gundulf of Rochester, effected the first translation of the relics of

---

[51] *GR*, II, 470: ". . . suadentibus amicis, ac maxime pontificibus. . . ."

[52] Mathilda certainly regarded Anselm as her spiritual father shortly after her marriage: *AO*, ep. 242. Cf. Anselm to Mathilda *AO*, ep. 243, ll. 14-16: "Memor est benigna vestra dignatio in epistola sua quod per me sit vestra celsitudo in coniugium legitimum desponsata et ad regni sublimitatem me sacrante coronata." See also above Ch. II, p. 67.

[53] Raine, ed., *Hist. of Church of York* (*RS*, 1894), I, 161ff.; II, 1ff.; Stubbs, ed., *Memorials of St. Dunstan* (*RS*, 1874), 162ff.

[54] See the dedication of one of Gosselin's works to Anselm, *MPL* 155, coll. 13-14.

[55] *MPL* 155, col. 57ff.

Edward the Confessor.[56] After exhumation, the body of the Anglo-Saxon King was found to be incorrupt, prima facie evidence for the sanctity of Edward, who was finally canonized in 1163.

Anselm did everything possible to expedite the marriage of Henry and Mathilda. The prime obstacle to the marriage was a rumor that Mathilda had taken the veil while at Wilton. Consequently, the Archbishop called a synod at Lambeth, at which evidence was taken and the rumor was declared false. On November 11, 1100, Anselm's policy was brought to a successful conclusion when he crowned Mathilda as Queen after her marriage to Henry.[57]

With the exception of the vexed question of lay investiture which was still to be decided, Anselm and Henry had now arrived at an harmonious understanding on church-state relations. The good old days of Lanfranc and William the Conqueror, when king and archbishop worked together in peace and friendship, appeared to be returning. On his part, Anselm would have been willing to come to an understanding with the King by which Henry would aid in the reform of the English Church, in return for non-intervention by the papacy in the affairs of the Church. The Archbishop had been disillusioned and disappointed by papal policy during the reign of Rufus. Now he would have preferred to act in cooperation with the King and in practical independence of Rome in order to reform the Church in England.

The Archbishop, as well as the King, at this time looked askance upon the entry of papal legates into England. Anselm's experience with Walter of Albano in 1096 had made him suspicious of papal legates, and after his return to England he did not hesitate to announce his hostility to them. When Rufus died, Paschal assumed that Urban's agreement with the English monarchy had been abrogated and in Au-

---

[56] Osbert of Clare, *Vita S. Edwardi*, ed. M. Bloch, *Analecta Bollandiana* 41 (1923), 122.
[57] *HN*, 121-26.

gust or September of 1100 he sent Archbishop Guy of Vienne to the royal court as legate in England and Scotland. Archbishop Guy, however, was ignored and rebuffed by the new King and left England immediately, probably before Anselm's return at the end of September. In his first letter to Paschal, Anselm protested the granting of legatory powers over the English Church to the Archbishop of Vienne as illegal; he claimed that the legateship in England should reside perpetually in the Archbishop of Canterbury.[58] This high opinion of the authority of the Archbishop of Canterbury, which resembles Lanfranc's view, appears to have been a reaction against Anselm's unfortunate experiences with Urban's legates. Certainly he had never protested the authority of Urban's legates when he had still hoped that they might assist him in his struggle with William II and his episcopal colleagues.

Paschal appears to have taken cognizance of Anselm's protest. The Pope did not give up sending legates to England, but he attempted to conciliate Anselm by limiting the legate's authority and by choosing one of the Archbishop's friends and disciples for the office. At the end of February 1101, he dispatched Cardinal Bishop John of Tusculum, assisted by Tiberius, a member of the papal household, to England to work with Anselm in the general reform of the English Church, in the collection of Peter's Pence, and in making peace between Henry and Robert Curthose. Cardinal John was one of Anselm's Bec disciples who could be expected to work amicably with the Archbishop. It appears that Paschal also sought to conciliate Anselm by withholding full legatory powers from Cardinal John and Tiberius. In Paschal's letter

---

[58] *HN*, 126; *AO*, ep. 214, ll. 17-30. See also Tillmann, *Legaten*, 22. For Anselm's statement on the legatory powers of the Archbishop of Canterbury, *AO*, ep. 214, ll. 17-21: Quando Romae fui, ostendi praefato domino papae [Urbano] de legatione Romana super regnum Angliae, quam ipsius regni homines asseverant ab antiquis temporibus usque ad nostrum tempus ecclesiam Cantuariensem tenuisse, quam necessarie ita esse oporteat, nec aliter nisi contra utilitatem ecclesiae Romanae et Anglicanae fieri possit."

to Anselm announcing their appointment, they are referred to
only as papal "envoys" and a specific statement of their *legatio* is lacking.[59] In spite of these concessions from Rome, Anselm showed no enthusiasm for working with the papal representatives. Although Cardinal John and Tiberius remained
in England at least until the beginning of September 1101,[59a]
there is no indication that Anselm allowed them to influence
or to intervene in his negotiations with the King on lay investiture in England.

As part of the new harmony in church-state relations, Anselm reached a reconciliation with the royal supporters among
the clergy. The appointment of the curialist clerk and royal
physician, the Italian Faricius, as Abbot of Abingdon, occurred
at the end of November 1100, at the very time when Anselm
was concluding the preparations for Henry's marriage to
Mathilda.[60] The King would not have made this appointment of Faricius, if it had not been acceptable to Anselm. At
the beginning of 1101 Anselm wrote to Paschal to obtain the
pallium for Gerard, to whom Henry had given the Archbishopric of York in fulfillment of his promise at the time of
his coronation. Anselm praised Gerard, the intellectual leader
of the curialist bishops, for his learning and ability. He assured the Pope that the "clergy and people" of York had
elected their new metropolitan.[61] There is indeed no reason

[59] It is significant that there is no mention in *HN* of Cardinal John and
Tiberius in England in 1101. Again Eadmer suppressed evidence indicating a difference of opinion between Anselm and the papacy. Information is,
however, supplied by Hugh of Flavigny, *Chronicon, MGH, SS,* VIII, 494,
and in Paschal's letter to Anselm at the end of February 1101: *AO*, ep.
213, ll. 13-24. See also Tillmann, *Legaten,* 22-23; Lunt, *Financial Relations,* 36-37. For Cardinal John's biography see Hugh of Flavigny, *loc.cit.,*
and H. W. Klewitz, "Die Entstehung des Kardinalkollegiums," *ZRG, KA,*
25 (1936), 211. Neither in Hugh of Flavigny nor in Paschal's letter is
there any mention of legatus or legatio. Paschal referred to John and
Tiberius as "nostris nuntiis" (*AO*, ep. 214, l. 19).

[59a] Farrer, "Itinerary," nos. 25, 26, 28, witness lists (September 3,
1101).

[60] Johnson, *Reg.,* no. 498; *Hist. Mons. de Abingdon,* ed. J. Stevenson
(*RS,* 1858), II, 44.

[61] *AO*, ep. 214, ll. 64-67: "Mortuo archiepiscopo Erboracensi, postquam

to doubt that the form of canonical election had actually been observed. At about the same time Henry appointed a monk of Caen to the abbacy of Glastonbury, "but with the convent's consent."[62] Henry and Anselm were working out a reasonable compromise on ecclesiastical elections. The real power of appointment still resided with the King, but the candidates were approved by the Archbishop of Canterbury and the "clergy and people." To a limited extent, Henry was accepting the Gregorian ideal of canonical election. As a result of his reconciliation with the curialist bishops, Anselm was gaining recognition as Primate of all Britain, a title which he had wanted to assume since the beginning of his pontificate. Bishop Samson of Worcester is known to have taken such an oath of canonical obedience to Anselm.[63]

In the midst of this cooperation between the King and Anselm, and the growing *rapprochement* between the Primate and his episcopal colleagues, Paschal's decision on lay investiture in England was received shortly after Pentecost of 1101.[64] Previously the Pope had sent his first letter to Anselm at the end of February, before receipt of Anselm's letter raising the question of mitigation of the papal decrees on lay investiture. In that letter, Paschal had urged Anselm, in general terms, to reform the English Church along the lines required by the reforming papacy.[65] Although Anselm's letter

---

reversus sum, electus est in locum eius episcopus Herefordensis, vir admodum litteratus et in ecclesiasticis disciplinis eruditus. In hac electione nos episcopi clero et populo eiusdem ecclesiae assensum praebuimus." Gerard was elected Archbishop at Christmas of 1100 (Sym. Dur., *HDE*, II, 232; *HC*, 366).

[62] Will. Malmesbury, *De Antiq. Glaston.*, ch. 66.

[63] *C.C.C. MS. 146* (Pontifical of Samson of Worcester), p. 1, contains Samson's oath of canonical obedience to Anselm as Primas totius Britanniae. The date of this profession of obedience by the Bishop of Worcester (1096-1112) is unknown but it is most likely that it was made shortly after Anselm's return to England in 1100.

[64] *AO*, ep. 216 n.

[65] *AO*, ep. 213 (J-L, no. 5883), ll. 8-11: "Primo, ut ecclesiarum in regno Anglico statum sendum Romanae ecclesiae sanctiones corrigi ac disponi facias. Dehinc de regis erga nos devotione ac fidelitate debita censuque beati Petri restituendo efficacius studeas."

had raised the investiture question in the most delicate manner, only presenting the fact that the King and magnates vehemently resisted prohibition of lay investiture, and not specifically asking for mitigation of the papal decrees,[66] the Pope appears to have been offended by the Archbishop's statement. Apparently concluding that Anselm did not subscribe to his own high Gregorian doctrines, Paschal ignored the Archbishop and wrote directly to the King alone.

Paschal refused to make any concession whatever to the King. Instead his letter to Henry presented a detailed statement of high Gregorian doctrine. Quoting St. Ambrose's principle that the palace belongs to the emperor, but the church to the priest, Paschal delineated the now familiar argument that the Church was the bride of Christ and must not be violated by laymen. He demanded the full implementation in Henry's kingdom of the papal decrees on lay investiture and homage of ecclesiastics.[67]

Before Henry could make any new decision on lay investiture, he had to face the grave threat of an invasion by his brother, Duke Robert of Normandy, which was finally being prepared in June of 1101. On July 21 Robert landed in England with his army and a number of the Anglo-Norman barons defected to the invader.[68] Anselm made the most of his opportunity. On the one hand, he wanted to preserve Henry on the throne, for Henry was an anointed king against whom rebellion was forbidden, according to the example of Saul

[66] *AO*, ep. 214, ll. 14-16: "Sensi et audivi quia nullo modo eam [i.e. prohibition of lay investiture] rex et principes eius vellent suscipere. Qua de re necessarium mihi vestrae celsitudinis consilium exspecto."

[67] *AO*, ep. 216 (J-L no. 5868), ll. 25-36: "Ad imperatorem palatia pertinent, ad sacerdotem ecclesiae [cf. Ambrose, ep. 20, *MPL* 16, col. 1041]. . . . Adulteria est enim quae non est legitimo Christi coniugio copulata. Audis, o rex, adulteram ecclesiam nuncupari, quae non legitime nupserit. Ecclesiae siquidem sponsus unusquisque aestimatur episcopus. . . . Si ergo ecclesiae filius es—quod utique omnis catholicus Christianus est—permitte matri tuae legitimum sortiri coniugium, ut non per hominem, sed per deum et hominem Christum legitimo sponso copuletur ecclesia."

[68] For the details of Robert's invasion, see David, *Robert Curthose*, 131-37.

and David. Furthermore, Henry had indicated his sympathy for Anselm's plan to reform the English Church, whereas in Normandy the church had languished during Robert's weak and ineffective rule.[69] On the other hand, however, Anselm realized that Paschal probably could not be induced to mitigate the prohibition of lay investiture, and hence he decided to use the opportunity provided by Henry's discomfiture as best he could. In return for support, Anselm made Henry promise to obey the commands of the apostolic see.[70]

Having secured the King's promise to abolish lay investiture, Anselm turned vigorously to his defense and became Henry's most vehement and effective supporter. Not only did Anselm give the King the knight service due him from Canterbury[71]; he joined Count Robert of Meulan, Henry's chief lay supporter, in attesting a writ sent out to the shire-moots demanding loyalty to the King.[72] Both privately and publicly the Primate inspired the barons to support Henry.[73] Anselm was probably one of the "twelve leading men" from both sides attesting the Treaty of Alton between Henry and Robert, which brought the Duke's invasion to a rapid conclusion.[74]

Anselm was almost too successful in securing Henry's throne. Now that the danger was past, the King broke his promise to obey the papal decrees. The investiture dispute gave Robert his opportunity for revenge upon the Archbishop, and he urged his brother not to surrender to Anselm and the Pope on the investiture issue. Upon the advice of the Duke and the disgruntled barons who had supported Robert's abortive invasion, Henry summoned the Primate to his court at

---

[69] On the Norman Church under Duke Robert, see Haskins, *Norman Institutions*, 62 ff.

[70] *HN*, 127: "Ipse [rex] igitur Anselmo jura totius Christianitatis in Anglia exercendae se relicturum, atque decretis et iussionibus apostolicae sedis se perpetuo oboediturum, summo opere promittebat." It is probable that Anselm demanded Henry's promise after receipt of Paschal's letter to the King rather than before, as Eadmer states (*HN*, 127-28).

[71] *HN*, 127.

[72] Farrer, "Itinerary," no. 24.

[73] *HN*, 127; *GP*, 106; *GR*, II, 471-72.

[74] Farrer, "Itinerary," no. 24.

Winchester in September 1101. In the presence of the great number of lay and ecclesiastical magnates attending the court, including the papal representatives Cardinal John and Tiberius, the King called upon Anselm to do him homage and consecrate the ecclesiastics who had been invested by the royal hand, or leave the kingdom.[75]

Clearly the King was not satisfied with these harsh measures which he had taken at his brother's urging. He still wanted to avoid a break with the Pope and the venerable Primate. Henry wrote to Paschal in the hope of pacifying the intransigent Pope. He expressed his intention to pay Peter's Pence, and declared that he was willing to give obedience and due honor to the apostolic see, although at the same time he wanted the usages and customs of his predecessors on the English throne to be preserved. Even should he himself want to give up these usages, Henry's appeal concluded, his magnates would never allow the abandoning of lay investiture.[76]

Again it was Anselm himself who saved Henry from an open conflict with the Pope and the reform party in the English Church. When the Archbishop suggested the sending of another embassy to Rome to seek mitigation of the papal decrees on lay investiture, the King readily agreed. If Cardinal John and Tiberius, at the Winchester assembly, had urged

---

[75] *HN*, 131; Farrer, "Itinerary," nos. 25 and 28 for large number of lay and ecclesiastical magnates present at Henry's court at Winchester, in September of 1101, to which Anselm was summoned.

[76] *AO*, ep. 215, ll. 6-15: ". . . Beneficium quod ab antecessoribus meis beatus Petrus habuit, vobis mitto, eosque honores et eam oboedientiam, quam tempore patris mei antecessores vestri in regno Angliae habuerunt, tempore meo ut habeatis volo; eo vidilicet tenore, ut dignitates, usus et consuetudines, quas pater meus tempore antecessorum vestrorum in regno Angliae habuit, ego tempore vestro in eodem regno meo integra obtineam. Notumque habeat sanctitas vestra quod me vivente deo auxiliante dignitates et usus regni Angliae non minuentur. Et si ego—quod absit!—in tanta me deiectione ponerem, optimates mei, immo totius Angliae populus id nullo modo pateretur." Although Schmitt dates this letter before receipt of Paschal's letter to Henry (ep. 215, n.) it appears to be written in reply to Paschal's letter. For in that letter, the Pope had expressed his disappointment that the King had not declared his obedience to him (ep. 216, ll. 3-4), which Henry offers in this letter.

Anselm to break immediately with Henry on the issue of lay investiture, it is clear that the Archbishop had rejected this advice. He still hoped to avoid another bitter controversy over church-state relations in England; his personal admiration for the young King made Anselm reluctant to break decisively with Henry. Accordingly, before the end of 1102, a joint embassy representing Anselm and the King started for Rome. The Archbishop was represented by two of his monastic disciples from the Canterbury *familia*, Baldwin and Alexander, and Henry by Gerard of York and two other curialist bishops, Herbert of Norwich and Robert of Chester, all of whom had diocesan business at the papal court.[77]

The letters which Anselm dispatched to Paschal at this time reveal the Archbishop's impossible position and his chagrin at being caught between the millstones of an intransigent high Gregorian Pope and a King who refused to give up lay investiture. In the reign of William II, the papacy had placed Anselm in a difficult position by refusing to support his reform endeavors in England. Now Paschal II was going to the other extreme of demanding changes in church-state relations which the King, the lay magnates and the great majority of the episcopate would not accept. In his letters to the Pope, Anselm pointed out how much he had already suffered during his pontificate, as a result of controversies with the royal authority and exile.[78] He complained that Paschal had not even deigned to answer his inquiry about lay investiture in England, but instead had begun to negotiate directly with the King.[79] He warned Paschal that not only the King and lay magnates, "but even the bishops and minor orders" would rather expel their Primate from the kingdom and cut themselves off from the Roman Church than abandon lay investiture.[80] Anselm tried

[77] *HN*, 131-32.
[78] *AO*, ep. 217, ll. 6-8; ep. 220, ll. 3-7.
[79] *AO*, ep. 218, l. 8.
[80] *AO*, ep. 219, ll. 8-11: After Anselm had said that he was bound by the papal decrees on investiture, "quod audientes rex et principes eius, ipsi etiam episcopi et alii minores ordinis, tam graviter acceperunt, ut asserent

hard to effect a reconciliation with the curialist bishops, but now the papacy was fomenting a renewed split within the episcopate. In an attempt to maintain his friendly relations with the curialist bishops, Anselm strongly supported the King's request that Paschal grant the pallium to Gerard while the Archbishop of York was at Rome.[81]

In spite of Anselm's endeavors to maintain harmonious agreement on church-state relations in England, it was apparent by the latter part of 1101 that only a sudden change of heart by Paschal would prevent a controversy over lay investiture in England similar to the dispute which had racked Germany for a quarter of a century. Now that his throne had been secured, Henry could afford to be firm in his defense of lay investiture. While the Primate again withdrew from the royal court until the return of the envoys from Rome in August/September of 1102,[82] the King set about establishing his complete control over the English Church and gaining the support of the episcopate, in preparation for the almost inevitable break with Anselm and Paschal over lay investiture. Ranulf Flambard was released from the Tower and given back the bishopric of Durham.[83] Henry placed the vacant see of Hereford in custody of his chaplain Bernard,[84] and was generous in royal grants to the curialist bishops and abbots.[85]

When the envoys from England arrived at the Lateran in

---

se nullo modo huic rei assensum praebituros, et me de regno potius quam hoc servarent expulsuros et a Romana ecclesia se discessuros." In view of such a strong statement as this, Fliche's thesis that the English investiture controversy was only the outgrowth of Lyons' claim to primatial authority (above, n. 1) appears quite erroneous.

[81] *AO*, ep. 220, ll. 19-22; ep. 221, ll. 3-5.

[82] From the dispatch of the envoys to Rome in September/October of 1101 until their return in August/September 1102, Anselm attested at the most one royal charter, and even this charter may be outside this period. See Farrer, "Itinerary," no. 29.

[83] Sym. Durham, *HDE*, I, 138. Ranulf witnessed a royal charter in September, 1101: Farrer, "Itinerary," no. 28.

[84] Round, *CDF*, no. 1138.

[85] Farrer, "Itinerary," nos. 25, 26, 28, 30, 35, 39, 40.

the second or third month of 1102, they found that Paschal had in no wise departed from his doctrinaire attitude on investiture in England. By this time Henry IV had been incapacitated in his war with the papacy by the revolt of his son[86] and Paschal, freed from the imperial threat, felt that he could afford to refuse any concession to Henry I. Since the time of Gregory VII and William the Conqueror, the papacy had tended to be conciliatory in its dealings with the English king, especially during the pontificate of Urban II. But now the reforming papacy's long-standing fear of fomenting a two-front war with both the German Emperor and English King had been alleviated by the prevailing weakness of the imperial power.

The English envoys found in Paschal a dour old monk and fanatical high Gregorian, a man of very different attitude from the wily and moderate Urban II. Paschal indignantly scolded the envoys for requesting mitigation of the apostolic decrees on investiture,[87] and instead dispatched several letters to England, which the envoys brought back with them when they returned at the end of the summer of 1102. Two of these papal letters reflect the slow growth of papal jurisdiction in England during Anselm's pontificate. Paschal wrote to Ranulf Flambard of Durham, demanding that he submit himself to Anselm's judgement on the rectitude of his personal life, and to Osbern of Exeter, supporting Anselm's metropolitan authority over that Bishop's diocesan administration.[88] Although these letters were written at Anselm's request, they indicate a new papal interest in the internal affairs of the English Church.

The most important of Paschal's letters were addressed to the King and Primate, and dealt with the investiture issue. Lay investiture was "the root of simoniacal depravity," Paschal wrote to Anselm. Even though the Archbishop had to exercise episcopal authority "among a barbarous people," he

---

[86] Meyer von Knonau, *Jahrbücher . . . Heinrich V*, v, 151ff.
[87] *HN*, 134.   [88] *AO*, epp. 225, 226.

ought not to let force dissuade him from carrying out the papal policy to its fullest extent.[89] Anselm's envoys had placed before the Pope several questions arising from the prohibition of lay investiture, which make clear the Archbishop's keen appreciation of the importance of feudal institutions in the life of the Anglo-Norman Church. Nor did he refrain from asking the fundamental question of how ecclesiastics could hold benefices and non-ecclesiastical possessions unless the churchman became a layman's *homo*.[90] To each of Anselm's questions, Paschal replied from an uncompromising Gregorian position. Already the Pope was envisaging that withdrawal of the Church from the framework of feudal institutions which was to startle Western Europe when fully expounded in the Concordat of Sutri of 1111. The Church was to be free, Paschal argued, and this meant the abolition of homage by ecclesiastics to laymen: "It is intolerable that a cleric, who has now been received into the order of God and has exceeded the dignity of laymen, should do homage to a layman for earthly wealth; lest perhaps, while addiction to secular service is repeated, the Church is empty and oppressed."[91]

Through his envoys, Anselm also pointed out to the Pope that in the history of the church, papal and conciliar decrees had often been relaxed out of necessity. Especially, he claimed,

---

[89] *AO*, ep. 222, ll. 8-12, 20-22: "Deo autem gratias quia in te semper episcopalis auctoritas perseverat, et inter barbaros positus non tyrannorum violentia . . . a veritatis annuntiatione desistis. Rogamus itaque, ut quod agis agas, quod loqueris loquaris. . . . Decreta renovavimus . . . ne quisquam omnino clericus hominium faciat laico aut de manu laici ecclesias vel ecclesiastica dona suscipiat. Haec est enim Simoniacae pravitatis radix. . . ."

[90] *AO*, ep. 223 (J-L, 5909), ll. 46-48: "Si nullus clericus debet fieri homo laici et aliqua beneficia aut possessiones non ecclesasticas debet tenere de laico, nec laicus vult ei dare, nisi fiat suus homo: quid fiet?" Cf. ll. 11-13, 37-40. This letter from Paschal to Anselm is arranged in the form of a dialogue, giving first Anselm's questions, as presented by his envoys, and then the Pope's answers.

[91] *AO*, ep. 223, ll. 49-52: "Liberam esse ecclesiam Paulus dicit. Indignum est igitur ut clericus, qui iam in dei sortem assumptus est et iam laicorum dignitatem excessit, pro terrenis lucris hominium laico faciat; ne, forte, dum repetitur servitii saecularis obnoxius, vacet aut gravetur ecclesia." Cf. ll. 14-18, 41-45.

should this be done in this case, "in a kingdom in which almost all things are corrupt and perverse."[92] In reply Paschal felt compelled to grant Anselm discretionary powers,[93] but by his inflexible stand on lay investiture and homage of ecclesiastics, he had made this concession a mere formality. The Pope's letter to Henry was in a similar vein. While praising the King for acts favorable to the freedom of the church at the beginning of his reign, the Pope added that this fine beginning would come to naught unless lay investiture were abandoned in England.[94]

One of the Roman cardinals added his voice to the conflict over church-state relations in England. A certain Cardinal John, probably the recent papal envoy in England, wrote to Anselm at the same time as Paschal to encourage him in his dispute with the King and the "false bishops."[95] The papal curia was making a concerted and all-out attack on the basis of the Anglo-Norman church-state system, the feudalization of the church which the Norman rulers had made the foundation of their ecclesiastical policy for a century.

A new and even more acrimonious controversy over church-state relations in England than had occurred in the previous reign was now imminent. Henry's supporters hastened to consolidate the royal position. With the example of the German holocaust before them, they realized that an investiture controversy in England would constitute a very grave threat to the power of the monarchy.

Gerard of York failed to gain his pallium from Paschal II

---

[92] *AO*, ep. 223, ll. 54-56: "Saepe necesse est aliquid de apostolicis et canonicis statutis pro compensationibus relaxare, et maxime in regno in quo fere omnia sic corrupta et perversa sunt. . . ."

[93] *AO*, ep. 223, ll. 63-67.

[94] *AO*, ep. 224 (J-L 5910), ll. 8-9, 14-24.

[95] *PU*, I, no. 5 (*AO*, ep. 284, ll. 21-33). Cardinal John could be either John, Cardinal Bishop of Tusculum, one of Anselm's Bec disciples (H. W. Klewitz, "Die Entstehung des Kardinalkollegiums," *ZRG, KA*, 25 [1936], 211) or John, Cardinal Deacon of St. Maria in Cosmedin, the later Gelasius II (*ibid.*, 220). John of Tusculum is the more probable author because of his long acquaintance with Anselm and because of his recent visit to England.

while at Rome. It is apparent that the Pope intended to use the grant of the pallium as a bargaining factor in his dispute with the King. Having failed to achieve any success at Rome, Gerard turned southward and visited Count Roger of Sicily.[96] The details of Gerard's meeting with Roger are unknown, but it is apparent that Henry was looking around for an effective ally in case his break with the Pope should become final and irrevocable. As has been shown in the previous chapter, Urban II had granted similar privileges to William II and Roger I, placing both the Anglo-Norman and Sicilian-Norman churches officially under the control of the secular rulers in each country. Paschal had already violated the agreement of 1096 between Urban and Rufus. He had sent a papal legate to England, and what was more important, he was attempting to destroy the foundations of the ecclesiastical policy of the Anglo-Norman kings. The reform of the church along Gregorian lines in the territory under Roger's rule could be the next object of Paschal's seemingly reckless policy. Gerard, acting as Henry's envoy, probably brought these facts to Roger's attention and sought to learn where the Count would stand in case of a conflict between the Pope and the English King.

When the envoys returned to England at the end of August, 1102, with the papal letters, it appeared that the final break between the King and the church reformers was inevitable and now imminent. But Anselm, by using any expedient he could find, succeeded in postponing it for yet another year. Gerard and two other curialist bishops, who had served as Henry's envoys, came back to England with a

---

[96] Gerard's visit with Roger in 1102 is mentioned only in a letter from the Archbishop of York to the Count in 1105. F. Liebermann, ed., *Quadripartitus* (1892), 159-60: "Licet mihi juxta preclaram excellentiae vestrae famam prius dilectus quam notus fueritis, ex quo tamen in notitiam vestram veni vestramque liberalitatem, dulcedinem et veritatem presens videre et quasi tangendo sentire potui. . . . De inpenso mihi a vobis in patria vestra honore dignas quidem grates reddere non sufficio." On Gerard's correspondence in the *Quadripartitus* see below, Ch. V, n. 110. Gerard's visit with Roger explains why the envoys to Rome were away from England for almost a year.

strange and wonderful tale. They reported that Paschal had told the envoys orally that in spite of his uncompromising attitude in his letters to Anselm and Henry, he would excommunicate no one in England because of lay investiture.[97] In view of Urban II's secret negotiations with William II in the previous decade, the story concocted by the royal envoys had some slight accoutrements of plausibility, enough at least to allow Henry to express his belief in it and hence demand that Anselm accept investiture from the royal hand.[98] Although Anselm's envoys had denied the report of Gerard and his colleagues,[99] the Archbishop employed it to patch up another truce with the King. He suggested that the investiture issue should be held in abeyance until yet another envoy could be sent to Rome to make sure of Paschal's opinion. Meanwhile the King could invest ecclesiastics without fear that the Primate would make use of his power of excommunication.[100] Henry gladly accepted Anselm's new proposal. Rejoicing in his substantial victory, for the Primate had not taken the word of his own envoys, the King proceeded to invest his chancellor Roger with the pastoral staff of Salisbury and to grant the symbols of the episcopacy of Hereford to the royal larderer Roger.[101]

By this concession Anselm had again won over the King to the cause of limited church reform, and probably his promise to refrain from excommunication was made with the understanding that Henry would accede to the calling of a reforming council of the English Church. Anselm had wanted to assemble such a council since the beginning of his pontificate. It met at Westminster Abbey at the end of September of 1102.[102] The text of this Council of London, as Eadmer and subsequent historians have called it,[103] reveals that in issues other than lay investiture, Gregorian ideas had gained

[97] *HN*, 137-38.   [98] *HN*, 140.   [99] *HN*, 138.   [100] *HN*, 140.

[101] *HN*, 141: "Tunc rex, tanquam cupitae potestati donatus, exultans et hilaris per dationem virgae pastoralis illico duos de clericis suis duobus epicopatibus investivit. . . ."

[102] *HN*, 141.   [103] *HN*, 144.

considerable support among the Anglo-Norman bishops and abbots.[104] Although Gerard refused to recognize Anselm's claim to the primacy,[105] the Archbishop of York and all but one member of the episcopate as well as the greater abbots were present at the London Council,[106] and they accepted the reforming decrees which Anselm proposed.

These decrees envisaged the drastic moral reform of the clergy in England. Several canons of the Council implemented Anselm's demand for celibacy in all ranks of the clergy down to and including subdeacons.[107] The Gregorian view that men in holy orders should be unmarried and celibate was not novel in England at this time, since in 1076 Lanfranc had issued a decree against married clergy. But sacerdotal celibacy had not been vigorously enforced in England, and several of the bishops, archdeacons, and cathedral canons at the time of Anselm's pontificate are known to have had children.[108] It was against these considerable vestiges of clerical marriage and concubinage and the attendant abuses, especially the inheritance of churches by priests' sons,[109] that Anselm now legislated. The Council of London marks an important step in the slow enforcement of clerical celibacy in England during the Gregorian reform period.

While in these and similar decrees on the morals of the clergy, Anselm was not imposing new ideals on the English

[104] The text of the canons of the Council of London is given in *HN*, 141-44.

[105] The preamble to the Council's canons refers to Anselm as Primate (*HN*, 141), but it is apparent from *HC*, 110 that Gerard refused to recognize Anselm's superior authority at the Council.

[106] *HN*, 141. Osbern of Exeter was ill.

[107] *HN*, 142: "Statutum quoque est . . . ut nullus archdiaconus, presbyter, diaconus, canonicus, uxorem ducat, aut ductam retineat. . . . Ut presbyter quamdiu illicitam conversationem mulieris habuerit, non sit legalis, nec missam celebret, nec, si celebraverit, eius missa audiatur. Ut nullus ad subdiaconatum aut supra ordinetur sine professione castitatis."

[108] C.N.L. Brooke, "Gregorian Reform in Action: Clerical Marriage in England 1050-1200," *Cambridge Hist. Journal* 12 (1956), 11-13; Brooke, "Married men among the English higher Clergy, 1066-1200," *ibid.*, 187.

[109] *HN*, 142: "Ut filii presbyterorum non sint haeredes ecclesiarum patrum suorum."

Church, some of the canons of the Council of London do reflect the more radical Gregorian aim of withdrawing churchmen from secular affairs. Ecclesiastics, especially bishops, were prohibited from undertaking judicial office, since that involved the shedding of blood. Abbots were precluded from becoming knights, and were required to eat and sleep in the same residence as their monks.[110] All these provisions remained dead letters. If they had been enforced, the development of English law, government, and monastic orders in the Middle Ages would have been greatly affected.

The very first canon of the Council of 1102 also contained radical Gregorian overtones, since it condemned "simoniacal heresy."[111] While Lanfranc's Council of 1075 had also prohibited simony, this was the first time in England that such acts were condemned in high Gregorian terms as heresy.[112] Unlike the other radical provisions of the Council of London, immediate steps were taken to implement this decree. The Council removed from office, on account of simony, no less than nine abbots, including the heads of the great monasteries of Ely, Ramsey, and Bury St. Edmund.[113] From the large number of deposed abbots, it is apparent that the Council's condemnation of simony was aimed at a real abuse which the King was maintaining in a flourishing state. It is known that the deposed Abbot of Bury St. Edmund was a Norman monk, the son of the Earl of Chester, who shortly before the Coun-

[110] *HN*, 142: "Statutum quoque est ne episcopi saecularium placitorum officium suscipiant. . . . Ne quilibet clerici sint saecularium praepositi vel procuratores, aut judices sanguinis." *HN*, 143: "Ne abbates faciant milites; et ut in eadem domo cum monachis suis manducent et dormiant, nisi necessitate aliquis prohibente."

[111] *HN*, 142: "Primum itaque ex auctoritate sanctorum patrum symoniacae haeresis surreptio in eodem concilio damnata est."

[112] On the history and meaning of the term simoniacal heresy, see the lucid study by J. Leclercq, " 'Simoniaca Heresis,' " *Studi Gregoriani*, ed. Borino, I (1947), 523ff. While the term was already used by Gregory I, it was the Gregorian reformers who popularized it, associated it with their reform doctrines, and clarified its meaning. Cardinal Humbert took the lead in defining the act of simony itself as an error in faith, constituting a departure from the teachings of the Church. Cf. Wilkins, *Consilia*, I, 363, col. 2, for Council of 1075.

[113] *HN*, 142.

cil had seized the abbacy with royal support.[114] This usurpation had undoubtedly brought a lucrative payment to the royal treasury.

On the other hand, the depositions revealed that the King and the curialist bishops were sincerely attempting to co-operate with Anselm in his reform of the English Church. While Henry himself appointed a new abbot for Ramsey,[115] a free election of a new abbot was allowed to take place at Bury St. Edmund.[116] Nor were the other abbots removed by the Council reinstated until the Pope absolved them in 1106-7.[117] Within the Province of York, Gerard attempted to carry out the Council's decrees on clerical celibacy, and gained Anselm's praise for his reforming zeal.[118]

The acceptance of the Gregorian prohibitions of simony by the Anglo-Norman episcopate and the King is in part explained by the presence at the Council of London of a highly respected religious from Normandy who was sympathetic to Gregorian doctrines. The *Vita* of St. Vital, later Abbot of Savigny, reveals that this Norman monastic reformer attended the Council of London.[119] St. Vital's attitude towards the monastic life resembled the principles of the later Cistercian order, which his monastery of Savigny, founded in 1105, eventually joined in 1147.[120] He is known to have been a supporter of at least the more moderate aspects of the Gre-

---

[114] R.H.C. Davis, "The Monks of St. Edmund, 1021-1148," *History* 40 (1955), 235.

[115] Farrer, "Itinerary," no. 56.

[116] R.H.C. Davis, *op.cit.*, 235.

[117] *AO*, epp. 397, 422; Johnson, *Reg.*, no. 771.

[118] *AO*, epp. 255, 256.

[119] E. P. Sauvage, ed., "Vitae BB. Vitalis et Gaufridi," *Analecta Bollandiana*, I (1882), 373-74. *HN* does not mention Vital at the Council of London, while the *Vita* gives Vital a prominent rôle in the Council.

[120] On St. Vital and the early history of Savigny, see J. Buhot, "L'Abbaye normande de Savigny," *Le Moyen Age* 46 (1936), 1ff.; J. Rambaud-Buhot, "L'Abbaye de Savigny," *Cahiers Léopold Delisle*, vol. II, fasc. I (1948), 3ff.; L. Janauschek, *Originum Cisterciensium* (1877), I, 95ff.; J. v. Walter, *Die ersten Wanderprediger Frankreichs* (1906), 61ff.; H. Sauvage, *St. Vital et l'abbaye de Savigny* (1895).

gorian reform program.[121] During his exile, Anselm had turned for assistance to the new and more rigorous monastic orders which were emerging on the Continent. Now one of the leaders of this new monastic movement had come over to England, probably at Anselm's invitation, to lend his prestige in the struggle for reform of the Anglo-Norman Church. Henry I admired the Norman monastic reformer,[122] and Vital's presence at the Council of London must account in part for Anselm's success in obtaining the condemnation of simony as heresy.

The reforms initiated by the Council of London were interrupted by the revival of the investiture controversy, and this time the break between Anselm and Henry was complete and was not entirely repaired until 1107. Although Anselm had promised that he would not excommunicate an ecclesiastic for accepting investiture from the King, he had not offered to consecrate the invested bishops. Indeed the papal decrees and Paschal's letters prevented him from doing this. In October 1102, the King appointed the Queen's chancellor Reinelm to the vacant bishopric of Hereford and made his clerk William Giffard Bishop of Winchester. He invested these bishops-elect with the ring and staff, but Anselm refused to consecrate them.[123] Annoyed by Anselm's intransigence, Henry ordered Gerard of York to consecrate the two bishops-elect, an act which would have been doubly uncanonical. Gerard could not legally consecrate a bishop in the Province of Canterbury, and his canonical power of consecration was vitiated without receipt of his pallium from the Pope. Nevertheless, the Archbishop of York revealed his basic hostility to the Gregorian doctrines on investiture by preparing to carry out these flagrantly uncanonical consecrations.[124] The bishops-

[121] A. Laveille, ed., *Histoire de la Congrégation de Savigny par Dom Claude Auvry* (*Soc. Hist. Norm.* 30), 1 (1896), 40-45, 84-91, 105.

[122] See Henry's grants and gifts to Savigny; below, Ch. VI, n. 233. Vital helped to make peace between Henry and Duke Robert in 1106.

[123] *HN*, 144-45. The royal larderer Roger, who had previously been appointed to Hereford, had died.

[124] *HN*, 145.

elect, fearing excommunication and the possibility of deposition by the Pope, forestalled Henry and Gerard and refused to accept consecration from the Archbishop of York. Reinelm returned his ring and staff to the King, while William Giffard was exiled by Henry and went to Normandy.[125]

The investiture controversy, which had been threatening for two years, had finally begun. Anselm withdrew from court until he left England at Easter of 1103.[126] Henry surrounded himself with the curialist bishops and abbots[127] and his chief lay supporter, the shrewd Norman baron Count Robert of Meulan.[128] Anselm complained to Henry that the King was now listening not to the reformers' advice, but to the opinions of "depraved and unfaithful counsellors," and appointing enemies of reform to ecclesiastical office.[129] The alliance of King and Primate, which had effected the partial reform of the English Church since the time of Henry's coronation, had completely disintegrated.

[125] *HN*, 144-45; *A-S Chron E, s.a.* 1102. Anselm informed William Giffard that he was willing to consecrate him (*AO*, ep. 229) but this must have been before William's investiture by the King.

[126] From the Council of London in September, 1102 (Farrer, "Itinerary," n. 58) until his departure from England shortly after Easter of 1103, Anselm attested only one royal charter. This was a grant to the Church of Rochester (Farrer, no. 69) in which Anselm, as Archbishop of Canterbury, had a special interest.

[127] These curialists were chiefly Roger of Salisbury, who appears to have held his chancellorship for a short time after becoming bishop (Dugdale, *Mon. Angl.*, I, 618, n. 18), Robert Bloet of Lincoln, Gerard of York, and the royal clerk William Warelwast. See Farrer, nos. 53, 54, 56-61, 67, 69, witness lists.

[128] Farrer, "Itinerary," nos. 56, 59, witness lists. *GR*, II, 473 identifies Robert of Meulan as the chief of the lay magnates opposing lay investiture. Anselm and Paschal regarded Robert of Meulan as their leading opponent in royal circles and he was excommunicated by the Pope in 1104 (see below, Ch. V, pt. 2).

[129] *AO*, ep. 228, ll. 8-12: "Ego vero . . . consulo vobis et obsecro, ne praeponedo ecclesiis dei personas, quales non debetis et aliter quam debetis et consilio, secundum quorum consilium hoc facere non debetis, attrahatis —quod absit!—iram dei super vos. Certum enim est quia iam in aliquibus pravi et infideles, quantum ad animam vestram, consiliarii aliter quam oportet vobis consuluerunt."

4. THE POLEMICAL LITERATURE OF THE
INVESTITURE CONTROVERSY

THE growing imminence of a controversy over lay investiture in England for two years before the final break at the end of 1102 induced both the reformers and the curialists to present theoretical defenses of their positions. In Germany the investiture controversy had resulted in a great flood of polemical literature on the freedom of the church, lay investiture and characteristics of kingship—the first instance of organized propaganda in medieval history.[130] In England the volume of theoretical literature defending or attacking the Gregorian reforms was much less than on the Continent, only because the English investiture controversy lasted for half a decade instead of half a century, as in Germany. By 1103, if not earlier, both sides in the investiture controversy were producing the same kind of polemical literature that marked the conflict between empire and papacy.

The polemical literature produced by the reformers was centered on Archbishop Anselm whose saintly reputation stood them in good stead. Already before Anselm's death his secretary Eadmer was hard at work on a life of Anselm, which he submitted to the Primate for his approval.[131] Possibly Eadmer's *Vita Anselmi* was begun during the investiture controversy in order to provide an apologia for the leader of the reformers. By 1108 Eadmer was at work on a more strictly historical study which presented the case for the reform party during the reigns of William II and Henry I. Shortly after Anselm's death in 1109, he published a comprehensive and unified account of his master's pontificate. It constitutes the first four books of the *Historia Novorum in Anglia,* which attained its final form just before Eadmer's death in 1122.[132]

[130] For a general survey, see C. Mirbt, *Die Publizistik im Zeitalter Gregors VII* (1894).

[131] Eadmer, *Vita Anselmi,* II, lxxii, ed. Rule, 422-23.

[132] F. Liebermann, "Ueber Eadmer," *Ungedruckte Anglo-Normannische Geschichtsquellen* (1879), 294-96. William of Malmesbury in *GR* used

4. Polemical Literature

Eadmer's history of Anselm's pontificate, which was a product of the investiture controversy,[133] was the first major historical work in Latin produced in England since the time of Bede.

Not only Anselm's secretary, but the Primate himself contributed to the polemical literature of the English investiture controversy. He sanctioned and supervised the publication of his collected correspondence with the intention of making known his views on church-state relations. Before the end of the English investiture controversy two collections of Anselm's letters were made by the Christ Church, Canterbury, monastic scribe Theodric.[134] The first of these collections was made in 1104 at the beginning of Anselm's second exile and the other in 1105-6 during the negotiations leading to the end of the English investiture controversy.[135] Anselm carefully took a hand in selecting the letters which went into his collected correspondence. One of Henry's letters to Paschal II from the period of the investiture controversy was excluded by Anselm from inclusion in his collected correspondence, because, as he wrote to Theodric, "I do not consider it would be advantageous if it should be preserved."[136] Not only did Eadmer suppress evidence in his account of Anselm's pontificate, but Anselm himself took care to prohibit documents not

---

this first edition of *HN*, consisting of the first four of the six books in the final edition of 1122.

[133] In the preface to *HN* (p. 2), Eadmer claimed that Anselm's opposition to lay investiture and homage of ecclesiastics to laymen was the cause of *both* of the Primate's exiles. This statement is palpably false, even according to Eadmer's own account, for there was no investiture controversy in William II's reign. But it reveals Eadmer's attempt to give his history a unified theme, by making Anselm the great opponent of lay investiture. There is thus some justification for Liebermann's description of *HN* as an "einheitliche Monographie" (*Geschichtsquellen*, 295).

[134] *MS Bodley 271* and *MS Lambeth 59*. See the excellent account of the making of these two collections of Anselm's correspondence by F. S. Schmitt, "Die Unter Anselm Veranstalte Ausgabe seiner Werke und Briefe," *Scriptorium* IX (1956), 64-75.

[135] Revealed by Anselm's letters to Theodric: *AO*, epp. 334, 379.

[136] *AO*, ep. 379, ll. 6-7: "Litteras quas quaeris regis ad papam, non tibi mitto, quia non intelligo utile esse, si serventur." Cf. Schmitt, *op.cit.*, 71.

altogether favorable to the reform cause from publication in his collected correspondence.

The publication of Anselm's letters giving the Primate's position on lay investiture, but not the King's, was the chief propaganda work of the reformers during the investiture controversy. Abbot Gilbert Crispin of Westminster, however, also provided a theoretical tract on simony.[137] Although Holtzmann's dating on the tract *De Simoniacis* as 1100-1103 cannot be improved,[138] Gilbert's treatise may have been written before the Council of London of 1102 in order to provide the intellectual justification for the condemnation of simony and the deposition of simoniacal abbots at the Council. The Abbot of Westminster addressed his work to Anselm,[139] and the tract undoubtedly presents Anselm's own opinion on simony.[140] It was probably written at the Archbishop's suggestion.

The *De Simoniacis* is an interesting early example of argument in the dialectical form, which had been employed by Berenger of Tours and Lanfranc in the middle of the eleventh century, but which was still rarely used. Gilbert began by asking Anselm's judgement on ecclesiastics guilty of simony, and proceeds to give the case on both sides.[141] Although he limited his definition of simony to the purchase of holy orders,[142] he accepted the Gregorian view of simony as heresy as a safe assumption.[143]

Citing pseudo-Ambrose as a statement of the radical position on simony,[144] Gilbert presented the view that the minis-

---

[137] W. Holtzmann, ed., "Der Traktat de Simoniacis des Abtes Gilbert von Westminster," *Neues Archiv* 50 (1933), 255ff. Holtzmann's introduction (246-255) is valuable. The tract was first published by J. A. Robinson, *Gilbert Crispin* (1911), 111ff.

[138] Holtzmann, *op.cit.*, 254.   [139] *De Sim.*, ed. Holtzmann, 255.

[140] Cf. Holtzmann, *op.cit.*, 253-54.

[141] *De Sim.*, ch. 1, 255.

[142] *De Sim.*, ch. 2, 255: "Symoniacos dicimus, qui munus dant pro sacris ordinibus; excludo munus a lingua, munus ab officio et si qua alia nobis sunt occulta exhibitionum genera."

[143] *Loc.cit.*: "Id equidem apud omnes convenit et constat de symoniacis, quia sunt heretici."

[144] *De Sim.*, ch. 8, 257. The pseudo-Ambrosian work is *Sermo de dig-*

trations of a simoniacal priest are invalid, and in fact worse than invalid, since such ministrations incur damnation.[145] The opposing moderate view was then taken up in the tractate, beginning with a conciliar text from pseudo-Isidore.[146] The benediction of a simoniacal priest "has and receives grace" since it is God and not the minister who grants sacramental grace.[147] In conclusion, Gilbert came out strongly on the moderate side, as might be expected of Anselm's disciple. The sacrament retains its power in spite of ministration by a simoniac, since it is God who effects the consecration. Christians ought to tolerate such heretical priests until they are removed by the church authorities, although no true believer ought to assent to heresy.[148]

The conflicting views on simony presented in this dialectical manner by Gilbert had been enunciated a half-century earlier by Humbert and Peter Damiani, the leaders of the radical and moderate groups in the papal curia.[149] Although Gilbert does not mention the treatises on simony by the two eminent reformers, nor actually quote from their works, it seems very

---

nitate sacerdotali, entitled *De Informatione Episcoporum* in some versions (*MPL*, 17, col. 657ff.; 139, col. 174ff.). Its exact date and authorship are still unknown, but a recent careful study by G. H. Williams, "The Golden Priesthood and the Leaden State," *Harvard Theol. Rev.* 50 (1957), 37ff., argues that this work, which presents many of the radical Gregorian doctrines, was written well before the tenth century, perhaps as early as the late fourth or fifth century. Cf. Holtzmann, *op.cit.,* 252-3, 257, n. 5. There was a copy of the pseudo-Ambrosian *Sermo* in the library at Bec, where Gilbert had received his education.

[145] *De Sim.,* ch. 8-15, esp. 14, 260: ". . . Symoniacus nichil ab ordinante accipit, nichil ipse ordinando aliquem illi tradit. Gratia enim Dei seu emi seu vendi non potest. Ipsa vero officiorum signa quae suscipit, quia furatur et rapit, nichil ei conferunt nisi maledictionem. . . ."

[146] *De Sim.,* ch. 16, 261.

[147] *Loc.cit.,* ". . . Symoniacus benedicendi quoque gratiam accepit et habet, quam aliis ex officio suo conferre potest." Cf. ch. 21, 263-64.

[148] *De Sim.,* chs. 31 and 32, 267-68. Although Gilbert does not definitely say that the moderate view is the correct one, he gives the more forceful arguments to the moderate side, so that the reader is left with no doubt as to which is the correct view of simony.

[149] The most recent study of the dispute between Humbert and Damiani is by F. Dressler, *Petrus Damiani* (*Studia Anselmiana* 34, 1954), 107ff.

probable that he was acquainted with their views.[150] The circumstances of the writing of Gilbert's tract may explain the absence of any reference to the dispute between Humbert and Damiani. The *De Simoniacis* was produced during the English investiture controversy, and Gilbert and Anselm may have considered the mentioning of disputes among the Gregorian reformers unsuitable for the English reform party's polemical literature.

The polemical literature produced by the reform party was countered by an even more comprehensive propaganda effort on the part of the royal curialists. The supporters of the King took advantage of the current popularity of the Anglo-Saxon heritage which the reformers themselves had fomented, and associated Anglo-Saxon kingship with Henry I in order to defend the power of the monarchy against Gregorian doctrines. In some instances, this defense was carried to extreme lengths, resulting in the elaboration of theories of theocratic monarchy which were rather archaic.

Henry's marriage to a descendant of the House of Cerdic, which Anselm had arranged, provided the theme for the royalist propaganda. The birth of an infant son to Henry and Mathilda in the summer of 1103 brought the association of the Anglo-Norman King with Edward the Confessor into sharp focus. Soothsayings and prophecies followed the birth of the heir to the English throne whose name, Guillaume Adelin (Aetheling), symbolized the union of the Anglo-Norman and Anglo-Saxon royal families.[151] The prophecy of the

---

[150] For Damiani's views on the ministrations of a simoniac priest, see *Liber Gratissimus, Lib. de Lite,* I, 21, ll. 33-36; 24, ll. 27-32. For Humbert's views, see *Adversus Simoniacos, Lib. de Lite,* I, 108, ll. 7-12; 237, ll. 25-27; 238, ll. 39-44. I have not been able to find any quotations from Damiani's and Humbert's works in Gilbert's tract. But the nature of the arguments he presents are identical with the conflicting views of the two cardinals. It seems certain that if Gilbert had not actually read Damiani's and Humbert's treatises, he was at least acquainted with their views at second hand.

[151] *GR,* II, 495. For a detailed account see Ritchie, *Normans in Scotland,* 109ff.

4. Polemical Literature

revival of the "green tree," which Edward the Confessor was supposed to have made on his deathbed, was recalled and applied to Henry's son.[152]

Edward the Confessor's thaumaturgical powers were also associated with Henry I by the court propagandists. It was claimed that Edward's power to touch for the King's Evil "did not proceed from personal sanctity but from the inheritance of the royal line."[153] As Edward's legitimate heir, Henry was held to possess thaumaturgical powers. He was the first Anglo-Norman king who touched for the King's Evil.[154] William of Malmesbury's complaint about "those who in our times assent" to the idea of thaumaturgical kingship[155] indicates that the royal supporters were successful in using the enthusiasm for Edward the Confessor, which the reformers themselves had inaugurated, to enhance the majesty of the King.

If the reformers could venerate the relics of the Confessor, the King and his supporters showed that they could honor Edward's regalia. The crown, ring, scepter, and sandals of the Anglo-Saxon King, which had been recovered after the opening of his tomb in 1102, were preserved at Westminster as tangible symbols of the Anglo-Saxon kingship, and the monks were forbidden to allow the removal of Edward's regalia

---

[152] The story of Edward's vision of the green tree on his deathbed is found at the end of the *Vita Edwardi Regis* (ed. Luard, *RS*, 431). For an excellent discussion of the meaning and history of the idea, see Ritchie, *op.cit.*, 110, n. 3.

[153] *GR*, I, 273: "Unde nostro tempore quidam falsam insumunt operam, qui asseverant istius morbi curationem non ex sanctitate, sed ex regalis prosapiae hereditate fluxisse."

[154] M. Bloch, *Les Rois Thaumaturges* (1924), 45ff.

[155] See *GR* quoted in n. 153. Bloch's thesis (*op.cit.*, 45-7) that the *Vita Aedwardi Regis* was commissioned by Henry and his counsellors to associate the King with Edward and thaumaturgical kingship has been disproved by R. W. Southern, *EHR* 58 (1943), 385ff., and E. Heningham, *Speculum* 21 (1946), 419ff., who have shown that the work was written shortly after the Conquest. But it is possible that Henry's supporters increased the circulation of the *Vita* and rescued it from obscurity, for their polemical purposes. The only surviving MS of the *Vita* (*B.M. MS Harl. 526*) is from the twelfth century.

from the royal abbey.[156] Thus, a revolution in ideas had occurred in England, brought on by the stresses of the investiture controversy. Whereas the hard-headed Norman conquerors had always shown only contempt for Anglo-Saxon culture, now even the curialists were engaged in a concerted attempt to enshroud Henry I in the mysticism of Old English kingship.

In order to accomplish this aim fully, it was necessary to revive the Edgar coronation order which Henry had rejected in 1100 in deference to the wishes of the reformers. The ideas of theocratic monarchy strongly reflected in the Edgar order would provide a theoretical defense of lay investiture against the condemnation of the papacy. The necessary resurrection of the Anglo-Saxon coronation order and delineation of the principles of theocratic monarchy were provided in some anonymous tractates stemming from the royal circle. Archbishop Gerard of York, the intellectual leader of the curialist bishops, was their probable author.

5. THE AUTHORSHIP OF THE Anonymous TRACTS

THE anonymous tracts in *Corpus Christi Cambridge MS. 415*, a codex belonging to the collection of manuscripts made by Archbishop Parker of Canterbury in the third quarter of the sixteenth century,[157] have been studied by several schol-

---

[156] P. E. Schramm, *Herrschaftszeichen und Staatssymbolik* (*MGH, Schriften* 13), III (1956), 757-58.

[157] For the circumstances of the making of the Parker collection, drawn mostly from dissolved religious houses, see M. R. James, *A Descriptive Catalogue of the Manuscripts in the Library of Corpus Christi College, Cambridge* (1912), introduction; W. W. Greg, "Books and Bookmen in Archbishop Parker's Correspondence," *The Library*, XVI (1935-36), 243-79; and C. E. Wright, "The Dispersal of the Monastic Libraries and the Beginning of Anglo-Saxon Studies," *Trans. Cambridge Bibliographical Soc.*, I (1951), 208-237. From these studies and from Parker's correspondence (ed. J. Bruce and T. Perowne, 1853, and in unpublished MS form in *C.C.C. MS. 114*) it is evident that Parker undertook his collection, which he left to Corpus Christi, his Cambridge college, not only for antiquarian and strictly scholarly reasons but also because he hoped to find in medieval works, especially those written before the thirteenth century, support for

ars. There is as yet, however, no complete edition of the tracts, which have been published in several different places, and a few fragments remain unpublished. Nor is there as yet a definitive study of the *Anonymous*, as the tracts may be called collectively. The contents of *C.C.C. 415* were first examined by K. Hampe for the *Monumenta Germaniae* in 1896,[158] and in the following year H. Böhmer published several of the tractates.[159] Böhmer assumed that all the thirty-one tracts were written by a single author, whom he identified as Gerard of York.[160] In publishing other tracts from this manuscript in 1899, however, Böhmer withdrew a definite ascription of the tracts to Gerard, but persisted in maintaining his thesis that the author was a York cleric with a Rouen background, whom he called the "Anonymous of York."[161]

Böhmer's interpretation of the authorship and provenance of the *Anonymous* tracts has been attacked in two ways. P. Funk argued in 1935 that the tracts were not of single authorship, but rather have a varied provenance.[162] The Cambridge codex would then be a miscellaneous collection of treatises

---

the Elizabethan church settlement (cf. Wright, *op.cit.*, 226-27). His principal agent in making the collection was his Latin secretary, John Joscelyn, who held offices at York and Exeter cathedrals and at Cambridge. There were, however, several other scholars and agents who assisted the Archbishop in compiling his collection, who appear to have been at work over various parts of the country and even, in one case, in Wales. While the supplying agent and even the ultimate provenance of several of the manuscripts in the Parker collection are mentioned in the Archbishop's voluminous correspondence, no reference to what is now *C.C.C. 415* has been found in these letters. Whoever sent the manuscript to Parker (if he did not discover it for himself) obviously realized that its defense of royal supremacy over the church and a married clergy would appeal to the Archbishop. But perhaps Parker found the views in *C.C.C. 415* too extreme since he did not publish it, as he did in the case of some other medieval writings.

[158] Hampe listed the contents of the *Anonymous* in *Neues Archiv* 23 (1897), 669-72. Another listing by James, *Descriptive Catalogue*, 305-8.

[159] *Lib. de Lite*, III, 645ff.

[160] *Ibid.*, 642-45.

[161] Böhmer, *Kirche und Staat*, 264.

[162] P. Funk, "Der fragliche An. von York," *Hist. Jahrbuch* 55 (1935), 251ff.

by various writers. Although H. Scherrinsky and G. H. Williams have severely attacked Funk's thesis, and have agreed with Böhmer on a single authorship for the tracts, they have located the anonymous author not at York but at Rouen.[163] G. H. Williams, in particular, has presented a detailed argument on behalf of Archbishop William of Rouen, or one of his immediate circle, as the author of the tracts.

These departures from Böhmer's interpretation deserve careful consideration. Funk's thesis of multi-authorship of the tracts has not been altogether demolished, as D. C. Douglas has pointed out.[164] Scherrinsky argued for stylistic unity of the tracts; Williams pointed out the reappearance of similar or identical key concepts and images in several of the tracts, and denied the validity of Funk's argument from a diversity of subject matter in the tracts to a diversity in authorship.[165] It may be questioned, however, whether stylistic and literary criteria afford better means of deciding authorship of early twelfth-century works than subject matter and content. The writers of Normandy and England in the first decade of the twelfth century, the date which all critics ascribe to the tracts, were all the products of a few monastic schools having the same traditions and offering the same education. It would only be remarkable if the style, images, allusions, quotations, etc. of all the Anglo-Norman and Norman writers of the period were *not* very similar. Anselm of Canterbury and Ralph d'Escures, Archbishop of Canterbury after Anselm's death, were both products of the school at Bec. Their styles are so similar that until recently Ralph's writings were attributed to Anselm. Many of the writings of John of Fécamp, from the middle of the eleventh century, are so similar in style to St. Bernard's homilies that until recently they were erroneously included

---

[163] H. Scherrinsky, *Untersuchungen z. sogen. An. von York* (1939); G. H. Williams, *The Norman Anonymous of 1100 A.D.* (Harvard Theol. Studies, no. 18, 1951).

[164] D. C. Douglas, *J. of Eccl. Hist.* 3 (1952), 111, in review of Williams' book.

[165] Scherrinsky, *Untersuchungen*, 114ff.; Williams, *Anonymous*, 33-36.

5. Authorship of Anonymous Tracts

in Bernard's *corpus:* Consequently, stylistic criteria are not very convincing as proof of the single authorship of the *Anonymous* tracts. Unity of style and repetition of certain concepts and images through several of the tracts would not necessarily exclude the possibility that some of the tracts were written by Gerard of York and others by William of Rouen. For Gerard was a Norman ecclesiastic who had been a canon of Rouen before coming to England, and the intellectual milieu of the two men was identical.

A strong argument for the multi-authorship of the tracts can be presented, not only on the basis of different subject matter as Funk contended, but also on the basis of conflicting views on church-state relations. At least six of the tracts in *C.C.C. 415* clearly present Gregorian reform doctrines, a fact which Williams overlooked. The content of these reform tracts will be discussed in the following chapter.[166] On the other hand, thirteen of the tracts take the anti-reform position. They attack papal authority and reject canonical election;[167] or they defend lay investiture and clerical marriage and expound the doctrines of theocratic monarchy,[168] or they attempt to discomfit the reformers Hugh of Lyons and Anselm of Canterbury through opposition to their claims to the primacies in France and England.[169] Some of these anti-reform tracts are directly related to the archdioceses of York or Rouen. Tract

---

[166] See below, Ch. V, pp. 244-46 and nn. 101-107.

[167] Against papal authority: Tract 1, *C.C.C. MS. 415*, pp. 1-2 (Böhmer, *KS*, 436-37); Tract 2, MS pp. 3-15 (*KS*, 437-449); Tract 4, MS 39-49 (*Lib. de Lite*, III, 656-662); Tract 12, MS 97-99 (*KS*, 457-62); Tract 23a, MS 139-42 (*KS*, 475-77); Tract 24d, MS 237-38 (Williams, 234-46); Tract 28, MS 265-278 (*Lib. de Lite*, 680-860); Tract 29, MS 279-84 (*KS*, 478-81; *Lib. de Lite*, 686-687). Against canonical election: Tract 13a, MS 100-01 (*KS*, 462-63).

[168] Defense of clerical marriage and right of priests' sons to obtain ordination: Tract 22, MS 128-39 (*Lib. de Lite*, 649-55); Tract 25, MS 239-47 (*Lib. de Lite*, 645-48). On lay investiture and theocratic monarchy: Tract 24a, MS 143-204 (*Lib. de Lite*, 664-79; Williams, 225-28; S. Hellman, *Sedulius Scotus*, 129-131; MS pp. 153-56, 159-171, 184-88 not published; for analysis of contents of tract see Williams, 229-33); Tract 28, MS 265-78 (*Lib. de Lite*, 680-86).

[169] Tract 2 (against Lyons); Tract 29 (against Canterbury).

29 states the Archbishop of York's defense against Canterbury's claim to the primacy.[170] Tracts 2 and 4 deny that the
Archbishop of Rouen has to recognize the primatial authority
of any other bishop in France.[171] One other tract is specially
localized: Tract 27 opposes Fécamp's claim to exemption from
the metropolitan authority of Rouen.[172] In addition, the content of Tracts 24a and 28 appears to refer to the English investiture controversy.[173] The remaining dozen tracts in the
Cambridge manuscript deal with questions of a general moral
or theological significance, especially predestination and grace,
and cannot be regarded as part of the polemical literature arising from the controversy over church-state relations.

The argument for multi-authorship of the tracts would
contend, therefore, that the tracts vary greatly in attitude
towards the Gregorian reforms, in the location of the arch-
diocese whose case is being pleaded, and in subject matter,
and hence the codex is a collection of treatises by various authors. Some were written by Gerard of York, or one of his
circle, others came from Rouen, yet others were produced by
a Gregorian author, and the provenance of the remainder of
the tracts is unknown.

Multi-authorship of the tractates would raise the question
of the date, location, and occasion of their collection into one
manuscript. In this connection C. R. Dodwell's claim that
C.C.C. 415 is in a Rouen hand would be of no assistance.[174]
M. R. James believed that the scribes who prepared the
manuscript used a Canterbury hand.[175] Without presuming to
be an authority on twelfth-century handwriting, I doubt if it
is possible for paleographers to state categorically what is a
Rouen or Canterbury script. In any case, it would be of little
help to localize the script used in the Cambridge manuscript,

---

[170] See above, n. 167.
[171] See above, n. 167.
[172] Tract 27, MS 264-45 (Scherrinsky, *Untersuchungen*, 150-51).
[173] See above, n. 168 and for a detailed discussion, see below, pp. 190-93.
[174] Williams, *Anonymous*, 32.
[175] James, *Descriptive Catalogue*, 303.

since it is obviously not an autograph. The scribes were merely copyists. In the latter part of the manuscript, a new scribe several times takes over even in the middle of a tract.[176] There is no certainty that the Cambridge codex was the earliest manuscript of the collected tracts.

The use of at least seven different scribes on the single manuscript[177] indicates that copying was done rapidly and for a special purpose. This hypothesis is supported by the rather careless and badly organized way in which the tractates were copied. Tract 10 appears to be unfinished.[178] Tract 26 is merely another recension of Tract 22,[179] and Tract 24b a condensed and useless version of 24a.[180] There is no apparent rational order according to subject matter among the tracts. It would appear that a group of scribes were handed a miscellaneous bunch of manuscripts and told to get busy and copy them as quickly as possible.

It will be shown that Tracts 24a and 28 were written to defend the King's position during the English investiture controversy, and it is possible that the entire collection was made at Henry I's behest in order to provide him with intellectual weapons against Anselm and the Pope. But there is no conceivable reason why the King would want to preserve the Gregorian treatises which are to be found in the Cambridge codex. The only alternative occasion for the making of the collection would be in the reign of Henry II. This hypothesis has not occurred to previous writers on the *Anonymous*, but it is worth considering.

In his controversy with Becket over the Constitutions of Clarendon in 1166, Henry II appealed to the past history of church-state relations in England and the precedent of his grandfather's authority over the church.[181] Because of this

---

[176] In Tracts 26, 28, 29. See MS, pp. 255, 265, 266, 280.

[177] Hampe, *op.cit.*, 699, identified seven or eight different hands.

[178] Tract 10, MS pp. 85-86 (Williams, 223-24). The last sentence and line on MS, p. 86 appears to be unfinished.

[179] MS, pp. 247-64.   [180] MS, pp. 204-35.

[181] Robertson, *Becket*, V, 71.

dispute over the nature of the church-state system of Henry I, it would have been feasible for Henry II's councillors to make a collection of royalist tracts from the period of the investiture controversy. The royal clerks and curialist bishops appealed to the ideas of theocratic monarchy as a rebuttal against Becket,[182] who could very well be termed the last Gregorian. The most learned of Henry II's propagandists, Peter of Blois, defended royal control over the church with the same argument used by the anonymous writer of Tract 24a: "I affirm that it is a holy thing to assist the lord king; for he is holy and anointed of the Lord; nor in vain does he receive the sacrament of holy unction. . . ."[183] Peter demonstrated the efficacy of royal unction by the king's thaumaturgical powers.[184] Becket's leading antagonist, Bishop Gilbert Foliot of London, used similar arguments in the diocesan letter attacking Thomas of Canterbury, which he published.[185]

It is conceivable, then, that Henry II's supporters commissioned a collection of royalist tracts from the reign of Henry I in order to provide themselves with a theoretical arsenal against Becket. Such a commission could account for the hasty and careless way in which *C.C.C. 415* was compiled. In the rush to compile tracts on church-state relations from the reign of Henry I, Gregorian works from the period were unintentionally mixed in with tractates defending the majesty of kingship, without careful scrutiny of the contents of the treatises. John of Salisbury complained that the King's supporters were willing to go to any lengths to defend Henry II's cause,[186] and this could possibly be taken as an oblique ref-

---

[182] R. Foreville, *L'Église et la Royauté en Angleterre sous Henri II Plantagenet* (1943), 248-49.

[183] *MPL* 207, col. 440D: "Fateor quidem, quod sanctum est domino regi assistere; sanctus enim et christus Domini est; nec in vacuum accepit unctionis regiae sacramentum. . . ."

[184] *Loc.cit.* Cf. Bloch, *Les Rois Thaumaturges*, 41.

[185] Robertson, *Becket*, V, 532-33. Cf. Foreville, *op.cit.*, 244-45. D. Knowles, *The Episcopal Colleagues of Thomas Becket*, 171ff., has shown that Gilbert Foliot was the author of *Multiplicem nobis*, the work here cited.

[186] Robertson, *Becket*, VI, 94.

erence to the collection of royalist tracts from the investiture controversy. There is, however, no certain evidence which proves that the collection was made in the reign of Henry II.

The argument for plural authorship of the *Anonymous* tracts is thus, to some extent, vitiated by lack of evidence for the occasion of the heterogeneous collection, as well as by the stylistic criteria presented by Scherrinsky and Williams. The other departure from Böhmer's original thesis, to the effect that all the tracts were written by "the Anonymous of Rouen," is even less satisfactory. All students of the *Anonymous* tracts must be indebted to G. H. Williams for the learning and care he has applied to determining the authorship of *C.C.C. 415.* Unfortunately, his arguments for Archbishop William Bona Anima of Rouen, or one of William's intimates, as the author of all the tracts are not convincing.[187]

It appears reasonable that the tracts defending the authority of the Archbishop of Rouen against Hugh of Lyons' claim to the primacy and Fécamp's exemption from metropolitan control were written by William Bona Anima or a member of his circle.[188] To these may be added the *Anonymous* tracts which defend clerical marriage and the right of priests' sons to obtain ordination.[189] For Gregory VII had claimed that William was the son of a priest and at first refused to grant him the pallium,[190] although as a matter of fact William's father took orders after he had become a widower.[191] It is difficult, however, to agree with G. H. Williams that the Archbishop of Rouen was the sole author of all the *Anonymous* tracts, including the longest and most substantial one, Tract 24a, which deals with lay investiture and theocratic monarchy.

What is known about Archbishop William indicates that he

[187] Williams, *Anonymous,* 35-36, excludes only Tract 10 of *C.C.C. 415* from Rouen authorship (see below, Ch. V, n. 102). Cf. E. H. Kantorowicz, *The King's Two Bodies* (1957), 42: ". . . the most recent study leaves no doubt that the 'Anonymous' was a Norman from Normandy and perhaps even a member of the Duchy's high clergy."
[188] Tracts 2, 4, 27.   [189] Tracts 22, 25.   [190] J-L no. 5135.
[191] Cf. F. Pommeraye, *Histoire des Archevêques de Rouen* (1686), 276.

was not a vehement opponent of Gregorian doctrine, like the author of the *Anonymous* tracts, but rather a moderate supporter of church reform. Orderic Vital regarded William as the defender of the clergy and "the light of the church."[192] He also had a high regard for Fulbert, Archdeacon of Rouen during Bona Anima's pontificate,[193] whom G. H. Williams considers also as a possible author of the *Anonymous* tracts.[194] Orderic's admiration for the Archbishop and Archdeacon of Rouen would not in itself prove that they were sympathetic to the Gregorian reforms, but other evidence reveals that his praise of William and Fulbert was not empty formality. In 1096, at the very time that Anselm was ignoring the decrees of the Council of Clermont, Archbishop William summoned a synod in Normandy which, among other decrees, prohibited the homage of priest to layman.[195] Archdeacon Fulbert promulgated the decrees of this reforming synod.[196] The ambiguous use of the term *presbyter* in the synodal decree, instead of specific reference to bishops and abbots does not lead to Williams' conclusion that the prohibition of homage was only for the lower clergy and therefore has little significance.[197]

The Archbishop of Rouen had been stirred by the Council of Clermont, but it would have been impossible to introduce the Council's decree on investiture in Normandy without precipitating a violent controversy. Hence, he revived the ambiguous prohibition of the homage of priests found in the canons of the Council of Lillebone of 1080,[198] and left the exact meaning of the prohibition an open question. By summoning the synod of 1096, Archbishop William had at least indicated his sympathy for the Gregorian reform program,

---

[192] *OV*, IV, 300. See also II, 313-15. For a similar high opinion of Archbishop William see *Acta Archiepiscopum Rotomagensium*, *MPL* 147, col. 780.
[193] *OV*, III, 433-34.
[194] Williams, *Anonymous*, 95ff.
[195] *OV*, III, 473 (Ch. 7): "Nullus presbyter efficiatur homo laici."
[196] *Loc.cit.*   [197] Williams, *Anonymous*, 114.
[198] Mansi, *Concilia*, XX, 555, ch. 10.

although ducal opposition prevented him from fully implementing these reforms in the Norman Church.[199]

Evidence which Williams apparently overlooked further reveals the Archbishop of Rouen's loyalty to the papacy. In the rite of episcopal ordination in the Province of Rouen, published by Mabillon[200] and dated by him as probably from the time of Archbishop William,[201] the Metropolitan asks the episcopal candidate if he is willing to be subject to St. Peter and the Holy Roman Church.[202] This attitude to the papacy hardly conforms to the *Anonymous'* attack upon the authority of the Roman Church. In the same rite, the Metropolitan asks the approval of his suffragan bishops before consecrating the bishop-elect,[203] in conformity with the principle of canonical election.

Not only does Archbishop William thus appear to be at least moderately sympathetic towards the Gregorian reforms, but there is no evidence that he was actually involved or even interested in the English investiture controversy, so as to account for the defense of lay investiture and revival of the Edgar *ordo* in Tract 24a. In the correspondence between Anselm and William Bona Anima, the subject of lay investiture is never mentioned. There is also no actual evidence, although Williams seems to assume that there is,[204] that the Archbishop of Rouen was involved in the investiture controversy between Paschal II and Duke Robert. Even if there was, it would not satisfactorily explain why William of Rouen wrote Tract 24a. In the first place, the Norman investiture dispute has been

---

[199] As evidence of Archbishop William's anti-Gregorian attitude, Williams (111, n. 366) cites Gregory VII's letter to the Archbishop of Rouen (J-L, 5204), complaining about his lack of respect for papal legates. It would be dangerous to make too much of such a letter. Even Anselm showed little respect towards papal legates. At this time, papal legates still constituted a new institution, and it was still possible for an ecclesiastic to be loyal to papal policy, while disliking the interference of legates in his diocese or province.

[200] *Ritus ordinandi episcopi in Metropoli Rotomagensi*, in Mabillon, *Vetera Analecta* (1733), 228-29.

[201] *Ibid.*, 229n. [202] *Ibid.*, 228, col. 2.

[203] *Ibid.*, 228, col. 1. [204] Williams, *Anonymous*, 117-18.

dated 1105 by C. W. David,[205] which would seem a bit late for the authorship of the *Anonymous* tracts. Secondly, there is no reason why the Archbishop of Rouen would support Duke Robert by quoting an Anglo-Saxon coronation order! This anomaly precludes the association of Tract 24a with any dispute over church-state relations in Normandy.

Anselm and William Bona Anima always remained on good terms, which would be very strange if the Archbishop of Rouen were the intellectual leader of the anti-Gregorians. They were both disciples of Lanfranc's Bec school, and in 1093 William commanded his friend, then Abbot of Bec, to accept the see of Canterbury.[206] When William was suspended from office by Paschal II, Anselm intervened on his behalf with the Pope.[207] Finally, in 1106 Paschal turned the judgement in William's case over to the Archbishop of Canterbury and William was restored to his office.[208]

The cause of William's suspension has never been satisfactorily explained. The Pope referred vaguely to bad acts.[209] Possibly he was making William responsible for scandals in Norman episcopal elections, for which Duke Robert was mostly to blame. William of Malmesbury is the only contemporary who provided an explanation; he said that Paschal had suspended William of Rouen because he had celebrated the illegal marriage of Bertrade de Montfort and Philip I in 1093.[210] Historians have rejected Malmesbury's account because other sources attribute the celebration of the marriage to Odo of Bayeux or Ursinus of Senlis, and because it seemed improbable that Paschal would punish William of Rouen for an act committed seven years previously.[211] Malmesbury's account of the illegal marriage and the Archbishop's suspension, however, is too detailed to allow easy dismissal on this point. It is perfectly conceivable that all three bishops had

---

[205] David, *Robert Curthose*, 154-55.   [206] *AO*, ep. 154.
[207] *AO*, ep. 388, ll. 26-29.   [208] *AO*, ep. 397, ll. 47-48; *GR*, II, 480.
[209] *MPL*, 163, ep. 178.   [210] *GR*, II, 480.
[211] A. Fliche, *Le Règne de Philip Ier* (1912), 48-50; Le Prevost, *OV*, III, 387, n. 5.

participated in the marriage ceremony, but that William of
Rouen, as the highest ranking church official involved, was
eventually made to suffer the Pope's wrath. Bertrade's brother
was William de Montfort, Anselm's successor as Abbot of
Bec,[212] and it was perhaps at his urging that the Archbishop
of Rouen consented to perform the marriage. Whatever the
reason for William of Rouen's suspension by Paschal, there
is no evidence that it was for writing the *Anonymous* tracts
attacking the Gregorian reform doctrines.

Against the view that the contents of Tract 24a and Tract
28 deal with issues involved in the English investiture controversy, Williams replies that this objection

can be easily removed both by the fact that the investiture Tractates use French, indeed Rouen, sources (the Robert Benedictional,
for example) and the fact that Frenchmen less directly concerned
with the English investiture controversy than a Norman wrote on
the subject, namely, Ivo of Chartres and Hugh of Fleury. But
more important than this, there is absolutely nothing in either
Tractate to connect them with specifically English affairs.[213]

Under careful consideration, this argument is seen to be
invalid. It will be shown in the next chapter that the long-
standing thesis, that Ivo of Chartres was concerned with the
English investiture controversy, is false.[214] Hugh of Fleury
was indeed concerned with it, but he appears to have been
bound to the family of William the Conqueror by some special loyalty, perhaps kinship, and considered it his duty to advise Henry I on the theoretical implications involved in the investiture dispute.[215]

Williams' argument that Tract 24a copied certain texts
from the *Benedictional of Archbishop Robert* is the keystone
of his Norman Anonymous thesis. It can be accepted that the
Winchester pontifical which goes by the name of the Benedictional of Robert of Canterbury was one of the many pontificals

212 J. Leclercq, *Ives. Correspondence*, I, 38, n. 3.
213 Williams, *Anonymous*, 123; see also 36ff.
214 See below, Ch. V, pts. 1 and 2.
215 See below, Ch. V, pt. 3.

produced in England during the Dunstinian revival of the late tenth century, and that it was transferred to Rouen before the end of the eleventh century.[216] To the Edgar coronation order and the *ordo* for episcopal consecration contained in the *"Robert"*[217] there was added at the end of the manuscript a new *ordinatio episcopi*,[218] in a hand which is probably of the eleventh century.[219] This text was apparently intended to supplement the original episcopal *ordo* in *Robert*, so as to make it especially applicable to the Province of Rouen. The bishop-elect is asked if he will be obedient to the Church of Rouen.[220]

Now it is a curious fact that in Tract 24a (*"De Consecratione"*), the *Anonymous* quotes the entire Edgar coronation order, the episcopal *ordo*, and four sections from the *ordo* which appears in *Robert* as a supplement.[221] It would therefore appear at first glance that the author of Tract 24a had before him the *Benedictional of Archbishop Robert* which he used as the source for his quotations from the three orders. Hence, it would be concluded, Tract 24a must have been written at Rouen Cathedral, where the Robert pontifical is known to have been located by 1100. This is the argument which G. H. Williams adopts,[222] but a collation of the texts in *Robert* and *Anonymous* proves that it is specious.

Williams' contention that the texts of the Edgar *ordo* in *Robert* and the *Anonymous* belong to the same recension, can be accepted for purposes of argument, although the number of variant readings is in fact not inconsiderable. But this in itself is not decisive proof. The text of the Edgar *ordo* became very widespread. At least nine manuscripts are extant

---

[216] H. A. Wilson, ed., *The Benedictional of Archbishop Robert* (1902), preface, pp. xvi-xxix; G. Ellard, *Ordination Anointings*, 78-80. The MS of *Robert* is Rouen Y.7., which I have examined from photographs.

[217] *The consecratio regis* is on p. 140ff. of Wilson's edition, and the *ordinatio episcopi* on p. 125ff.

[218] Wilson, *Robert*, 162ff.

[219] *Ibid.*, 162, n. 1.   [220] *Ibid.*, 163.

[221] C.C.C. MS *415*, pp. 163-166 (episcopal *ordo*); 166-68 (supplementary *ordo*); 169-172, 189-194 (Edgar coronation *ordo*).

[222] Williams, *Anonymous*, 40-41.

5. Authorship of Anonymous Tracts

in England and France.[223] The *Anonymous*, in using the same recension as *Robert*, is following a text known at Winchester in the tenth or early eleventh century, for it was at Winchester that this part of *Robert* was written. It is not remarkable that a recension known at Winchester in c.1000 should be known at York in c.1100.

It is in his collation of the texts of the episcopal *ordo* in *Robert* and the *Anonymous* that Williams is in error. A comparison of the variants in the two texts shows that they could not possibly belong to the same recension. Two whole sections of the *Ordinatio Episcopi* in *Robert* are not quoted in Tract 24a, while *Robert* lacks a section which is in *Anonymous*. There are many more variants.[224] It would be impossible, then, to

---

[223] J. Wickham Legg, *Three Coronation Orders* (1900), preface, p. xxxix; Ward, "Coronation Ceremony," *Speculum* 14 (1939), 167-68.

[224] Comparison of texts of *ordinatio episcopi* in *Anonymous* and *Robert*:

Anonymous (C.C.C. MS 415)	*Robert* (ed. Wilson)
p. 164: Domine sancte pater omnipotens eterne. Deus honorem omnium, etc.	p. 125: [missing]. Deus honorem omnium, etc.
p. 164: Illius namque sacerdotii anterioris *cultus* ad nostrae mentis *habitum* ornatus est.	p. 126: Illius namque sacerdotii anterioris *abitus* nostrae mentis ornatus est.
p. 164: *Et idcirco* huic famulo tuo *N* quem	p. 126: *Proinde* huic famulo tuo quem
p. 164: Hic mutet vocem *et dicat quasi orationem penens oleum in capite mixtum cum crismaque.* Ungatur et consecretur caput *tuum caelesti benedictione in ordine pontificali in nomine patris et filii et spiritus sancti.*	p. 126 (in margin, fol. 146r): Hic mutet vocem *dicens* unguatur et consecretur caput *usque amen. Pax tibi et cum spiritu tuo.*
p. 164: Comple in sacerdote	p. 126: Comple *domine* in sacerdote.
p. 165: Finita unctione persequatur episcopus.	p. 126: [missing]
p. 165: ad evangelizandum *verbum tuum.* ad evangelizandum bona tua	p. 126: ad evangelizandam *pacem*; ad etc.
p. 165: in *verbo* et factis *in virtute signorum et prodigiorum*	p. 126: in *verbis* et factis et *virtutibus et signis et prodigiis.*

187

argue that the *Anonymous* author used the *Benedictional of Archbishop Robert* as his source book. On the contrary, since the *Anonymous* contains a different recension of the episcopal *ordo*, it is certain that Tract 24a was not written at Rouen.

But the supplementary Rouen episcopal order remains to be discussed. Surely, it could be argued, if the *Anonymous* contains sections also to be found in the special Rouen supplement to *Robert*, this is proof that Tract 24a made use of the *Robert* text. A study of the content of these sections, however, reveals that this conclusion is not inevitable. The sections of the supplementary episcopal *ordo* in *Robert* which are also found in *Anonymous* are the last four sections of the *ordo*.[225] But when the contents of these final sections are examined, it becomes apparent that they are not specially related to the Church of Rouen, nor do they have any organic unity with the rest of the *ordo*. They are merely prayers asking for benediction on the episcopal hands, staff, ring, and throne. The first three of the four prayers have been found in at least one

---

p. 165: *humilitatem* diligat

[missing]

[missing]

[missing]

p. 166: Sicut unxit spiritus sanctus *divina virtute corda apostolorum.*

p. 166: Accipe baculum pastoralis officii *signum ut in corrigendis vitiis sis seviens et cum iratus*

p. 166: Accipe evangelii et vade praedica populo tibi commisso, potens est enim. Deus tibi augere gratiam qui vivit et regnat in saecula saeculorum. Amen.

p. 126: diligat *veritatem.*

p. 127: whole section of several lines beginning Pater sanctae

pp. 127-8: whole section of several lines beginning Spiritus sanctus

p. 128: rubric Consecratio manuum . . . et crismate

p. 128: Sicit unxit spiritus sanctus per suos *flatus manus suorum apostolorum*

p. 128: . . . *officii et sis in corrigendis vitiis seviens in ira iudicium* sine ira tenens cum iratus.

[missing]

[225] Wilson, *Robert*, 165; *C.C.C. MS 415*, pp. 166-68. In the *Anonymous*, these four sections do not appear consecutively.

other pontifical.[226] As to the fourth, the variant readings between *Robert* and *Anonymous* texts create doubt that they belong to the same recension.[227] Consequently, Williams' conclusion that the *Anonymous* in Tract 24a quoted from "the
eleventh-century Supplement to the *Benedictional* . . . for use
in the Province of Rouen"[228] is not proven. Both the *Anonymous* and *Robert* independently of each other could have used
prayers commonly found in pontificals. It is not necessary to
assume that one copied from the other. The evidence provided
by these prayers does not vitiate what was proved by comparison of the texts of the episcopal *ordo*—that Tract 24a was not
written at Rouen.[229]

Williams' final argument was a denial that Tracts 24a and
28 were related to the English investiture controversy. But he
himself has to admit that there appear to be allusions in *De
Consecratione* (Tract 24a) to Paschal's letter to Henry I in
1101.[230] The theory of theocratic monarchy delineated in
Tract 24a is a careful rebuttal of the high Gregorian principles which Paschal had presented in his letter to the English King justifying the prohibition of lay investiture. In a

---

[226] Wilson, *Robert*, 197: in a Bescançon pontifical.

[227]

MS C.C.C. *415*, p. 168	Wilson, *Robert*, p. 165
rubic Benedictio Cathedrae	[missing]
Episcopalis	
[missing]	
	in unitate eiusdem spiritus sancti deus

[228] Williams, *Anonymous*, 40.

[229] Other arguments presented by Williams to support his Rouen thesis
need not be discussed in detail since they are only supplementary. Quotation
by the *Anonymous* from Ivo of Chartres' letter on investiture (Williams,
55ff.) would not prove a Rouen provenance. As a matter of fact, however,
it is highly improbable that the *Anonymous* knew Ivo's letter (see below,
Ch. V, n. 93). Quotations by the *Anonymous* from pseudo-Isidore and the
collection of law known as the Hiberniensis (Williams, 47-52) are not
conclusive evidence for the *Anonymous*' provenance, as Williams admits
(p. 52). Williams' suggestion of Bishop William Giffard of Winchester as
the possible author of the *Anonymous* tracts (p. 90ff.) is based on a misunderstanding of Giffard's biography during the investiture controversy
(see below, Ch. V, n. 133).

[230] Williams, *Anonymous*, 60-62.

similar way, Tract 28 (*"De Romano Pontifice"*) appears to allude to papal interference in the affairs of the English Church. The author attacks papal insistence that bishops make frequent visits to Rome.[231] This had been a controversial issue in Anglo-papal relations since the pontificate of Gregory VII. If Gerard of York be taken as the most likely Anglo-Norman author of this tract, this complaint has special relevance, since Gerard had been forced to go to Rome to obtain his pallium, and even after fulfilling papal demands in this regard, he had been unsuccessful in obtaining the metropolitan insignia. The author's further complaint against papal excommunication of bishops[232] also had special relevance to the English investiture controversy. For Paschal's violent denunciations of lay investiture made clear that any bishop who dared to accept investiture from the royal hand would immediately incur papal excommunication. One bishop-elect had already resigned his see, and another had left the country because of this fear of papal excommunication.

The extensive quotations in Tract 24a from the Edgar coronation *ordo* and the Dunstinian rite of episcopal consecration must be looked upon as one of the more ambitious aspects of the attempt by the King's supporters to associate Henry I with the mysticism of Anglo-Saxon kingship. It has been shown how assiduously the royalists pursued this theme as a reaction against papal demands for the freedom of the church from lay control. Gerard of York was especially involved in these propa-

---

[231] *Lib. de Lite*, III, 680, l. 34 to 681, l. 2: "Et tamen Romanus pontifex multa alia mandat, quae non mandavit Christus, multa alia adnuntiat, quae nullus adnuntiavit apostolus. Mandat enim et sacramento compellit omnes archiepiscopos per singulos annos visitare limina apostolorum, mandat et conpellit episcopos Christi ire Romam sine ulla necessitate et causa rationabili, sed solo libitu propriae voluntatis et ostentatu dominationis."

[232] *Ibid.*, 684, ll. 5-11: "Veniamus nunc ad aliud, quod Romanus pontifex facit non sine magno quidem ecclesiae scandalo et populorum periculo. Excommunicat enim episcopos, quos Deus unxit et sanctificavit oleo sancto suo, quibus etiam dedit potestatem ligandi atque solvendi, sicut et illi. Quos cum excommunicavit, apostolos Christi et christos Domini excommunicat et ita et unctionem et sanctificationem eorum in irritum redigit et ecclesiarum, quibus presunt, capita amputat, quod absque interitu corporum nequit fieri."

ganda efforts. He had participated in the crowning of Henry I in 1100, and was conscious of the surrender which the King had been forced to make to the reformers on the nature of the coronation order. He now made a concerted endeavor to revive the Edgar *ordo* with its stronger implications of theocratic monarchy. The learned Archbishop of York believed that the best way to counter high Gregorian theory was to go to the other extreme and emphasize the early medieval ideal of kingship, which was well past its peak of popularity in 1100.[233] It was probably at Gerard's suggestion that a royal clerk, who was his close friend and eventually his literary executor, attempted to codify the laws of Edward the Confessor.[234] Gerard's own contribution to the polemical antiquarianism of the royal court was the writing of the tracts in defense of theocratic monarchy and royal control over the church, of which the most eloquent is Tract 24a of the *Anonymous*:

By divine authority and the institution of the holy fathers, kings are consecrated in God's Church before the sacred altar and are anointed with holy oil and sacred benediction to exercise the ruling power over Christians, the Lord's people, . . . the Holy Church of God. . . . The power of the king is the power of God, but it is God's through nature, the king's through grace, and whatever he does is not simply as a man, but as one who has been made God and Christ through grace. . . . No one by right ought to take precedence over the king, who is blessed with so many and such great benedictions, who is consecrated and deified by so many and such great sacraments. No one receives greater or better blessings or is consecrated and dedicated to God with greater or higher sacraments, not even indeed with as many and equal sacraments, and because of this no one is the king's equal. Wherefore he is not to be called a layman, since he is the anointed of the Lord [Christus Domini] and through grace he is God. He is the supreme ruler, the chief shepherd, master, defender and instructor of the Holy Church, lord over his brethren and worthy to be "adored" by

[233] On the decline of the idea of theocratic monarchy in the early twelfth century, see R. W. Southern, *The Making of the Middle Ages* (1953), 92-96.

[234] Liebermann, *Quadripartitus*, 36, 88-89.

all, since he is chief and supreme prelate. Nor is he to be spoken of as inferior to the bishop, because the bishop consecrates him, since it often happens that superiors are consecrated by their inferiors. . . .[235]

It inevitably follows from this view of kingship that so-called lay investiture is not contrary to the law of God:

It is manifest that kings have the sacred power of ecclesiastical rule over the bishops of God and power over them. . . . Therefore it is not against the rule of sanctity, if kings confer on bishops the signs of holy rule, that is the staff and ring of honor. . . .[236]

In Tract 28 the same doctrine of the king as the chief of all priests and the Lord's anointed is presented. The king has received a divine investiture and he in turn has the right to invest bishops with the symbols of ecclesiastical office:

This is indeed a sublime and glorious investiture, by which God has invested emperor or king, that he may have power from heaven granted to him over all men. . . . Whoever then strives to deprive kings of this investiture is striving to act contrary to the ordinance

---

[235] *Lib. de Lite*, III, 663, ll. 14-17; 667, ll. 36-39; 679, ll. 12-20: "Auctoritate divina simulque sanctorum patrum institutione reges in ecclesia Dei ordinantur, et ad sanctum altare sacra unctione et benedictione consecrantur, ut habeant potestatem regendi populum christianum, populum Domini . . . qui est ecclesia sancta Dei. Potestas enim regis potestas Dei est, Dei quidem est per naturam, regis per gratiam. Unde et rex Deus et Christus est, sed per gratiam, et quicquid facit non homo simpliciter, sed Deus factus et Christus per gratiam facit. . . . Nullus est iure preferendus, quia nullus pluribus vel melioribus benedictionibus benedicitur, nullus pluribus et maioribus sacramentis consecratur et deificatur, immo nec tot nec paribus, ac per hoc nullus est ei coaequandus. Quare non est appelandus laicus, quia christus Domini est, quia per gratiam Deus est, quia summus rector est, quia pastor et magister et defensor et instructor sanctae ecclesiae summus est, quia fratrum suorum dominus est et ab omnibus adorandus est, quia presul princeps et summus est. Nec ideo minor est dicendus pontifice, quia consecrat eum pontifex, quia plerumque fit, ut minores consecrent maiorem. . . ." On the political theory and Christology of the *Anonymous*, see E. H. Kantorowicz, "Deus per Gratiam, Deus per Naturam," *Harvard Theol. Rev.* 45 (1952), 253ff., and *The King's Two Bodies* (1957), ch. 3; Williams, *Anonymous*, 127ff.

[236] *Lib. de Lite*, III, 676, ll. 27-30: "Unde manifestum est reges habere sacrosanctam potestatem ecclesiastici super ipsos etiam pontifices Domini et imperium super eos. . . . Non est igitur contra regulam sanctitatis, si eis conferunt signa sacri regiminis, id est baculum et anulum honoris."

and judgement of God. . . . When the king grants this investiture it is not as a layman but as the Lord's anointed. . . .[237]

Gerard can be regarded as the author of at least another of the works in *C.C.C. 415*, Tract 29, which defends the Archbishop of York against Canterbury's claim to the primacy.[238] Even at the Council of London in 1102 this issue had been raised and Gerard had refused to take a seat lower than Anselm's.[239] Yet Williams would even deny the authorship of this tract to Gerard. He notices "the Anonymous' want of fire in defense of York . . . which may well be a clue to the distance of the writer from the scene."[240] Williams is particularly struck by the ending of the tract,[241] in which the author claims that if any English bishop has a right to primacy over York, it is the Bishop of London, not Canterbury, according to a letter of Gregory I.[242] This is indeed a moderate conclusion, and the whole tract refrains from any violent denunciation or abuse. But this "want of fire" can be easily explained.

In the first place, Gerard, like all contemporaries, undoubtedly had a high personal regard for Anselm,[243] with whom he had been on good terms from the time of the Archbishop's return from exile to the final break on lay investiture. He would not be inclined to indulge in a violent attack on the Archbishop of Canterbury, nor would this have been effective propaganda, in view of Anselm's great reputation for sanctity. Secondly, in April 1103, the year when Tract 29 was quite

[237] *Ibid.*, 685, ll. 33-34, 37-38, 42-43: "Et haec quidem sublimis et gloriasa investitura est, qua Deus imperatorem sive regem investit, ut habeat potestatem celitus datam super omnes. . . . Qui ergo hanc investituram eis auferre nititur, contra Dei ordinationem iudiciumque agere molitur. . . . Cum autem hanc investituram rex tribuit, non laicus, sed christus Domini tribuit. . . ." On the *Anonymous'* views on investiture, see further below, Ch. V, pp. 239-42.

[238] Böhmer, *Kirche und Staat*, 478-80.   [239] *HC*, 110.

[240] Williams, *Anonymous*, 63.   [241] *Ibid.*, 65.

[242] *KS*, 480-81: "Si ergo Eboracensis archiepiscopus istis vult exibere obedientiam, non debet, nisi cogatur, de his respondere archiepiscopo Cantuariensi, quae potius iure debet ecclesiae Londoniensi."

[243] See esp. Gerard's letter to Anselm shortly after the Council of London: *AO*, ep. 255.

possibly written, Paschal belatedly attempted to win over Gerard to the reform side by granting him some important privileges. The Pope not only gave the pallium to the Archbishop of York, but also confirmed the possessions of his see, and ordered the bishops of Scotland to render him obedience.[244] Upon receipt of these favors for his see, Gerard would not be inclined to be overly critical of Canterbury's claim to the primacy. Thirdly, the assertion that London had a greater right to the primacy than Canterbury can probably be taken as an ironic remark related to the English investiture controversy. The Bishop of London was Gerard's old curialist cohort Maurice; the Archbishop of Canterbury was the leader of the reform party in the English Church, with whom Gerard strongly disagreed on the investiture issue.

Consideration of the criticisms which have been directed against Böhmer's original thesis on the authorship of the *Anonymous* tracts has on the whole vindicated Gerard of York as the author. The tracts may possibly be by more than one author, but at least Gerard is left with the authorship of several of the tracts. With the exception of the tracts related to the Church of Rouen, there is no evidence for the circle of Archbishop William Bona Anima as the provenance of the tracts. It becomes necessary to return to the original thesis.

Gerard is the only prominent ecclesiastic in England or Normandy whose biography suits him for the role of author of the *Anonymous* tracts.[245] Even the Rouen tracts are not excluded from possible ascription to the Archbishop of York, for he had been a canon of Rouen Cathedral before coming to England in 1096. He would want to defend the Church of Rouen against Lyons' claim to the primacy because he recognized that Hugh of Lyons was the leader of the high Gregorian party north of the Alps. He took Henry's side in the investiture controversy and was willing to consecrate uncanoni-

---

[244] Raine, *Docts.*, nos. 8, 11.
[245] For Gerard's biography, see Böhmer, *Lib. de Lite*, III, 642-44; KS, 261-65.

cally the bishops-elect whom the King had invested. Anselm and other contemporaries regarded Gerard as an unusually learned man,[246] and he had the intellectual ability to write the tracts in defense of theocratic monarchy and lay investiture. Finally, as will be shown in the next chapter, Gerard changed his views in 1105-6 and came over strongly to the Gregorian position. The tracts in *C.C.C. 415* which delineate Gregorian principles would then have been written by him during this final period of his intellectual development.[247]

Gerard's change of sides from curialist to reformer could account for the remarkable fact that the *Anonymous* tracts were mentioned by no one not only in the twelfth century but for the whole medieval period. The existence of these treatises, the joy of historians of medieval political theory, is referred to by no writer from the period of the English investiture controversy, let alone a later medieval period. They survive in only one manuscript. It must be concluded from these facts that the *Anonymous* tracts were never really published, that is, circulated outside their immediate place of authorship. On the contrary, they appear to have been suppressed and hidden away by their author who had decided, for some reason, that their publication would be harmful to himself. If Gerard is accepted as the author of the *Anonymous* tracts, the reason for their suppression is evident. By the time he had completed the polemical tracts defending theocratic monarchy and attacking the papacy, he had begun to swing over to the reform side. Naturally, he did not want to publish his efforts on behalf of royalist propaganda when he was trying to achieve a reconciliation with Anselm and Paschal II. He produced new tracts from the Gregorian side, but fearing the King's wrath, he considered it prudent to suppress these works as well.

In retrospect, it is necessary to guard against exaggerating the importance of the *Anonymous* tracts. They provide a con-

---

[246] For Anselm's opinion on Gerard, see above, n. 61. In *B.M. MS Cotton Titus D. XXIV*, fol. 61, there is a poem with a heavy classical flavor ascribed to Gerard.

[247] See below, Ch. V, pp. 244-48.

venient source-book for the historian of early medieval political ideas, but for the conception of kingship prevalent among
Anglo-Norman churchmen at the beginning of the twelfth
century they are not altogether reliable as a source. The
heavy emphasis upon theocratic monarchy in Tracts 24a and
28 must be regarded as an extreme statement produced by the
polemical conflicts of the period and the needs of royal propaganda. The old conception of the kingship still had influence
among learned curialists, and it still continued to play a part
in political life. But Henry and his bishops were also capable
of thinking along other lines, or else the acceptance of the
Anselm *ordo* in 1100 and the abolition of lay investiture in
1107 would have been impossible. If a statement of a typical
Anglo-Norman bishop's attitude to the King is desired, it
would be historically more accurate to quote from the letters
of Herbert Losinga of Norwich than from the mystical ful-
minations of the *Anonymous* tracts:

I am yours [Herbert wrote to Henry I] and all that I have is
yours, and for the things which are yours I am bound continually
to do you service. . . . All that I have has been collected through
your favor, and is preserved to me by your protection. . . . I implore our Redeemer and Savior . . . that He would bestow upon
you, in return for the favor you have confirmed, a worthy recom-
pense. And may the King of kings . . . after many long and happy
years, crown your soul, when it is absolved from the frailties of
an earthly existence, with the diadem of incorruption, in the glory
of the saints triumphant . . . among His Constantines, Theo-
dosiuses, and Gratians, and among all other emperors and nobles
who have been sound in the faith. . . .[248]

[248] *Herb. Epistolae*, ed. Anstruther, ep. 11: "Ego vester, et omnia mea
vestra sunt, et vobis de vestris continuo serviendum. . . . Omnia quippe mea
vestra ex gratia collata sunt et vestra tuitione conservantur. . . . Interminis
deprecationibus nostri Redemptoris et Salvatoris exoro clementiam, ut . . .
idem vobis dignam vestrae mihi collatae gratiae restituat retributionem. Et
Rex Regum qui ab hominibus propter homines, archano humanae redemp-
tionis consilio, ineffabili patientia spinis coronari voluit, iisdem inter suos
Constantinos, Theodosios, Gratianos aliosve sane fidei Imperatores ac pa-
tricios, post diuturnos felices annos, in triumphantium gloria sanctorum
. . . vestram coronet animam diademate impassibilitatis. . . ."

6. *Anselm's Second Exile*

In Herbert Losinga's attitude to the King, devotion and gratitude are the main themes, but within a more traditional Christian framework than in the quasi-heretical tendencies of the *Anonymous* tracts.

6. ANSELM'S SECOND EXILE

THE extreme views expressed in the polemical literature of the English investiture controversy were reflected in the uncompromising attitudes adopted by Anselm and Henry I after their decisive break in October 1102 over the issue of the consecration of invested bishops. Hitherto, Anselm had adopted a conciliatory and tolerant attitude towards Henry's ecclesiastical policy. By the beginning of 1103, the Archbishop's dismay at Henry's precipitate action in ordering Gerard of York to perform the uncanonical consecration of the invested bishops,[249] and the influence of Paschal II and Hugh of Lyons, the leaders of the high Gregorians on the Continent, had induced Anselm to abandon his moderation and to adopt an intransigent Gregorian position on church-state relations.

Anselm's new hostility towards Henry I led him to hold up King Baldwin of Jerusalem and Count Robert of Flanders as examples of ideal Christian rulers. Count Robert had refrained from investing Flemish abbots. King Baldwin had also demonstrated that he regarded the church as the bride of Christ, and respected its freedom. Only princes of this kind, who preserved the liberty of the church, could be assured of heavenly reward.[250] The situation in England was very different, Anselm implied. The King had turned to the "counsels of princes," rather than the leaders of the church,[251] and

---

[249] *AO*, ep. 265, ll. 8-9.

[250] *AO*, ep. 235, l. 18ff.; ep. 248, l. 10ff.; ep. 249, l. 10ff.

[251] *AO*, ep. 246, ll. 7-10 (Anselm to Mathilda) "Oro etiam ut sic faciat vestram bonam intentionem proficere, quatenus per vos cor domini nostri regis avertat a consiliis principum, quae reprobat, et consilio suo, quod in aeternum manet, adhaere faciat."

197

he had destroyed the harmony in church-state relations which had existed since the beginning of his reign. The exile of William Giffard for his refusal to accept an uncanonical consecration was, in Anselm's opinion, particularly unjust.[252] He requested Duke Robert and Archbishop William of Rouen to provide a haven of refuge for the Bishop-elect of Winchester, who had been so grievously wronged by his King.[253] Anselm's return to an uncompromising high Gregorian position at the end of 1102 is also revealed by the steady deterioration of his relations with the curialist bishops. In reply to the bishops' appeals for mitigation of the reform decrees of the Council of London, Anselm demanded their full implementation, and to assure this, sent out copies of these decrees to the episcopate.[254] By the early months of 1103, Anselm was ready to welcome warmly Hugh of Lyons' expression of sympathy and his invitation to take up exile again at Lyons.[255] In the previous three years Hugh had been serving as papal legate in the East. The absence of his influence in part explains Anselm's conciliatory attitude towards Henry I during that period. Now Hugh's vehement devotion to the ideals of Gregory VII began again to induce Anselm towards a doctrinaire position.

In order to accept fully the Gregorian tenets of his friend the Archbishop of Lyons, Anselm only needed to be reassured that the Pope had made no secret deal with Henry I on lay investiture, of a kind reported by Gerard of York and the other royal envoys in 1102. At the Rockingham council in 1095, Anselm had vehemently expressed his loyalty to Gregorian principles, but his subsequent disillusionment by Urban II's concessions to William Rufus had taught him to put little trust in popes and to attempt to work in harmony and friendship with Henry I. Now that he had broken with the English King, Anselm was ready to return to his previous

[252] *AO*, ep. 265 (Anselm to Henry), ll. 3-8.
[253] *AO*, ep. 273, l. 3ff.; ep. 274, l. 7ff.
[254] *AO*, ep. 253 (to Gerard of York), ll. 13-15; ep. 254 (to Herbert of Norwich), ll. 3-6, 15-19.
[255] *AO*, epp. 260, 261.

6. Anselm's Second Exile

Gregorian position, provided that the Pope demonstrated his complete sincerity and good faith. Consequently, in the latter part of 1102 the Archbishop again sent representatives to Rome to learn if there was any truth in the report of the royal envoys that Paschal had promised orally not to exercise excommunication because of lay investiture.

I fear neither exile, poverty, torment, nor death [Anselm wrote to the Pope] since, with God's comfort, my heart has been prepared for all these things on behalf of obedience to the apostolic see and the freedom of my Mother, the Church of Christ. I request only such great certitude that I may know without any ambiguity what position I ought to hold according to your authority.[256]

Paschal reassured Anselm immediately that he had made no secret deal with Henry I. The Pope took an oath that the report of the royal envoys was false, and affirmed that any bishop who accepted royal investiture would be excommunicated.[257] In order to make evident his full support of Anselm in the Archbishop's dispute with Henry I, Paschal demanded that Gerard of York make his profession of obedience to Anselm as Primate.[258] The Pope now regarded Anselm as the representative of the high Gregorian party in England, and he was trying to bring the whole of the English Church under the complete authority of the Archbishop of Canterbury.

With this assurance of full papal support, Anselm was prepared to take a completely doctrinaire and uncompromising position on lay investiture. When Henry came to Canterbury during Lent of 1103, with the intention of forcing a favorable decision on the investiture issue, he found that Anselm's attitude was very different from what it had been during the

---

[256] *AO*, ep. 280, ll. 32-36: "Non timeo exsilium, non paupertatem, non tormenta, non mortem, quia ad haec omnia deo confortante paratum est cor meum pro apostolicae sedis obedientia et matris meae, ecclesiae Christi, libertate. Certitudinem tantum quaero, ut sciam absque omni ambiguitate quid auctoritate vestra tenere debeam."

[257] *AO*, ep. 281, ll. 13-18, 41-47.

[258] *AO*, ep. 283.

previous three years. Anselm could now inform the King that the report of the royal envoys had been declared false by the Pope and that Paschal was willing to make no concession whatever to Henry. The Primate demanded obedience to the apostolic decrees, and sharp words were exchanged between him and the King.[259] Henry could see only one way of postponing a conflict with the papacy; he asked Anselm himself to go to Rome and plead the royal case for mitigation of the investiture prohibition. The magnates of the realm seconded Henry's appeal to Anselm.[260]

After Easter of 1103, the Archbishop left England and went to Rome in accordance with these requests,[261] but with little intention of trying to dissuade the Pope from a policy with which Anselm was now in substantial agreement. At the papal curia, it was the royal envoy William Warelwast who represented Henry while Anselm, apart from a perfunctory statement of Henry's views, kept silent, and allowed Paschal to reply to Henry's representative in his characteristically vehement and dogmatic manner.[262] In more moderate tones than he had used in addressing William Warelwast, Paschal wrote to the King, explaining once again that England could not be made an exception to the papal condemnation of lay investiture, and demanding that Henry recall the Primate to England.[263] For his part, Anselm was not eager to return to England to face a bitter quarrel with the King. He obtained from Paschal a privilege giving official recognition to Canterbury's claim to the primacy,[264] which had been one of his chief aims since the beginning of his pontificate in 1093, and left Rome to take up residence at Lyons at the end of 1103.[265]

The beginning of Anselm's second exile signified the failure of Henry's plans, carefully nurtured since his coronation, for gaining the support and the cooperation of the reform party in the English Church. The King was left to grieve that An-

[259] HN, 146-47.   [260] HN, 147-48.   [261] HN, 149.
[262] HN, 152-53; AO, ep. 308, ll. 3-5.   [263] AO, ep. 305, l. 12ff.
[264] HN, 154; AO, ep. 303.   [265] HN, 154, 157-58.

6. Anselm's Second Exile

selm would not assume the role of Lanfranc in his father's reign,[266] and through his envoy William Warelwast he begged Anselm to return to England and reestablish the harmony which had existed between his predecessor and the Conqueror.[267] The exiled Primate blandly replied that such a request was tantamount to declaring that the King did not want him to return to England.[268]

During his pontificate Anselm had wavered between playing the roles of Lanfranc and high Gregorian reformer; now the Gregorian aspect, which had receded somewhat into the background between 1100 and 1102, had become dominant in his mind. Under the influence of Paschal II and Hugh of Lyons, Anselm had given up all thought of cooperating with Henry, unless the King completely surrendered to Gregorian principles. When Henry seized the temporalities of Canterbury early in 1104,[269] he signified his acknowledgement of this situation, and indicated that he was prepared to defy the Primate and the Pope in defense of lay investiture. The only uncertain aspect of the situation now prevailing was whether England would be subjected to a long conflict between King and Pope such as still was ruining Germany, or whether the English investiture controversy could still be brought to an early conclusion.

[266] AO, ep. 318, ll. 3-7 (Henry to Anselm, 1104): "Mandasti mihi quod ad me venire non poteras, nec mecum esse sicut Lanfrancus, antecessor tuus, cum patre meo multis annis fuit. Unde valde doleo quod facere non vis. Quia si facere voluisses, libenter te susciperem et omnes illos honores et dignitates et amicitias, quae pater meus antecessori tuo fecit, tibi fecissem."

[267] HN, 157, AO, ep. 308, ll. 12-17.

[268] AO, ep. 308, ll. 17-18.

[269] HN, 159.

CHAPTER V

THE ENDING OF THE INVESTITURE
CONTROVERSY, 1104-1109

I. THE IVO OF CHARTRES THESIS

THE ENGLISH INVESTITURE CONTROVERSY was brought to an end by the so-called "concordat" of London of August 1107. The only surviving account of this agreement (it was never called a concordat by contemporaries) which gives any detailed statement of the terms of the settlement arrived at is to be found in Eadmer's *Historia Novorum*. According to this account, the investiture controversy in England was terminated by a compromise: ". . . The King granted and commanded that from that time and henceforth no one should be invested in England with a bishopric or abbacy by the gift of the pastoral ring and staff from the royal or any lay hand. And Anselm also conceded that no one elected to a prelacy should be deprived of receiving the honor through consecration because of the homage he made to the King."[1]

The terms of this compromise are of special interest because they bear close resemblance to the more famous Concordat of Worms of 1122 which ended the German investiture controversy.[2] Consequently, historians have attempted, since the publication of Bernheim's pioneering work on the Concordat of Worms in 1878, to determine the origins of the English

---

[1] *HN*, 186: ". . . Annuit rex et statuit ut ab eo tempore in reliquum nunquam per dationem baculi pastoralis vel anuli quisquam episcopatu aut abbatia per regem vel quamlibet laicam manum in Anglia investiretur, concedente quoque Anselmo ut nullus in praelationem electus pro homnio quod regi faceret consecratione suscepti honoris privaretur."

[2] *MGH, LL, sectio 4 Const. et acta I*, 159 (imperial grant): "1. Ego Heinricus . . . dimitto Deo et sanctis Dei apostolis Petro et Paulo sanctaeque catholicae aecclesiae omnem investituram per annulum et baculum . . ." Papal grant: "2. Electus autem regalia [absque omni exactione] per sceptrum a te recipiat et quae ex his iure tibi debet, faciat."

compromise on lay investiture, which apparently indicated to men on the Continent how the vexed question of lay investiture might finally be laid to rest. The compromise of 1107 has received more attention from historians of the period than any other aspect of the English investiture controversy.

At the present time scholars unanimously attribute the ending of the English investiture controversy by the agreement of 1107, to the wisdom, learning, and influence of Bishop Ivo of Chartres, the greatest canonist of his day. From 1878 to 1957, a series of historians including E. Bernheim, F. Liebermann, A. Fliche, A. L. Poole, J. Leclercq, G. H. Williams, K. Hampe, F. Barlow, A. Becker, and E. H. Kantorowicz have propounded or at least accepted an interpretation which may be termed the Ivo thesis on the ending of the English investiture controversy. A careful examination of the evidence, however, must lead to a rejection of this widely-held thesis.

That Ivo's doctrines on church-state relations were the source of the English agreement of 1107 (and, subsequently, of the Concordat of Worms) was first suggested by E. Bernheim in 1878.[3] The first detailed statement of the Ivo thesis was made, however, by Felix Liebermann in his valuable study of the relations between Anselm and Hugh of Lyons, published in 1886. Ivo, Liebermann held, was the "geistige Vater des Englischen Concordats."[4] This great scholar never abandoned this view of the ending of the English investiture controversy. In 1901 he concluded again that "the great canonist Ivo was induced to prepare the way for the English concordat of 1105 [*sic*] partly by his personal relations to the Conqueror's daughter Adela, Countess of Blois."[5] The only other detailed statement of the Ivo thesis was made by Augustin Fliche in his history of the Gregorian reform period, first published in 1940.[6] Although Fliche does not refer to Lieber-

[3] *Zur Geschichte des Wormser Konkordats* (1878), p. 12.

[4] "Anselm von Canterbury and Hugh von Lyon," *Aufsätze G. Waitz Gewidmet* (1886), 194-6. Quotation from p. 194.

[5] *EHR*, XVI (1901), 498.

[6] *La Réforme Grégorienne et La Reconquête Chrétienne* (1940), 340-1.

mann's work on the subject, the lines of his argument are, for the most part, the same as Liebermann's in his 1886 article. More recently, the Ivo thesis has been stated by Mr. A. L. Poole in the *Oxford History of England*, although in a rather cursory way.[7] A critical examination of the Ivo thesis must, therefore, consider primarily the arguments of Liebermann and Fliche.

Liebermann was such a great scholar, one of the very best of all German medievalists, that his delineation of the Ivo thesis deserves very careful, in fact, point-by-point consideration. It should be noted at the outset, however, that Liebermann's historical judgement, as distinguished from his unsurpassed erudition in medieval English history, was not always particularly profound. His views on the Anglo-Saxon witan, for instance, have been in great part negated by the work of later historians and his historical introductions to his truly monumental editions of Anglo-Saxon and Anglo-Norman laws are at times not always entirely reliable.

Liebermann's delineation of the Ivo thesis (and in this he is followed by all later writers on the subject) falls into two parts: 1) the direct influence of Ivo on the ending of the English investiture controversy; and 2) the influence which the Bishop of Chartres exercised through his friend, Countess Adela, the sister of Henry I.

Liebermann states his argument on behalf of Ivo's direct influence on the ending of the English investiture controversy in this way: "Der Ruhm wird also Ivo gehören, dessen Ansichten ja auch den Deutschen Investiturstreit beeinflussten [citing, Bernheim, *Wormser Concordat* (1878), p. 12] der

---

[7] From *Domesday Book to Magna Carta* (1951), 179. Among the other historians mentioned on p. 203, the following repeat the Ivo thesis only briefly: G. H. Williams, *The Norman Anonymous* (1950), 37; J. Leclercq, *Ives. Correspondence*, I (1949), XXIV-XXV; K. Hampe, *Das Hochmittelalter*, 2nd ed. (1953), 166; F. Barlow, *The Feudal Kingdom of England* (1955), 180. For the views of A. Becker, *Studien zum Investiturproblem in Frankreich* (1955), 100-01, 107, 121, see below, n. 25. For a discussion of the interpretation by E. H. Kantorowicz, *The King's Two Bodies* (1957), 44, see below n. 34a.

einen ähnlichen Compromiss dem Papsts empfahl [citing Ivo, ep. 190], anderseits aber auf Heinrich den I [citing Ivo, ep. 106] und dessen ersten Rathgeber Robert von Meulan in kirchlichen Sinne einzuwirken suchte [citing Ivo, ep. in *Bibl. de l'école des Chartes*, 4th ser., I (1855), p. 464]."[8] This statement is either unproven or false from beginning to end.

In the first place, far from Ivo having received renown for ending the English investiture controversy, the Bishop of Chartres was never mentioned in this regard by Anselm, Eadmer, Paschal II, Henry I, or any other contemporary. The only twelfth-century English writer who mentioned Ivo's views on investiture was Hugh the Cantor, Archdeacon of York, writing in the 1130's.[9] While Hugh approved of Ivo's views, this isolated and late instance cannot be introduced as evidence that the Bishop of Chartres' theory on lay investiture influenced the making of the compromise of 1107.

Surely if the agreement of 1107 had actually been made under Ivo's influence, as detailed a work as the *Historia Novorum* would have mentioned this fact. Eadmer and Anselm, who gave his approval to his secretary's official history, had no cause to deny to the great canonist, a friend of the Archbishop of Canterbury, recognition for his role in ending the English investiture controversy. But Ivo is never mentioned by Eadmer in that connection. Only once does his name appear in the *Historia Novorum*; he is said to have received the English Primate when he passed through Chartres in 1103.[10] Eadmer does state that Anselm accompanied Countess Adela to Chartres in 1105, but it is significant that Ivo is not mentioned in connection with this visit.[11]

As for the three letters of the Bishop of Chartres which Liebermann cites in support of his thesis that Ivo influenced

---

[8] Liebermann, "Anselm u. Hugo," 195.   [9] *HC*, 110-11.

[10] *HN*, 151. The only extant correspondence between Anselm and Ivo is a letter written by Ivo in 1094. It reveals, as might be expected, that they were on friendly terms. (*AO*, ep. 181).

[11] *HN*, 165. On Adela's part in the ending of the English investiture controversy, see further below, pt. 2.

the ending of the English investiture controversy, they completely fail to support his argument. In ep. 190 Ivo writes to Paschal requesting that the Archbishop of Rheims be allowed to make an oath of homage to the King of France, since this was the custom of the French kingdom.[12] At first sight this statement bears some resemblance (as Liebermann thought)[13] to the English compromise of 1107. Even if it did, however, ep. 190 could not be introduced as evidence for the Ivo thesis on the ending of the English investiture controversy since this letter was written in 1109/10, or at least two years after the settlement at London in 1107.[14] But Ivo's statement on the right of the Archbishop of Rheims to make an oath of fidelity to the French King must be seen in the context of the letters, written both before and after 1107, in which he delineated more completely his theory on lay investiture. As will be shown later, Ivo's theory was quite different from the one embodied in the English settlement of 1107.[15]

The other two letters of the Bishop of Chartres which Liebermann cites in support of the Ivo thesis are completely worthless as evidence in support of his argument. Ep. 106 was written in 1100 or 1101 to Henry I, congratulating the King on his accession to the throne. After urging the continuance of peace between church and state, Ivo advanced the general Gelasian argument that the earthly kingdom should be subordinate to the heavenly. Ivo's real reason for writing this letter, as is indicated by the closing section, was to obtain Hen-

[12] Ivo, *Epistolae, MPL* 162, coll. 196 C-D-197A: "Sed reclamante curia plenariam pacem impetrare nequivimus, nisi praedictus metropolitanus per manum et sacramentum eam fidelitatem regi faceret, quam praedecessoribus suis regibus Francorum antea fecerant omnes Remenses archiepiscopi, et caeteri regni Francorum quamlibet religiosi et sancti episcopi. . . . Petimus ergo flexis genibus cordis, ut hoc eodem intuitu charitatis et pacis veniale habeat paterna moderatio, quod illicitum facit non aeterna lex, sed intentione acquirendae libertatis praesidentium sola prohibitio."

[13] "Anselm u. Hugo," 196.

[14] Dated by L. Merlet, *Saint Yves, évêque de Chartres. Lettres* (1886), n. to ep. 191 (=MPL ep. 190).

[15] See below p. 208ff.

ry's patronage for the Church of Chartres. No mention is made in it of the problem of lay investiture.[16]

The same silence on the investiture controversy characterized the letter to Robert of Meulan which Liebermann cites. This letter, written in 1102, indicates that Ivo was not interested in the English investiture controversy, or at least adopted an impartial attitude in that dispute. Ivo complained in his letter that Ranulf Flambard had usurped the Bishopric of Lisieux for his nephew, a minor, in complete violation of canonical principles, but he said nothing about Henry's continuance of lay investiture, which was an uncanonical practice in the eyes of the reformers.[17] The Bishop of Chartres was concerned about the condition of the church in the neighboring diocese of Lisieux, but never in any of his writings did he discuss or even mention the problem which was disturbing the peace of the English Church, the dispute between Henry and the church reformers over lay investiture. Not only did Ivo refrain from attacking Henry and Robert of Meulan for their defiance of the papacy on the question of lay investiture, but all through Anselm's pontificate the Bishop of Chartres

[16] *MPL* 162, coll. 124-5. Fliche, *op.cit.*, 348, also wrongly interprets this letter as relating to the investiture controversy.

[17] L. Merlet, ed., "Lettres d'Yves de Chartres et d'autres Personnages de son Temps," *Bib. de l'École des Chartes*, XVI (1855), 464. Ivo begins his letter by remarking that Robert is a favorite of the English King but "many ecclesiastical persons" claim that Robert is more interested in advancing his own interests than those of the king of the angels. Robert has been regenerated by the sacraments of the church; therefore he ought not to offend the divine majesty or diminish the liberty of the church. It might appear that this is a reference to the English controversy over church-state relations. That it is not is indicated by the rest of the letter. Ivo goes on to complain about the situation in Normandy, not in England. "Sustained by the violence of the King of the English," Ivo complains, Ranulf Flambard has invaded the church of Lisieux. Ivo implies that Robert must bear part of the blame for this since he is the King's chief counsellor. Merlet, *Yves. Lettres*, p. 277, dates this letter 1105. That is quite possible, but it would have to be before Robert's excommunication in March of that year since Ivo knows nothing of Robert's excommunication. If the letter was written in 1105, Ivo's silence on the English investiture controversy is even more remarkable than if this letter had been written in 1102, the dating given by Liebermann. The 1102 dating is probably the correct one, since Ranulf's usurpation at Lisieux occurred in 1101.

remained on friendly terms with Anselm's most determined opponents, the curialist bishops. Ivo's letters to Walkelin of Winchester, Samson of Worcester, and Robert of Lincoln[18] are as amiable as his correspondence with the Archbishop of Canterbury. Ivo never interfered in the controversy over church-state relations in England which marked Anselm's pontificate, and there is no evidence that he used his influence to bring the controversy to an end by the compromise of 1107.

The silence of contemporaries on Ivo's role in ending the English investiture controversy does not rule out the possibility that Ivo exercised such influence on the theoretical level. It might be argued that Ivo's doctrines on lay investiture presented the model for the English compromise of 1107. This argument was suggested by Liebermann in the passage already quoted and has been vigorously affirmed by Fliche who contends that the compromise of 1107 "strictement conforme à la théorie chartraine."[19] The central part of the Ivo thesis, this argument was first suggested by Bernheim who regarded Ivo's theory on lay investiture as the source of both English and German concordats.[20] But the argument is erroneous. Ivo's

[18] To Walkelin: J. Leclercq, *Yves de Chartres. Correspondance*, 1 (1949), no. 39 (1094-5). To Samson: *PML* 162, no. 165 (date unknown; Samson was bishop from 1097-1112, so that this letter could have been written during the investiture controversy). To Robert: *MPL* 162, ep. no. 278 (date unknown. Leclercq places it after 1098 since he has omitted it from the first volume of his definitive edition of Ivo's correspondence which only goes down to that year. Robert was bishop 1092-1112). In each case Ivo praised the curialist bishop's munificence and liberality but said nothing about the current controversy over church-state relations in England.

[19] Fliche, *op.cit.*, 351. Cf. A. L. Poole, *op.cit.*, 179: "It is more than a mere probability that the settlement, which was finally reached in England and was sanctioned by a council at London in August of the same year, followed on lines suggested by him [i.e. Ivo]." Fliche first stated his thesis on the influence of "la théorie chartraine" in *Rev. Ben.* 46 (1934), 283ff. He believed that Ivo's doctrines on investiture also brought to an end the investiture controversy in France in 1107. (*La Réforme Grég.*, 352-3). For a discussion of the validity of this latter thesis, see below, n. 35.

[20] In his 1878 study of the Concordat of Worms. It is noteworthy, however, that in a later work on the origins of the Concordat of Worms (*Das Wormser Konkordat und seine Vorurkunden*, 1906), Bernheim was more

theory on lay investiture is quite different, and is based upon a contradictory premise, from the theory embodied in the English compromise of 1107.

Ivo's views on the vexed question of lay investiture were never propounded in a systematic tract, but rather in three letters dealing with particular instances of investiture and homage of bishops, as they happened to arise. Such was his fame as an authority on canon law, however, that his letters dealing with lay investiture were copied and received quite extensive circulation.[21] Ivo's doctrine on lay investiture was first presented in 1097, in a letter to the papal legate in France, Archbishop Hugh of Lyons. Hugh had prohibited Ivo and his cosuffragans from consecrating their Primate Daimbert, the Archbishop-elect of Sens, because Daimbert had received investiture with ring and staff from the hands of the French king. Although Ivo denied, perhaps not with complete honesty, that he had known about Daimbert's action,[22] he went

---

cautious about attributing to Ivo the theoretical basis for the compromise of 1122. He says that Ivo prepared the way for the Concordat by maintaining that lay investiture was not forbidden by canon law but was only to the disadvantage of the church. (Bernheim, p. 58, and see further, below, p. 212f). That was certainly Ivo's view, but it was also the opinion of all the anti-Gregorians that lay investiture was not forbidden by canon law. There is no reason why Ivo should be viewed as the originator of the idea. Henry IV and his supporters had claimed this from the beginning and had contended that Gregory VII, in condemning lay investiture, was acting as a revolutionary. Cf. Tellenbach, *Church, State, and Christian Society*, 102 and 115.

21 The three letters were written in 1097, 1109/10, and 1112, with those of 1097 and 1112 being the most important. These two letters were published by E. Sackur in *Lib. de Lite*, II, 640ff. For the 1097 letter, however, I quote from the latest edition by J. Leclercq, *Yves. Correspondance*, no. 60. The letter of 1109/10 (so dated by L. Merlet; see above, n. 14) is to be found only in *MPL* 162, coll. 196-7 (ep. 190). That Ivo's letters referring to the question of lay investiture were widely circulated is indicated by the large number of extant copies in manuscript (listed by Sackur for the 1097 and 1112 letters in *Lib. de Lite*, II, 641 and 649). For a rebuttal of G. H. Williams' contention (*The Norman Anonymous*, 55-57) that the author of the anonymous tract in *C.C.C. MS 415* was acquainted with Ivo's letter on lay investiture and "a member of the Ivonian circle," see below, n. 93.

22 Ivo, ep. 60, Leclercq ed., p. 246.

on to discuss the question of investiture generally in reply to Hugh's prohibition of Daimbert's consecration. It would appear that Ivo's intention was to negate the view of lay investiture which had recently been presented by Geoffrey, Abbot of Vendome, in his tract *De ordinatione episcoporum et investitura laicorum*.[23] Geoffrey's theory was in the high Gregorian vein; his tract owes much to the doctrines of Cardinal Humbert. He claimed that the investiture of a bishop or abbot with ring and staff is a sacrament and, therefore, that investiture given by a layman is a sacrilegious usurpation and an heretical act.

Ivo argued in reply that the investiture of bishops by the king carries no force of a sacrament at the election of a bishop but merely puts those elected in possession of their bishoprics.[24] He could see nothing wrong in the ceremony of investiture of a bishop by a king since by it kings claim to give nothing spiritual, but only accede "to the voice of the electors or concede to the elect the ecclesiastical domain and other exterior gifts which churches hold from royal munificence."[25]

[23] Suggested by A. Esmein, "La question des investitures dans les lettres d'Yves de Chartres," *Bibl. de l'École des Hautes-Études, Sciences Religieuses*, 1 (1889), 151ff. My account of Ivo's theory on lay investiture agrees with the interpretation given by Esmein. He did not, however, discuss the relation of Ivo's theory to the English compromise of 1107. Geoffrey's tract is in *MPL* 157, col. 216ff.

[24] Ivo, ep. 60, Leclercq ed., p. 246: "Quod autem scripsistis praedictum electum investituram episcopatus de manu regis accepisse nec relatum est nobis ab aliquo qui viderit nec cognitum. Quod tamen si factum esset, cum hoc nullam vim sacramenti gerat in constituendo episcopo vel admissum vel omissum, quid fidei, qui sacrae religioni officiat ignoramus, cum post canonicam electionem reges ipsos auctoritate apostolica a concessione episcopatuum prohibitos minime videamus. Legimus enim sanctae recordationis summos pontifices aliquando apud reges pro electis ecclesiarum ut eis ab ipsis regibus concederentur episcopatus ad quos electi erant intercessisse, aliquorum, quia concessiones regem nondum consecuti fuerant, consecrationes distulisse."

[25] *Ibid.*, 246-8: "Quae concessio, sive fiat manu, sive fiat nutu, sive lingua, sive virga, quid refert? Cum reges nihil spirituale se dare intendant, sed tantum aut votis petentium annuere aut villas ecclesiasticas et alia bona exteriora, quae de munificentia regum obtinent ecclesiae, ipsis electis concedere." The most recent discussion of Ivo's theory of investiture in ep. 60 by A. Becker (*Studien zum Investiturproblem in Frankreich*), who also

1. The Ivo of Chartres Thesis

Urban disapproved of Ivo's statement on lay investiture and the Bishop of Chartres desisted from quarreling with the papacy on this fundamental point.[26] It is significant, however, that Ivo did not attend the Council of Troyes of 1107 which condemned lay investiture again.[27] The illness which he presented as his excuse for his absence[28] was probably diplomatic. For Ivo never came to accept the Gregorian condemnation of lay investiture as heresy.

In 1112 he again stated his theory that lay investiture was not heresy since it proceeded not from the heart, the repository of faith and error, but only from the hands "which are able to do good and bad, but cannot believe or be in error in [matters of] faith."[29] In other words, lay investiture was a

---

accepts the Ivo thesis on the ending of the investiture controversy in England (p. 121), presents the ingenious interpretation that Ivo was not referring to the actual investiture of the staff from the king's hand but only to the concession of the bishop's temporalities by the king "nicht mehr persönlich, sondern durch Erlass, oder etwa durch entsprechende Erklärung des Königs gegenüber Boten und Gesandtschaft des betreffenden Kapitels. . . ." (p. 107). But reference to the text of Ivo's letter shows that Becker's interpretation is false. Ivo did not deny to the king the personal investiture of the bishop with the grant of the staff from the royal hand. (See the first sentence quoted from Ivo, ep. 60, in this note and the first two sentences quoted in n. 24). Similar to Becker's view is the interpretation of Ivo's theory presented by A. Scharnagl in his fundamental study of *Der Begriff der Investitur in den Quellen und der Literatur des Investiturstreites* (1908), a pioneering work which, while very useful in its day, is now badly in need of revision in the light of recent scholarship. Scharnagl contended (p. 88) that Ivo, working for the freedom of the church, wanted to replace investiture, with its association with the proprietary church system, with a looser *concessio*. As in the case of Becker's interpretation, this view has no foundation in the actual texts of Ivo's pronouncements on lay investiture.

[26] See Ivo ep. to Urban in 1097/8 (Leclercq ed. ep. 66, p. 290: ". . . quid fecerim, unde mansuetudinem vestram exasperaverim. . . .") For a full account of the disagreement between Urban and Ivo see Fliche, *Rev. Ben.* 46 (1934), 288-92. In his letter on investitures (Leclercq ed. p. 246) Ivo, with either naïveté or guile, had claimed that Urban took the same position as himself on the investiture question.

[27] Esmein, *op.cit.*, 157.   [28] *MPL* 162, epp. nos. 175 and 176.

[29] *Ivonis Epistola ad Loscerannum Archiepiscopum Lugdenunsem, Lib. de Lite*, II, 653, ll. 24-26: "Et fides et error ex corde procedunt. Investitura vero illa, de qua tantus est motus, in solis est manibus dantis et accipientis, quae bonae et mala agere possunt, credere vel errare in fide non possunt."

political, not a religious issue.[30] Only a layman who believed the contrary while investing an ecclesiastic was a heretic:

If any layman should rush to this madness, that in the giving and receiving of the staff he should think himself able to grant the sacrament or a thing pertaining to the ecclesiastical sacrament, then we judge him a heretic, not because of the handing of investitures, but on account of diabolical presumption.[31]

Since lay investiture was not a religious issue, Ivo continued, it was not a matter which was established one way or another by eternal law. Rather it was one of those things that could be instituted or prohibited for the good of the church as the particular occasion arose. To give lay investiture its right name, it could be said that it was a sacrilegious presumption which for the sake of the liberty of the church ought to be abolished.[32] But in some places lay investiture was so deeply bound up with social custom and political order that this was not always possible. In 1109/10 Ivo had defended the Archbishop of Rheim's homage to the French king on the grounds that this was the custom of the realm.[33] Likewise, in 1112 he contended that the theories of the reformers had to be subordinated to the sanction of custom on the issue of lay investiture. When this institution had such extensive support that it could not be abolished without a schism, the reformers had better be content with a protestation.[34] It is not surpris-

[30] Esmein, op.cit., 161.
[31] Lib. de Lite, II, 654, ll. 8-11. "Si quis vero laicus ad hanc prorumpit insaniam, ut in datione et acceptione virgae putet se posse tribuere sacramentum vel rem sacramenti ecclesiastici, illum prorsus iudicamus hereticum non propter manualem investituram, sed propter presumptionem diabolicam."
[32] Ibid., ll. 4-7, 11-14 "Cum ergo ea, quae aeterna lege sancita non sunt, sed pro honestate et utilitate ecclesiae instituta vel prohibita pro eadem occasione ad tempus remittuntur, pro qua inventa sunt, non est institutorum dampnosa prevaricatio, sed laudabilis et saluberrima dispensatio. . . . Si vero congrua volumus rebus nomina dare, possumus dicere, quia manualis illa investitura per laicos facta alieni iuris est pervasio et sacrilega presumptio, quae pro libertate ecclesiae et honestate salvo pacis vinculo si fieri potest funditus abscidenda est."
[33] See above, n. 12.
[34] Lib. de Lite., II, 654, ll. 14-16: "Ubi ergo sine scismate auferri potest,

ing, in view of his distinctively non-Gregorian doctrine on lay investiture, that Ivo never came to the support of the Gregorian reform party in England.

Back of the English compromise of 1107 lay the dispute between reform and royal theorists which the investiture controversy had engendered. The reformers claimed that lay investiture was heretical since it involved the performance of a spiritual function by a layman. The supporters of the royal position had denied this on the grounds that a consecrated king had received priestly powers and could perform the spiritual function of granting the ring and staff. Neither side doubted that investiture was a religious act; the dispute centered on the question of whether or not the king possessed sacerdotal powers. The agreement of 1107 accepted the Gregorian doctrine that lay investiture was contrary to Christian doctrine and consequently abolished it. By the terms of the compromise, the king admitted that he was only a layman and could not perform the spiritual office of investing a bishop with ring and staff. A division was made, however, between granting the bishop the insignia of his office, a spiritual function which was beyond the scope of royal powers, and granting the bishop his temporalities through royal acceptance of his homage, a function which it was proper and indeed necessary for the king to perform.

These views on lay investiture reflected in the London agreement of 1107 are precisely the opposite of the doctrines on the subject delineated by the Bishop of Chartres. Ivo never admitted that there was any necessity for abolishing lay investiture, since that practice only pertained to external, political, non-spiritual matters. In 1112 he was willing to concede that it might be advantageous to the church to abolish

---

auferatur. Ubi sine scismate auferri non potest, cum discreta reclamatione differatur." Cf. Ivo, ep. 233 (*MPL* 162, col. 236A): "Quocumque autem nomine talis pervasio proprie vocetur, qui investituras laicorum defendere volunt, scismaticam iudico." To Abbot Henry of St. Jean d'Angeli. Dated 1111 by A. Scharnagl, *Begriff der Investitur* (1908), 86.

lay investiture, but in the first formulation of his doctrine, presented in 1097, he had not even conceded this. Even if Ivo had advanced to his 1112 position by the time of the ending of the English investiture controversy (1105-1107), he would not have envisioned the prohibition of lay investiture in England. In the first place, it was the custom of the realm which sufficed to endorse an institution, not proscribed by eternal law, against the theories of the church reformers. Secondly, the investiture controversy had produced a virtual schism in the English Church between reform and anti-reform parties, and as it turned out, the schism was only brought to an end by the surrender of the leaders of the anti-reform group. Yet Ivo wrote in 1112 that lay investiture should be prohibited only where a schism over the issue would not occur.

Finally, and most important, investiture with ring and staff and the homage of a bishop to the king were, in Ivo's view, the same species of non-religious act. The Bishop of Chartres never suggested, either before or after 1107, the division between investiture and homage which is the essence of the agreement of 1107. That compromise could not have been achieved according to Ivo's theory. He claimed that investiture was necessary to put elected bishops in possesssion of their bishoprics, to hand over to them their ecclesiastical domains. The English and German concordats are founded upon the idea that the same end can be achieved through the feudal institution of homage. Only when an elected bishop becomes the king's man can he assume control over the temporalities of his see and therefore really enter into possession of his bishopric. The act of homage thus achieves the same ends that Ivo claimed had to be achieved by investiture. In order to arrive at the compromise of 1107 it was necessary to perceive that investiture is a purely religious act which the king can afford to surrender, provided he is willing to abandon the principle of theocratic monarchy, and that the political act of homage in itself suffices to put a bishop in possession of his bishopric and thereby allows the king to exercise a veto over the person of the bishop-elect. Since Ivo maintained to the end that investiture was a purely non-religious but a necessary political act, he never perceived the fundamental distinction between investiture and homage which made possible the compromise of 1107.[34a]

In his last letter on lay investiture, Ivo continued to defend that institution, although it had been prohibited in England five years before. Not only is it false to say that Ivo was the intellectual father of the English compromise of 1107, but also it is necessary to conclude that the Bishop of Chartres never accepted the doctrine of division between investiture and homage even after it had been made known by the terms of the agreement of London. Ivo's theories neither ended the English investiture controversy nor are

---

[34a] The most recent formulation of the Ivo thesis by E. H. Kantorowicz in *The King's Two Bodies* (1957), 44, merits special consideration since it is more subtle than most of the other statements of the Ivo thesis: "It is significant, however, that a seemingly so obvious distinction as that between the spiritualities and temporalities of a bishop, with which the problem of investiture had been almost hopelessly entangled, could be established only with great difficulty, and that it was due chiefly to the clear thinking of a legal authority, Ivo of Chartres, that the logical conclusion finally was drawn: the recognition of a bishop's dual status. Under Ivo's sponsorship the problem of the bishops' investiture with the temporalities, sided [*sic*] by the ecclesiastical consecration, was regulated in England by the concordat of 1107, and from that time onwards the dual status of the English bishop-barons was clearly defined." This view attributes to Ivo ideas already widely held, at least in England: the dual status of a bishop as priest and baron, and the resulting distinction between the spiritualities and temporalities of a bishop (see below, pt. 4, p. 250). To the Anglo-Norman higher clergy such principles were reflected in the facts of everyday life since the 1070's and especially in the practices of the *curia regis*; they did not learn them from Ivo of Chartres. The problem with investiture was to decide whether this institution fell under the spiritual or secular aspects of the bishop-baron's office. Ivo tended to believe that investiture was connected exclusively with the bishop's temporalities (see above, notes 24, 25, 31), which is precisely the opposite of the conclusion reflected in the concordat of 1107. Ivo indeed advocated "investiture with the temporalities" but this idea was an anathema to the Gregorians and is certainly not the principle found in the concordat of 1107. The learned Bishop of Chartres failed to perceive the necessary distinction between investiture and homage and to relate these institutions to the obvious dual aspects of a bishop's status.

they the source of the same compromise embodied in the Concordat of Worms.[35]

2. ROYAL PROVENANCE OF THE INVESTITURE COMPROMISE

A SUBSIDIARY aspect of the Ivo thesis on the ending of the English investiture controversy centers on the activity of Adela, Countess of Blois in 1105. Adela, the daughter of William the Conqueror and the sister of Henry I, became the wife of Stephen of Blois in 1081.[36] In her nature, the piety which had been a dominant characteristic of many of the Norman dukes, including her father, was brought to its fullest expression. Although Ivo of Chartres did not always agree with her in matters involving church-state relations in Blois,[37] he

[35] An identical "Ivo thesis" on the ending of the French investiture controversy in 1107 has been presented by Fliche (*Réf. Grég.*, 352-3) and by a recent writer on the subject A. Becker (*Studien zum Investiturproblem in Frankreich*, 121-2). From April 30 to May 3, 1107, Paschal II negotiated at St. Denis with the French rulers Philip I and Louis VI concerning the "status ecclesiae." (Suger, *Vita Ludovici*, ch. 10). Suger's account is the only description of the meeting. He says nothing about a compromise on the investiture dispute, and mentions only that the pope conferred on friendly terms with the king: "Cum quibus [regibus] de statu ecclesiae ut sapiens sapienter agens, familiariter contulit." It would be impossible to make anything out of this vague remark. Becker does go so far as to admit that no formal concordat was made at St. Denis. But because Suger mentions (ch. 10) that Paschal visited Ivo at Chartres before the meeting at St. Denis with the French rulers, and because he accepts the common and erroneous interpretation of Ivo's views on investiture, Becker agrees with Fliche that a compromise was reached at St. Denis on investiture, prohibiting lay investiture but accepting homage of ecclesiastics to laymen. This Ivo thesis on the French investiture controversy is false. In the first place, there is no evidence from Suger's account that a compromise was reached on lay investiture at St. Denis. Secondly, as I have shown above, Fliche and Becker have misinterpreted Ivo's views on lay investiture. Ivo would not have advised Paschal to effect a compromise on investiture in France such as had been achieved in England. Finally, in Ivo's letter to Paschal recalling the Pope's visit to Chartres (*MPL* 162, ep. CLXXV) there is no mention of a discussion between the Bishop and Pope on investiture. Orderic Vital (IV, p. 4) noted that the purpose of Paschal's visit to Ivo was the confirmation of the privileges of the Church of Chartres at the Bishop's request.

[36] For Adela's lineage see Leclercq, *Yves. Correspondance*, I, 15, n. 4.

[37] This fact is frequently overlooked. Some instances of disagreement between Adela and Ivo are pointed out by Raine and Dixon, *Fasti Eboracenses* I (1863), 187-8.

nevertheless had a high regard for the Countess, and they were always on friendly terms.[38] Her pious disposition led her to have a great admiration for the saintly English Primate, and she regarded Anselm as her spiritual adviser.[39] In spite of her religious bent, Adela was very capable in secular affairs, a characteristic which she also inherited from her father. After she had virtually forced her husband to leave Blois as a rather reluctant leader of the First Crusade, she ruled the country during Stephen's absence in a highly effective manner.[40] Adela must have watched the course of the dispute between her brother and her spiritual adviser with mixed emotions. But it was not until 1105 that she made an attempt to intervene in the English investiture controversy.

It appears that at the very end of 1104 or the beginning of 1105, Paschal II decided that the English King would never surrender to the papal reform decrees unless drastic steps were taken. Accordingly, in December 1104 or shortly thereafter, he wrote to Queen Mathilda, another feminine ruler renowned for piety. The Pope demanded that Henry give up lay investitures and receive Anselm back into the see of Canterbury. If the King persisted in his refusal to obey these papal demands, Paschal warned that the excommunication of Mathilda's husband and his counsellors would necessarily follow.[41] At the same time, Paschal promised to aid

---

[38] See especially Ivo's laudatory letter to Adela in Leclercq, ep. 5 (1091). Cf. *OV*, II, 392: "Adelidis pulcherrima virgo iam nubilis devote Deo se commendavit. . . ."

[39] While Anselm was still Abbot of Bec, he referred to himself as "*servus et amicus animae vestrae*" in writing to Adela. *AO*, ep. 10, ll. 19-20. This letter also indicates that Adela looked upon Anselm as her spiritual father.

[40] For Adela's biography during the First Crusade see Runciman, *Crusades*, I, 165. A letter from Count Stephen to Adela in 1097 is published in Hagenmeyer, *Kreuzzugsbriefe*, 138.

[41] *AO*, ep. 352, ll. 8-15, 19-20: "Nunc autem per investituras ecclesias occupavit, et eundem religiousum virum, Anselmum episcopum, quia eius nequam actibus contradicebat, regno abegit, et sibi consiliarios perditionis assumpsit. Qua in re saluti eius multum timemus, quia multum eum pro priori bona exhibitione diligimus. Te ergo, filia carissima, rogamus circa eius custodiam sollicitus vigilare et cor illius a consiliis pravis avertere, ne tantopere velit dei adversus se iracundiam provocare. . . . Alioquin ulterius

Henry "against all enemies" if the King would obey the papal demands.[42] The Pope was probably aware of Henry's designs on Normandy and the enemy referred to was likely Robert Curthose.

Both the papal threat and promise of aid failed to move the King from his determined opposition to the Gregorian decrees. Heretofore Paschal had made no attempt to bring sanctions against Henry. Hence the King and his counsellors must have decided to ignore Paschal's letter to Mathilda in the hope that the Pope would not carry out his threat.

But at the end of March 1105 Paschal revealed that he had been fully in earnest in his letter to the English Queen. In a council held at the Lateran, he excommunicated Henry's chief counsellor, Count Robert of Meulan, and Robert's unnamed "confederates" who together had driven the King "to that shameful act of investiture." Those who had been invested by the King, although they were not named, were also declared excommunicate. These decrees of excommunication were made known in simultaneous letters to the exiled English Primate and to Archbishop Gerard of York.[43] Gerard

---

pati non possumus, quin ipsum cum consiliaris suis, et eos qui per ipsum ecclesias invadunt, perpetuo anathemate feriamus." This letter is also published in *PU*, I, no. 8 by Holtzmann, who dates it December 1104-March 1105. But it is unlikely that it was written after January 1105 since Paschal's decree of excommunication against Robert of Meulan and other royal counsellors was issued in March (see below, n. 43). It is very probable that the Pope would have allowed two months to see if his letter to Mathilda had had any effect before acting on his threat of excommunication.

[42] *Ibid.*, ll. 21-23: "Verum enimvero, si oboedire consenserit, omnipotentis dei et apostolicae sedis auxilium contra omnes adversarios obtinebit, ecclesiarum ipsarum libertate in regni tuitionem per dei gratiam potietur."

[43] The two letters are *AO*, epp. 353 and 354 (=J-L 6028 and 6029). The letter to Anselm (ep. 353) is dated March 26, 1105. The letter to Gerard is undated, but appears to have been issued at exactly or approximately the same time. The account of the excommunications is very similar in both letters. The following is the account in the letter to Anselm (ep. 353, ll. 11-16) "Unde in concilio nuper habito ex communi fratrum et coepiscoporum sententia delibertatum est regis consiliarios, qui ad investiturae flagitium illum impellunt, et eos qui ab eo investiti sunt, ab ecclesiae liminibus repellendos, quia de libera facere conantur ancillam. Quam nimirum sententiam nos sancti spiritus iudicio in comitem de Mellento et eius

was reprimanded by Paschal for not aiding his senior colleague against the King. He was ordered to make known to all the decrees of excommunication.[44] In both letters, the Pope concluded with the observation that the sentence of excommunication against the King was being delayed in order that Henry could send envoys to Rome, who ought to arrive at the Lateran at Easter.[45]

By these letters and decrees, Paschal had clearly assumed for himself the leadership of the Gregorian attack on the prevailing system of church-state relations in England. Yet his attitude was not as rigorous and vehement as his letters might indicate at first reading. Of all those excommunicated, only Robert of Meulan was mentioned by name. Paschal still believed that Henry could be made to surrender to the papal demands, and the purpose of the decree of excommunication was to frighten the King into this surrender. Paschal was certainly not trying to duplicate Gregory VII's role in the German investiture controversy by deposing the King and stirring up rebellion in England. When Henry did not send envoys to Rome at Easter, nothing happened.[46] What Paschal's decree and letters of March 1105 did make clear was this: the chief royal counsellor had now been excommunicated; the excommunication of the King was the next logical step that the papacy would take in bringing sanctions against Henry. Paschal implied that for the moment he was content with the legal fiction that the King's evil counsellors had misled Hen-

---

complices promulgavimus, et eandem ipsam in eos qui sunt investiti a rege, eiusdem spiritus sancti iudicio confirmamus."

[44] *AO*, ep. 354, ll. 8-12, 17: "Nostrae vero mansuetudinis oblitus, nec eundem fratrem [Anselmum] adiuvare curasti, nec pro officii tui debito iniquitati regiae obviasti, immo favorem diceris adhibere. Nos tamen adhuc te sedis apoltolicae mansuetudine sustinemus, eo nimirum tenore ut excessus tuos corrigas, vitam emendes praeteritam, et nobis sicut dignum est satisfacias. . . . [Following the account of the excommunications:] Quod per te omnibus annuntiari praecipimus."

[45] *AO*, ep. 353, ll. 16-17; ep. 354, ll. 17-19: "Regis vero sententia ea ex causa dilata est, quia suos ad nos nuntios in praeteriti Paschae tempore debuit destinare."

[46] The Easter envoys to Rome are not mentioned again in any source.

ry. This fiction gave Henry the opportunity to make a diplomatic withdrawal from his opposition to the high Gregorian
theory on lay investiture. But this fiction would not be long
sustained by the papal curia, and the King was required to
make his surrender to the papal demands. While Henry never
made this complete surrender demanded by Paschal, the
excommunication of Robert of Meulan in March 1105 did
have far-reaching ramifications. It set in motion the series of
events which resulted in the agreement of 1107.

It was probably just after he had received word of Paschal's
decree of excommunication that Anselm visited the Countess
Adela at her castle in Blois. He informed her that her brother's excommunication could no longer be delayed. Fearing
for the safety of Henry's soul, Adela determined to bring about
a reconciliation between the English King and Primate.[47]

These facts have led proponents of the Ivo thesis to conclude that Adela henceforth acted as an intermediary for the
Bishop of Chartres in the negotiations leading up to the compromise of 1107. Liebermann held that Adela brought Anselm to Chartres in the spring of 1105, and that Anselm then
heard from Ivo the doctrine on lay investiture and homage
which was eventually embodied in the London agreement of
1107.[48] A. L. Poole has proposed a slightly different thesis:
Adela herself acted as spokeswoman for Ivo's theory on lay
investiture. This would appear to be the implication of his
statement that "in the negotiations and meetings which took
place between Henry I and Anselm an important part was
played by the King's sister, Adela, Countess of Blois, who
was on terms of intimate friendship with Ivo, Bishop of
Chartres, the famous canonist."[49] Since Ivo's theory on lay

[47] *HN*, 165: "Anselmus comitissae . . . Henricum videlicet regem Anglorum, pro injuria quam Deo sibique iam per biennium et ultra fecerat
excommunicare veniebat, non celavit. Quod illa audiens, fraternae dam-
nationi vehementer indoluit, ac ut potius illum pontifici concordaret operam
dare disposuit."
[48] Liebermann, "Anselm u. Hugo," 194.
[49] Poole, *Domesday Book to Magna Carta*, 179.

investiture, as has been shown, differs radically from the compromise of 1107, it is a priori impossible to maintain that he influenced the negotiations leading up to the compromise through an intermediary, Countess Adela. There is, further-more, detailed evidence to disprove Liebermann's and Poole's views on Adela's importance in the ending of the English investiture controversy.

Even if Adela had not decided to effect a reconciliation between her brother and Anselm, the King himself would have arranged a meeting with the exiled Primate in the summer of 1105. Henry was in Normandy from February until August of that year, engaged in a war with his brother Robert for possession of the duchy.[50] According to the *Historia Novorum*, the Countess' envoys informed the King that he was in imminent danger of excommunication. Henry, after consulting with his counsellors, sent word that he desired an interview with Anselm, which Adela thereupon arranged.[51] In the *Vita Anselmi* Eadmer never mentioned the Countess, but instead attributed the initiative for the meeting between the King and Anselm in 1105 to Henry alone.[52] It seems very probable that Henry was about to seek an interview with Anselm even before he had received Adela's message. For even without Anselm's warning to Adela it was abundantly clear that Henry's excommunication would shortly follow the withdrawal of the sacraments from Robert of Meulan and other royal counsellors.

In the Archbishop's own account of the negotiations preceding his meeting with the King, given in a letter to Paschal II, Anselm implied that he was anxious to talk with Henry and that he made Adela his intermediary for the purpose of arranging the meeting.[53] It is thus evident that Henry and An-

---

[50] Johnson, *Reg.*, p. XXIX; no. 682.
[51] *HN*, 165.
[52] *Vita Anselmi*, ed. Rule, 411: ". . . Relicta Burgundia, Anselmus Franciam ivit. Quod ubi regi Anglorum Henrico innotuit, rogatus ad eum in Normanniam venit."
[53] *AO*, ep. 388, ll. 7-11: "Postquam auctoritas vestra comiti de Mellento

selm desired to meet with each other for the purpose of
terminating their dispute before the King's impending excommunication by the Pope. Both regarded Adela as the con-
venient intermediary who could arrange the meeting. The
Countess did not act on her own initiative; she acted at the
urging of both her brother and her spiritual adviser.

From Adela's castle at Blois, while Henry's reply to Adela's envoys was still awaited, Anselm and the Countess, according to a simple statement in the *Historia Novorum*, went
to Chartres.[54] Liebermann expanded this fact into the thesis
that Adela took Anselm to an interview with Bishop Ivo,
and that Ivo proposed to Anselm his solution for ending the
investiture controversy, which was then adopted by Anselm
and Henry at their meeting.[55] This thesis has the whole force
of evidence against it. Bishop Ivo was not mentioned by Eadmer in connection with this visit of Adela and Anselm to
Chartres; there appears to be no reason why Eadmer would
have intentionally ignored Ivo in his account. On his way to
see Adela, Anselm had previously stopped at Chartres, but
it was not for the purpose of talking with Ivo, but rather to
visit a cell of Cluniac monks.[56] Supposing that Adela did arrange an interview between Anselm and Ivo, it is not necessary to assume that they discussed the subject of investiture.
Even supposing that Ivo did expound to Anselm his views
on lay investiture, it is certain that Anselm did not agree with
them. It is possible to determine Anselm's view of the investiture problem at this time. His view was neither Ivo's
theory nor the idea which some scholars have erroneously
believed to be Ivo's, and which is incorporated in the agree-

---

et aliis impedientibus apud regem iussionem vestram introitum ecclesiae
prohibuit, appropinquavi Normanniae, et factum est per comitissam Car-
notensem, sororem regis, fidelissiman ecclesiae dei et vestris praeceptis oboe-
dientem, ut ad colloquendum rex et ego cum quadam spe boni eventus con-
veniremus."

[54] *HN*, 165.
[55] Liebermann, "Anselm u. Hugo," 194.
[56] *HN*, 164.

ment of 1107. Anselm's view at the time of his meeting with Henry was strictly Gregorian.

This meeting took place during the last week of July 1105 at Laigle, in Normandy. A personal reconciliation between the King and the Primate was achieved and Henry restored to Anselm the temporalities of his see. On the question of lay investiture and homage of prelates, Henry would negotiate with the Pope by means of an envoy before Christmas.[57]

During the course of the negotiations at Laigle, Henry indicated to Anselm that he was willing to give up lay investitures, but not the homage of bishops to the king. In a letter to Hugh of Lyons, reporting on his situation as a result of the Laigle meeting, Anselm revealed that the King had made such a proposal, which is, of course, the essence of the agreement adopted two years later:

> The whole difficulty of the case between the King and me now appears to consist chiefly in this, that the King, although he will, I hope, allow himself to be conquered as to ecclesiastical investitures by the apostolic decrees, yet does not wish, he says, to give up the homage of prelates. Concerning this, he is inquiring from the apostolic see by his embassy, so that he may thence obtain leave to carry out his own will in this matter.[58]

This is the first time that the division between lay investiture and homage of ecclesiastics to the King was broached.

[57] *HN*, 166: "Deinde habito inter eos colloquio Anselmum rex de reddibus sui pontificatus revestivit, et in pristinam amicitiam utrinque recepti sunt." *AO*, ep. 388, ll. 11-15 (Anselm to Paschal): "Ubi me de archiepospicatu, unde me spoliaverat, revestivit, et de iis in quibus dissentiebamus, scilicet de investituris ecclesiarum et hominii praelatorum—de quibus simul et similem in Romano concilio audivi prohibitionem—se apostolicam sedem per legatum suum ante proximam Nativitatem domini requisiturum constituit." *HN*, 166 adds that the King wanted Anselm not to exclude from his communion those ecclesiastics who had violated the prohibition of lay investiture, but the Archbishop would not accept this condition. Eadmer gives July 22 as the date of the Laigle meeting.

[58] *AO*, ep. 389, ll. 17-21: "Tota difficultas causae inter regem et me iam in hoc maxime videtur consistere, quia rex, quamvis de investituris ecclesiarum apostolicis decretis se vinci, ut spero, permittat, hominia tamen praelatorum nondum vult, ait, dimittere. Qua de re sua legatione sedem requirit apostolicam, quatenus in hoc suae voluntatis impetret ab ea licentiam."

V. Ending of the Controversy, 1104-1109

The compromise proposal came not from Anselm and the Gregorians who supported him, but from the King's side. Anselm's letter makes clear that Henry wanted this compromise to constitute the final settlement of the English investiture controversy. Hence he was sending an embassy to Rome to secure papal approval for the compromise he had presented. The King's will, not Anselm's, was behind the proposed compromise. In the Primate's view, the merits of Henry's proposal at Laigle were highly dubious. Even if the compromise were actually instituted in England, it would leave problems unsolved. If the Pope accepted Henry's proposed compromise, Anselm wrote to Hugh of Lyons, "I doubt what I ought to do, if any elected religious should refuse to be made the King's man for a bishopric or abbacy."[59]

At Laigle Anselm had not been sure, as he subsequently explained to Paschal II, whether he should have prohibited Henry from sending a legation to Rome for the purpose of presenting his compromise proposal to the Pope.[60] But finally Anselm gave his approval to the royal embassy. He reasoned that the decision on ending the English investiture controversy rested with the Pope. The Primate wrote Paschal that he too would send an envoy to Rome to learn about the papal attitude to the proposed compromise.[61]

Anselm thus accepted for himself a subordinate position to Paschal and Henry in further negotiations leading to the ending of the English investiture controversy. He was not unwilling to do so, since he could see no way to end the controversy, except by the complete surrender of the King on

[59] *Ibid.*, ll. 21-23: "Quam si adeptus fuerit, dubito quid me facere oporteat, si aliquis religiosus electus homo regis pro episcopatu vel abbatia fieri respuat."

[60] Anselm was also hesitant about receiving back his archbishopric while the investiture controversy was not settled (*AO*, ep. 388, ll. 16-17): "Non autem intellexi me debere aut legationem eius prohibere aut revestituram meam respuere."

[61] *Ibid.*, ll. 18-20: "Et quoniam totius causae finis de vestro pendet arbitrio, misi simul legatum nostrum, ut cognoscam quomodo vobis et regi conveniat et quid mihi iussio vestra praecipiet."

both lay investiture and homage of ecclesiastics, and it was apparent by 1105 that Henry would never make such a complete surrender. Anselm had certainly not acted as Ivo's representative at Laigle. As his letter to Hugh of Lyons makes clear, the compromise proposal which has mistakenly been attributed to Ivo of Chartres was presented by the King at Laigle. Nor did Anselm have any sympathy with the doctrines on lay investiture really held by Ivo. He continued to hold without qualification the Gregorian view on these issues. He still wanted the King to give up the homage of ecclesiastics as well as lay investiture. He insisted that he would rather follow the advice of Archbishop Hugh of Lyons, an uncompromising high Gregorian, "than that of any other man I have ever known." He requested Hugh to advise the Pope on "how to set right this matter [of lay investiture, etc.]."[62] Anselm himself could not yet accept the validity of a compromise, but he realized that a compromise might be the only way to end the controversy over church relations in England. He left it to others, therefore, to work out the terms of the compromise settlement.

Adela of Blois had accompanied Anselm to Laigle, but it is doubtful if she was even present at the negotiations between her brother and the Primate.[63] If she did, however, act as the representative of Ivo of Chartres at this time, and brought Ivo's views on lay investiture and homage to the attention of Henry and Anselm, it is obvious that both of them turned deaf ears to Ivo's doctrines. The Countess had nothing to do with later meetings between Anselm and Henry which led up to the agreement of 1107. Adela's part in the ending of the English investiture controversy was therefore

[62] *AO*, ep. 389, ll. 7-8, 10-12: "Quoniam autem in omnibus meis actionibus vestro vellem, si fieri posset, super omnes homines quos novi uti consilio. . . . Audeo etiam rogare ut, si sanctitati vestrae videtur convenire, aliquid domino papae suggerat, prout ipsi negotio intelliget expedire."

[63] From Eadmer's account (*HN*, 165-6) it appears that Adela accompanied Anselm to Laigle, but was not present at the actual negotiations between Henry and Anselm.

a very modest one. She only served as an intermediary in arranging the initial meeting between her brother and Anselm which, in any case, the King and Primate would have brought about by themselves.

3. THE HUGH OF FLEURY THESIS

It is evident that the first proposal of the terms of the compromise which eventually formed the famous "concordat" of 1107—the King would give up the investiture of bishops and abbots with ring and staff but their homage to him for their lands would be retained—came not from the reformers but from the King's side. Did this compromise idea originate with Henry or one of his councillors? Or did it come from outside the immediate royal circle and was then adopted by royal theorists and the King himself?

Following A. Fliche's interpretation of the ending of the English investiture controversy, the latter alternative must be accepted as the right one. In a corollary to his Ivo thesis, Fliche maintained that the compromise idea was made known in a tract written by Hugh, a monk of Fleury on the Loire, which was dedicated to Henry I. Fliche argues that Ivo, constrained to silence by the apostolic see, left it to his friend and disciple Hugh of Fleury to develop his ideas "et il est plus que vraisemblable que le *De regia potestate et sacerdotali dignitate*, qui a vu le jour en 1103, est à l'origine du compromis qui allait mettre fin à la querelle des investitures en Angleterre."[64] Fliche's interpretation of the importance of Hugh of Fleury's tract requires careful consideration.

The author of the tract on royal power and sacerdotal dignity, which was dedicated to Henry I, designated himself in the preface to his work as Hugh, monk of St. Benedict of Fleury.[65] He was a friend and disciple of Ivo of Chartres.[66] But

---

[64] *Réf. Grég.*, 348.

[65] *Hugonis Monachi Floriacensis Tractatus De Regia Potestate et Sacerdotali Dignitate*, ed. E. Sackur, *Lib. de Lite*, II, 465ff. See the dedication at the beginning of the *Prologus* (*Lib. de Lite*, II, 466, ll. 18-20): "Hen-

3. The Hugh of Fleury Thesis

Hugh was also on good terms with the house of William the Conqueror. One of his histories had previously been dedicated to Henry's sister, Adela of Blois, and later he dedicated another historical work to Henry's daughter, Empress Mathilda.[67] The editor of Hugh's tract, E. Sackur, was unable to discover the reason for this close association of Hugh and Henry's family. He suggested as a possible cause the tradition of close relations between Fleury and England since the time of St. Dunstan and Abbo in the late tenth century.[68] This is

---

rico Anglorum regi gloriosissimo frater Hugh monachorum omnium extremus, sanctissimi Benedicti Floriacensis monachus, pacis perpetuae munus." In one of his other works, Hugh designates himself by his full name of Hugo de Sancta Maria, monk of St. Benedict of Fleury. (*MGH, SS*, IX, 345, n. 41) Very little is known about the author of the treatise on royal power and sacerdotal dignity, and the problem of his biography is complicated by the existence of a contemporary "Hugo de Floriaco," Abbot of St. Augustine's, Canterbury, in the first decade of the twelfth century. G. Waitz long ago investigated the problem of whether the two Hugh of Fleurys were the same man, and concluded (*SS*, IX, 345, n. 40) that they certainly were not. Following Thorne's Chronicle of St. Augustine's (Twysden, *SS*, II, 1794), Waitz gave the date of the abbacy of Hugo de Floriaco as 1091-1124. (Cf. Knowles, *MO*, 420 and 424, n. 3 for the same dating). But Thorne made a peculiar slip in dating. This is apparent even from Thorne's account, because that early fourteenth-century historian said that Hugh of Fleury was consecrated Abbot of St. Augustine's while Anselm was in exile, and Anselm was not even Archbishop in 1091. According to the unpublished chronicle of Thomas Sprott (c.1230), which was one of the sources of Thorne's work, Hugh became abbot in 1099. (*B.M.*, *MS Tiber. A. IX*, fol. 125r; *MS Harl.* 692, 106r. This date is also given by Thomas of Elmham, *R.S.*, p. 30). Since Anselm was in exile in 1099, this year can be accepted as the beginning of Hugh of Fleury's abbacy. Sprott gives little information about Abbot Hugh, but Thorne, apparently relying on an additional source which is no longer extant, gives a long account. Abbot Hugh was originally an illiterate Norman knight, a kinsman of William Rufus, who experienced a conversion to the religious life and became a monk of St. Augustine's. From the monastic community he was chosen as abbot by Rufus (Twysden, *SS*, II, 1794). For two reasons, therefore, it would appear that the two contemporary Hugh of Fleurys were not the same person. A Hugh of Fleury became Abbot of St. Augustine's in 1099. But in the early years of the reign of Henry I, Hugo de Sancta Maria was still a monk at Fleury. Secondly, the biography of Abbot Hugh given by Thorne is not compatible with the biography of the learned monk Hugh of Fleury. While Waitz did not investigate the problem with sufficient thoroughness, his conclusion was nevertheless correct.

[66] Waitz, *MGH, SS*, IX, 338 and 341.
[67] *Ibid.*, 337-8; Sackur, *Neues Archiv*, XVI, 375.   [68] Sackur, *loc.cit.*

plausible, but it does not satisfactorily explain Hugh's devotion to the Anglo-Norman royal house. A better explanation would be the existence of some sort of kinship between Hugh and Henry I's family, but evidence of this has not been discovered. The tract is undated, but Sackur's dating of 1102-5, based on internal evidence, is highly probable.[69]

Hugh intended that his tract should be read by Henry and his "wise men."[70] In its content, the work presents a typical Cluniac view of church-state relations. King and priest ought to work together in peace and harmony for the welfare of the church. For the sake of right order and preservation of discipline, the royal majesty is superior to the priestly dignity. Hugh attacks Gregory VII for denying the divine origin of royal power; he quotes Romans, XIII, and Gelasius to substantiate the legitimacy of royal power. The monk of Fleury was a conservative. He attempted to negate the revolutionary doctrines of the Gregorians with the political theory of the early middle ages, which the Benedictine monks associated with Cluny continued to uphold:

Considering Lord King, the crisis of discord, in which the holy church is directed concerning the royal power and sacerdotal dignity, which indeed separate and divide from one another in turn, goaded by pious care and fraternal love I have determined to write this pamphlet, in which this dispute may be somewhat laid to rest, and the error, which is spreading far and wide, may be equally alleviated: the error, I say, of those who rashly separating the priestly dignity from the royal dignity, overturn the order arranged by God, while they imagine that they know what they do not know. For they think that the arrangement of the earthly kingdom should be ordered and arranged not by God, but by men. And therefore they place the sacerdotal dignity above the royal majesty, when the former ought to be subject to the latter on account of order, not on account of dignity. . . . Our maker and savior the Lord Jesus Christ was worthy to be called at once king and priest by most

[69] Sackur, *op.cit.*, 385 and in *Lib. de Lite*, II, 465-6.

[70] *Tractatus, Prologus, Lib. de Lite*, II, 467, ll. 4-6: "Precor denique excellentiam celsitudinis vestrae, ut illud et seorsum et cum viris sapientibus, qui vobiscum sunt, retractetis et diligenter examinetis, et ut quaecunque in eo confutanda videritis, detegere satagatis."

3. The Hugh of Fleury Thesis

holy mystery, in order that it might be shown to us, by how much the king and priest ought to join to each other in turn by compact and union. . . . I know certain men in our times [i.e. Gregory VII in his letter to Hermann of Metz] who. assert that kings had their origin not from God but from those who ignoring God, strove by pride, rapine, perfidy, murder, and finally almost universal crimes, at the devil's instigation in the beginning of the world, to dominate men who were their equals with blind cupidity and indescribable presumption and temerity. How frivolous this opinion is, is made clear by the apostolic document, which said: "There is no power but of God. The powers that be are ordained of God." By this opinion, therefore, it is certain that not by men but by God the royal power was ordained and arranged on earth. . . . "The two principal powers, by which this world is ruled, are the royal and priestly." These two powers the Lord Jesus, who was king and priest at the same time, decreed to bear in his own person only by most sacred mystery. . . . The king in the body of his kingdom is seen to obtain the image of the Omnipotent Father, and the bishop that of Christ. Whence as the Son is discovered to be subject to the Father not by nature but on account of order, all bishops of the kingdom are rightly seen to be subject to the king, so that the community of the kingdom might be reduced to one origin. . . . The office of the king is to amend from error the people subjected to him and recall them to the narrow path of equity and justice. . . . Omnipotent God is known to have preferred the king to other men, with whom he has one condition of being born and dying, in order that by his terror he may restrain from evil the people subject to himself and in order that he may subdue them rightly by laws. . . . What the priest does not prevail to achieve through the word of doctrine, the royal power achieves and commands through the terror of discipline.[71]

[71] *Lib. de Lite*, II, 466, ll. 20-28: "Considerans, domine rex, discrimen discordiae, in quo sancta versatur aecclesia de potestate regia et sacerdotali dignitate, quas quidem ab invicem secernunt et dividunt, libellum istum pia cura et fraterno compunctus amore condere statui, quo contentio haec aliquatenus sopiatur et error, qui longe lateque diffunditur, pariter mitigetur: error, inquam, illorum, qui sacerdotalem dignitatem a regia dignitate temere secernentes ordinem a Deo dispositum evertunt, dum opinantur se scire quod nesciunt. Putant enim, quod terreni regni dispositio non a Deo, sed ab hominibus sit ordinata sive disposita. Et ideo sacerdotalem dignitatem maiestati regiae praeferunt, cum ei subesse ordine, non dignitate, debeat. . . ." *Ibid.*, 466, ll. 34-37: "Nam ideo noster conditor et salvator dominus Iesus Christus rex simul et sacerdos sacrosancto misterio vocari dignatus est, ut nobis ostenderet, quanto foedere vel affinitate rex et sacerdos sibi

Hugh's tract is thus much more moderate in its defense of royal power than some of the Anonymous treatises in *C.C.C. 415*. Instead of upholding the Carolingian, Ottonian, and Anglo-Saxon ideal of the king-priest, he advocated the dichotomy of royal and sacerdotal dignities. But because the monk of Fleury maintained, on pragmatic grounds, the ultimate supremacy of the royal power, he must be placed among the conservative ecclesiastics who were resisting the revolutionary Gregorian doctrines.

While Hugh did not specifically mention the English investiture controversy, in accordance with his generally moderate attitude, he attempted to find a middle ground on the vexed questions of canonical election and lay investiture:

By the inspiration of the Holy Spirit the King can, I believe, bestow the honor of the prelacy upon a religious cleric. But the archbishop

---

invicem debeant convenire. . . ." *Ibid.*, I, 1; 467, ll. 25-31: "Scio quosdam nostris temporibus qui reges autumant non a Deo, 'sed ab his habuisse principium qui Deum ignorantes, superbia, rapinis, perfidia, homicidiis et postremo universis pene sceleribus in mundi principio diabolo agitante supra pares homines dominari caeca cupiditate et inenarrabili affectaverunt praesumptione' [Gregory VII to Hermann of Metz] vel temeritate. Quorum sententia quam sit frivola liquet apostolico documento, qui ait: 'Non est potestas nisi a Deo. Quae enim sunt a Deo ordinatae sunt.' [Rom., 13:1] Constat igitur hac sententia, quia non ab hominibus, sed a Deo potestas regia in terris est ordinata sive disposita. . . ." *Ibid.* I, 2; 468, ll. 22-24: " 'Principales etiam potestates, quibus hic mundus regitur, duae sunt regia et sacerdotalis.' [Gelasius I paraphrased] Quas duas potestates in sua sola persona ipse dominus Iesus Christus sacrosancto mysterio gestare decrevit, qui rex simul est et sacerdos. . . ." *Ibid.*, I, 3; 468, ll. 27-31: "Verumptamen rex in regni sui corpore Patris omnipotentis optinere videtur imaginem, et episcopus Christi. Unde rite regi subiacere videntur omnes regni ipsius episcopi, sicut Patri Filius deprehenditur esse subiectus, non natura, sed ordine, ut universitas regni ad unum redigatur principium. [The early use of the term, *universitas regni*, popular in thirteenth-century England, is worthy of note]. . . ." *Ibid.*, I, 4; 468, ll. 39-40: "Regis igitur ministerium est populum sibi subiectum ab errore corrigere et ad aequitatis atque iusticiae semitam revocare. . . ." *Ibid.*, 469, ll. 4-9: "Ideo, inquam, Deus omnipotens caeteris hominibus regem, cui cum eis una nascendi moriendique conditio est, praetulisse cognoscitur, ut et suo terrore sibi subiectum populum a malo coherceat, et ut ad recte vivendum legibus subdat. Unde per terrenum regnum sepe caelesti proficit, dum quod sacerdos non praevalet efficere per doctrinae sermonem, regia potestas hoc agit vel imperat per disciplinae terrorem."

ought to give him [the bishop-elect] the care of souls. . . . Where however the bishop was elected by clergy and people according to ecclesiastical custom, the king ought reasonably to inflict no force or disturbance on the electors through tyranny, but he should add his consent to the legitimate ordination. . . . After the election, the elected bishop ought to receive from the royal hand not the ring or staff, but the investiture of secular things, and from his archbishop he ought to receive, through the ring or staff, among his [ecclesiastical] orders, the care of souls, so that a matter of this kind may be accomplished without dispute, and the privilege of his authority may be preserved by both earthly and spiritual powers.[72]

This is the passage in Hugh's tract which Fliche regarded as the source of the agreement of 1107. On the question of canonical election, Hugh was able to offer no real compromise as an effective solution. On the question of lay investiture, which was the vital issue in England, his proposal was more satisfactory: the king should grant "the investiture of secular things," the archbishop the care of souls through the bestowing of the symbols of ecclesiastical office. But was this a workable solution? Which was to come first, the royal or archiepiscopal grant? Presumably the royal grant, since Hugh mentions that first, but he is too vague on this point.

Most important of all, what did Hugh mean by "investiture of secular things"? Following Fliche's interpretation, it must be presumed that the monk of Fleury meant the homage of the bishop to the king for his lands.[73] But there is no valid

---

[72] *Lib. de Lite*, I, 5; 472, ll. 14-15, 19-22, 25-30: "Igitur rex instinctu Spiritus sancti potest, sicut existimo, praesulatus honorem religioso clerico tribuere. Animarum vero curam archiepiscopus debet ei committere. . . . Ubi vero elegitur episcopus a clero vel populo secundum morem aecclesiasticum, nullam vim ac perturbationem eligentibus rationabiliter rex per tyrannidem debet inferre, sed ordinationi legitime suum adhibere concensum. . . . Post electionem autem, non annulum aut baculum a manu regia, sed investituram rerum secularium electus antistes debet suscipere, et in suis ordinibus per annulum aut baculum animarum curam ab archiepiscopo suo, ut negotium huiusmodi sine disceptatione peragatur, et terrenis et spiritalibus potestatibus suae auctoritatis privilegium conservetur."

[73] Because Fliche believed that Hugh's treatise was the origin of the compromise of 1107. (See above, p. 226.) Bernheim, *Gesch. Wormser Con-*

reason to assume this. "Investiture" was, in the twelfth century, the technical term for the symbolic corporeal act, involved in enfeoffment, which created a property right of one kind or another.[74] It is significant that Hugh remains silent on the reciprocal act of homage which was a definite and meaningful act, by which the bishop-elect became the king's vassal. As A. Scharnagl pointed out,[75] Hugh nowhere in his tract mentioned the oath of homage or the feudal duties of the bishop to the king. Standing by itself, and used without reference to some term such as *homagium* or at least *fidelitas*, "investiture of secular things" can mean only the grant of royal permission to the bishop to enter into the temporalities of his see, involving no reciprocal act of homage on the part of the bishop. Perhaps Hugh had not considered the problem sufficiently to realize the significance of the formal act of homage. Or possibly, he comprehended the significance of the technical word *homagium* and did not use it because he wanted to deprive the king of the bishop's vassalage. The word *homagium*, or *hominium*, was known in France and England in Hugh's day[76] and his omission of the term or at least some other word designating the feudal oath of obedience to the king, such as the old term *fidelitas*, may express an intention to deprive the king of the vassalage of bishops as well as lay investiture. This interpretation, however, is not compatible with Hugh's generally conservative, anti-Gregorian, and moderate royalist attitude. The declared purpose of his treatise was to "confirm the privilege of royal authority."[77] Hence it

---

cordat, 17, states explicitly that Hugh advocated the homage of prelates to the king, which is certainly an error.

[74] F. L. Ganshof, *Feudalism* (1952), 110-11. H. Mitteis, *Lehnrecht und Staatsgewalt* (1933), 500ff.

[75] Scharnagl, *Begriff der Investitur*, 91, n. 2.

[76] See, in general, *DuCange, s.v. homanagium*; Imbart de la Tour, *Élections Épiscopales*, 352ff.; Scharnagl, *Begriff*, 57. The word *hominium* was used by Anselm in describing Henry's proposed compromise at Laigle, and by Eadmer in describing the terms of the agreement of 1107. (See above, n. 1 and n. 58.)

[77] *Tractatus, Lib. de Lite*, II, 466, l. 40-467, l.1: "Proinde, domine rex,

is unlikely that he wanted to diminish royal authority in a drastic manner by abolition of ecclesiastical homage. His omission of homage from his proposed compromise most probably stems from the simple failure to comprehend clearly how Henry I or any other king could give up lay investiture and still maintain control over the episcopate through feudal ties.

It must be concluded, therefore, that Hugh only went part way towards the delineation of the terms of the agreement of 1107. He dissented from the opinion of his teacher and friend, Ivo of Chartres, that lay investiture was merely a political act.[78] He perceived clearly that this ceremony had spiritual significance; investiture of ring and staff by laymen was condemned by ecclesiastical theory and law and must be given up. The monk of Fleury felt vaguely that the solution to the investiture controversy involved the separation of spiritual and temporal grants to the bishop-elect. But he failed to perceive how this might be accomplished in a manner acceptable to the English King. If lay investiture was to be abolished, the king needed to maintain his hold over the episcopate through feudal ties. The key to the eventual compromise of 1107 was the maintenance of homage by ecclesiastics to the king, and the precedence of the formal act of homage over the formal grant of the symbols of ecclesiastical office by the archbishop, so that the king could exercise a veto over the person of the bishop-elect. Hugh appears to have been groping towards this solution, but he failed to achieve it.

In 1103, while the monk of Fleury was writing his treatise, an imperial writer, Sigebert of Gembloux, in a public letter addressed to Paschal II, was defending as canonical the swearing of fealty by an imperial bishop to the German Emperor

---

idcirco vobis opus hoc assignare vel dedicare decrevi, ut auctoritatis vestrae privilegio confirmetur et corroboretur. . . ."

[78] Cf. the erroneous opinion of Fliche (*Réf. Grég.*, 349) which is based on his misunderstanding of Ivo's theory and an inadequate comprehension of Hugh's views on investiture.

in return for receipt of his *regalia.*[79] But Sigebert failed to perceive the significance of his own defense of episcopal homage to the secular ruler. He did not envision the retention of homage as the key to the compromise for ending the investiture controversy in the Empire. In any case, there is no indication that his tract was known in England, and his defense of the homage of a bishop to the king had no influence on the ending of the English investiture controversy.

As a matter of fact, there is also no evidence that Hugh of Fleury's treatise had any influence on Henry I and his councillors, or even that it was read by the Anglo-Norman curialists, for whose eyes it was intended. The tract survives in no English manuscript,[80] and is referred to by no contemporary in England or Normandy. Presuming, however, that Hugh's work was read by some of the more important members of the *curia regis*, it would not have provided them with the compromise proposal presented by the King at the Laigle meeting with Anselm. Hugh's treatise was a possible startingpoint for speculation on the way of ending the investiture controversy, but the King and his councillors would have found it necessary to go on from there, and to consider the problem in a more careful and practical manner.

4. ROBERT OF MEULAN, GERARD OF YORK,
AND HENRY I IN THE ENDING OF THE
INVESTITURE CONTROVERSY

IN THE FIRST DECADE of the twelfth century, excommunication was still a very potent weapon in the spiritual armory of the

---

[79] Sigebert of Gembloux, *Epistola Leodicensium Adversus Paschalem Papam*, ed. E. Sackur, *Lib. de Lite*, II, 458, l. 40 to 459, l.2. (7): "Dominus noster episcopus communicat regi et imperatori suo, cui ex regalibus eius acceptis fidelitatem iuravit. Nimium effluxit tempus, quo haec consuetudo incepit; et sub hac consuetudine migraverunt a seculo sancti et reverentes episcopi, reddentes caeseri que erant cesaris et Deo quae erant Dei." On Sigebert and his views on investiture, see Scharnagl, *Begriff*, 93-4; Mirbt, *Publicistik*, 73, 514-5.

[80] Hugh's treatise survives in two MSS: *Paris Lat. 1977*, a twelfth-century MS which is possibly an autograph, and a thirteenth-century MS which is copied from this one. On these MSS, see Molinier, *Catal. des manuscr. des départ.*, X, 12 and Sackur, *Lib. de Lite*, II, 466.

papal curia. Paschal II's letters of March 1105, excommunicating Robert of Meulan and other unnamed royal councillors and reprimanding Archbishop Gerard of York for failing to aid his colleague Anselm, had the effect of bringing about the collapse of the curialist party which had successfully opposed Anselm's attempts to reform the English Church from the beginning of his pontificate. The effectiveness of Paschal's drastic action makes Urban II's procrastination and prevarication in his dealings with Anselm and William II in the previous decade all the more culpable.

Although the solidarity of opposition to the Archbishop of Canterbury on the part of the leading ecclesiastical and lay curialists was destroyed by the papal action, the King's advisers could still not bring themselves to surrender completely to Paschal's and Anselm's views on church-state relations. They sought some compromise by which the Pope could be pacified and the excommunication removed and yet by which the prevailing royal domination over the English Church would not be fundamentally altered. Hence it is to this curialist group which constituted the King's close friends and advisers in 1105 that the origins of the compromise proposal made by the King at Laigle must be traced.

The effects of Paschal's intervention in the English investiture controversy had fallen hardest on the head of the eminent Norman house of Beaumont, the Count of Meulan. He alone had been named in the papal excommunication on the grounds that he had urged the King to maintain lay investitures.[81] This selection of Robert of Meulan as the leader of opposition to the Gregorian reforms in England was well justified. He had long been known as a vigorous opponent of Anselm. He was renowned as the closest friend and adviser of the King.[82] Through most of 1103 and 1104 Robert had been absent from Henry's court. During this period he was acting as the King's representative in Normandy.[83] But he re-

---

[81] See above, p. 218.   [82] See *GR*, II, 483.
[83] *OV*, IV, bk. XI, chs. 6 and 7. Robert witnessed no royal charters during this period.

V. Ending of the Controversy, 1104-1109

turned to England in time for the Christmas court of 1104[84] and undoubtedly he urged Henry to ignore Paschal's threatening letter to Queen Mathilda, which arrived in England early in 1105.

Because he had been singled out by the Pope for excommunication, Robert stood to gain more than anyone else by the reconciliation effected between Henry and Anselm at Laigle in July 1105. At this time, in fact, the Archbishop did release the Count of Meulan from his excommunication. It is uncertain whether Robert accompanied the King to Laigle. But he did, in any case, communicate with Anselm at about that time, whether in person, by envoy, or by letter. Robert promised to try to make the King comply with "the liberty of the church." In return for this promise, Anselm restored the count to communion in the church.[85]

Robert's apparent surrender must have been made with the full consent of the King. For after Henry's return to England in August 1105 the Count of Meulan continued to be a leading member of the *curia regis*.[86] His apparent acceptance of the reform program did not result in any loss or diminution of the King's friendship towards him. Anselm himself was not completely convinced that the Count of Meulan had gone over to the side of the reformers. When Henry delayed the sending of an embassy to Rome, as he had promised at Laigle, Anselm wrote Robert to warn him that the King had to fulfill his promise, lest the anger of God descend on the King and his councillors. Anselm's letter implied that the continuance of Robert's freedom from excommunication was con-

[84] Johnson, *Reg.*, no. 681, witness list.
[85] See Anselm's report to Paschal II on the Laigle meeting: (*AO*, ep. 388, ll. 21-24): "Comiti de Mellento per auctoritatem cartae vestrae quam illi direxistis, in qua legi quia, si vobis oboediret, gratiam vestram obtineret: concessi introitum ecclesiae, quoniam promisit se conaturum, ut rex iussionibus vestris ad libertatem ecclesiae obtemperet." Robert accompanied Henry to Normandy (*OV*, iv, 199) and therefore could have been present at Laigle.
[86] Johnson, *Reg.*, nos. 689, 706, 712, 713, 716 (August-December 1105), witness lists.

tingent on the dispatching of the royal envoy to Rome to settle the investiture controversy.[87]

Robert's release from excommunication was thus closely
related to the reconciliation between the King and Archbishop
at Laigle. It is highly probable, in view of the fact that he
was the leading royal counsellor, that Robert had worked to
achieve this reconciliation from which he stood to gain personally more than anyone else. The papal excommunication
had placed him in a predicament. On the one hand, there was
no doubt that he would have to make some sort of surrender
to papal demands. On the other, he was hostile to the prospect
of the abolition of royal control of the Anglo-Norman Church,
which he had always vigorously defended. It may very well,
then, have been Robert of Meulan who originated the compromise proposal which the King presented at the Laigle
meeting. It was enough of a surrender, Robert would hope,
to pacify the Pope and Archbishop. He could stand forth as
an advocate of the liberty of the church, and thereby obtain
release from excommunication. At the same time, through
maintenance of ecclesiastical homage, the royal power would
suffer no great loss, and Henry would not regard the Count
of Meulan as a turncoat. The compromise proposal made by
the King at Laigle fits in so well with the needs of Robert,
that the idea may have originated in his shrewd mind.

While papal intervention in the English investiture controversy only brought about the partial surrender of Robert of
Meulan, and that on grounds of necessity, Paschal's support

[87] Although Anselm addressed the count as his "friend," it is apparent
from the text that he did not trust Robert completely. (*AO*, ep. 369, ll. 3-
7, 15-18): "Vos scitis quia, quando rex et ego convenimus apud castrum
Aquiliae, dictum fuit quod rex mitteret legatum suum Romam, pro iis in
quibus concordare non poteramus nisi per dominum papam. Quod intellexi
ut ita fieret, quatenus anti proximam Nativitatem domini legatus rediret.
Videtis autem quia dominus meus rex hoc quod tunc dixit facere moratur.
. . . Quapropter dico vobis quia valde timeo, ne ipse super se provocet iram
dei et super eos, quorum consilio differt tam necessariae rei, tam rationabili
succurrere, cum ad illum hoc pertineat et facere possit, ut nihil perdat de
iis quae secundum deum ad regiam pertinent potestatem."

of Anselm had a very decisive effect on the attitude of the leading curialist bishop, Gerard of York. Between 1104 and the ending of the investiture controversy in 1107, Gerard made a complete *volte-face* in his attitude towards lay investiture and was sincerely converted to the Gregorian reform program. This reversal on the part of the leading anti-Gregorian theorist in England and Normandy is one of the most remarkable aspects of the ending of the English investiture controversy.

It has been shown in a previous chapter that Archbishop William of Rouen could not possibly have been the author of the *Anonymous* tracts in *C.C.C. 415*, as G. H. Williams and others have contended. The weight of the evidence supports H. Böhmer's original thesis that among the leading churchmen in England and Normandy at the time, Gerard of York is the most likely candidate for the authorship of several, and perhaps all, of the *Anonymous* tracts.[88]

From the moment of Henry's coronation, which had been performed by the Bishop of Hereford along with the Bishop of London, until that latter part of 1104, Gerard can be regarded as Henry's leading supporter, next to Robert of Meulan. In 1101 and 1102 he was in frequent attendance at the royal court and served as Henry's envoy to Rome. Although Gerard indicated his intention of carrying out the decrees of the Council of London of 1102, his general hostility to the Gregorian reforms and his refusal to help Anselm in his quarrel with the King were painfully evident to the Archbishop of Canterbury and the Pope. It was during these four years to the latter part of 1104, and probably during 1101-2, that the *Anonymous* tracts on lay investiture and theocratic monarchy were written. Gerard's eloquent defense of the early medieval ideals of kingship drew upon theories which had originated in Byzantium, had been popular in the West since Carolingian times, and had been embodied in the Anglo-Saxon "Edgar" coronation order, which the author of the *Anonymous* tracts quoted extensively.[89]

[88] See above, Ch. IV, pt. 5.   [89] See above, Ch. IV, n. 221.

4. Robert, Gerard, and Henry I

But even in the two tracts (24a and 28) obviously inspired by the English investiture controversy there can be found, amid the welter of arguments on behalf of lay investiture, some deep doubts in the author's mind about the validity of the investiture of churchmen with the symbols of ecclesiastical office by laymen. Gerard was, after all, not a naïve antiquarian living in the Byzantine, Carolingian, and Anglo-Saxon past. Anselm had freely praised the high quality of his colleague's intellect and erudition.[90] Gerard was a very active ecclesiastic statesman with a long and distinguished record of service at both Rouen and York. He was well aware of the arguments of the Gregorian theorists and the new attitudes towards church-state relations which had steadily been gaining adherents in Western Europe during the previous half-century. While Gerard rushed to the defense of lay investiture and the whole ideal of theocratic monarchy with which that institution was connected, he could not altogether free himself, even in his anti-Gregorian period, from lingering doubts that the Gregorian principles did have some validity.

In the midst of Gerard's two tracts in defense of lay investiture, there is, in each case, a remarkable passage which contradicts his general line of argument and attempts to protect his thesis against Gregorian rebuttal by conceding the partial validity of the Gregorian position. The result is not felicitous for coherent and cogent argument. While students and admirers of the *Anonymous* tracts have attempted to gloss over and explain away these self-contradictory passages in Tracts 24a and 28,[91] their disturbing presence cannot be denied or ignored. They reveal that even when Gerard was arguing most eloquently, even violently, on behalf of lay investiture and theocratic monarchy by summoning up all the traditions of early medieval kingship, his learned and sensitive

[90] See above, Ch. IV, n. 61.
[91] Cf. Williams, *Norman Anonymous*, 188-9, for this approach. On the other hand, H. Böhmer, after some hesitation, finally concluded that the *Anonymous* was confusing and contradictory on this point (*KS*, 229, 232-33).

mind was already troubled by agonizing doubts that his Gregorian opponents, who were negating the traditions of early medieval kingship, might actually have right and law on their side.

The king as the anointed of God, Gerard argues in these two passages, had the prerogative of conferring the ring and staff upon the bishop-elect. But in performing this act, the king is not conferring sacerdotal powers upon the bishop, but only the power of ruling the church, the Christian people, and the temporalities of the church.[92] By this dichotomy, Gerard vitiated the major thesis of the two tracts, the defense of theocratic monarchy. For if the king is indeed *Christus Domini* why cannot he perform a spiritual act? Of course, only Christ can grant sacerdotal powers. But if the king was a member of the *sacerdotium* as a result of his anointment, as Gerard had contended at great length, he should be able, acting as the minister of Christ, to confer sacerdotal powers on the bishop-elect in the ceremony of investiture with ring and staff. The author of the *Anonymous* tracts in this way involved himself in a logical fallacy and self-contradiction.

The two passages in Tracts 24a and 28, in which Gerard contradicted the mainstream of his argument in defense of theocratic monarchy, presented an interpretation of lay investiture identical with the famous theory propounded by Ivo of Chartres in 1097: lay investiture is a political, not a spiritual act. Nevertheless, Gerard was not writing under Ivo's influence. He began with the same patristic text as Ivo had in

---

[92] *Lib. de Lite*, III, 667, l. 41-668, l.2 (Tract 24a) : "Sed nunc videamus, quid rex conferat homini, qui creandus est episcopus per prerogativam baculi pastoralis. Estimo, quia neque ordinem, neque ius sacerdotii confert illi, sed quod sui iuris est et regni terrenarum, videlicet rerum dominationem et tutelam ecclesiae et potestatem regendi populum Dei, qui est templum Dei vivi et ecclesia sancta sponsa Christi domini nostri." *Ibid.*, III, 685, ll. 37-43: "Qui ergo hanc investituram eis auferre nititur, contra Dei ordinationem iudicimque agere molitur. Iustum quippe est, ut eadem manus quibus sacerdotes a Deo commissi sunt, ut eis etiam dominetur ipsis sacerdotibus, partem investiturae huius eisdem sacerdotibus largiatur; investiture dico huius regiminis videlicet et dominationis in populum et possessionis temporialium rerum, non sacerdotii et sacerdotalium gratiarum."

240

4. Robert, Gerard, and Henry I

evolving his views on lay investiture—a passage in one of St. Augustine's sermons—and independently developed the same theory. It is very probable that Gerard did not know Ivo's letter on lay investiture.[93]

Ivo's views on lay investiture, it has been shown, are distant from the theory implicit in the agreement of 1107. By the

[93] My view, that the author of the *Anonymous* tracts was not under the influence of Ivo of Chartres, is in opposition to the conclusion of G. H. Williams (*The Norman Anonymous*, p. 57): "The Anonymous must be counted a member of the Ivonian circle, however much he remained an exponent of the pre-Gregorian usages in Church and State." The strongest evidence for this sweeping statement is that the same extracts from certain papal decretals appear in Tracts 28 and 29 and in Ivo's letter to Hugh of Lyons on lay investiture in 1097. (Cf. *Lib. de Lite*, III, 683, l. 23ff. and Böhmer, *Kirche und Staat*, 480 with *Lib. de Lite*, II, 642, l. 32-643, 1.29). But it is not necessary to suppose that the anonymous author was quoting from Ivo's letter. It is possible that both authors are quoting from a common source, most likely a canon law collection. When the *Anonymous'* statements on lay investiture quoted in n. 92 are compared with Ivo's views in his letter to Hugh of Lyons, it is evident that the author of the *Anonymous* tracts was not dependent on Ivo, and very probably had never read the Bishop of Chartres' letter on lay investiture. For although the views of the two writers are virtually identical, the author of the *Anonymous* tracts did not mention Ivo in support of his argument.

The anonymous author had in fact arrived at the same theory as Ivo independently. He began with the same source—a passage in St. Augustine's sermon on John—and quoted this passage in support of his argument (*Lib. de Lite*, III, 668, ll. 4-23). Ivo also quoted from this passage in Augustine's sermon (*Lib. de Lite*, II, 645, ll. 7-16), but his quotation is considerably shorter than the one given by the anonymous author. Therefore, the latter could not possibly have lifted his quotation of Augustine's sermon from Ivo's letter on lay investiture. The anonymous author arrived at the same conclusion as Ivo in the passages quoted in n. 92, but he did so without any apparent knowledge or use of Ivo's work. Even in the *Decretum* of Ivo, the quotation from the passage in Augustine's sermon is more abbreviated than in the *Anonymous* Tract 24a (*MPL* 161, ch. 194, col. 244). It would appear that the anonymous author was quoting Augustine from an independent source, and from none of Ivo's works. (Cf. Williams, *Norman Anonymous*, 56, whose discussion of this problem I find totally unconvincing: "In this case it would appear that the Anonymous consulted the original source, but the text may well have been suggested by Ivo. In any event its presence in 'De Consecratione' probably attests familiarity with, and some proximity to, canonical thought going on in Chartres.") Williams' final evidence (56-7) that *Anonymous* made use of Ivo's *Pannormia* can be accepted, at least until the Lanfranc canon law collections have been investigated as the source of the decretals quoted by the anonymous author. But this hardly makes the *Anonymous* "a member of the Ivonian circle."

same token, the two passages in Gerard's tract which deny the spiritual significance of lay investiture could not be the source of the compromise ending the English investiture controversy. Even during the period when he was the intellectual leader of the anti-Gregorians in England, that is, down to the latter part of 1104, Gerard was troubled by the force of the reformers' arguments against lay investiture. He even attempted to defend the institution of lay investiture by claiming it was a political, not a spiritual act. This view vitiated his own defense of theocratic monarchy, but it could never satisfy the Gregorians and serve as the basis of compromise. Between 1104 and 1107, Gerard was driven to accept the whole Gregorian position and to admit that lay investiture was in fact a spiritual act, which the king had no right to perform.

From the latter months of 1104 until the Council of London in August 1107 Gerard was absent from Henry's court and remained at his see in York.[94] Probably his growing doubts about the validity of his originally anti-Gregorian position and the ideals of theocratic monarchy caused his withdrawal to York. During these three years the Archbishop of York was completely converted to the doctrines of the Gregorian reformers. The admonishments which Gerard received from Paschal II and the friendly letters which he received from the exiled Archbishop of Canterbury helped to bring about this conversion. At the time of Robert of Meulan's excommunication in March 1105 the Pope wrote to Gerard to reprehend him for his reluctance to support Anselm and to order him to publish the decree of excommunication in England.[95] Shortly after receipt of Paschal's letter, Gerard replied in very deferential terms. He claimed that he had been unjustly defamed; he expressed his devotion and obedience to the Pope and insisted (untruthfully) that he had al-

---

[94] Gerard witnessed no royal charters between autumn 1104 (Johnson, *Reg.*, no. 677) and 1 August 1107, the assembly at London which ended the investiture controversy (*ibid.*, no. 828). Through most or all of this period he was at York (*ibid.*, nos. 686, 705, 709, 720).

[95] *AO*, ep. 354. See above, n. 45.

ways favored Anselm's cause.[96] In a similar vein Gerard wrote to Anselm in the summer of 1105. He expressed his willingness to undergo exile along with Anselm if his "father," as he addressed his colleague, should desire it.[97]

As a religious whose actions were governed by Christian love, Anselm readily forgave his erring colleague. In replying to Gerard's letter at the end of 1105 or the beginning of 1106, Anselm made no reference to Gerard's past support of Henry I. Instead he praised Gerard's zeal and looked forward to the restoration of peace and harmony between the King and the episcopate.[98]

By the end of 1105 Gerard had been completely converted to the Gregorian position. Anselm's letter showed him that the old Primate had forgiven him, and he could make a full confession of his past errors without fear of punishment. He admitted in writing to Anselm that previously, by supporting lay investiture, he had been in danger of involving himself in "heresy."[99] Gerard was thus not content with accepting the views of the more moderate reformers. By condemning lay investiture as heresy, he indicated his acceptance of the revolutionary doctrines of Humbert and Hildebrand. He was also fully aware of the consequences: conflict with the King. He wrote Anselm that while he rejoiced at the peace between

---

[96] *AO*, ep. 362, ll. 9-10, 15-16: "Si quid amarius dulcedini litterarum vestrae sancitati interfuit, falsa de me relatio ut hoc interesset effecit. . . . Venerabilis et summi Cantuariensis archiepiscopi causam votis semper fovi. . . ."

[97] *AO*, ep. 363, ll. 1, 10-11: "Patri filius salutem et oboedientiam. . . . Exulat animus meus tecum, paratus et corporeum, si iusseris, subire exilium."

[98] *AO*, ep. 372, ll. 5-7, 12-13: "Quod autem et verbis per multos et vestris litteris vestram voluntatem zelo dei accendi contra mala, quae in ecclesia dei fervent et pullulant, intelligo. . . . Spero in deo quia dominus noster rex, sicut ipse mihi deo inspirante promittit, ad omne bonum nobis adiutor accedet. . . ."

[99] *AO*, ep. 373, ll. 6-11: "Tunc demum pericula partis, cuius corpori adhaerebam, intueri attentius coepi, vidique et video, nec falli timeo, quia non longe ab haeresi recedit, quicumque in his quae ecclesiae sunt dissentit, et adversari nititur generalibus conciliis de ipsius rei prohibitione factis eiusque sententiae, cuius vox et persona apostolorum principem Petrum mundo repraesentat. . . ."

the King and Archbishop of Canterbury, he was afraid of incurring Henry's wrath. For Gerard now did not want to give communion to the King's followers who had put themselves outside the church by their support of lay investiture.[100]

In his theoretical works as well, Gerard's full acceptance of the Gregorian doctrines is evident. In the *Anonymous* tracts in *C.C.C. MS. 415* there are at least six tracts which are Gregorian in tone and which contradict the doctrines of theocratic monarchy found in several of the other tracts in the same codex.[101] It has been noticed by G. H. Williams that Tract 10, on the basis of the Gelasian theory, argues that priestly power is superior to royal power. But Williams too readily dismisses this tract as an "extraneous work," not by the author of the other tracts, which was copied into the codex by mistake.[102] A careful reading of all the tracts, however, reveals that five of them, besides Tract 10, are Gregorian in attitude. Tract 8 presents Cardinal Humbert's neo-Donatist principle that the ministration of the sacraments by an unworthy priest is invalid. The author contends that a pastor who was not canonically elected and who administers his office in an uncanonical and unworthy manner "does not have

---

[100] *AO*, ep. 373, ll. 42-4, 48-9: "Sed ecce dum medicus abest, languor meus invalescit, dum eis communicare cogor, quos sententia Romani et pontificis et concilii vel a communione fidelium penitus alienavit, vel a liminibus ecclesiae solummodo expulit. . . . Da consilium, fer auxilium, ne acriorem iram regis incurram, si eis non communicem. . . ."

[101] The tracts are: nos. 8 (MS. pp. 56-7), 9 (MS. 57-8), 10 (MS. 85-6), 18 (MS. 114-18), 21 (MS. 121-7), 31 (MS. 285-302). Tract 7 (MS. 55-6) possibly also belongs to this group.

[102] Tract 10, ed. Williams, *Anonymous*, 223: "*Duo sunt quibus hic mundus principaliter regitur, sacerdotalis auctoritas et regalis potestas*. Sed sacerdotalis auctoritas potestate regali maius habet privilegium atque praestantius, tanto siquidem quanto terrenis caelestia et corporibus animae et divina humanis." The last sentence of the tract is incomplete and the leaf is not filled (MS. p. 86). Because of this fact and his belief that this is the only tract presenting a reform argument in the codex, Williams (*op.cit.*, 35) takes the view that Tract 10 "is an extraneous leaf that was perhaps mistakenly copied into our Codex." But in view of the five other tracts which expound Gregorian principles, this view is untenable. One tract could have been copied in error, but not six.

power of binding and loosing."[103] Tract 18 returns to the same theme. A man consecrated to ecclesiastical office who remains polluted with sin had not really been consecrated.[104]

Three of the tracts attack the ideals and institutions of Anglo-Norman kingship. Tract 9 presages the revolt of Becket and John of Salisbury against the striving for legal omnipotence by the Anglo-Norman state. The author complains about the harsh administration of justice. He argues that secular judgement is an institution of the sons of Belial, and, in accordance with a decree of the Council of London of 1102, he concluded that no Christian should live by this profession, since it involves the exercise of cruelty. He also advocates the freedom of the clergy from secular courts, and the independence of ecclesiastical courts from lay control.[105] Tract 21, by

[103] Tract 8, ed. Böhmer, *KS*, 452-3: "Hic est, qui nec a Christo eligitur nec a clero uel populo expetitur, sed inuitis preponitur, qui digamus, qui uiduae maritus, qui inphamiae masculis aspersus, qui christianae legis preuaricatur, qui canonum contemptor, qui omnes non recipit, qui non est imitator apostoli, qui reprehensibilis est nec talis est, qualem precipit apostolus in sacerdotium eligi. Hic non habet potestatem ligandi atque soluendi. Huius ergo nec timenda nec tenenda est sententia."

[104] Tract 18, v, ed. Böhmer, *KS*, 473: "Omnis consecratus santificatus est et iustificatus. Consecratio enim sanctificat et iustificat. Alioquin nichil uidetur operari, si sanctitatem et iusticiam non tribuit, et si non tollit uicia et emundet a peccatis. Nam, quam diu homo plenus est uiciorum et pollutus peccatis, non est consecratus, id est sanctificatus et iustificatus. Quae temerarium est, ut illum arbitremur esse consecratum, quem non uidemus sanctificatum et iustificatum, sed plenum uiciis et peccatorum sorde pollutum. Consecratio enim mutat et efficit meliorem, et si non mutat nec efficit meliorem, non est consecratio."

[105] Tract 9, ed. H. Scherrinsky, *Untersuchungen zum sogenannten Anonymous von York* (1939), 131, 132, 134, 146, 147-8: "Omne iudicium aut in ecclesiasticis situm est negotiis aut in secularibus. . . . Omne vero quod in secularibus negotiis positum est, id exterioris tantum hominis utilitatem attendit, interioris vero aut parum aut nichil. . . . Qui hoc facit, a Christo desciscit, et in partem Belial et tenenbrarum cedit, et portionem suam ponit cum infidelibus. . . . Quare nulli Christiano secularia licet gerere iudicia, quin nec negotia. . . . Tot necesse est sub iudice supplicia mortis evenire quot pene sunt. . . . Sed non expedit Christiano ut crudelitatis professione vivat. . . . Ut autem ad propositum revertamur, qui iure tantum caeli servus est, is iure saeculi liber est. . . . Nunc autem adversus laicos agendum est, qui ministris Dei audent dicere: Vos, inquam, nullam iusticiam vel potestatem habetis in terra nostra. . . . Hos contra, si sollempniter agere possumus ut dicamus: audite o vos omnes filii Dei et videte quam praesumptuose loquuntur

questioning the necessity for earthly rulers,[106] follows the Gregorian (originally Augustinian) tendency to negate, or at least ignore, the Pauline political tradition of the early Middle Ages. Tract 31 takes a high Gregorian attitude towards kingship and dismisses entirely the ideal of theocratic monarchy:

He who wishes to rule in the kingdom which is of this world, he who seeks to be a prince or judge, does not wish to have a place in the Kingdom of Christ, does not wish to be inscribed in the book of the living with the saints, does not wish to be designated in the number of the disciples. . . . You, o man, who desire dominion in this world, you do not wish to be a subordinate or minister, but you wish to rule like the kings of the Gentiles and like those who, having power over others, are called "privileged" (Luke 22:25). Therefore you are not a disciple of Christ, you are not His member, you are a disciple and member of the Devil.[107]

Of all the leading churchmen in England and Normandy at the time, only Gerard of York could have been the author

---

homines isti in patrem vestrum et dominum vestrum. Non enim is sum ego vel filius hominis contra quem loquuntur, sed Deus sempiternus, neque negotium istud meum est, vel hominis, sed Dei omnipotentis, cuius in hoc officio nichil aliud sum quam servis atque minister, ipse vero iudex et dominus. . . . Sunt autem et qui volunt et in curiam eorum veniamus ex consuetudine propter iusticiam Dei. Sed dum hoc volunt, Deum sub necessitatem redigere volunt, suam iusticiam anteferre iusticiae Dei volunt, et convenire adversus Dominum et adversus Christum eius volunt."

[106] Tract 21 ed. Scherrinsky, *Anonymous*, 149: "Si Deus omnia regit et moderatur, et omnem rationalem creaturam regit et moderatur. . . . Sed quemcumque Deus regit et moderatur, omnipotenti bonitate, et perpetua ratione, summaque sapientia, et ordine et modo, quo melior cogitari non potest, ea regit et moderatur. . . . Sed his ita se habentibus, quae est necessitas, ut homines hominibus praeponatur, qui eos regant et moderantur? An ut melius et rationabilius et sapientius atque ordinatius et modestius hac faciunt? Sed hoc ad ignominiam Dei fierit. Si vero ut deterius et minus rationabiliter, minusque sapianter et ordinate minus atque modeste hoc faciant, ad detrimentum eorum fit et iniurias."

[107] Tract 31 (numbered xxx by Böhmer), ed. Böhmer, *KS*, 483: "Qui autem in regno, quod est de hoc mundo, querit dominari, quaerit princeps aut iudex fieri, non uult habere sortem in regno Christi, non uult in libro uiuentium cum sanctis asscribi, non uult in numero discipulorum assignari. . . . Tu autem, o homo, qui in hoc mundo principatum desideras, non uis fieri sicut iunior et minister, sed uis dominari sicut *reges gentium* et sicut hi, *qui potestatem habent super eos* (Luke 22:25), beneficus [*sic*. cf. Luke 22:25 benefici] uocari. Non est igitur discipulus Christi, non est menbrum eius, sed diaboli es et menbrum et discipulus."

of these Gregorian tracts, and a little earlier, the author of treastises defending the ideal of theocratic monarchy, the antithesis of the Gregorian doctrines. Only Gerard's intellectual development underwent such a radical change. In his earlier period he had quoted extensively, in his tract dealing with lay investiture, from the "Edgar" coronation order, which embodies the ideals of early medieval kingship. Now that he had lost his enthusiasm for kingship, Gerard quoted from the theological works of Anselm, the leader of the reforming party in the English Church.[108] In Tract 10 Gerard also quoted from the same work cited by Gilbert Crispin in his treatise on simony, the pseudo-Ambrosian *Sermo de dignitate sacerdotali*, the metaphor which compares royal power and sacerdotal privilege to lead and gold.[108a] Gilbert had used this *Sermo*, with its doctrines of extreme sacerdotalism, to present the radical Gregorian view on simony. Consequently, the *Sermo* must have been well known in the circle of the Anglo-Norman reformers. Its quotation again in Tract 10 of the *Anonymous* is additional evidence in favor of the English provenance of these tracts.

In Gerard's case, the anonymity of the tracts is readily explained. In his earlier period, when he was writing tracts defending the old order of church-state relations against the Gregorian reformers, he was afraid lest Anselm and the Pope discover his propaganda efforts on behalf of Henry I, and excommunicate him for his opposition to the decisions of reforming councils. Between 1104 and 1107, when he was writing his Gregorian tracts, Gerard preferred not to subscribe his name to these works, lest he incur the King's wrath. Gerard's preference for anonymity during this period carried over to his

---

[108] Tract 21, *MS. C.C.C. 415*, p. 122. For Tract 24a's quotations from the Edgar *ordo*, see Ch. IV, n. 221.

[108a] The quotation from pseudo-Ambrose in Tract 10 has been shown by G. H. Williams in his valuable study, "The Golden Priesthood and the Leaden State," *Harvard Theol. Rev.* 50 (1957), 57-58. However, Williams overlooks the significant fact that pseudo-Ambrose had also, and in all probability previously, been cited by Gilbert Crispin (see above, Ch. IV, n. 144).

correspondence. In his letter to Anselm in 1105 in which the Archbishop of York announced his complete break with the King, he remained completely anonymous, and in the succeeding letter in which he branded lay investiture as heresy, Gerard designated himself only by his initial.[109]

Gerard's position in the latter half of 1105 and in the following year was very precarious. There is indeed evidence that he was terror-stricken at the thought of Henry's wrath and wanted to flee the country, but was not able to do so. Between the middle and end of 1105 he wrote to a friend in the papal curia begging him to intercede with Paschal II. Gerard explained that if the Pope would not free him from the prohibition against communicating with certain of Henry's supporters, he would have to flee from his homeland. He added, however, that he was not even free to do this.[110] In the following year the Archbishop of York tried to leave Henry's kingdom by enlisting as a crusader in the expeditionary force which Bohemond was trying to assemble in France at that time. He wrote Bohemond that he was ready to set out as a crusader,[111] but apparently Henry prevented Gerard from leaving England.

Because of his very precarious position, the Archbishop of York, during 1105, was eager to see the final ending of the

[109] *AO*, epp. 363 and 373. The letters are preserved in the *Quadripartitus*, whose author may have copied them from Gerard's register.

[110] F. Liebermann, ed., *Quadripartitus* (1892), 160: "De his quos in regno Angliae dominus noster papa removit ab ecclesia, peto ut circa me mitius agat, quia quibus rex communicat, his sine intolerabili corporis mei detrimento non communicare non possum, ita ut alterum mihi sit necesse: vel quibus rex communicat communicare, vel de patria fugere. Liber enim abire non possum; mirum videtur quod dico, sed verum est." Gerard's letter was written to his "lord and friend" Peter Leoni, consul of the Romans, whom he had met at the papal curia on the occasion of his trips to Rome in 1095 and/or 1102. The text of Gerard's letter is appended to the early twelfth-century lawbook, the *Quadripartitus*, whose author was a *clericus regis* friendly to Gerard. (Liebermann, 36-7).

[111] Also appended to the *Quadripartitus*, ed. Liebermann, 161: ". . . Litteris vestris et harum portitore mihi innotescat iterum vestra in me voluntas et terminus itineris vesti, et quomodo et quando me vultis ire. . . . Me etenim totum habetis, non separabit a vobis adversitas vel prosperitas." On Bohemond's crusade, see below, p. 262ff.

4. Robert, Gerard, and Henry I

English investiture controversy. His motives were as strong as those of Robert of Meulan for suggesting the compromise to Henry which the King presented at his conference with Anselm at Laigle in July 1105. Nevertheless the weight of the evidence is against designating Gerard as the originator of the compromise which ended the English investiture controversy. There is no evidence that he did suggest the compromise proposal, and furthermore his known views on lay investiture were along quite different lines. At the beginning of the investiture controversy he was a vehement defender of theocratic monarchy and a staunch supporter of the King. For a short while he sought a compromise and arrived independently at the same theory as the one presented by Ivo of Chartres. This satisfied no one and was far from the compromise presented by Henry at Laigle and later adopted in the agreement of 1107. In 1105 Gerard accepted the Gregorian view of lay investiture as heresy and thereby admitted that he could find no middle ground between the royalist and Gregorian views. At the end, he could only despair at the unfortunate circumstances which had brought him into conflict with the King.

Robert of Meulan and Gerard of York had compelling personal motives for suggesting the compromise principle which eventually ended the English investiture controversy. The one wanted to escape from excommunication, the other from the dire consequences of his break with the King. But behind Henry's concession to Anselm at Laigle that he would give up lay investiture while retaining ecclesiastical homage, lay also a compelling *raison d'état*. The ending of the investiture controversy in England and the restoration of peace with the papacy would greatly aid Henry in his projected conquest of Normandy. Hence not only one of his chief councillors, but the King himself could have been the author of the compromise proposal.

Henry I was regarded by contemporaries as an intellectual. No doubt the extent of his learning was greatly exaggerated, but he was literate, the first educated man on the English throne since Alfred.[112] His intellectual ability was sufficient to originate the compromise proposal without any assistance from his councillors. Henry could have derived the idea for the compromise presented at Laigle from the usages of his own court. Since his father's reign it had been the practice of the *curia regis*, in the pleas before it, to separate a bishop's position as tenant-in-chief from his episcopal office. The precedent for this dichotomy was established at the famous trial of Odo of Bayeux at Pennenden Heath in the 1070's. Archbishop Lanfranc accused Odo of usurping Canterbury lands, and Odo was tried as Earl of Kent.[113] The report of the trial of William of St. Calais, Bishop of Durham, for treason in 1088, in the *De Iniuste Vexatione Willelmi* makes Lanfranc say to the bishop: "We are judging you concerning your fee, not your bishopric." In this account Lanfranc appeals to the precedent of the trial of Odo of Bayeux.[114] Similarly, in 1095 Anselm was summoned to the *curia regis* at Rockingham to answer Rufus' complaints concerning the deficiency of Canterbury knight service.[115] The dichotomy between the bishop's ecclesiastical and feudal offices, which was at the basis of the compromise on the investiture dispute, was already evident in the practices of the *curia regis*.

[112] V. H. Galbraith, "The Literacy of the Medieval English Kings," PBA, XXI (1935), 13-14.

[113] J. Le Patourel, ed., "Reports of the Trial on Pennenden Heath," *Studies . . . Presented to F. M. Powicke*, 33, Text A: "Huic interfuerunt . . . comes Cantiae, videlicet praedictus Odo Baiocenis episcopus."

[114] Sym. Durham, HDE, I, 184: "'Nos non de episcipio sed de tuo te feodo judicamus. . . .'" William of Malmesbury, GR, II, 361 gives a similar remark by Lanfranc to Odo of Bayeux in 1088. H. S. Offler, EHR, 66 (1951), 321ff. has shown that there are good grounds for concluding that the version of the *De Iniuste* which we have is a "product of the brilliant literary activity at Durham in the second quarter of the twelfth century" (341). But it seems reasonable to accept as authentic the statement attributed to Lanfranc. J. Leclercq, *Yves. Correspondance*, I, xxiv and F. Barlow, *Feudal Kingdom*, 180, have credited Lanfranc with originally suggesting the principle upon which the English investiture controversy was settled. Lanfranc, however, was only enunciating the practice of the Anglo-Norman *curia regis*.

[115] See above, Ch. II, pt. 3.

4. Robert, Gerard, and Henry I

Henry thus had good precedents upon which he could develop the separation between ecclesiastical office and homage. He also had good reasons for wanting to obtain a reconciliation with Anselm in the summer of 1105. The meeting with Anselm at Laigle fitted in perfectly with his plans for the conquest of Normandy from Robert Curthose. It was the culmination of a shrewdly conceived and carefully executed policy. In 1105 Duke Robert became involved in an investiture controversy with Paschal II. There had recently been two scandalous usurpations of ecclesiastical office in Normandy, and the Pope placed the blame, not unjustly, on the Duke. He accused Robert of violating the spouse of Christ by performing investiture of ecclesiastics with ring and staff. Robert appears to have stood firm on the custom of his ancestors.[116] Paschal's letter was probably known in England; it survives only in an English manuscript[117] and a copy may have been sent to England. At any rate, Henry's subsequent actions indicate that he was fully aware of the dispute between Robert and Paschal.

At the beginning of 1105 the Pope had promised to aid Henry against all his enemies if he would obey the papal demands on lay investiture.[118] Undoubtedly this was a veiled reference to Henry's careful preparations for his invasion of Normandy which he had been making in 1104.[119] When the dispute between Robert and Paschal became known, Henry saw how he could avail himself of the Pope's offer and undertake the conquest of Normandy in the guise of a protector of the Norman Church. Robert as a crusader had an initial moral superiority over his brother. But if Henry were willing

---

[116] Paschal's letter was published by W. Levison in *DA*, 35 (1910), 428: "Tu autem te ipsum ostium efficisti et per annulum et virgam investituram ecclesiae non ut sponse Christi, sed sicut ancille hostibus tradis eius regimen usurpantibus, deserentibus Deum, qui vere ostium est, per quem qui non ingreditur fur est et latro." For analysis of Paschal's letter to Robert and dating, see C. W. David, *Robert Curthose* (1920), 154-5.

[117] *MS. B.M. Harl.* 633, f. 66v-67r.

[118] See above, n. 43.

[119] On these preparations, David, *Robert Curthose*, 155-9.

to make concessions on the vexed issue of lay investiture, while Robert stood firm on the custom of his predecessors, it would be the English King who would gain ecclesiastical support for his seizure of his brother's Duchy.

This is exactly what happened. Henry's successful invasion of Normandy between Easter and August of 1105, which brought a large part of the Duchy under his rule,[120] was conducted under the subterfuge of saving the Norman Church from the rapacity of an unjust ruler. In following this course Henry had a good precedent: his father had conquered England under the papal banner. Shortly after his invasion of Normandy in Holy Week of 1105 a great assembly was held at Henry's camp in the village of Carentan in the Cotentin. Here the respected old Serlo, Bishop of Séez, delivered a long harangue justifying Henry's invasion. In accordance with the early medieval conception of kingship, Serlo justified Robert's deposition on grounds that the Duke's government had been totally ineffective and therefore the church in Normandy had been at the mercy of rapacious laymen such as the notorious Robert of Bellême. Serlo also maintained that Robert was personally unworthy to be the duke. Let the King, he concluded, gain his rightful inheritance with the sword of justice.[121] Henry in turn solemnly promised to undertake the conquest of the Duchy in order to "seek peace for the church."[122] Orderic Vital's dramatic account of this assembly, if it does not report the exact words used on the occasion, certainly makes clear that Henry undertook the conquest of the Duchy in the guise so popular with all his predecessors since Richard I, that of reformer and defender of the church.

Henry's concession at Laigle was the culmination of this policy. There he demonstrated that whereas the unworthy Duke remained in opposition to the papacy on lay investiture, the King of England, as a loyal son of the church, was willing

---

[120] *Ibid.*, 168.   [121] *OV*, IV, 204-6.

[122] *Ibid.*, 206: "In nomine Domini, pro pace ad laborem exsurgam, et quietem Ecclesiae, vobis adjuvantibus, summopere perquiram."

to obey the papal prohibition. By retaining ecclesiastical homage, Henry felt that the substance of his power over the English Church could be saved. Of course, by giving up lay investiture he was abandoning the idea of theocratic monarchy which was its basis. This was a real concession in the long run. But in the short run the prize to be gained was very great—the Duchy of Normandy—and Henry, who had desired it so strongly and planned for the conquest so carefully, figured that the immediate gain was the greater one. Henry's plan was successful. The meeting at Laigle did not end the English investiture controversy. But, on the other hand, the Pope did not interfere to prevent Henry's seizure of the rightful patrimony of a crusader. In fact, it was rumored in England that the Pope had urged Henry to undertake fratricidal conflict.[123] The King's prestige had been greatly enhanced by his apparent rapprochement with the church.

5. THE HIGHER CLERGY, PASCHAL II, AND THE AGREEMENT OF 1107

BY THE END of 1105 conditions had become suitable for ending the investiture controversy in England by some sort of compromise. Both the curialist bishops who had supported the King and the small group of reformers in the English Church had lost their enthusiasm for Gregorian and anti-Gregorian slogans and theories. By 1105 the investiture controversy was rapidly receding into the background as the critical issue in the English Church, and was replaced by an almost universal demand for the ending of Anselm's second exile and the return of the church to normal conditions.

The long absence of the Primate from the country was creating havoc in the life of the English Church. Only the

[123] The story told by William of Malmesbury, *GR*, II, 474. No papal letter confirming William's account survives. But no doubt Paschal had indirectly encouraged Henry to undertake his conquest of Normandy, by promising to help him against all his enemies, provided Henry obeyed the papacy on the investiture question.

V. Ending of the Controversy, 1104-1109

Archbishop could consecrate the bishops-elect in his province and by 1107 no less than five bishops-designate for widowed sees were waiting to be consecrated by Anselm,[124] who grieved over the suffering his exile was bringing upon his church.[125] The King, too, was aware that the church was in dire need of peace and tranquillity.[126] Henry's pious Queen implored Anselm, her spiritual father, to return to England.[127] But it was the bishops and leading abbots themselves who were most vociferous in the demand for restoration of peace in church-state relations and the consequent return of the head of the English Church from exile. In 1105 and 1106 the curialist and reform parties in the English Church disintegrated and the higher clergy united in asking Anselm to return to England.

During these years Henry temporarily lost the support of the majority of the episcopate which Anglo-Norman kings had always enjoyed. Gerard of York is only the most outstanding example of this change. The curialist bishops were no longer eager to support the King in his dispute with the papacy. There were three reasons for this change. In the first place, the unconsecrated bishops-elect wished to escape from their

---

[124] *HN*, 187. The five bishops were: William Giffard, Winchester; Roger, Salisbury; Reinelm, Hereford; William Warelwast, Exeter; Urban, Glamorgan (Wales). All but one of the seven abbots suspended from office in 1102 were reinstated by Paschal in April 1106 (*AO*, ep. 397, l. 15ff). Richard of Ely was reinstated a year later (*AO*, ep. 422, l. 10).

[125] Anselm to Robert of Meulan in 1105 (*AO*, ep. 369, ll. 10-14): "Unde quidam opinantur et dicunt quia rex non multum curat festinare, ut ego redeam in Angliam, et ecclesia Dei, quam Deus illi custodiendam commendavit, quae iam fere per tres annos desolata est, suo vivo pastore, eius reditu et praesentia consoletur, et pro consilio animae suae, . . . laetificetur."

[126] Henry to Anselm after the battle of Tinchebrai, September 28, 1106 (*AO*, ep. 401, ll. 14-18): ". . . Pater venerande . . . te deprecor, ut supernum iudicem, cuius arbitrio et voluntate triumphus iste tam gloriosus et utilis mihi contigit, depreceris, ut non sit mihi ad damnum et detrimentum, sed ad initium bonorum operum et servitii Dei, et sanctae Dei ecclesiae statum tranquilla pace tenendum et corroborandum. . . ."

[127] *AO*, ep. 395, ll. 6-8: "Vestri etenim reditus optati terminus, quanto celerior et proprinquior a pluribus mihi promittitur, tanto magis a me, vestra frui optante praesentia et locutione, desideratur."

anomalous position and fully enter into possession of their sees. The royal chancery between 1103 and 1107 rarely distinguished between "bishop-elect" and "bishop," which indicates that the King was willing to allow the unconsecrated bishops-elect to assume their positions as ecclesiastical magnates.[128] But in doing this, the bishops-elect incurred the danger of excommunication. The second reason for the change of heart on the part of the curialist bishops was the heavy taxation which Henry was levying upon the church for the support of his expeditions in Normandy. His treasury went so far as to use the prohibitions of the Council of 1102 against married clergy, and to levy fines on married priests and canons.[129] This measure aroused Anselm's wrath and probably annoyed the episcopate also, since it involved royal interference with their diocesan authority.[130] Finally, in the case of Gerard of York and perhaps one other instance, there was a genuine conversion by a royalist ecclesiastic to Gregorian reform principles.

By 1105 the curialist bishops were trying to achieve a reconciliation with Anselm. Already in 1103, the former royal clerk William Giffard, Bishop-elect of Winchester, had left England and gone into exile in Normandy rather than accept uncanonical consecration from the hands of Gerard of York.[131] In the following year, while Anselm was at Lyons, the Primate and Bishop-elect had a falling-out. Anselm accused William of willingness to go to almost any lengths to gain the King's favor and his lucrative bishopric.[132] It appears that

[128] Johnson, *Reg.*, p. xxv.

[129] *HN*, 171-2.

[130] Anselm to Henry, *AO*, ep. 391, ll. 7-8, 11-14: "Audio quod vestra excellentia vindictam exercet super presbyteros Angliae et forisfacturam exigit ab eis, quia non servaverunt praeceptum concilii. . . . Non enim pertinet secundum legem Dei huiusmodi culpam vindicare, nisi ad singulos episcopos per suas parochias, aut, si et ipsi episcopi in hoc negligentes fuerint, ad archiepiscopum et primatem." Henry acceded to Anselm's demand, although somewhat reluctantly (*AO*, epp. 392 and 394).

[131] See Ch. IV, pt. 3.

[132] *AO*, ep. 322, ll. 26-28: ". . . Si hoc faceretis quod a vobis rex exigit, nullus posset extinguere execrabilem famam quia hoc factum esset propter

V. Ending of the Controversy, 1104-1109

William took Anselm's advice, for the Primate's next letter to him was more cordial.[133] In 1106 William, who had by this time returned to England, joined Gerard of York and four other former curialist bishops in drafting a letter to Anselm which cautiously asserted their support of "God's cause" and begged their pastor to return to his flock.[134] In reply, Anselm expressed appreciation for the bishops' support, although he would not return to England until his dispute with Henry had been finally settled.[135]

William Giffard had an ulterior motive for his reconciliation with Anselm and his desire to see the end of the investiture controversy. Only with Anselm's return to England could he obtain canonical consecration as bishop and enter into the wealthy see of Winchester. But if Eadmer can be believed, the case of the royal clerk William Warelwast is similar to the *volte-face* of Gerard of York—William was sincerely converted to Gregorian reform principles. This royal clerk had been a devoted servant of Rufus and Henry in their quarrels with Anselm.[136] In 1105 William Warelwast suddenly emerges as an advocate of the "liberty of the church."[137]

For more than a decade Anselm had been quarreling with

---

episcopatus, quem perdere timeretis, redemptionem." Henry wanted William Giffard to turn over to him a castle which William was holding in Normandy from Duke Robert.

[133] *AO*, ep. 344. G. H. Williams, in his account of William Giffard's career (*Norman Anonymous*, 90-92) has overlooked this letter, which indicates a rapid reconciliation between Anselm and the Bishop-elect of Winchester.

[134] *AO*, ep. 386, ll. 12-13, 17-18: "Ut quid enim peregrinaris, et oves tuae sine pastore pereunt? . . . Non enim iam in hac causa non quae nostra, sed quae nostra, sed quae Dei sunt quaerimus." The other four bishops were Robert of Chester, Samson of Worcester, Ralph Luffa of Chichester, and the old simoniac Herbert Losinga of Norwich.

[135] *AO*, ep. 387, ll. 8-13: "Bonum tamen est et gratum mihi . . . quia promittitis mihi auxilium vestrum, non in mea sed in Dei causa, et invitatis me non pigriter venire ad vos. Quamvis enim hoc modo facere non possim, quia rex non vult me esse in Anglia adhuc, nisi discordem a iussione papae et eius concordem voluntati. . . ."

[136] See Ch. II, p. 108; Ch. IV, pp. 200-01.

[137] *HN*, 181: "[Willelmus] erat enim iam tunc ad libertatem ecclesiae Dei cor habens. . . ."

these curialist bishops, who had constantly supported the King and rejected his pleas for the reform of the English Church. But the satisfaction which he could now derive at their reversal was limited. For the Archbishop's own supporters in the English Church, who had always been very few, had also grown weary of the continued dispute over church-state relations and were vociferous in their demands that Anselm return to England and restore peace to the English Church. Gilbert Crispin, the Norman Abbot of Westminster, had been one of Anselm's first supporters in England and a member of the Archbishop's circle of monastic disciples. He had been an ardent supporter of reform, the author of a tract which presented Anselm's moderate Gregorian views on simony.[138] But during Anselm's second exile, Gilbert appears to have broken with the Archbishop. It is significant that no correspondence between Gilbert and Anselm survives from this period. While Gilbert was at the *curia regis* in 1104, a lawsuit between a baron and Westminster was decided, in the King's presence, in favor of the Abbey.[139] Apparently Gilbert was on good terms with Henry by this time. In the following year the Abbot of Westminster addressed a poem to Anselm, which inquired in forthright terms why the pastor remained absent from his flock when the English Church was in need of his leadership.[140] At the same time Anselm received an anony-

---

[138] See Ch. IV, p. 170ff.

[139] Gilbert Crispin appears on the witness list of a royal charter in 1104 (Johnson, *Reg.*, no. 677) in which Westminster had no interest. Armitage-Robinson (*Gilbert Crispin*, 160) consequently regarded the charter as spurious. But Round and Johnson accept it as genuine (*EHR*, XVI, 721ff; Johnson, *Reg.*, *loc. cit.*). Gilbert probably witnessed this charter while he was at the royal court for the plea involving possession of a manor, claimed successfully by Westminster. The royal writ announcing the result of this plea can be dated 1104 (Johnson, *Reg.*, no. 818).

[140] *AO*, ep. 366, ll. 1-10, 72-78: "Quae modulando clara solebat dicere laudes fistula vestras murmare rauco nunc canit, atque lugubris extat: dicit et: unde vos ab ovili pastor, abestis? . . . Quando revisa regna perampla ista fuere? Nemo revisit: annus et praeteriere: ergo timendum." The literary form of Gilbert's letter would indicate that it was intended for circulation. But it survives only in two collections of Anselm's correspondence (Schmitt, *AO*, V, p. 309n.) and in a twelfth-century collection of Gilbert's works (*MS. B.M.Add.*, 8166, f. 26b).

mous letter, possibly from his diocesan ordinary, Gundulph of Rochester, which claimed that the whole English Church was in danger of destruction because of the continued lack of leadership, and implied that Anselm ought to end his dispute with the King and return to England.[141]

Although the English Church by 1105 was united in its demands for the end of the investiture controversy, it was not until two years after the meeting at Laigle that the compromise proposal presented there by Henry was officially ratified by the *curia regis* and accepted as the terms for ending this dispute between the King and Primate. The reasons for this long delay were, first of all, the reluctance on the part of the King to give up lay investiture, which he had offered to do at Laigle; secondly, Henry's expedition in Normandy in 1106-7; and finally, Anselm's repeated illnesses.

It was not until the beginning of 1106 that the embassy to Rome which Henry, at Laigle, had promised to send before Christmas, finally set off on the arduous two-month journey. Until December Henry was able to procrastinate by taking a long time to decide on the number and personnel of the embassy. Finally he and Anselm agreed to dispatch the royal clerk William Warelwast and Baldwin, Anselm's secretary.[142] In the middle of December, Henry found a new excuse for delay. He had heard, so he wrote to Anselm, that there were now two popes in Rome, and perhaps Anselm ought to retain the envoys, who by this time were with him in Normandy.[143]

---

[141] *AO*, ep. 365, ll. 1-6: "Carissime Pater et domine, quamvis optime sciatis quid facere debeatis et quid facere velitis, videtur tamen omni fere homini sano sensu sapienti omnino nihil aliud esse id quod inter vos et regem sub tam morosa exspectatione agitur, nisi diabolicae fraudis illusio et illudens dilatio, et—ut manifestius dicam—totius Anglorum ecclesiae ac religionis et legis Christianae cotidiana diminutio et summa destructio." The letter was obviously written by someone very close to Anselm, possibly Gundulph of Rochester or perhaps Gilbert Crispin.

[142] *AO*, epp. 367, 368, 370, 371.

[143] *AO*, ep. 377, ll. 3-4, 6-7: "Plurimum relatione didicimus et maxime per Robertum, clericum cancellarii mei, rumores de apostolico. . . . Dicunt enim Romae—quod absit—duos esse apostolicos, et ad invicem bellicosam seditionem inter se obtinere." The chancery clerk Robert was Robert Malet,

5. The Agreement of 1107

Anselm replied coolly that there was only one legal pope and finally sent William and Baldwin on their way.[144] It is true that an anti-pope had been elected in November, but Henry was clearly not very anxious to see the embassy leave for Rome. He had made the concession on lay investiture at Laigle at a time when his leading counsellor and general was under excommunication, and when he needed the church's support for his conquest of Normandy. Now that Robert of Meulan was restored to communion, and his conquest of Normandy was well on the way to a successful conclusion, Henry was reluctant to present his compromise to Paschal, lest the Pope accept it.

Lay investiture was still a very meaningful institution. While retention of ecclesiastical homage would allow the King to retain his power over the English Church, the surrender of lay investiture meant the virtual abandonment of the idea of theocratic monarchy in England. This surrender of the intellectual basis of royal control over the church Henry was in no hurry to make.[144a] It is true that the idea of theocratic monarchy was past its prime and slowly becoming archaic, but it still was a powerful force in the political life of Europe. The kings of the twelfth century were to base their power

---

an important landholder in Normandy and England who in 1106 supported Robert Curthose and was exiled from England. (On Robert, see G. H. White, *Burke's Complete Peerage*, x (1949), appendix F, p. 51; Johnson, *Reg.*, p. xiii). The moot point as to whether Robert had the title of Master Chamberlain appears to be settled in the negative by Henry's reference to him as *clericus cancelarii*. The anti-pope Silvester IV was elected in the middle of November 1105 (*MGH, SS.*, xix, 281). Henry's letter was written c. December 18 (Johnson, *Reg.*, no. 716). I have not been able to determine how and why Robert Malet knew about the anti-pope within a month after his election.

[144] *AO*, ep. 378, ll. 11-13: "Hoc tantum dico quia apostolicus Paschalis secundum deum ecclesiastice est electus, et per totam ecclesiam catholicam iam susceptus et confirmatus."

[144a] In 1108, Henry heard a rumor that Paschal was allowing Henry V of Germany to retain lay investiture without danger of excommunication, and complained to the Pope that he had received very different treatment on the investiture issue (*AO*, ep. 451, ll. 26-29). Paschal hotly denied that the rumor was true (*AO*, ep. 452).

not on the divinity that doth hedge a king, but on the efficiency of their administrations and law courts. Henry I must have sensed, however dimly, that this was the way the political currents were running and, if absolutely necessary, investiture could be surrendered. But in giving up lay investiture, Henry was turning his back on the early medieval idea of kingship and the political tradition of centuries. It is understandable that he hoped he could avoid fulfilling the offer he had made at Laigle.

According to Gerard of York, who was in a good position to know the situation at the *curia regis*, there was hope at Henry's court in the latter part of 1105 that the old Primate would soon finally die, and one of the King's intimates, probably Roger of Salisbury, was already looking forward to his election as Archbishop of Canterbury.[145] It appears, then, that Henry's delay in sending the embassy to Rome was caused by his reluctance to surrender lay investiture, and by the hope that Anselm would die and one of Henry's intimates would become head of the English Church. But the sick old monk grimly held on to his life, and by the end of 1105 Henry could procrastinate no longer and the embassy finally set off for Rome.

In June, William Warelwast and Baldwin returned from Rome, and found Anselm at Rouen.[146] They brought with them the letter from Paschal II to Anselm, written at the end of April, which set forth the results of the embassy. It is a very subtle and highly interesting document. Nearly all of its seventy-odd lines (in modern print) inform Anselm in

[145] Gerard to Anselm, *AO*, ep. 373, ll. 31-35: "Dolorem istum ille non sentit, qui inani spe honoris tui inflatus in te conspirat, morti tuae quasi iam proxime aspirat, ut sanguine et lacrimis pauperum delibutus thronum tantae dignitatis ascendat. Unde iam quasi archiflamen inter sodales suos incendit et, dum vix oculos humo attolit, inter labia nescio quid sententiarum submurmurat, cum necdum noverit quid sit sententia." Schmitt (*AO*, v,317n.) believes Gerard is referring to Ranulf Flambard, but Liebermann's suggestion that Roger of Salisbury was the ecclesiastic intended (*Quadripartitus*, 158, n. 4) is more probable.
[146] *HN*, 177.

considerable detail how he should restore peace to the English Church by restoring to communion and absolving from penance and sin the magnates who had violated the papal decrees on lay investiture. And then, squarely in the middle of the letter, in one sentence, comes the important point—Paschal's acceptance of Henry's compromise proposal:

If some people should have received prelacies without the investitures of churches [i.e. lay investiture], even if they should have done homage to the King, by no means on account of this should they be cut off from the gift of benediction, until, through the grace of omnipotent God, the royal heart may be softened by the rain of your preaching to omit this [act of homage].[147]

Paschal's reply to the embassy, then, was the immediate and forthright acceptance of Henry's compromise proposal. As long as lay investiture was abolished, the homage of bishops-elect to the King should not prevent their consecration. The Pope qualified his acceptance in only one way. The retention of homage was not ideal, and Anselm should continue to try to persuade the King to abandon it, but not, it is implied, by engaging in more acrimonious disputes with Henry.

Why did Paschal II make this concession to the English King? Why did he accept Henry's compromise proposal? The Pope was not convinced of the canonical validity of the retention of ecclesiastical homage, since he still hoped that Anselm might convince Henry to abandon it. That Paschal was not very happy about the terms of the settlement of the English investiture controversy is indicated by the way he declared his acceptance of it—in a single sentence in the middle of a long letter. All through the English investiture controversy Paschal had been intransigent in his refusal to make any concessions to the English King, even at Anselm's request. He made no such concession to the German Emperor. In an interview

[147] *AO*, ep. 397, ll. 25-28: "Si qui vero deinceps praeter investiturae ecclesiarum praelationes assumpserint, etiam si regi hominia fecerint, nequaquam ob hoc a benedictionis munere arceantur, donec per omnipotentis dei gratiam ad hoc omittendum cor regium tuae praedicationis imbribus molliatur."

with the envoys of Henry V at Chalons in May 1107, Paschal reiterated his demand that the Emperor give up both lay investiture and the homage of ecclesiastics.[148] What, then, was the cause of Paschal's remarkable concession to Henry I? This has never been satisfactorily explained by historians.

The Pope's acceptance of the compromise ending the English investiture controversy appears to have been the result of a special papal project in 1106—Bohemond's crusade against Byzantium. Late in the year 1105, Bohemond I of Apulia, who had become the ruler of the crusaders' principality of Antioch, came to Rome and laid before Paschal II his plans for a holy war to be undertaken by Latin Christendom against the Emperor Alexius. Paschal's enthusiastic acceptance of Bohemond's plan is indicated by the rank of papal legate which the crusader received from the Pope, to help him preach the holy war and raise an expeditionary force in France. Bohemond received a warm welcome in France, where he arrived early in 1106, especially from King Philip, whose daughter he married, and from "that eager Crusader-by-proxy," as Runciman calls her, Adela of Blois.[149]

Before leaving Italy, Bohemond had sent envoys to England requesting permission to visit Henry's court.[150] It was probably in this way that Gerard of York heard about Bohemond's projected crusade and subsequently volunteered his services.[151] Henry was well aware of the reason for Bohemond's intended visit, and apprehensive lest Bohemond recruit some of his best knights, which were needed for his conquest of Normandy, the King sent word to the crusader

[148] Suger, *Vie de Louis VI*, ed. Waquet, 58: "Si sacratas Dominico corpori et sanguini manus laici manibus gladio sanguinolentis obligando supponant, ordini suo et sacre unctioni derogare." Cf. Meyer von Knonau, *Jahrbücher . . . Heinrich IV u. Heinrich V*, VI (1907), 45-7.

[149] On Bohemond's crusade against Byzantium, see S. Runciman, *A History of the Crusades* (1952), II, 47-49; R. B. Yewdale, *Bohemond I, Prince of Antioch* (1922), ch. 7. W. Holtzmann, "Bohemund von Antiochen und Alexius I," *Neues Archiv*, 50 (1933), 270ff., has proved conclusively that Paschal enthusiastically supported Bohemond's crusade against Byzantium.

[150] *OV*, IV, 211.   [151] See above, n. 111.

not to risk the dangers of a winter crossing. Instead he offered to meet Bohemond in Normandy at Easter.[152] It is unlikely that this meeting took place.[153] But Anselm, probably acting as Henry's representative, had an interview with Bohemond late in the spring of 1106.[154]

Although several Norman knights took the cross in Bohemond's ill-fated expedition against Byzantium,[155] Henry appears to have been successful in preventing any of his own knights from setting out for the east. The failure of the Anglo-Norman knights once again to enlist in a holy war under the papal banner must have come as a disappointment, especially to Paschal II. For it is readily apparent that Paschal's concession to Henry I in the investiture controversy was related to his support of Bohemond's crusade. The embassy bearing Henry's compromise proposal arrived in Rome in February or March of 1106. At the end of April, Paschal dispatched his reply to Anselm, accepting the compromise and conceding the retention of ecclesiastical homage.[156] Only a cause of the highest urgency for the papacy would have forced Paschal to depart from his ordinarily dogmatic attitude. At the same time that Paschal was preparing his reply to Henry's proposal, Bohemond was in France, seeking an interview with the English King, and hoping for his support in the papal-sponsored war against Byzantium. England had remained aloof from the First Crusade. But in 1105 a considerable number of English pilgrims had set out for the Holy Land,[157] which could be taken to indicate a new crusading fervor in England. Paschal regarded Henry's concession on lay investiture as an indication of a new obedient attitude on his

---

[152] *OV*, IV, 211: "At contra providus rex, metuens ne sibi electos milites de ditione sua subtraheret, mandavit ei ne discrimen hibernae navigationis subiret. . . ."

[153] Runciman, II, 48 asserts that it did. This is in accordance with Orderic's account. But Henry's charters show that he was in England at Easter and did not go to Normandy until the beginning of August (Johnson, *Reg.*, nos. 749, 750; p. xxix).

[154] *HN*, 179-80.   [155] *OV*, IV, 213.

[156] *AO*, ep. 397, dating clause.   [157] Runciman, *Crusades*, II, 91.

part towards the Holy See. Now Paschal intended that his own remarkable concession ending the dispute over church-state relations in England, and restoring amity between the papacy and the English King, would induce Henry to support Bohemond's crusade.

By the time Paschal arrived in France, in the spring of 1107, Bohemond had assembled his army at Brindisi, where he built a fleet. He was not ready to sail until September 1107.[158] All this time Paschal was hoping that Henry would yet do something to support the holy war against Byzantium. But already by the end of May 1107 there is an indication that he was disappointed in the English King and regretful that he had made the bootless concession to Henry. Baldwin and William Warelwast were present as representatives of Anselm and Henry at the council which Paschal held at Troyes in May of 1107,[159] and from them the Pope probably learned that England would make no contribution to Bohemond's crusade. At any rate, by this time it was abundantly clear that Paschal would gain nothing from his remarkable concession to Henry I. His letter to Anselm, written just after the council ended, reveals the Pope's disgust and chagrin in its closing sentence: "Let care for your good sense and religion arrange, in accordance with the barbarousness of the people and the advantages of the church, the other things which must be arranged in that kingdom on account of the urgency of the times."[160]

Among these "other things" which Paschal did not specifically mention was the official ending of the investiture controversy. It is evident that by now the Pope was regretting his acceptance of Henry's proposal. He tried to qualify it by emphasizing its temporary nature and depicting it as a concession to the supposed backward condition of England. Hence he did

---

[158] Yewdale, *Bohemond*, 114.
[159] *HN*, 184; *AO*, ep. 422, l. 11.
[160] *AO*, ep. 422, ll. 14-16: "Cetera etiam quae in regno illo pro necessitate temporis dispensanda sunt, iuxta gentis barbariem, iuxta ecclesiae opportunitates, sapientiae ac religionis tuae sollicitudo dispenset."

not want a formal written concordat between the papacy and
the English King, but left it to Anselm to work out the final
settlement with Henry. This would emphasize the temporary,
special nature of the agreement. Later the papacy could withdraw support for the agreement on the grounds that a new
set of circumstances had arisen. Nevertheless, Paschal could
not very well back out now from the concession he had made
in the previous year, and the way was open for the official
ending of the investiture controversy in England.

This ending was delayed until the summer of 1107 by
Henry's war against his brother in Normandy and Anselm's
frequent illnesses. The results of the embassy to Rome were
reported to the King in July of 1106 by William Warelwast,[161] who was rewarded for his services with the vacant
Bishopric of Exeter.[162] Although Henry immediately summoned Anselm back to England, the old Archbishop was too
ill to travel.[163] Consequently Henry asked Anselm to await
his own return to Normandy. In the meantime, Anselm was
appointed the King's regent in Normandy.[164] Late in July,
Henry crossed the Channel to complete the conquest of his
brother's duchy and on the Feast of the Assumption of the
Blessed Mary (August, 15, 1106), a holy day especially dear
to Anselm and his monastic disciples, the King and Archbishop met at Anselm's former Abbey at Bec. As a sign of the
peace and concord re-established between them, the King
promised that all the temporalities of Canterbury would be
returned to Anselm after his return to England.[165]

Then the King and Archbishop parted, the former to continue his campaign against his brother, the latter to return to

[161] HN, 181.

[162] William Warelwast is referred to as Bishop of Exeter in a writ of
July 1106 (Johnson, Reg., no. 779).

[163] HN, 181-2.

[164] AO, ep. 399, ll. 8-9: "Volo autem et praecipio, et ubique per omnes
possessiones meas Normanniae imperetis sicut per vestras dominicas. . . ."

[165] HN, 182-3. A royal writ from the summer of 1106 (Johnson, Reg.,
no. 756) reveals Henry's administration carrying out this restoration of the
Canterbury lands.

V. Ending of the Controversy, 1104-1109

England. A little over a month later, on September 28, came Tinchebrai, Henry's final and complete victory. In a letter to Anselm after the battle, Henry attributed his victory to divine dispensation.[166] Anselm expressed his joy upon receipt of Henry's letter, and hoped that the King would go on "from earthly exaltation after this life to the heavenly kingdom and eternal glory."[167] From the verge of excommunication two years previously Henry had risen to the highest moral position. He had learned that more was to be gained through subtle negotiations and cautious cooperation with the church than by flagrant opposition to its leaders. He was to apply this lesson with great skill for the rest of his long reign.

Until the beginning of April 1107, Henry was concerned with affairs in his new Duchy.[168] During this period Anselm acted as his regent in England.[169] Following Henry's return shortly before Easter, the official ending of the investiture controversy was again postponed until Whitsuntide because of Anselm's illness.[170] Finally, on August 1, 1107 a great meeting of the *curia regis* was held in the royal palace at London. Present were all the principal disputants in the English investiture controversy, with the exception of the Pope—not only Henry and Mathilda, but Anselm, Gerard of York, eight other bishops, Abbot Gilbert Crispin of Westminister and several other abbots, and a considerable number of lay magnates headed by Robert of Meulan.[171] The only detailed accounts we have of the proceedings are from the pens of Eadmer, in the *Historia Novorum*, the official history of the reform party, and Anselm, in a letter to the Pope.[172]

[166] *AO*, ep. 401, ll. 12-13: "Hoc autem non elationi vel arrogantiae nec viribus meis, sed dono divinae dispositionis attribuo."

[167] *AO*, ep. 402, ll. 11-15: "Oro autem ore et corde . . . ut de terrena exaltatione post hanc vitam ad caeleste regnum et gloriam aeternam vos perducat."

[168] David, *Robert*, 178-9; Johnson, *Reg.*, p. xxix.

[169] Anselm to a Norman abbot, *AO*, ep. 407, ll. 14-15: "Quod audistis quia dominus meus rex mihi commendavit regnum suum et omnia sua. . . ."

[170] *HN*, 185.   [171] Johnson, *Reg.*, no. 828, witness list.

[172] *AO*, ep. 430, ll. 4-10: "Rex qui dominatur Anglis et Normannis,

5. The Agreement of 1107

These are not entirely impartial accounts, but taken together with a perceptive remark by William of Malmesbury,[173] it seems possible to establish what happened at the London council. Henry arrived back in England in very good humor, ready to make his concession on lay investiture ·the law of the land. But at the London council he decided to put the matter to a discussion first and gain the general consent of magnates. Anselm withdrew, and a discussion ensued which lasted through three days. A minority of the bishops were alarmed that Henry was intending to depart from the ecclesiastical practices of his father and brother. But the reformers emphasized that the Pope also had made an important concession. Then the lay magnates led by Robert of Meulan had their say, and Count Robert insisted that Henry fulfill his promise to Anselm and Paschal and give up lay investiture. Presumably Robert feared that he would be blamed if the King backed down now. Or, if he was indeed the originator of the compromise principle, he had a vested interest in defending it. When Henry felt that he had the general consent of

---

oboedienter suscipiens vestram iussionem, investituram ecclesiarum, renitentibus multis, omnino deseruit. Quod ut faceret, Robertus, comes de Mellento, et Ricardus de Redveri, ut fideles vestri et filii ecclesiae, vestris attracti monitis, vehementer institerunt. Rex ipsi in personis eligendis nullatenus propria utitur voluntate, sed religisiorum se penitus committit consilio." It is significant that the agreement on the process of ecclesiastical election, which falls far short of canonical election, is omitted in Eadmer's official history. Richard de Redvers was a baron from the Cotentin serving in Henry's administration. He was for a time justiciar in the Isle of Wight and Devon (Johnson, *Reg.*, p. xviii; *DNB*, 47, p. 385). Eadmer's account of the London assembly is in *HN*, 186: ". . . Per tres continuos dies, absente Anselmo, inter regem et episcopis satis actum de ecclesiarum investituris, quibusdam ad hoc nitentibus ut rex eas faceret more patris et fratris sui, non juxta praeceptum et oboedientiam apostoloci. Nam papa in sententia quae exinde promulgata fuerat firmus stans, concesserat hominia quae Urbanus papa aeque ut investituras interdixerat, ac per hoc regem sibi de investituris consentaneum fecerat. . . . Dehinc, praesente Anselmo, astante multitudine, annuit rex et statuit. . . ." Then follow the terms of the agreement between Henry and Anselm quoted in n. 1 above.

[173] *GP*, 117: "Venit igitur rex sullimi tropheo splendidus, et triumphali gloria Angliam invectus, investiturasque ecclesiarum Anselmo in perpetuum in manum remisit."

his court for the compromise, Anselm was called back and the exact terms of the agreement were worked out. There is no necessity, in the absence of an extant document, to assume that the agreement was made into a formal written concordat.[174] The King and Primate each made formal oral promises; in early twelfth-century law this would have sufficed.

The promises made by Henry and Anselm were such that the procedure for episcopal and abbatial election in England was henceforth to be as follows: There would not be full canonical election by clergy and people, but the King, in appointing the bishop or abbot, would take "the counsel of religious persons," apparently the more important bishops. Then the bishop-elect or abbot-elect would do homage to the King for the temporalities of his see and, finally, he would receive consecration and symbols of spiritual office from his ecclesiastical superior. The King thus had a double veto over the person of the bishop or abbot elected. It was he who made the choice in the first instance, albeit supposedly with good advice. Secondly, if the King did not approve of the person selected for ecclesiastical office, he could refuse to accept the homage of the bishop-elect or abbot-elect. Then, presumably, a new candidate would have to be found whom the King was willing to accept as his *homo*. Under this system of election, it was a priori impossible that anyone could become a bishop or one of the greater abbots without the King's approval. The history of episcopal and abbatial elections for the rest of Henry's reign was to show that this was also true in practice.

Although the Pope heaped praise on Henry for the concession he had made[175]—under the circumstances, Paschal could not very well do anything else—the victory gained by

---

[174] An unnecessary assumption made by Poole, *Domesday Book to Magna Carta*, 180: "No authoritative text has survived to inform us of the precise nature of the agreement of 1107."

[175] *AO*, ep. 457, ll. 3-5: "Omnipotenti Deo gratias agimus, quod talem te regem nostris temporibus constituit, qui et terrenum regnum sapienter ad honorem Dei gubernas et aeterni regis sollicitudinem ante oculos mentis portas."

the reformers in England was in fact a limited one. It is true that Henry had been forced to abandon the idea of theocratic monarchy, but this conception of kingship was past its prime anyways. In practice, church-state relations in England were not fundamentally altered by the agreement of 1107. The firm control over the affairs and personnel of the church which the Norman rulers had possessed for more than a century was retained by Henry I.

In the long run, Paschal II made a serious error in not attempting to work out with Henry I a detailed and permanent concordat on church-state relations in England. Paschal might have been able to include in such a formal document some statement on episcopal electoral procedure which would have secured for the English Church in the future a real measure of canonical election. By envisaging the nature of the settlement with Henry as temporary, special and limited, Paschal left it for custom to decide the general procedure and the majority of the institutions of church-state relations in England. This custom was all on the side of royal power. It is curious that the papacy was to make the same mistake again when it tried to reach a settlement with Henry V in 1122. In the case of the Concordat of Worms as well as the "concordat" of London, the relations between the royal government and the church were left by the papacy to be determined by the custom of the realm, which favored the continuance of royal control over the church.[176]

Although the papacy missed a great opportunity in 1106-7, the way had been opened by the investiture controversy for further close relations between Rome and the English Church. In this fact lies the importance of the investiture controversy in the history of medieval England. Now for the first time since the Norman Conquest the English Church had been brought into a real and relatively close relationship with the

---

[176] On the effect of the Concordat of Worms on the German Church, see A. Hofmeister, "Das Wormser Konkordat. Zum Streit und seine Bedeutung," *Festschrift Dietrich Schäfer* (1915), 64ff., esp. 94-118.

papal curia. This relationship was not to decrease during the remaining two decades of Henry I's reign. On the contrary it was to grow. An archbishop of York with the support and aid of the pope would defy Canterbury and the King himself for several years. Papal confirmation of the privileges of ecclesiastical corporations in England would become common in the 1120's and 1130's. Papal legates would be allowed to enter the country and attempt, albeit with little success, to reform the English Church.[177] These innovations are the indirect consequences of the investiture controversy. During the investiture controversy the Anglo-Norman bishops and abbots had become accustomed to look to Rome for decisions on doctrinal matters. They had received papal letters and some had gone to the papal curia as envoys of Anselm or the King. Between 1100 and 1107 England was at last brought within the effective orbit of papal administration.

It was to be characteristic of the English Church for the rest of Henry's reign, however, that while an increasing amount of ecclesiastical business was conducted at Rome, this was limited to secondary and usually routine matters. On important issues affecting the life of the English Church, the King and Primate, working together, made the important decisions. This tendency was already evident before Anselm's death in 1109.

The venerable and sick Primate and the King, after Anselm's return to England, again worked together in harmony and friendship as they had done before the investiture issue became crucial in 1103. Anselm again expressed his personal admiration for the King,[178] while Henry appointed the Primate his regent in England while he was on the Continent in 1108.[179] Another reform council was called for London in 1108, at which the King and Primate, with the support of the higher clergy and magnates, created the new episcopal see of

[177] See below, Ch. VI, pts. 1, 3, 4.
[178] AO, ep. 462, l. 5ff.
[179] AO, ep. 461, ll. 21-25.

Ely, by division of the diocese of Lincoln.[180] Papal confirmation for this important change in the life of the English Church was requested, but only after King and Primate had already acted.[181] Paschal could only confirm the *fait accompli*.[182]

While the investiture controversy had brought the English Church into contact with Rome, the development of the possibilities of this situation depended largely on the Primate. If he chose to act in continued close cooperation with the King, the papal curia would be able to derive only limited advantages from its expanded relations with English ecclesiastics. This was the path that Anselm adopted in the short period between the ending of the investiture controversy and his death in April 1109.

Through more than a decade of bitter controversy over church-state relations in England, Anselm had faced the power of the monarchy with very little support from the English higher clergy. Urban II's duplicity had made him suspicious of papal policy, and the prestige of the papacy in his eyes could not have been entirely restored by Paschal II's sudden shift from an uncompromising attack on the Anglo-Norman *Landeskirche* to concessions and compromise. In 1093 Anselm had wanted to reform the English Church along Gregorian lines. Obedience to ecclesiastical superiors, above all the pope, had become natural for a man who was always at heart a monk; hence he felt obligated to carry the Gregorian reform program to England and to attempt to force its acceptance against almost universal opposition. Furthermore, there is ample evidence that he believed in the validity of at least the more moderate Gregorian doctrines; had he lacked conviction in the righteousness of his cause, the Archbishop would not have been able to maintain his struggle for so long and against such vehement and able opponents. But by 1107 Anselm was exhausted and ill, and perhaps also a little confused and dis-

[180] *HN*, 195-96. [181] *AO*, ep. 441, ll. 9-20.
[182] J-L, no. 6212.

illusioned. Possibly Lanfranc's support of the Norman church-state system was prudent after all; the first two years of Henry's reign had demonstrated anew what could be accomplished by King and Primate cooperating in the moral and intellectual improvement of the English clergy. These ideas may have occurred to the old Archbishop when, in the last two years of his life, he again worked in harmony with the King for whom he had such deep personal admiration.

Anselm's episcopal colleagues of course approved of the Archbishop's moderation at the end of his pontificate; this was the policy they had long urged him to follow. His successors as leaders of the English Church for the rest of Henry's reign, even his disciple Ralph d'Escures, who became Archbishop of Canterbury in 1114, ignored Anselm's heroic struggle for the freedom of the church from royal control. Occasionally they gave utterance to Gregorian terms, or favored ecclesiastical reform which did not conflict with royal authority. But the concluding chapter of this work will show that they allowed and even assisted the King to strengthen his authority over the English Church.

As an interesting appendix to Anselm's career as a reforming bishop, it is worth noting that one of Anselm's Canterbury disciples continued the struggle for the reform of church-state relations along radical Gregorian lines into the second decade of the twelfth century, but in Germany rather than in England. This disciple was the famous "Honorius Augustodunensis," one of the most prolific and influential theologians of the early twelfth century. Honorius' provenance remains completely obscure, but he is now known to have been one of Anselm's monastic disciples at Canterbury in the last decade of the eleventh century.[183] By the 1120's, if not earlier, Honorius was located at Regensburg where shortly after the Concordat of Worms he published his *Summa Gloria*,[184] a contribution to the German investiture controversy from the

---

[183] Y. Lefèvre, *L'Elucidarium et les Lucidaires* (1954), 219-222.
[184] *Lib. de Lite*, III, 63-80.

radical Gregorian position.[185] Some of the extreme statements
on behalf of papal power made by the decretalists of the fourteenth century were anticipated in Honorius' tractate, and this
undoubtedly accounts for the fact that the contribution made
by Anselm's disciple to the polemical literature of the German investiture was read in southern Germany and Austria
until the fifteenth century.[186] It is indicative of the general attitude prevailing among leaders of the English Church after
1109 that the only one of Anselm's disciples who continued
to argue vehemently on behalf of papal authority and against
royal interference in ecclesiastical affairs was the one who
migrated to Germany. It is also significant that the radical
Gregorian Honorius had been Anselm's student during the
early years of his pontificate, before the Archbishop's reforming zeal was affected by weariness and disillusionment.

[185] For discussion of Honorius' theories, see R. W. and A. J. Carlyle,
History of Medieval Political Theory, IV (1922), 286-297; E. M. Sanford, "Honorius, Presbyter and Scholasticus," *Speculum*, 23 (1948), 418-
419; W. Ullmann, *Growth of Papal Government in the Middle Ages*
(1955), 414-420.
[186] Sanford, *op.cit.*, 418.

CHAPTER VI

HENRY I, THE ENGLISH CHURCH, AND THE
PAPACY, 1109-1135

I. THE EXTENT OF GREGORIAN IDEAS AFTER
ANSELM'S DEATH

THE quarter of a century following Anselm's death and coinciding with the latter part of the reign of Henry I lacks the dramatic conflicts between the leaders of church and state, which dominate the great theologian's pontificate. But the period 1109-35, while placid on the surface, is not an entirely obscure one. Nor is it devoid of developments significant for the later history of the English Church. Definite patterns and cross-currents of development can be traced in the life of the English episcopate and greater abbots, in the relations between King and ecclesiastics, in papal policy towards England, which together comprise the history of church-state relations in the period.[1]

Anselm's death did not mark the complete abandoning of reform ideas and endeavors within the English Church. In the remainder of Henry's reign, there are definite indications that some of the more moderate and least controversial doctrines of the Gregorian reformers had been widely accepted in England. The visits of such leaders of the English Church as Archbishops Ralph, William of Corbeil, and Thurstan, Bishop Robert of Hereford, and Abbot Hugh of Reading, to Rome,[2] the attendance of English ecclesiastics at the Council

[1] Cf. R. W. Southern's view of the period: "During the twenty years after Anselm's death, the policies of the archbishops and the character of the English episcopate is extremely obscure; except for the continuing dispute between York and Canterbury no crisis occurred to reveal the tendencies of the time." *Medieval and Renaissance Studies*, I (1941), 28-9.
[2] Ralph in 1117 (*HN*, 241-3); William of Corbeil in 1123 and 1125 (*A-S Chron. E, s.a.*); Thurstan in 1123 (*HC*, 201-6); Robert of Hereford

of Rheims in 1119,[3] the coming of papal legates to England,[4] the visits to England of Peter the Venerable, Abbot of Cluny,[5] and Hugh de Payen, the founder of the Templars,[6] all helped to keep the English Church in touch with trends on the Continent. The new dynastic connection between England and the German Empire following the marriage of Henry V to Mathilda in 1114 worked towards the same end. In the second decade of the century, the English court and church were fully informed of the course of the struggle between the papacy and Henry V over lay investiture.[7] But the investiture question was considered settled as far as England was concerned, with the result that Archbishop Ralph of Canterbury, while visiting Rome in 1117, could presume to take an impartial position between Emperor and Pope.[8]

A concerted attempt was made, however, to abolish some forms of simony and other abuses within the English Church. The English Council of 1125, meeting under the direction of the legate Cardinal John of Crema, prohibited simony, payment for sacraments and the holding of ecclesiastical preferment by inheritance.[9] The purchase of benefices, of holy orders, and of admission to religious houses, were prohibited by the Council of 1127, at which the Primate and legate William of Corbeil presided.[10] The King confirmed the decisions of

---

in 1134-5 (*PU*, II, no. 15); Hugh of Reading in 1128 (*PU*, III, no. 21).

[3] *HN*, 255-6; *HC*, 165-6. William of Exter, Ranulf of Durham, Bernard of St. David's, Urban of Llandaff, Thurstan of York, Ralph of the Orkneys, and Archdeacon John of Canterbury were at Rheims.

[4] For the legates in this period, see Tillmann, *Legaten*, 23-38. The important ones are: Anselm of St. Saba's, 1115-16; Peter, 1121; John of Crema, 1125.

[5] *A-S Chron. E*, *s.a.* 1130.   [6] *Ibid.*, *s.a.* 1128.

[7] Florence of Worcester is one of the chief sources for the abortive compromise plan of 1111 put forward by Paschal. On the significance of this, see W. Holtzmann in *Neues Archiv*, 50 (1933), 282ff. It is apparent that Henry I maintained a close watch on the development of the German investiture controversy. Cf. *AO*, ep. 451, ll. 26-32 for additional evidence of this.

[8] *HN*, 242. See below, p. 305.

[9] *JW*, 20-1, canons 1, 2, and 5.

[10] *JW*, 23-5, canons 1, 2, and 3.

this Council.[11] In the previous decade Henry had again made an attempt to enforce the law of clerical continence established by Anselm's Council of 1102.[12] Archdeacons and priests were again ordered to give up their wives at the Council of 1129.[13]

The Gregorian reform doctrine of canonical election of bishops by the "clergy and people"[14] was widely known in England in the second and third decades of the twelfth century. Although never really put into practice in this period as the effective procedure in episcopal elections, it was at least recognized as the reform ideal demanded by the papacy and therefore as a principle of canon law. It was felt in some instances that the consent of the clergy and people of the see gave to the appointment of a new bishop a special canonical force. As early as 1109 the canons of York, in petitioning the Primate for consecration of the Archbishop-elect, Thomas II, stated that he had been elected by clergy and people.[15] In 1114 Ralph was "received" as Archbishop of Canterbury and Ernulf as Bishop of Rochester by the clergy and people of their respective sees.[16] The right of *cleri et populi* to assent to a bishop designated by the King seems to have been recognized in the case of the appointment of Gilbert the Universal to London in 1128.[17] The concept of canonical election was sufficiently known in England for Calixtus II, in 1119, to commend Thurstan to *clero et populo Eboracensis*.[18] Similarly in 1134/5 Innocent II exhorted the clergy and people of Hereford to receive and support Bishop Robert de Bethune returning from the Holy See to England.[19] While not the important factor in the appointment of bishops, election by clergy and people was a phrase not infrequently appealed to, so that the doctrine must have been common knowledge in the Eng-

---

[11] JW, 25.   [12] HN, 213.   [13] A-S Chron. E, s.a. 1129.

[14] On the general importance of the concept of canonical election for the Gregorian reform period, see P. Schmid, *Die Begriff d. Kanon. Wahl* (1926).

[15] Raine, *Docts.*, III, 32.   [16] HN, 223 and 225: "receptus."

[17] JW, 26: "annuente clero et populo."

[18] Raine, *Docts.*, III, 38.   [19] PU, II, no. 15.

lish Church of the period. One chronicler refers to the great multitude of *cleri et populi* at the Council of 1125.[20] Although for Henry's reign it is of little or no practical consequence, the doctrine of canonical election could have an important effect on episcopal elections, whenever the royal power became weak in the future.

Reform ideas from the Continent continued to be disseminated in England through the medium of collections of law. It is only to be expected that the royal justice who, in the latter part of the reign of Henry I, drew up the legal miscellany known as the *leges Henrici Primi*, should attempt to ignore the ecclesiastical legislation of Anselm's pontificate, and in accordance with Henry's policy, should reiterate the ecclesiastical law of the Conqueror's reign.[21] In the same period, however, ecclesiastical legists were incorporating reform ideas in other collections of law. The author of the *leges Edwardi Confessori* which probably can be dated as written in the last five years of Henry's reign, was much under the influence of Gregorian doctrines of *libertas ecclesiae*.[22] An attempt was made to gloss Lanfranc's collection so as to make Anselm's appeal to the pope a canon law principle.[23] The English Church was aware of the expanding corpus of canon law on the Continent, and did not remain satisfied with the collection made by Lanfranc.[24] Copies were made in England, in the

---

[20] *JW*, 20. For clergy and people in election of David of Bangor, see *HN*, 259.

[21] See F. Liebermann, *Über das Englische Rechtsbuch Leges Henrici* (1901), 43.

[22] See especially *Leg. Ed. Conf.*, I: (Liebermann, *Gesetze*, I, 628): "De pace et libertate sanctae ecclesiae: a sancta igitur ecclesia exordium sumentes . . . pacem illius et libertatem concionati sunt dicentes." For dating, Liebermann, *Über Leg. Ed. Conf.* (1896), p. 20.

[23] P. Fournier, *RHDFE*, 4th ser., XII (1933), p. 130.

[24] The history of canon law in England in the first half of the twelfth century remains to be written. The following are important contributions to the subject, in order of publication: Brooke, *En. Ch. & Papacy* (1931); Fournier and Le Bras, *Hist. d. Collections* (1931); Fournier in *RHDFE*, 4th ser., XII (1933); H. E. Lohmann, "Die Collectio Wigorniensis," *ZRG, KA* 22 (1933); S. Kuttner, *Repertorium, Studi e Testi*, 71 (1937); G. Barraclough, rev. of Kuttner in *EHR*, 53 (1938), 492-5; W. Holtzmann,

early twelfth century, of Ivo's *Tripartita* and *Panormia,* the newest and most complete canon law collections in France.[25] Even the royalist but eclectic *leges Henrici Primi* borrows several clauses from Ivo's *Panormia.*[26] Attempts were made to keep up to date the older canon law collections known in England, those of Lanfranc and Burchard of Worms, by adding the canons of the English Councils of 1108, 1125, and 1127,[27] Paschal's decree of 1112 on investiture,[28] and the canons of the first Lateran Council of 1123.[29]

Too much significance should not, however, be attributed to this dissemination of canon law in England. As yet these collections, deriving from Continental sources for the most part, remained in the realm of private opinions and claims. No English ecclesiastic in Henry's reign regarded them as the established law of the English Church. Although Ernulf, Bishop of Rochester, was learned in canon law, he was only interested in establishing the rights and privileges of the Church of Rochester.[30] This was about as far as the legal interests of the other English bishops extended.

The first half of the twelfth century, as is well known, was an age of great legal activity in Western Europe when con-

---

"Über ein Ausg. d. papstl. Dekretalen d. 12 Jhdts.," *Nachricht. d. Ak. d. Wiss. in Göttingen, Phil.-Hist. Kl.,* 1945, 15ff.; Kuttner, "Notes on a projected Corpus of twelfth century decretal letters," *Traditio,* VI (1948), 345ff.; Kuttner and E. Rathbone, "Anglo-Norman Canonists," *Traditio,* VII (1949-51), 279ff.; Holtzmann, "Dekretensamm. d. 12 Jhdts.," *Feier . . . Göttingen,* 1951, vol. II; S. Mochi-Onory, *Fonti Canonistiche* (1951), esp. 21ff.; Holtzmann and E. Kemp, *Decretals,* Lincoln Rec. Soc., 47 (1954).

[25] Manuscripts mentioned in this note and in notes 27, 28, and 29 were pointed out by Brooke, *E. Ch. & Pap.,* 231-3, 242-4. *Tripartita: Bodl. 16, 934 (d'Orville 46); Panormia: Jesus Coll. Oxf. 50; B.M. Cotton Vittelius, A. XIII.*

[26] Noted in Liebermann's edition, *Gesetze,* I, 549ff.

[27] *Hereford Cathed. Lib. o.2.vii* (Burchard of Worms).

[28] *BM. Royal 11.D.VIII,* f. 249 (Lanfranc's collection).

[29] *Peterhouse 74* (Lanfranc's collection).

[30] On Ernulf as a canonist and on his role in the making of the *Textus Roffensis,* see F. Liebermann, "Notes on the Textus Roffensis," *Archael. Cantiana,* XXIII (1898), 101-12, esp. §§ 11a and 26.

certed attempts were made, in many cases for the first time, to define the conflicting jurisdictions which had grown up under feudal conditions.[31] The English episcopate were eager not only to establish their positions as feudatories, but also to secure royal and papal confirmation for the rights and privileges of their sees. The *Textus Roffensis* and other cartularies of the period, and the many papal confirmations of the 1120's, are the results of this intention.[32] Aside from legislation of church councils, the English episcopate made no attempt in Henry's reign to define the law of the church. The spread of Continental canon law in England kept the English Church in touch with the doctrines of the Continental reformers and abetted the slow spread of reform ideas. As yet its effect was not greater than this.

2. THE KING'S INFLUENCE ON THE COMPOSITION AND INTERESTS OF THE HIGHER CLERGY

ADHERENCE to some reform doctrines by English ecclesiastics was concomitant with a period of almost unchallenged royal supremacy over the English Church. As Henry was able to develop the powers implicit in his status as liege lord to the highest degree,[33] so was his ascendancy in church-state relations accepted. It was assumed even by ecclesiastics of reforming inclination that he was the "natural lord" of his vassals;[34] scarcely less was the King lord of bishops and abbots in their ecclesiastical capacities. Without the occasion of a large-scale feudal *diffidatio* to aid any ecclesiastics concerned about the freedom of the church, the last twenty-six years of Henry's reign mark the efflorescence of the Anglo-Norman "territorial church" system as well as Anglo-Norman feudalism.

[31] The best study of the history of feudal law in twelfth-century Europe is by H. Mitteis, *Lehnrecht und Staatsgewalt* (1933).

[32] The edition of the *Textus Roffensis* is still that of Th. Hearne (1720). Many of the papal confirmations have recently been re-edited by Holtzmann, *PU* (see below, nn. 247–262).

[33] F. M. Stenton, *The First Century of English Feudalism*, 216ff.

[34] *HN*, 248.

An increased English interest in Roman law, which is revealed by William of Malmesbury's collection of extracts from the Theodosian Code of c.1130,[35] undoubtedly helped to enhance the status of the King. For in Roman law Henry could be viewed not only as a liege lord but also as a *princeps*. And in fact, in the *leges Henrici Primi*, under the influence of Roman law concepts, the English King is *gloriosus Caesar Henricus* from whom divine and secular law radiate throughout the kingdom.[36]

Reform doctrines from the Continent had not made sufficient progress in England to bring about a clear distinction between *regnum* and *ecclesia*. The church was still part of the "whole kingdom" which the administrative ability of the Conqueror and his sons had created. In 1116 the bishops and abbots were called upon to promise to "translate" the crown to Prince William after Henry's death.[37] In similar fashion the great ecclesiastics swore fealty to Mathilda in 1128.[38] At the same time it was assumed that laymen should participate in important ecclesiastical decisions. In 1115 for the general council at which the legate Anselm of St. Saba's was supposed to present measures for the correction of religion, Henry summoned to the *curia regis* not only all the bishops but also *principes totius regni*.[39] In 1121 the King told the legate Peter that he could not allow any important decision on the affairs of the English Church to be made without calling "*episcoporum, abbatum, procerum . . . totius regni conventum*."[40] While the King was in Normandy, his council decided ecclesiastical questions relating to England, and in 1116 refused entry to a papal legate.[41] Especially in episcopal elections were the

---

[35] *MS. Bodl. 3362* (*MS. Arch. Selden B.16*). I am following the dating given in the *Bodl. Lib. Catalogue*. There is a possibility that William made use of a Roman law collection in the possession of Aldhelm of Malmesbury in the seventh century. Cf. M. R. James, *Two Ancient English Scholars* (1931), 121.

[36] *Leg. Hen. Pr.*, I, *Gesetze*, I, 547, following *Quadripartitus*, II, 14, *Gesetze*, I, 543.

[37] *HN*, 237: "coronam . . . in eum . . . translaturos."   [38] *JW*, 26-7.

[39] *HN*, 231.   [40] *HN*, 295.   [41] *HN*, 245.

voices of the lay magnates important. It was stated as a theory that the election of a new bishop involved the participation of the magnates as well as clergy and people.[42] The election of the primate in 1114 involved an assembly *totius Anglici regni* meeting in the King's presence.[43]

Wherever the King happened to be was considered the proper place for episcopal elections. In 1125, when Henry was in Normandy, two bishops were elected there for English sees.[44] A concerted attempt was made in this period to carry further the visible sign of royal control over the church, and to establish the King's chapel as the proper place of consecration for bishops and abbots. Perhaps this attempt was encouraged by some lingering tradition of theocratic monarchy which regarded the royal chapel as a church of special sanctity. At any rate, Count Robert of Meulan, Henry's chief counsellor and a bitter enemy of Gregorian reform doctrines, demanded in 1115 that Bernard, bishop-elect of St. David's, should be consecrated "in accordance with custom," in the royal chapel.[45] This claim was stoutly opposed by the new Primate, and Henry, never a man to insist too much on theoretical questions, let Ralph have his way.[46] But Ralph himself, seven years later, consecrated a bishop in the royal chapel.[47] These two episcopal candidates had been royal chaplains,[48] so that their consecration in the royal chapel may have been viewed as representing their dependent relationship to the King as their patron. But in the 1120's this claim was taken a step further by the new Primate William of Corbeil, who refused to consecrate the Abbot of St. Augustine's, Canterbury, except *in capella regis* and demanded this as a custom of St. Anselm.[49]

---

[42] See the case of the disputed election of Ralph of the Orkneys in 1128 (*JW*, 25-6): "Qui Radulfus quoniam nec principes terrae, nec cleri, nec plebis electione vel assensu fuerat ordinatus. . . ."

[43] *HN*, 227: Letter of monks of Christ Church to Paschal, requesting the pallium.

[44] *JW*, 18. [45] *HN*, 235-6. [46] *HN*, 236.

[47] *HN*, 290-1. [48] *HN*, 235 and 290.

[49] *Thorne's Chronicle, Twysden SS.*, 1798.

Whatever the place or manner of election or consecration, the King's control over ecclesiastical appointments was real and final. When the King's decision was given, as it was in 1121 on behalf of Everard of Montgomery for the see of Norwich, the Primate and episcopate hastened to please the King.[50] Before an English ecclesiastic could accept a foreign bishopric in the gift of another king, as in the case of Eadmer who was offered the Bishopric of St. Andrews by Alexander, King of the Scots, it was necessary for the Primate to intercede with Henry and obtain his consent.[51] Of course the selection of bishops and abbots was not always made directly by Henry; many abbots, in particular, were elected in a more or less canonical manner.[52] In 1119 the monks of St. Alban's elected an abbot before the King could interfere and managed to obtain Henry's approval of their candidate.[53] But the King always possessed a veto power over abbatial elections on account of the feudal status of the abbots: the latter had to do homage to the King for their lands, as required by the compromise of 1107.

The King might decide not to interfere in an episcopal election. In 1123 Henry left the election of the new primate to the decision of lay and ecclesiastical magnates.[54] Or he might decide, after the royal candidate had been rejected by the *totum regnum*—a very rare case, that of Faricius in 1114—to accept the bishop-elect, should he seem likely to be compliant to the royal will, as Ralph was.[55] The King might be presented with a fait accompli by some recalcitrant monastery and decide it was not worth the trouble to interfere, as in the case of Peterborough in 1132.[56]

---

[50] *HN*, 294.   [51] *HN*, 279-81.

[52] D. Knowles in *Downside Review*, XLIX (1931), 252-78.

[53] Walsingham, *Gesta Abb.* (R,S.), I, 73.

[54] *A-S Chron. E, s.a.* 1123: "The King ordered them to elect as Archbishop of Canterbury for themselves whomever they wished, and he would grant it to them."

[55] *HN*, 223. Thanks was given to God for having changed the King's mind. See also below, pp. 304-05.

[56] *A-S Chron. E, s.a.* 1132.

2. King's Influence on the Clergy

But it was assumed that if the King wished to exercise the royal will in an ecclesiastical appointment, it would be effective. After the death of Abbot Gilbert Crispin in 1117, and while Henry was still in Normandy, the monks of Westminster attempted to elect the leader of the reform party in the convent, the Prior Osbert of Clare, as abbot. But after the King returned to England in 1120, he appointed Herbert the Almoner as abbot and interfered in the monastery to secure the banishment of Osbert to Ely.[57] At Eadmer's urging in 1123,[58] after the death of Bishop Theulf, the monks of Worcester, desiring to obtain a bishop from their own order, petitioned the King for the "free election" of the new prelate. But in this case Henry chose not to relinquish his right of appointment, and Simon, a secular clerk, was elected.[59]

The King might allow the chapter to go through the forms of canonical election, but the monks or canons would be required to elect the royal candidate. This is what happened at Ely in 1133.[60] The Peterborough author of the Anglo-Saxon Chronicle reflects the contemporary view of royal supremacy over the church when he makes all ecclesiastical appointments directly due to the King's gift.[61] The decision as to the filling of vacant bishoprics was Henry's to make and he could force an unwilling appointee, like Ernulf in 1114, to accept the office thrust upon him.[62] The manner of ecclesiastical appointment was not affected by the provenance of the appointee; it was not contingent upon whether or not the candidate for episcopal office was a royal clerk. Roger de Clinton, an archdeacon, became Bishop of Chichester in 1129 *"ex dono regis."*[63] In the case of the appointment of Robert de Bethune, Prior of Llanthony, as Bishop of Hereford, in 1128, royal approval of

---

[57] E. Williamson, ed., *Letters of Osbert of Clare* (1929), ep. 1, p. 47. See J. A. Robinson's introduction to this edition, pp. 2-9, where the incident and the evidence for it are fully discussed.
[58] Wharton, *Anglia Sacra*, II, 238.   [59] *Ibid.*, 238n.
[60] *Historia Eliensis, Anglia Sacra*, I, 618-19.
[61] See especially *A-S Chron. E, s.a.* 1114.
[62] *Loc.cit.*   [63] *GP*, 311.

him was the first requisite for his appointment. Only after this had been obtained was the opinion of the Primate sought.[64]

Even an alien and a pluralist could impose himself on a leading English religious house for several years, as long as he had royal support to overcome the bitter opposition of the monks. The long and lugubrious account in the *Chronicle* of the history of Peterborough in the 1120's reveals this clearly.[65] Henry, in fact, is said to have preferred to appoint alien abbots to religious houses,[66] in order to prevent abbots from identifying themselves with the interests of the monks and the traditions of the monasteries.

Whether or not the King did actually appoint foreign ecclesiastics as a matter of conscious policy, it is certain that Henry had the cosmopolitan outlook characteristic of a Norman. Neither the King nor his barons nor the episcopate could have seen anything exceptional in appointing a theologian from Lyons and Paris, Gilbert the Universal, to the see of London, or a French Cluniac, Henry of Blois, as Bishop of Winchester.[67] In 1116/17 the King was seriously thinking of appointing Abbot Anselm of St. Saba's in Rome, the nephew of St. Anselm, to an English bishopric.[68]

Royal control over ecclesiastical appointments encouraged the perpetuation of the practices long condemned by the Gregorian reformers. At least one bishop, Theulf of Worcester, confessed on his deathbed in 1123 that he had bought his way into his see.[69] In spite of the legislation of English councils,

[64] *Vita* of Robert, pt. I, 11, in *Anglia Sacra*, II, 304-5.

[65] Henry of Poitou, Abbot of St. Jean d'Angely, succeeded in imposing himself on Peterborough from 1127-32 with the help of Henry I, whose relative he was. See *A-S Chron.* E for these years and especially for 1127, and also *The Peterborough Chronicle of Hugh Candious*, ed. Mellowes (1941), p. 100.

[66] According to Eadmer, *HN*, 224.

[67] On Gilbertus Universalis, see B. Smalley in *Recherches de théologie ancienne et médiévale*, VII (1935-6). On Henry of Blois, the study of L. Voss, *Heinrich von Blois* (1932), and Knowles, *Monastic Order*, 281-97.

[68] According to the unpublished chronicle of St. Edmundsbury, *B.M. Harl. 1005*, cited by Williamson, *Letters of Osbert of Clare*, 193.

[69] *GP*, 290n.

simony seems to have been rife throughout the hierarchy. Even the Primate, William of Corbeil, was accused of demanding a simoniacal payment from the Abbot-elect of St. Augustine's.[70] On the local level, the purchase of consecrated oil, while prohibited by the Council of 1125, seems to have been accepted as a commonplace.[71] As during Anselm's pontificate, Henry's apparently sincere intention to establish a celibate clergy was vitiated by the Exchequer's plan to make a profit out of the weakness of the flesh.[72] Like his brother before him, Henry kept Canterbury and other sees vacant and *in manu regis* in order to enjoy the profits of their temporalities.[73] In the pipe roll of 1130, the farms of the Bishoprics of Durham and Hereford, and the Abbey of Glastonbury, are accounted for like any other regular source of royal income.[74] Usually, as in the instances of Durham and Hereford, special royal agents were appointed to direct the farming of the see.[75]

[70] *Thorne's Chronicle, Twysden SS*, 1799.

[71] I. H. Jeayes, ed., *Descriptive Catal. of the Charters and Muniments belonging to the Marquis of Anglesey* (*Will. Salt Soc.*, 1937, no. 15), pp. 11-12: "Confirmation by Theobald, Archbishop of Canterbury . . . to the mother church of Burton, of all the liberty which that church has held from ancient times, and, which Robert, Bishop of Chester has granted to it, that is, that it should not pay any custom for consecrated oil . . . in respect of the parish of Burton. . . ." The Bishop Robert referred to is either Robert de Limesey, 1082-1121, or Robert Peche, 1121-1129.

[72] See *A-S Chron. E, s.a.* 1129: The law of the Council of 1129 against the marriage of priests and archdeacons "availed nothing. They all kept their wives by the permission of the king as they had done before." It cannot be said that the episcopate, especially the curialist bishops, set a very good example in the matter of celibacy. Roger of Salisbury lived openly with a mistress, and his son, Roger le Poer, became chancellor under Stephen (*DNB*, XVII, 106). Robert Bloet of Lincoln appointed his son Dean of the cathedral. (Henry of Huntingdon, *De contemptu*, pp. 305-6.)

[73] In 1109 Henry took into his dominium "omnia ad episcopatum quidem Cantuariensem perinentia" (*HN*, 221) and kept the see vacant for five years. Other long vacancies were at Coventry (1126-9), Ely (1131-3), and Durham (1128-33). The *ius spolii* is known to have been exercised at London after the death of Bishop Gilbert (Henry of Huntingdon, *De contemptu*, 308).

[74] Ed. J. Hunter, pp. 68, 130-1, 140.

[75] Geoffrey the chancellor was in charge both of the farms of Durham and Hereford (*Pipe Roll 1130*, 130-1, 140), although at Durham he was assisted by another royal agent (continuation of *Symeonis Historia Dunelmensis Ecclesiae*, ed. T. Arnold, *R.S.*, I, 141).

VI. The Church and the Papacy, 1109-1135

The constant attendance of many of the leading ecclesiastics at the *curia regis* must have had a harmful effect on the administration of sees and monasteries. Not only did curialist bishops like Robert Bloet of Lincoln and Roger of Salisbury constantly attend at court and follow the King about England,[76] but the archbishops of Canterbury and York were with him for long periods in Normandy.[77] Anselm of St. Saba's who eventually became Abbot of St. Edmundsbury was a royal favorite,[78] and was also in attendance on Henry at court. In one letter the Prior and convent of St. Edmundsbury implore their Abbot to return from Normandy; the monastery is in danger without him, and if one of his sheep perished, it will be no excuse to plead *"curia regis."*[79]

The close interrelationship between church and state in England meant that the greater ecclesiastics came into contact with royal administrative power in every phase of life. Not only in ecclesiastical affairs did they have cause to fear or to be grateful to the King but also in their capacities as feudal lords and magnates of the realm. No bishop could afford to displease Henry for long, for as a tenant-in-chief he might have to appeal to the royal chancery for a writ which would secure him the knight service owed him. Nigel of Ely required such a writ.[80] Without royal support, Bishop Godfrey of Bath could have neither judgement nor justice against an archdeacon who had usurped the lands of the canons of the cathedral chapter.[81]

Both as ecclesiastic and as tenant-in-chief, a bishop owed military and financial obligations to the King and his exchequer.

[76] As revealed by their very frequent attestation of royal charters. Johnson, *Reg.*, index, *s.n.*

[77] Ralph 1116-1120 (*HN*, 239-59); Thurstan 1117-1118 (*HC*, 140-50), and 1120 (*HC*, 190); William of Corbeil 1123 and 1125 (*JW*, 17-19).

[78] "deliciae regis": *Letters of Osbert*, ep. 5.

[79] Chronicle of Bury St. Edmund, *Morgan Library Holford MS*, foll. 2-3, published in part by Williamson, *Letters of Osbert*, 195.

[80] E. Miller, *The Abbey and Bishopric of Ely* (1951), p. 166, n. 1.

[81] J. Hunter, ed., *Historiala de primordiis episcopatus Somersetensis* (*Camden Soc.*, vol. 8, 1840), p. 23; *Anglia Sacra*, I, 560.

2. King's Influence on the Clergy

The bishop might find that the manifold burdens, coming at once, were so heavy that he had no recourse but to throw himself on the King's mercy, as Herbert Losinga of Norwich felt at one time that he might have to do.[82] The many and long wars of Henry's reign entailed enormous expenditures which were financed, aside from exactions from urban communities, from the *placita* and *conventiones* owed by the magnates,[83] among whom were of course the episcopate. Of £66,000 accounted for in the pipe roll of 1130, the Bishop of Ely alone was charged £1,500 for various fines and agreements.[84]

Always vulnerable in their financial obligations to the crown, the bishops and abbots found it prudent not to displease the King by an excessively zealous attitude in church reform. When the papal legate Peter came to England in 1121, Henry was able to command effectively that no church or monastery should receive him.[85] From 1114 to 1120, when Archbishop Thurstan was offending Henry by refusing profession to Canterbury and by receiving consecration from the Pope, he received no grants or privileges or lands from the King.[86] Even afterwards, Henry's grants to Thurstan are remarkably few and meagre.[87] The fate of the Archbishop of York was undoubtedly a salutary lesson for his episcopal colleagues. Also the canons of a cathedral, such as the Dean and chapter of Salisbury, were dependent upon the King as the

---

[82] *Epistolae*, ed. R. Anstruther, ep. 26.

[83] J. Prestwich, "War and Finance in the Anglo-Norman State," *TRHS*, 5th ser., IV (1954), 19-45, esp. 36.

[84] *Ibid.*, pp. 23 and 36.

[85] *HN*, 295.

[86] See W. Farrer, *Early Yorkshire Charters*, vol. I. Aside from no. 19, dated generally 1114-1135 by Farrer, the earliest royal charter to Thurstan is in 1121-2, no. 94.

[87] *Ibid.*, no. 19 (1114-35): grant of liberties in royal forest; 61 (1131-33): confirms Thurstan's grants to Fountains Abbey; 94 (1121-22): increases length of Beverley fair; 96 (1124-33): confirms Thurstan's grants to church of Beverley; 115 (1123-35): allows fair at Ripon. The King also disseized Thurstan in 1119 (*HC*, 172).

wealthiest magnate for the founding of prebends and grants of privileges and special jurisdiction.[88]

Whether it was a question of churches and ecclesiastical customs and tithes, of lands and knights, of taxation and judicial jurisdiction, or a special private privilege, the bishops required a royal writ. To take the wealthy bishopric of Lincoln as an example,[89] Henry's writ grants to Bishop Alexander license to assign the third part of the service of the knights of the see to Alexander's castle at Newark.[90] The King brings the Abbot of Peterborough and the Bishop of Lincoln into agreement in the plea that was between them touching the parish church of Peterborough.[91] A royal writ allows the Bishop to use as his private lodging the tower over the gate of Lincoln.[92] The King commands the barons, vavasours, and all the lords who hold lands within a certain wapentake to come to the Bishop's pleas.[93]

The contemporary lack of a conscious distinction between church and state operates on the most local level as well as in the relations between king and bishops. The system of proprietary churches (*Eigenkirchen*) may have been ultimately due to a deep-rooted conception in Germanic private law that possession of a piece of land implies ownership of whatever is built on that land.[94] Or it may have been simply due to the accidents of feudal history, to the patronage of churches by lay

[88] W. R. Jones and W. D. Macray, eds., *Sarum Charters and Documents* (*R.S.*), nos. 1-4.

[89] W. Foster, ed., *Registrum Antiquissimum of Lincoln* (*Lincoln Record Society*, vol. 27, 1931). On lands and knight service: nos. 18, 23, 24, 28, 29, 36, 42, 50, 51, 53, 56, 59, 70, 72. On churches and ecclesiastical customs and tithes: nos. 19, 20, 27, 33, 35, 38, 39, 40, 41, 52, 67, 68, 69, 71, 74. On taxation and judicial jurisdiction: nos. 22, 30, 32, 60. On private privileges granted to the bishop: nos. 21, 25, 26, 46, 48, 49, 51, 54a, 55.

[90] *Ibid.*, no. 51 (1123-33).

[91] *Ibid.*, no. 52 (1133-35).

[92] *Ibid.*, no. 49 (1130-33).

[93] *Ibid.*, no. 60 (1123-33).

[94] U. Stutz, *Die Eigenkirche als Element des mittelalterlich-germanischen Kirchenrechts* (1895), trans. G. Barraclough, *Medieval Germany* (1938), II, 38-46, 67-70. This essay is an introduction to Stutz's many works on the proprietary churches.

lords, and to attempts to bring all property, whether real or otherwise, under lordship.[95] At any rate, the Domesday survey shows the widespread existence of proprietary churches in England,[95a] an institution in which churches like any other property are accepted as matters of seisin. Three or four decades after Domesday, there seems to be no attenuation of this institution.[96] The King's writ gives seisin of churches as well as landed possessions.[97]

The royal writ, therefore, runs on all matters which interest a great ecclesiastic and the securing of the King's favor is alone the way to wealth and power. When Bishop Robert Bloet of Lincoln, the eminent curialist and close companion of the King,[98] can summon the King's writ on his own behalf,[99] he is one of the wealthiest men in the kingdom. His manner of life was magnificent, and his household, in which noble youths were trained, was large and splendid.[100] He made his own son Dean of Lincoln.[101] But when he displeased the King and was heavily amerced by the exchequer, he was a ruined man, and in his grief died of apoplexy.[102] The rise and fall of great English ecclesiastics in the second and third decades of the twelfth century can usually be reduced to such a simple story as this. Henry, says Orderic Vital in a famous passage,

[95] P. Imbart de la Tour, "Les paroisses rurales dans l'ancienne France," *Revue historique* (1898), vol. 67, 1ff., esp. 23-24; vol. 68, 1ff., esp. 40-42. Cf. P. Thomas, *Le droit de propriété des laïques sur les églises* (1906), 29-34.

[95a] W. Page, "Churches of the Domesday Survey," *Archaeologia*, vol. 66 (1914-15), 96ff.

[96] As is revealed in H. Böhmer, "Das Eigenkirchentum in England," *F. Liebermann Festschrift* (1921), which remains the only study of the subject. There are some valuable observations in F. Barlow, *Durham Jurisdictional Peculiars* (1950).

[97] *Reg. Ant. Lincoln*, no. 39 (1114-16): Writ of Henry I commanding Ralf de Rehart and his fellows to place the Bishop of Lincoln in seisin of two churches named.

[98] Farrer, "Itinerary" and *A-S Chron. E*, 1123: Bishop Robert died while he was accompanying the King.

[99] *Reg. Ant. Lincoln*, no. 29.

[100] See *DNB*, II, 685-6 and sources there cited.

[101] Henry of Huntingdon, *De contemptu*, 305-6.

[102] *Ibid.*, 299-300.

raised men from the dust to wealth and power in the royal administration.[103] And the King's will could crush them and return them to the dust just as easily.

Illustrative of the King's importance in the life of the higher clergy during this period is the history of the family of Belmeis, which between 1109 and 1135 provided a bishop of London and a number of canons and prebendaries of St. Paul's Cathedral. The Belmeis history consists of the successful combination of royal service and ecclesiastical office to obtain wealth and power for a family originally not of the first rank.[104] Richard de Belmeis, the founder of the family, was originally a follower of Roger de Montgomery, Earl of Shrewsbury.[105] Having served the King as Sheriff of Shropshire,[106] in 1108 he became Bishop of London. He had already founded an important Shropshire family descending from his brother,[107] and in the decades succeeding Richard's elevation to the see of London, many of his relatives became canons of St. Paul's, London. While holding their prebends from St. Paul's, many of them engaged in royal administration. The absentee cathedral dignitary, serving the King and expecting to be rewarded with promotion in the church, was becoming an accepted institution.[108]

Henry, indeed, had a long memory: special service to him, if only in a single instance, could bring a great reward. Gilbert the Universal became Bishop of London in 1128 not so much on account of his learning, but because he had served the English King faithfully as a lawyer at the papal curia.[109] Like-

---

[103] *OV*, iv, 164.

[104] For the history of the Belmeis family see Stubbs intro. to his edition of *Ralph de Diceto (R.S.)*, xxi ff., R. W. Eyton, *Antiquities of Shropshire*, ii, 193ff.; L. C. Lloyd, *The Origins of Some Anglo-Norman Families, Harl. Soc. Public.*, CIII (1951), p. 13, who summarizes the previous work on the subject.

[105] Lloyd, *op.cit.*, 68-9, 13. [106] *OV*, iv, 275.

[107] Lloyd, *op.cit.*, 13.

[108] C.N.L. Brooke, "The Composition of the Chapter of St. Paul's, 1086-1163," *Cambr. Histor. Journal*, x (1951), 111ff., esp. 120 and nn. 50, 51, 57, p. 124 and n. 71.

[109] *HC*, 215 and Smalley, *Recherches*, vii (1935), 238-9.

wise Siffrid d'Escures, Ralph's brother and Abbot of Glastonbury, became Bishop of Chichester in 1125, after having acted as a royal envoy at Rome.[110] The legate John of Crema had helped to secure the dissolution of William Clito's marriage. Hence he had a claim on Henry's gratitude and was the only legate of the period allowed to call a reform council in England.[111] Another agent in Henry's diplomatic victory over William Clito, the French abbot Henry, became for a time Abbot of Peterborough. He was also the King's kinsman.[112] Ecclesiastical offices were always ready on hand to provide for Henry's relatives. Henry of Blois, the King's nephew, became Abbot of Glastonbury and later Bishop of Winchester.[113]

In the period of Henry's reign which follows the death of Anselm there is a noticeable increase in the proportion of bishops-elect who did not come directly from the royal administration. Of the nine bishops appointed in the period 1100-1109, only one, Ralph of Rochester, the diocesan ordinary of Canterbury, was not a royal clerk or chaplain. In the remaining twenty-six years of Henry's reign, only eight of the bishops appointed, or slightly less than half the total bishops-elect, are definitely known to have come from the royal chapel and chancery.[114] The remaining appointments to the episcopate are divided equally between monks and cathedral dignitaries—five from each group. Two Austin canons were among these ten appointments to the episcopate.[115] The promotions to the

---

[110] GP, 265.

[111] Suggested by Tillmann, Legaten, 28.

[112] A-S Chron. E, s.a. 1127, where Henry of Poitou is regarded as a "principal man" in dissolving William Clito's marriage.

[113] See works cited in n. 67 above.

[114] Godfrey, Bath (1123): Anglia Sacra, I, 560, n. f., and Henry of Huntingdon, Hist. Angl., 245; Robert Peche, Chester (1121): GP, 310; Theulf, Worcester (1115): GP, 290 n.; Thurstan, York (elected 1114, consecrated 1119): HC, 129; Geoffrey Rufus, Durham (1133): contin. of Sym. of Durham, I, 141; Nigel, Ely (1133): see below, p. 298 and nn. 154-5; Robert de Capella, Hereford (1121): GP, 304; Simon, Worcester (1125): GP, 290 and JW, 18.

[115] I have included the two Austin canons among the monks, but it should be noted that "regular canons were ranked, in theory at least, not with the monks, but with the regular clergy." (J. C. Dickinson, The Origins of the

episcopate of royal clerks and chaplains are spread quite evenly
through the period: one in 1114, one in 1115, two in 1121,
one in 1123, one in 1125, two in 1133.[116] There was no change
of royal policy, therefore, in episcopal appointments within
the period 1109-1135. The change in the provenance of the
bishops-elect came after Anselm's death when Henry felt his
control over the English Church no longer threatened by a
reforming primate.

But it would be a mistake to exaggerate the significance of
the change in the composition of the episcopate. Siffrid d'Escures, an abbot, and Gilbert the Universal, a schoolman and
cathedral dignitary of Lyons, become bishops because of their
service to the King as royal envoys at Rome.[117] While Everard
of Montgomery, Bishop of Norwich, was at the time of his
election in 1121 Archdeacon of Salisbury,[118] he was also at
one time a royal clerk.[119] In fact, given the prevailing system
of absentee cathedral clergy working in the royal administration, it is not impossible that he held the two offices at the same
time. This might also be true of some other cathedral clergy
who became bishops, if more could be known about them.
While Alexander of Lincoln was Archdeacon of Salisbury in

Austin Canons, 1950, p. 201). They were so ranked at least at the time of
the election of the Primate in 1123. See below, p. 294. The two Austin
canons were William of Corbeil, Prior of St. Osyth's (Canterbury, 1123.
On him see Dickinson, *op.cit.*, ch. III, *passim*) and Robert de Bethune, Prior
of Llanthony (Hereford, 1131. On him see B. J. Parkinson, *MS. B. Litt.
thesis*, Oxford, 1951, where the vita published in *Anglia Sacra*, II, is also
newly edited). The black monks among the bishops-elect were Siffrid d'Escures, Abbot of Glastonbury (*JW*, 18. Chichester, 1125), Ernulf of Peterborough (Rochester, 1115), Henry of Blois, Abbot of Glastonbury (Winchester, 1129). The following are the cathedral dignitaries who became
bishops during the period: Gilbert the Universal, London (1128); Roger
de Clinton, Chester (1129. "archidiaconus," *JW*, 29); John, Rochester
(1125, Archdeacon of Canterbury. *HN*, 231 and 257. *JW*, 19); Everard
of Montgomery, Norwich (1121, Archdeacon of Salisbury. *GP*, 429);
Alexander, Lincoln (1123. Archdeacon of Salisbury. *DNB*, *s.n.*) I have
not been able to discover the provenance of Geoffrey de Clive (Hereford,
1115).

[116] See above, n. 114.   [117] See above, n. 109 and n. 110.
[118] *GP*, 429.   [119] *HN*, 293.

succession to Everard at the time of his appointment as bishop in 1123, he had been trained since youth for royal service and episcopal office by his uncle, Roger of Salisbury.[120]

The change in the composition of the episcopate in this period was thus caused not so much by a decrease in Henry's custom of rewarding his administrators with bishoprics, as by an increase in the tendency to combine the holding of royal and ecclesiastical offices. Royal administrators who became bishops must be looked for not only among the royal clerks and chaplains, but also among abbots and cathedral dignitaries who had served the King at one time or another. From another point of view, the increasing tendency to combine ecclesiastical office and royal service is revealed by Geoffrey Rufus' retention of his chancellorship after he became Bishop of Durham in 1133, the first member of the English episcopate since the Conquest to do so.[121]

As far as future developments are concerned, the most significant change in the composition of the English episcopate in the latter part of the reign of Henry I was the appointment to it of two men trained in the French schools, Robert of Hereford and Gilbert of London.[122] Henceforth a new group makes its appearance among the English higher clergy, the products of the French schools. The education provided by these schools was already considered an excellent start for an ecclesiastical career. From 1118 to 1130 John of Salisbury was studying at Paris and in 1135 Thomas Becket went there.[123] In reference to the closing years of Henry's reign, it is impossible to speak, as H. Böhmer does,[124] of the existence of a

---

[120] Henry of Huntingdon, *Hist. Angl.*, 280.

[121] G. H. White, *TRHS*, 4th ser., xxx (1941), 131, 135.

[122] For Robert, see *Vita* in *Angl. Sacra*, I, 4. For Gilbert, see Smalley in *Recherches*, VII. Alexander of Lincoln and Nigel of Ely also studied for a short time at Laon (*MPL* 156, col. 983), but they can scarcely be regarded as schoolmen.

[123] L. Maître, *Les Écoles Épiscopales et Monastiques* (1924), 97.

[124] H. Böhmer, *Kirche und Staat*, 307-8: "Einige der angesehensten Bischöfe, wie Heinrich von Winchester, Robert von Hereford, Thurstan von York, waren ihr [i.e. the papal curia] schon so ergeben, dass man sie direkt

"Gregorian" party among the English episcopate. There is no contemporary evidence that any English bishop was critical of Henry's control over the church.[124a] But the education of some of the coming generation of English ecclesiastics at Paris in these years was bringing future leaders of the English Church into close contact with reform ideas on the Continent.

The inevitable competition between the regular and secular clergy for promotion to the episcopate developed, in the second and third decades of the century, into a vocal and acrimonious controversy. The secular clergy claimed that an excessive number of monks had been made bishops, especially primates. The monks, in defending the aspersions cast upon their order, turned the controversy, in part, into a dispute over the right of free election of bishops by the cathedral chapters.

Although one of Anselm's monastic disciples, Bishop Ralph d'Escures of Rochester, was chosen as Archbishop of Canterbury in 1114, already on this occasion the bishops and some of the magnates, undoubtedly headed by Robert of Meulan, pressed unsuccessfully for an archbishop *"de ordine clericali aut clericum aliquem de capella regis."*[125] In 1123, however, Henry allowed the *totum regnum* to choose the new archbishop, and led by Roger of Salisbury, the secular clergy succeeded in obtaining the election of an Austin canon, William of Corbeil.[126] Regular canons were ranked not with the monks but with the secular clergy.[127] The monks bewailed the aban-

---

als Gregorianer bezeichnen kann." I do not believe that there is any evidence to support this interpretation, nor does Böhmer give any.

[124a] A. L. Poole (*Domesday Book to Magna Carta*, 182, n. 4) cites the complaints which the bishops made at the beginning of Stephen's reign about the oppression of the church by Henry I (*Gesta Stephani, R.S.,* p. 17). I doubt that these complaints can be taken at their face value and regarded as the attitude of the episcopate during Henry's reign. There is no contemporary evidence from the period 1109-1135 to indicate episcopal opposition to Henry's authority over the English Church.

[125] *HN,* 222.

[126] *A-S Chron. E, s.a.* 1123.

[127] Dickinson, *Austin Canons,* 201.

doning of an ancient custom because of the "jealousy of clerks,"[128] and the monks of Canterbury at first feared William "since he was a clerk."[129] The alignment at Rockingham in 1095 was repeated at the election of 1123 when the lay magnates supported the monks against the majority of the bishops, the magnates' chief competitors for power and wealth.[130] An attack of "malignant men" from the ranks of the secular clergy upon the monastic order was also involved in the Worcester election of 1125, resulting again in the defeat of the monks and the appointment of a secular clerk as bishop.[131]

During the last two decades of Henry's reign, cathedral canons launched a conscious propaganda attack upon the monastic life.[132] A poem by a cathedral dignitary of York pointing out the corruptions of the Cluniacs has survived.[133] An appeal was made to Bishop Herbert Losinga to assume the role of Anselm as defender of the regular clergy and to write a tract on behalf of the monastic life.[134] Herbert had been both a royal clerk and a monk in his time, and in the current dispute he preferred to remain impartial. He politely declined the invitation extended him and did not refrain from stating his opinion that the monks had little to complain about.[135] A cathedral dignitary of Salisbury, on the other hand,

---

[128] OV, IV, 431.   [129] GP, 146.

[130] A-S Chron. E, s.a. 1123: "The monks and earls and thegns, nearly all that were there, opposed him" (William).

[131] Eadmer, letter to monks of Worcester, in Anglia Sacra, II, 238.

[132] Epis. Herbert Losinga, ed. Anstruther, ep. LIX, p. 103 (letter of Richard, Abbot of Ely [?] to Herbert): "Nonnulli perversae mentis canonicae feritatis oblatrantes, monachicae invidentes religioni. . . ." I take the "canonicae" to be probably cathedral canons, but Goulburn and Symonds, Herb. Los., I, 262, n.s., assume regular canons are meant. Their interpretation may possibly be the correct one. See Ph. Schmitz, "Le Monachisme Bénédictin au XIIe Siècle," in S. Bernardo, Pub. d. Un. Cattolica del S. Cuore, n.s. vol. XLVI (1954), p. 9: "Une autre querelle caractérise encore le XIIe siècle monastique, celle qu'il fallut soutenir avec les chanoines réguliers, nouvellement fondés."

[133] A poem by Hugh the Cantor, in Cotton, Vitellius A.XII, f. 135.

[134] Epis. Herb. Los., LIX, p. 104.

[135] Ibid., ep. LX, p. 106ff. It would be wrong to imply that all of the secular clergy were hostile to the monks. Thurstan's friendship with the

felt it necessary to write a treatise defending his own order.[136] In the course of this controversy, the disputants drew sharp distinctions between various orders in society. *Reges, laici, sacerdotes, canonici, monachi* are the orders referred to in the appeal to Bishop Herbert.[137] One of the canons of the Council of 1127 also envisages several different orders.[138] The sharp distinction within the ranks of the English clergy, reflected in this polemical literature, was to some extent a legacy of Anselm's pontificate. For the majority of Anselm's supporters in his attempts at church reform had come from the regular clergy, while the Archbishop's most vehement opponents had been his episcopal colleagues.

The struggle between the monks and secular clergy was in the 1120's resolved into a dispute over the reintroduction of the Feast of the Conception of the Virgin.[139] On the one side, favoring the Feast, were the younger Anselm, Abbot of St. Edmundsbury since 1121,[140] Eadmer,[141] Osbert of Clare, Prior of Westminster, who was responsible for the celebra-

---

regular clergy of his province and, in particular, his support of the early Cistercian foundations are well known (see his letter to William of Corbeil on behalf of the Cistercians in J. S. Walbran, *Memorials of Fountains Abbey*, Surtees Soc., 1863, p. 11ff.; and in general, Knowles, *Monastic Order*, 230-9). Everard of Montgomery, Bishop of Norwich, 1121-1145 (Herbert Losinga's successor) left a tradition at Norwich of friendship with the monks there (*First Register of Norwich Cathedral Priory*, ed. Saunders, *Norwich Rec. Soc.*, XI, 1939, p. 56).
[136] Godwin, precentor of Salisbury Cathedral, *MS. Bodl. Digby 96. Meditaciones Godwini Cantoris Salesberie, ad Rainilvam Reclusam*. Dated by K. Edwards as "about 1140," (*The English Secular Cathedrals in the Middle Ages*, 1949, p. 5).
[137] *Epist. Herb. Los.*, ep. LIX, p. 103.
[138] Canon 1; *JW*, 23.
[139] E. Bishop, *Liturgica Historica* (1918), 242-50; Gasquet and Bishop, *The Bosworth Psalter* (1908), 43-53; H. Thurston in *The Month* (1904), 1-16; R. W. Southern, *Making of the Middle Ages*, 251, have discussed the history of the Feast and Bishop deals fully with the controversy over it.
[140] *Letters of Osbert of Clare*, ep. 7, p. 65, where Anselm's zeal for the Feast is assumed. See also Williamson in *ibid.*, pp. 191-200, and works of Thurston and Southern cited in n. 139.
[141] See his treatise on the Feast of the Conception of the Virgin, *MPL* 159, col. 301ff.

tion of the Feast at Westminster in 1127 or 1128,[142] and the monks generally, who were in closer touch with the English tradition than the more cosmopolitan bishops. On the other side were the secular clergy and especially the great bishops, former royal clerks, who were now, in Eadmer's description, pre-eminent in church and state, and the wealthy ones of the land. Imbued with the new learning, they prided themselves on their position of authority and were contemptuous of "the poor in spirit," "the simple folk."[143] The leading opponents of the Feast were apparently Roger of Salisbury and Bernard of St. David's, who attempted to prevent its celebration, and claimed that it was forbidden by a church council.[144]

This dispute was terminated only by royal intervention on the side of the monks. Perhaps because of his personal esteem for the younger Anselm,[145] perhaps because his first wife Mathilda had been devoted to the Virgin,[146] perhaps because he was becoming generally more sympathetic to the monastic reformers,[147] Henry sided with the advocates of the Feast and ordered Abbot Hugh to celebrate it at Reading.[148] The Feast was legitimized by the Council of 1129.[149] Even in this dispute between the regular and secular clergy over a doctrinal matter, the King's decision was the important and final one.

Roger of Salisbury assumed the role of leader of the secular clergy in their controversy with the monks. He frustrated the regular clergy at the election of the primate in 1123 and attempted to prevent the celebration of the Feast of the Conception of the Virgin. Roger was par excellence the humble Norman priest who rose through the King's service to become *"secundus a rege."*[150] Although almost illiterate he was an as-

---

[142] *Letters of Osbert*, ep. 7 and Williamson's note, p. 201.

[143] *MPL* 159, coll. 301-3.   [144] *Osbert*, ep. 7, p. 65.

[145] Williamson, *Letters of Osbert*, 193-4.

[146] As is revealed in Herbert Losinga's letter to the Queen. *Epis. Herb. Los.*, ep. xxv.

[147] See below, notes 231-234.

[148] *Letters of Osbert*, ep. 7, p. 67.   [149] *JW*, 29.

[150] Henry of Huntingdon, *Hist. Angl.*, 245. The best study is still C. L. Kingsford in *DNB*, XVII, 103-106. The earlier work of Boivin-Champeaux

tute and shrewd man. From royal steward he rose to be chancellor, Bishop of Salisbury, and finally chief justiciar and head of the administration.[151] He was the constant companion of the King when Henry was in England, and in the 1120's was responsible for the administration of the country while the King was absent across the Channel.[152] Roger was able to found a dynasty of great administrative ecclesiastics. He brought up his nephews Alexander and Nigel with care and secured for them the bishoprics of Lincoln and Ely. Alexander became famous for the magnificent manner with which he wasted the revenues of his wealthy see.[153] Nigel served in the exchequer, and although not Treasurer before the death of Henry I,[154] became the reorganizer of the exchequer after the civil war.[155] Roger's illegitimate son, Roger le Poer, became chancellor during Stephen's reign.[156]

Until the early 1120's, the Bishop of Salisbury had strong rivals both in church and state. But after the deaths of Robert of Meulan in 1118, and of Robert Bloet, the other great curialist bishop of the period, in 1123,[156a] Roger's influence over

---

(*Roger Le Grand*, 1878) is of no value. The few pages devoted to Roger by K. Norgate add nothing to previous knowledge. The account given of him by A. L. Poole, *Domesday Book to Magna Carta*, is meagre. Roger's place in the royal administration is discussed by Tout, *Administrative History*, I, 87ff. and by G. H. White, "Financial Administration under Henry I," *TRHS*, 4th ser., VIII (1925), esp. p. 68.

[151] *DNB*, XVII, 103-4 and sources there cited; White, *op.cit.*, p. 68.

[152] William of Malmesbury, *GR*, II, 484. See Johnson, *Reg.*, index, for his very frequent attestation of charters. William of Malmesbury also points out that Roger was "pontifex magnanimus, et nullis unquam parcens sumptibus, dum quae facienda proponeret, aedificia praesertim, consummaret" (*GR, loc.cit.*).

[153] See the poem in praise of Alexander's "munificence" by Henry of Huntingdon, *Hist. Angl.*, 246. Alexander seems to have been something of a literary patron. Both Geoffrey of Monmouth's *History of Britain* and Henry of Huntingdon's *Historia Anglorum* were dedicated to him. Both Henry and Geoffrey were cathedral dignitaries of Lincoln.

[154] According to White, *op.cit.*, p. 70.

[155] C. Johnson, ed., *Dialogus de Scaccario* (1950), p. 50.

[156] *DNB*, XVII, 106.

[156a] On Robert Bloet, see above, p. 289: On Robert of Meulan and his influence on the King, see *HN, passim*; Henry of Huntingdon, *De con-*

the King was unchallenged. Henry appointed bishops "out of love" for Roger,[157] and made several grants to the Church of Sarum on behalf of its bishop.[158] As long as Ralph of Canterbury lived, Roger's eminence within the episcopate was still challenged and his attempt to officiate at Henry's second marriage in 1121 was successfully opposed by the Primate.[159] But the new Primate chosen in 1123, partly due to Roger's influence, was an inconspicuous nonentity,[160] and henceforth the Bishop of Salisbury dominated the episcopate as well as the royal administration. Even in the previous decade, Herbert Losinga had written to Roger as *"ovis Norwicensis"* to *"pastor Salisberiensis,"* begging him to alleviate the financial burdens which the exchequer had placed upon the see of Norwich.[161] Herbert had been very eager to be in the good graces of his episcopal colleague.[162] In the 1120's Roger's eminence within the episcopate was even more marked. At Henry's Christmas court of 1126, when the magnates swore allegiance to Mathilda, it was Roger who was foremost in recommending the oath.[163] Again it was Roger, along with his nephew Alexander of Lincoln, and not the Primate, who helped the monks of Peterborough to get rid of the alien abbot the King had imposed upon them.[164]

The substitution of Bishop Roger for Count Robert of Meulan as Henry's chief counsellor undoubtedly encouraged

---

temptu, 306; *GR*, II, 483. William says of Robert's influence on Henry that "habebaturque eius consilium quasi quis divinum consuluisset sacrarium."

[157] Appointments of Alexander to Lincoln and Godfrey to Bath in 1123. *A-S Chron. E, s.a.*

[158] W. R. Jones, ed., *Register of St. Osmund* (R.S., 1883), I, 200-202, 206, 208. Jones and Macray, *Sarum Charters*, no. 6.

[159] *HN*, 292.

[160] Henry of Huntingdon, *De contemptu*, 314: ". . . Willelmus, cuius laudes dici nequeunt quia non sunt." Cf. view of William in *HC*, 219: he was a good and religious canon who was spoiled by being raised to high office.

[161] *Epis. Herb. Los.*, XXI.

[162] *Ibid.*, ep. XXV: Herbert asks the Queen to speak well of him to Roger.

[163] *JW*, 26.

[164] *A-S Chron. E, s.a.* 1132.

Henry to adopt a more conciliatory policy towards the English Church, since Robert had been the implacable enemy of the higher clergy.[165] Although the easing of tension in church-state relations in England became most pronounced in the 1120's when Pope and King reached an understanding, it was already apparent in the previous decade. The controversies of Anselm's pontificate did not settle the fundamental question on the relative power of papal *auctoritas* and royal *imperium* over the English Church. But for the rest of Henry's reign, this question did not disturb relations between church and state, because with one exception, that of Thurstan of York, the great ecclesiastics supported the King against papal interference in England.

3. ROME, CANTERBURY, AND YORK, 1109-C.1124

THE case of Archbishop Thurstan of York, the only English ecclesiastic in this period who dared to appeal to Rome over the King's objection, was the outgrowth of the long-standing dispute between the two English metropolitans over primatial authority. Anglo-papal relations between 1109 and about 1124 are inextricably involved with this dispute between Canterbury and York.

In 1109, in accordance with Anselm's views made known to them shortly before his death, the bishops demanded that Thomas II, Archbishop-elect of York, should make a profession of obedience to the see of Canterbury.[166] As was customary in England, such an important issue was left to be settled in the royal court. Count Robert happily envisaged the

---

[165] During the investiture controversy Robert had been Anselm's bitterest opponent, and had been excommunicated by Paschal II. For further evidence of Robert's ecclesiastical policy, see above, n. 45, and below, n. 167, and Henry of Huntingdon, *De Contemptu*, 306-7.

[166] *HN*, 206. The Canterbury-York dispute is here discussed only from the point of view of church-state relations. For a full account, see M. Dueball, *Der Suprematstreit* (*Ebering's Hist. Stud.* 184, 1929) whose value, however, is somewhat diminished by a lack of adequate criticism of the sources.

prospect of a dispute between the King and the episcopate.[167]
But Henry, after wavering, came out on the side of the bishops, much to their relief.[168] He demanded that Thomas should
make his profession of obedience in accordance with the authority and privileges of the apostolic see and the customs of the
kingdom.[169] Faced with the united opposition of "pontiff, king,
the holy orders of the kingdom, and the magnates,"[170] the
Archbishop of York surrendered. Thomas' profession of obedience to Canterbury was written down in the King's presence
and secured with the royal seal.[171] The papal legate Cardinal
Ulric, *"audito rege curiaeque regis consilio,"*[172] gave the pall,
with which he had come to England, to the new Archbishop
of York, and quietly left the kingdom. But the *salvo* clause
of Thomas' profession of obedience to Canterbury clearly reveals the dual loyalty of the English episcopate, which had
so much disturbed church-state relations during Anselm's pontificate. Thomas stated that he owed allegiance to his lord
King and obedience to the holy Roman Church.[172a]

For five years after Anselm's death, Paschal II was too concerned with the German investiture controversy to attempt
to press claims of papal jurisdiction over the English Church.[173]
But after Ralph's election as Primate in 1114, Paschal again
asserted these claims in Gregorian terms. The envoys sent to
Rome to obtain the pallium for Ralph were coldly received at
Rome, and it was perhaps only the intercession of Anselm of
St. Saba's with the Pope which saved the *dignitas regni Anglorum.*[174]

Anselm brought with him to England in 1115 letters from
Paschal to the monks of Christ Church and to the King which

---

[167] *HN,* 208.   [168] *HC,* 114, 119, 121.   [169] *HN,* 209.
[170] *HN,* 209.   [171] *HN,* 211.

[172] *HN,* 210. Henry had requested that a legate be sent to England to
help settle the dispute, according to *HC,* 118.

[172a] *HN,* 210.

[173] Paschal was also undoubtedly wary of making Henry I the ally of
his son-in-law, Henry V, in the latter's war against the Hildebrandine
papacy.

[174] *HN,* 228.

complained that bishops, such as Ralph, were being trans-
lated to other sees in England without the Pope's consent, or
even without his knowledge, that papal legates were not being
admitted into England, except by Henry's permission, and
that no appeals were brought from England to the papal
curia.[175] Christ had given to Peter and Paul the rule over his
disciples throughout the world and especially in Europe. How
could the vicar of Peter obey Christ's command to Peter,
"feed my sheep," when the Pope neither knew, saw, nor heard
from the English bishops?[176] Paschal continued to make these
claims upon the English Church for the rest of his pontificate. In 1116 he demanded that the episcopate and abbots
should receive his legate Anselm and pay Peter's Pence.[177]

Before the new Primate Ralph, in 1115, took the pallium
from the altar where it had been placed by the legate Anselm,
he first professed "fidelity and canonical obedience to the Roman pontiff."[178] In view of the dual loyalty of the English
episcopate, and the claims over the English Church which
Paschal was again asserting, the way was open for a repetition
of the controversies and confusions of Anselm's pontificate.
This did not occur, however, for two reasons. The papacy was
too weak in power and prestige to assert effectively its claims.
Secondly, the Primate supported the King in opposing Paschal's demands.

Until the Concordat of Worms in 1122, the continued existence of the Hildebrandine papacy was seriously threatened
by imperial armies and anti-popes. Any demands which Pas-
cal II or his successors might make upon the English Church
were effectively mitigated by the *"controversia quae inter ecclesiam et regnum est"*[179] which absorbed almost all the ener-
gies and attention of the papal curia elsewhere. When Ralph
did finally go to Rome in 1117 to see Paschal, he found that
the Pope had fled from the advancing imperial army to Bene-

---

[175] J-L, 6547. *HN*, 231-3.   [176] *HN*, 232.
[177] *HN*, 244-6; J-L, 6525.   [178] *HN*, 230.
[179] Letter of Gelasius II to the faithful "per Gallium": *HN*, 247.

vento.[180] A letter was received in England in 1118 from Gelasius II begging for support against the imperial anti-pope.[181] In 1119 there was even doubt in England as to who was the rightful pope.[182] The unseemly wars between popes and anti-popes could not but lower papal prestige in England, especially when the issues involved did not appeal to the sympathy of English ecclesiastics. Eadmer either ignored or did not recognize the fact that Pope and Emperor were in conflict over the same question, that of lay investiture, which had divided Anselm and Henry I.[183] In general, the second and third decades of the twelfth century see the beginning in England of cynical attitudes towards papal aims and methods. William of Malmesbury believed that the unsuccessful legates of the second decade of the century made great profits from their offices.[184] The Peterborough chronicler asserted that gold and silver were very influential at Rome.[185] Henry of Huntingdon enjoyed repeating a scandalous story about a papal legate.[186]

In rejecting effective papal jurisdiction over the English Church, Henry was supported and even encouraged by the Primate. Ralph d'Escures had become Abbot of Séez in 1089, and was known in Normandy for his learning, eloquence, and jocularity. Forced to flee in 1103 from the depredations of Robert of Bellême, he came to England and was kindly received by Henry.[187] In England, Ralph became a member of the circle of Anselm's monastic disciples,[188] and gained the friendship of Gundulf, whom he succeeded at Rochester in

---

[180] *HN*, 242.   [181] *HN*, 247.   [182] *HN*, 249.

[183] He merely refers to the "discordia" between Pope and Emperor. *HN*, 242.

[184] *GP*, 128.   [185] *A-S Chron. E, s.a.* 1123.

[186] Abbot John of Crema (*Hist. Angl.*, 246): ". . . Cum igitur in concilio severissime de uxoribus sacerdotum tractasset . . . cum meretrice post vesperam interceptus est." But as A. L. Poole (*op.cit.*, 183, n. 2) points out, Gilbert Foliot had a high opinion of John (Robertson, *Becket*, v, 539).

[187] *Gallia Christiana*, XI, col. 718-19.

[188] R. W. Southern, "St. Anselm and His English Pupils," *Medieval and Renaissance Studies*, I (1941), 3ff., esp. 24-29; A. Wilmart in *Archives*, II (1927), 21-22.

1108.[189] As diocesan ordinary of Canterbury, he administered the see during the five years' vacancy after Anselm's death.[190] Although he was certainly not at this time a curialist bishop,[191] the King must have come to know him well while he was administering the archiepiscopal see, and found that Ralph was a man given to moderation and compromise. Hence Henry's assent was easily obtained for Ralph's election as primate in 1114.[192]

Ralph was anything but a Gregorian. On church-state relations he seems to have held quite different views from his teacher Anselm. He felt that he could make up his own mind on these matters and that he was not bound to obey papal decrees. In reply to Paschal's demands Henry maintained that entry of a papal legate into England violated English custom and royal privileges.[193] In 1116 he detained Anselm of St. Saba's in Normandy,[194] and in 1121, after magnificently receiving the legate Peter, he politely bowed him out of the country.[195] Ralph not only supported Henry in this policy, but even suggested to Henry that he should claim for England freedom from effective papal jurisdiction. As soon as Anselm appeared in Normandy in 1116, intending to cross over to England, Ralph went to the King and informed him of "the ancient custom and liberty of the kingdom."[196] He offered to go to Rome in order "to demolish these innovations."[197] In 1121 he was probably one of those who counselled the King on how to deal with the legate Peter.[198] It might be argued on Ralph's behalf that his hostility to papal legates was founded on the precedent of Archbishop Anselm's similar attitude. But Anselm had only become embittered against the

---

[189] *MPL* 159, col. 833; *OV*, III, 309.   [190] *HN*, 221-22.

[191] Between 1109 and 1114 Ralph attested only two royal charters (Farrer, "Itinerary," nos. 230 and 260) and the first of these was on the occasion of the erection of Ely into an episcopal see in 1109, when the whole episcopate was present.

[192] *HN*, 222-23 for Ralph's election in preference to the royal candidate Abbot Faricius of Abingdon, and Henry's assent.

[193] *HN*, 239 and 295.   [194] *HN*, 239.   [195] *HN*, 296.
[196] *HN*, 239.   [197] *HN*, 239.   [198] *HN*, 295.

legates because of their secret negotiations with William II and their surprising concessions to that King. It is impossible to find any such extenuating circumstances for Ralph's hostility to papal legates.

Furthermore, there are several other incidents which indicate Ralph's distinct lack of enthusiasm for the reforming papacy. Ralph generally seems to have preferred the company of king and emperor to that of pope and legate. He was absent from his see and with the King for four years (1116-1120) in Normandy.[199] When he went to Rome, in 1117, he pleaded illness for not going further to meet Paschal at Benevento. But he did spend eight days with Henry V in his camp near Rome, with the Emperor, that is, who had just expelled Paschal from the apostolic see and set up an anti-pope.[200] Ralph's companion on his trip to Rome and his envoy to Paschal at Benevento was none other than Herbert Losinga, who sixteen years previously had been Henry's representative at Rome.[201] King and Primate were in perfect accord. Ralph now had no difficulty cooperating with the curialist bishops.[202]

After Calixtus II's support of Archbishop Thurstan of York in his controversy with Canterbury, Ralph's sympathies with papal policy, if there were any to start with, no doubt greatly decreased. Henceforth his sole interest was the securing of the privileges of Canterbury, real and supposed. He had a search made at Christ Church, Canterbury, for evidences bearing upon the rights of his see.[203] He set forth the papal privileges to Canterbury, several of them forged, in a long complaining letter to Calixtus in 1119,[204] and had these privileges and professions of new bishops to Canterbury collected together in a

---

[199] *HN*, 239-259. See especially Ralph's letter to the monks of Christ Church during his absence (*HN*, 250).

[200] *HN*, 242-3.   [201] *HN*, 241-2.

[202] The curialist bishops helped him to consecrate bishops-elect. *HN*, 230, 260, 291, 294, 298.

[203] *HN*, 260. It is possible that some of the Canterbury forgeries, which Böhmer attributed to Lanfranc, really date from this occasion.

[204] Raine, *Docts.*, II, 228ff.

single manuscript in the following year.[205] When the legate
Peter appeared at Canterbury in 1121, Ralph again lodged a
complaint against the harm which Calixtus had done to his
see.[206]

As long as King and Primate were unanimous in rejecting
effective papal jurisdiction over the English Church, the controversy of Anselm's pontificate could not reoccur. But in view
of the papal claims, the way was always open for an English
ecclesiastic to appeal to Rome when he found royal policy detri-
mental to his interests. The dispute over Thomas' profession
of obedience to Canterbury in 1109 had once more revealed the
two claims upon the loyalty of the English prelates. His successor Thurstan, a former royal clerk and a particular favorite
of Rufus and Henry,[207] also refused to make the required profession of obedience, and successfully played off Pope against
King. In 1116, as soon as it became apparent that the new Primate would insist on his profession, Thurstan sent envoys to
Rome to ask Paschal to absolve him from the necessity of declaring obedience to Canterbury.[208] Then for five years Thurstan and Ralph attempted to settle the issue by appealing, now
to the King, now to the Pope. Henry and the papacy saw in the
dispute the question of ultimate supremacy over the English
Church, and each made use of the various appeals by the two
archbishops to them, as occasions for asserting their respective
authorities.

In 1116 and 1117 Thurstan, Ralph, and the canons of York
all appealed to Paschal for a papal decision to settle the dis-

---

[205] *B.M. MS. Cotton Cleopatra E. I*, ff. 16-31, 38-55. For dating and full
discussion see *New Paleographical Soc.*, 1st. s., I (1903); intro. to plates 60-
62. During William of Corbeil's pontificate, the Canterbury scriptorium
continued to collect the privileges granted, or at least claimed for, the see.
Ralph's letter to Calixtus and Honorius II's confirmation of the privileges of
Canterbury were added to a copy of Lanfranc's collection. (*B.M. Claudius
E.V*, f. 249 and f. 255). It would seem, therefore, that T. S. R. Boase is
in error when he dates this MS 1114-22 (*English Art*, 1100-1216 [1953],
p. 42).
[206] *HN*, 296.
[207] *DNB*, *s.n.*; *HC*, 129.
[208] *HN*, 238.

pute between Canterbury and York.[209] For the first time since Anselm's death an opportunity was provided for papal intervention in the affairs of the English Church. Paschal wrote to Henry that he would settle the dispute between the two archbishops "in our presence."[210] The King, busy with his Continental wars, was willing to comply, but Paschal died early in 1118, before he could summon Ralph and Thurstan to Rome.[211] When his successor, Gelasius II, was in Burgundy in the same year, Ralph sent envoys to him, and Thurstan left England with the intention of appealing to the Pope personally, but was detained at Rouen by Henry.[212]

It was inevitable that in a jurisdictional dispute between the two archbishops an appeal should have been made to Rome. Ralph had first relied only on the King's power to force Thurstan into submission, but from 1119 he depended as well on the "authority and privileges of the Roman Pontiffs."[213] In the 1120's Thurstan was also provided with papal confirmations of his metropolitan rights. These freed the Archbishop of York from necessity of making profession of obedience to Canterbury, and made the Scot bishops the suffragans of York. Possibly these papal privileges went so far as to allow the Archbishop of York the right to carry his cross before him at all times and gave him also the right to crown the King.[214]

---

[209] HC, 134; HN, 243-4. HN and HC naturally differ on some details of the controversy. According to HN, 238, when Henry insisted on Thurstan's submission, the Archbishop resigned his see, but subsequently regretted his hasty action and went to Henry in Normandy and asked to be "re-invested." According to HC, 140, the King refused to accept Thurstan's resignation.

[210] HN, 244.   [211] HN, 244.

[212] HC, 150-53; HN, 248-49.   [213] HN, 260-61.

[214] The important papal privileges confirming the metropolitan rights of York are J-L, 6831=Raine, Docts., III, no. 23 (Calixtus II, 1120); J-L, 7226 & 7227 = Raine, III, no. 33 (Honorius II, 1125); and Innocent II's confirmation of the previous privileges in 1131 (PU, II, no. 13). The provisions about the Archbishop's cross and right of crowning the King would seem to make these documents suspect, and J-L in a note to 6831 mark that document "textus interpolatus." But Holtzmann in his note to PU, II, no. 13 appears to accept them as genuine. The documents are preserved in Hugh the Cantor's History of the Archbishops of York and

Once more "royal will" and "apostolic authority" clashed.[215] Neither for the loss of his crown nor under threat of excommunication, Henry asserted, would he abandon his demand that Thurstan should make his profession of obedience to the Primate.[216] He could not accept papal absolution from his oath to assure Thurstan's profession because that would be contrary to "royal honesty."[217] Hence he could not allow Thurstan to return to his see nor receive him as his friend until the Archbishop had made his profession of obedience.[218] Calixtus II was Henry's kinsman. Against the protests of Louis VI at the Council of Rheims in 1119, he subsequently declared that he approved of Henry's actions in Normandy.[219] Nevertheless, he saw clearly that it would be advantageous to papal policy if he supported Thurstan. He consecrated the Archbishop of York at the Council of Rheims and informed Henry that he would not confirm to him the customs of the Conqueror until he took back Thurstan into his friendship.[220]

The dispute between Ralph and Thurstan was never really settled. After the disaster of the White Ship, Henry required the unanimous support of the higher clergy in order to secure the throne for his daughter.[220a] While he dismissed Thurstan from his court in disgrace,[221] the King allowed him to take possession of his see without making a profession of obedience to Canterbury.[222] Nevertheless, Thurstan's recalcitrance had

---

in the fourteenth century *Reg. Magnum Album of York*, which are of course partisan sources. A careful study of the genuineness of the York documents is needed. For the papal letters making Thurstan the metropolitan of the Scot bishops, see J-L, 6785, 6787, 6943, 6944, 6945, 6976, 6982, 7204, 7224, 7225, 7514, 7515, 7650.

[215] *HN*, 254 and 256.   [216] *HN*, 256.
[217] *HN*, 258.   [218] *HN*, 258-9.
[219] *OV*, IV, 398-9. See also A. L. Poole, *op.cit.*, 124-5.
[220] *HN*, 258; *HC*, 185-6.
[220a] The account given by Hugh the Cantor suggests two other reasons for Henry's partial reconciliation with the Archbishop of York. Thurstan was the close friend of Countess Adela of Blois, Henry's sister (*HC*, 183-4) and he was very helpful to Henry in negotiating peace with Louis of France in 1120 (*HC*, 188).
[221] According to *JW*, 22 (1126).   [222] *HC*, 196-7; *HN*, 291-2.

shown how far a single bishop could go in opposing the King, as long as he had papal support. When Thurstan violated his promise to Henry and accepted consecration from Calixtus at Rheims, it was rumored in England that he had done so with tacit royal consent, such was the surprise at his audacity.[223] Thurstan had demonstrated a fundamental weakness in royal control over the English Church, no matter how imposing and effective it remained in this period.

4. DECLINE OF THE GREGORIAN REFORM MOVEMENT AND THE TRIUMPH OF HENRY I, C.1124-1135

HENRY I was fortunate in that the last two decades of his reign coincided with a change in the attitudes and aims of the leaders of the Western Church, affecting eventually even the papal curia. This change, which only slowly became evident amid the confusion of the latter stages of the investiture controversies, consisted of the decline of the Gregorian reform movement, for all practical purposes, and precluded any strong challenge to Henry's authority over the English Church.

By the middle of the second decade of the twelfth century, the Gregorian reform movement had spent its force even at its vital center, the papacy, but in the life and writings of St. Bernard, the Gregorian doctrines of the freedom of the church under papal authority and the moral reform of the church were revivified.[224] Due to his personal influence, enthusiasm for Gregorian ideas may seem greater in the 1120's and 1130's than in fact it was. Certainly among the theorists of the period, the revolution in theories of church-state relations which Humbert and Hildebrand had brought about, was not challenged.[225] But if the period is surveyed at a distance, and too

---

[223] *HN*, 257.

[224] A. Fliche, "L'influence de Grégoire VII et des idées grégoriennes sur la pensée de Saint Bernard," in *Saint Bernard et son temps* (1924), I, 138ff. See also Commission d'Hist. de St. Ber., *Bernard de Clairvaux* (1953), ch. XI.

[225] For the history of Gregorian doctrine in the twelfth century, see G. B.

much significance is not attributed to the activities of St. Bernard, which were certainly not those of a typical Cistercian monk,[226] it can be seen that a conservative, monastic reaction had set in against Gregorian ideas.

Gregory VII's attempt to bring the Church into the world and to set up a papal monarchy had been violently resisted by the vested interests of the old order, not only by laymen but also by many ecclesiastics who adhered to the early medieval dualism between the world and the monastery. The Hildebrandine papacy brought to the Church not peace but a sword. Hence many of the best spirits of the second and third decades of the twelfth century, like the Englishman Stephen Harding, the third Abbot of Citeaux and the author of the *Carta Caritatis*,[227] again turned from the world and sought their peace with God outside the world in the many new religious orders.[228] Through the emergence of these new monastic orders, the Gregorian doctrine of a unified Christian world-system (*"Christianitas"*) was rejected, incidentally, and tacitly rather than consciously, in favor of a return to early medieval dualism in which the men of God seek their own salvation apart from the world and leave the government of the world to laymen. This was, in a sense, a return to the view of church-state relations held by the Cluniacs, who had always been rather cool towards Gregorian doctrines. Henry of Huntingdon, more influenced by Gregorian attitudes than perhaps he

---

Ladner, "The concepts of 'ecclesia' and 'Christianitas' and their relation to the idea of papal 'plenitudo potestatis' from Gregory VII to Boniface VIII," *Miscellanea Historiae Pontificiae*, XVIII (1954), 49ff.; and P. E. Schramm, "Sacerdotium und Regnum im Austausch ihrer Vorrechte," *Studi Gregoriani*, II (1947), 408ff.

[226] Stated most strongly by E. Bishop in *Downside Review*, LII (1934), 221.

[227] On Stephen Harding, see Knowles, *Monastic Order*, 199-200.

[228] See the Cistercián history of *Saint Bernard de Clairvaux* (1953), p. 188: "On pourrait même dire qu'aucune époque peutêtre ne fut plus riche en sainteté monastique que cette fin du XIᵉ siècle et ce début du XIIᵉ où se développent les instituts nouveaux: Chartreux, Grandmontains, Fontrevistes, Cistercians, Prémontrés, sans parler des congrégations ou chapitres de chanoines réguliers."

realized, might regard Henry of Blois, who was both knight and monk, as a "monstrous" anomaly.[229] But this kind of aristocratic monk was typical of the Cluniac order, which at this time, under its great Abbot Peter the Venerable,[230] was expanding in numbers, wealth, and power.

Henry I's personal predilection for Cluny is well known. Not only did his great foundation of Reading Abbey have a Cluniac observance,[231] but Henry was one of the greatest benefactors of Cluny itself in the period. He assigned an annual gift from royal revenues to Cluny, and along with Alfonso VI of Castile was regarded as the *"constructor"* of the new basilica at Cluny.[232] In the 1120's he also appears as a patron and protector of the new monastic orders in England and Normandy: Savigny, Tiron, the Cistercians, the order of Fontrevalt.[233] Especially remarkable is the role of Henry and the royal entourage in the founding of houses of Austin canons.[234] The conservative monastic reaction against Gregorian doctrine ideally suited Henry's attitude to the church. Like his father, he was a pious man who wanted to found and support establishments of religious, but at the same time assumed that the government of England, including the English Church, should be left to himself.

In the last decade of Henry's reign, the papacy finally complied with his demands and seldom interfered in church-state relations in England. During the greater part of the period

[229] Henry of Huntingdon, *De contemptu*, 315: "Henricus . . . qui futurus est novum quoddam monstrum ex integro et corrupto compositum, scilicet monachus et miles."

[230] The best study of Peter is by J. Leclercq: *Peter le Venerable* (1946).

[231] Knowles, *Monastic Order*, 282.

[232] On Henry's gifts to Cluny, Bernard and Bruel, *Recueil des chartes de Cluny*, no. 4015; J-L, 7476; Round, *CDF*, nos. 1383-1389. On Henry as "constructor" of the new basilica at Cluny, Bernard and Bruel, no. 4183. See also G. Duby, in *Annales Econ. Soc. Civ.*, n.s., VII (1952), pp. 165 and 167, n. 3.

[233] Henry's gifts to Savigny: Round, *CDF*, nos. 795 and 797. To Fontrevalt, *ibid.*, no. 1460. On Henry and the early Cistercian foundations in England, A. Cooke in *EHR*, VIII, 650-1.

[234] See Dickinson, *Austin Canons*, 108-131, esp. 128-130.

1109-1135, the papacy was under duress of one kind or another. Until 1122, it had to be wary of antagonizing the English King too much, lest he become the ally of his German son-in-law in the latter's war against the Hildebrandine popes. In 1130 came a new danger with the double papal election of that year and the resulting schism of Anacletus,[235] which necessitated Innocent II's appeal to the English King and Church for support.[236] Only Honorius II (1124-1130) enjoyed peace and security. The calm prevailing during Honorius' pontificate was not, however, entirely fortuitous. Under his leadership a fundamental change in papal policy occurred. A much more conciliatory attitude towards the secular rulers of Western Europe emerged in the papal curia, as a new generation of cardinals, more interested in slow administrative improvements than in fundamental ideological conflicts, came to power. The profound peace in church-state relations throughout almost all of Western Europe, beginning with Honorius' pontificate, marks the end of the reforming papacy and the Gregorian revolution and the beginning of a new era.[237]

England was no exception to this new papal policy. Calixtus II had tended to continue Paschal's policy of interference in the affairs of the English Church. He had firmly supported Thurstan, had summoned English as well as French bishops to the Council of Rheims in 1119,[238] and when William of Corbeil came to Rome in 1123 to obtain his pallium, had exacted from him an oath of "obedience in all things that the Pope imposed upon him."[239] Honorius began by following

---

[235] A. Fliche, *Histoire de l'Église*, IX, pt. 1 (1948), 50ff.

[236] J-L, 7407 (1130). Similar letters to Germany at the same time: J-L, 7403, 7411, 7413.

[237] On the decline of reforming ideals in the papal curia during the pontificate of Honorius II, see the excellent study by H. W. Klewitz, "Das Ende des Reformpapsttums," *DA*, 3 (1939), 371ff. Cf. Fliche, *op.cit.*, 49: ". . . jamais la paix entre l'Église et les États n'a été aussi profonde."

[238] J-L, 6722, 6723, 6724 for summoning of English bishops; J-L, 6725 for French bishops.

[239] *A-S Chron. E, s.a.* 1123. According to the Peterborough chronicler,

this policy and sent his legate Cardinal John of Crema to hold a reform council in England in 1125. But after the English Primate had protested against the precedence which John had taken over him,[240] Honorius gave up the attempt to reform the English Church through the conciliar activities of legates. He informed the ecclesiastical and lay magnates in England and Scotland that he had appointed the English Primate as his legate in those countries.[241]

It would be a mistake to exaggerate the extent of papal surrender to the demands of the English King and episcopate and to regard the appointment of Archbishop William as legate as papal recognition of the unique quasi-independence of the English Church from Rome. The English Primate was still after all the representative of the papacy: "*apostolicae auctoritatis suffragio.*"[242] In France and Germany as well as in England, in this period, the papacy was following a policy of occasionally appointing native bishops as papal legates.[243] Nevertheless, the appointment of William as papal legate does mark a point of departure in papal policy towards the English Church. Honorius II also virtually employed Abbot Hugh of Reading, who was on very good terms with the King, as a papal legate. In 1128 the Pope summoned Hugh to Rome,[244] and in sending him back to his monastery in the following year placed him in charge of collecting Peter's Pence in England.[245] Innocent II continued to impose this office on

---

Thurstan tried to prevent the grant of the pallium to William. *HC*, 202, gives just the opposite account: Thurstan intercedes with Calixtus on William's behalf.

[240] *JW*, 12.

[241] J-L, 7284. Cf. J-L 7366 (1129) where Honorius addresses William as "apostolicae sedis legatus."

[242] Honorius II (1126) in *PU*, II, no. 9.

[243] In 1108, Paschal II made Gerard of Angoulême permanent legate in north-western France (J-L, 6262). On Gerard, see H. Claude in *Mélanges Saint Bernard* (1954), 8off. In 1137 Innocent II granted legatine power to Adalbert of Trier (J-L, 7852). According to *HC*, 178, William of Exeter requested legatine power in Britain for Ralph from Calixtus II in c.1120, but Calixtus refused. No other source mentions this incident.

[244] *PU*, III, no. 15 (1128). [245] *PU*, III, nos. 22 and 23.

Hugh.[246] These acts mark the final step in the papal curia's departure from Paschal II's policy of attempting the overthrow of the Anglo-Norman church-state system. They indicate a new desire on the part of the Pope to achieve an understanding with the English King which would gain certain concessions for Rome but which would not seriously impair royal authority over the English Church.

This conclusion is not at all vitiated by the rapid increase in papal confirmations and grants to English churches and monasteries during the last two decades of Henry's reign. Rather these papal privileges reveal clearly the nature of the settlement between the English King and the papal curia.

In an age in which the privileges of ecclesiastical corporations throughout Western Europe were written down and collected, it was only to be expected that churches and monasteries should turn to Rome for confirmation of their rights and possessions. The English Church was not behind the churches of France and Germany in this process, but it does not appear either that the numerous English appeals to the curia in the 1120's and 1130's for confirmation of privileges were in any way exceptional.[247]

The *arenga* of these papal confirmations frequently contains Gregorian claims to universal papal jurisdiction. The holy Roman and apostolic Church is the *caput et cardo ecclesiarum omnium*;[248] its office is to provide for the peace and advantage of all churches;[249] its *honor* must be preserved so that it may protect the *dignitas* of every church.[250] The papal confirmations sometimes afforded opportunity for legislation along the lines of reform principles, which were contrary to current practice in church-state relations in England. In confirming the temporal possessions of the Church of Canterbury in 1126, at the request of Archbishop William, Honorius II

---

[246] *PU*, III, no. 25.

[247] See especially the large number of confirmations for churches and monasteries in France and in Germany as well as in England by Innocent II in J-L, I, 852-61, *passim*.

[248] *PU*, II, no. 7.   [249] *PU*, II, no. 14.   [250] *PU*, II, no. 13.

forbade the *ius spolii*.[251] He granted the right of free elections of their abbot to the monks of St. Mary's in Kenilworth in a confirmation of privileges.[252] He ignored the royal government and directly ordered the lay magnates of the diocese of Lincoln to preserve the temporalities of the canons of the cathedral.[253] The confirmations allowed the papacy occasionally to legislate for the internal organization of the English Church. Calixtus freed the Church of St. Peter and St. Paul from domination by Christ Church.[254] In taking the monastic houses of Westminster, Reading, and Durham under papal protection, he removed them partially or completely from episcopal control.[255]

This papal legislation for the English Church was only made, however, at the request of the churches or monasteries which stood to benefit from it, or at the request of the great ecclesiastics or lay magnates who were their founders or benefactors. The curialist bishops Roger of Salisbury and Alexander of Lincoln,[256] and lay magnates like Humphrey of Bohun,[257] as well as bishops in high favor at Rome, such as Thurstan and Robert of Hereford,[258] requested the papal confirmations. In several instances the papal chancery issued these documents during, or shortly after, the visit in Rome of an English bishop or abbot—Herbert Losinga, William of Corbeil, Thurstan, Hugh of Reading.[259] Founders of new religious houses, even the King, sought papal confirmation of the possessions and liberties they had bestowed on their foundations.[260]

---

[251] *PU*, II, no. 9.   [252] *PU*, III, no. 14.   [253] *PU*, II, no. 10.
[254] *PU*, I, no. 10.
[255] *PU*, I, no. 17; II, no. 5 and no. 11; III, no. 29.
[256] *PU*, II, no. 7 and J-L, 7241.   [257] *PU*, I, no. 15.
[258] Robert: *PU*, I, no. 16; II, no. 14. Thurstan: *PU*, I, no. 14; III, no. 13, no. 24.
[259] Herbert Losinga went to Rome in 1117 not only as a royal envoy, but also to obtain papal confirmation for the privileges of the Church of Norwich (*First Reg. of Norwich Cathedral Priory*, ed. Saunders, pp. 54-56). The papal confirmations granted on behalf of the three other English ecclesiastics mentioned are also approximately concomitant with their visits to Rome.
[260] Confirmation of privileges and possession of Reading at request of

In making these confirmations the papacy was not trying to diminish the efficacy of royal charters. The papal curia conceded that royal and papal grants worked concurrently,[261] and that the protection of the churches of the kingdom was a function of royal dignity as well as papal authority.[262] Although Henry was at one time concerned lest Honorius infringe upon his rights in his own foundation of Reading,[263] he did not regard the papal confirmations in general as threats to royal control over the church. In his reign, apart from the papal grants sought and obtained by both sides in the York-Canterbury dispute, it was not yet apparent that a class of documents had been issued by the papal chancery which would inevitably require litigation at Rome.

In the latter years of Henry's reign, the papacy spoke of the pious King only in glowing terms. He was a "beloved son" and "glorious king" who by his support of Innocent against Anacletus had sustained the holy Roman Church.[264] He was even kept informed of papal policy in Wales.[265] Henry in his turn was inclined to be conciliatory and moderate in his relations with the English higher clergy and with Rome. His major aim had always been the conquest of Normandy, and he was no doubt grateful to the papacy for sanctioning this conquest, and for dissolving the marriage of William Clito to the daughter of his enemy, Count Fulk of Anjou.[266] By the 1120's he was an old man, only interested in securing the succession to the throne for his dynasty. In order to achieve this, he could not afford to antagonize the papacy and the higher

---

Henry: *PU*, III, no. 9. Confirmation of possessions of new Augustinian house of Kirkham founded by a lay magnate: *PU*, III, no. 10.

[261] *PU*, III, no. 8: "regia libertate donatum apostolica quoque libertate donamus" (to Bury St. Edmunds, 1123).

[262] *PU*, I, no. 17: "Et quoniam tuae regiae dignitatis est ecclesias in tuo regno constitutas diligere, exaltare et eas a malignantium infestatione defensare" (to Westminster, 1133).

[263] See Henry's letter to Honorius (1128): *PU*, III, no. 16.

[264] *PU*, III, no. 5 and no. 9 (Calixtus) and no. 27 (Innocent).

[265] J-L, 7367 (1129).

[266] A. L. Poole, *op.cit.*, 125-6.

clergy in England. He was content that the bishops and abbots should join the lay magnates in swearing fealty to his
daughter Mathilda at London in 1128.[267] The death of Robert
of Meulan in 1118 and the influence upon the King of new
favorites, Bishop Roger of Salisbury and Abbot Anselm of
St. Edmundsbury, must have also encouraged him towards
a softening in his attitude towards the church.[268] Not only did
he allow John of Crema to hold a reform council in England,
but he seems to have taken a less prominent part in all the
English councils of the 1120's than he had in previous councils.[269] He supported Bishop Urban of Llandaff in his appeal
to Rome against Bernard of St. David's,[270] and reluctantly
allowed Abbot Hugh of Reading to obey Honorius' summons
to the papal curia.[271] Henry warmly welcomed Hugh the
Templar;[272] he was on friendly terms with St. Bernard;[273]
and, as has been seen, he gained the gratitude of Innocent II
by supporting him in the papal schism of 1130.[274] In 1129,
Henry's conciliatory policy towards the papacy resulted in his
offer to make up any arrears in Peter's Pence from the royal
treasury.[275]

By the 1130's the controversies of the first decade of Henry's reign had thus completely given way to agreement and
cooperation between the leaders of church and state. On the
one hand, the King, inspired by the traditional piety of his
house, had emerged as a great patron and protector of the

[267] *JW*, 26-7.   [268] See above, pp. 299-300.
[269] *JW*, 20-1, 23-5 and *A-S Chron. E, s.a.* 1129.
[270] *JW*, 28-9.
[271] Henry at first refused to allow Hugh to obey Honorius' summons (*PU*,
III, nos. 16, 18). But it is evident from *PU*, III, nos. 21 and 22, that he
eventually allowed Hugh to go to Rome.
[272] *A-S Chron. E, s.a.* 1128.
[273] See St. Bernard's letter to Henry on behalf of Innocent II: *MPL* 182,
ep. 138. St. Bernard attested one of Henry's charters to Cluny (Farrer,
"Itinerary," no. 640).
[274] *PU*, III, no. 27. Innocent to Henry (1133) thanking him for his support.
[275] *PU*, III, no. 23. Hugh of Reading to Honorius II (1129): ". . . Si
debitores reddere negligerent, ipse rex de thesauro suo eas mihi redderet ex
integro."

church, especially of the monastic order. On the other hand, the Gregorian revolution had run its course as the reforming papacy was replaced by the papacy of the high Middle Ages, which limited its endeavors to establishing the administrative and jurisdictional supremacy of the Roman curia over the Western Church. Previously Urban II had indicated a reluctance to pursue reform to its doctrinaire limits and to raise troubling questions about church-state relations within various countries. From the time of Honorius II's pontificate this moderate attitude became dominant in the papal curia. As long as the English King rendered to Peter the things that were Peter's—Peter's Pence, occasional appeals to Rome, papal privileges for English bishoprics and abbeys—the authority over the English Church exercised by the Conqueror and his sons would not be challenged.

Henry I had found that he could not entirely overcome the tendency of the English higher clergy to look towards Rome, which was a legacy of Anselm's pontificate. In order to maintain his effective control over the English Church, the King had to come to an understanding with the papacy which would give some minor concessions to Rome, while leaving church-state relations fundamentally unchanged. In other words, he attempted to repeat the victory he had gained in 1107. Because of the decay of the Gregorian reform movement in the last decade of Henry's reign, the King was able to achieve his aim. By 1135 the English Church had been set on the miserable road to Becket's martyrdom.

5. SUMMARY AND CONCLUSION

AT THE TIME of the death of Henry I in 1135 the royal authority over the English Church, which William I and Lanfranc had established, had not been removed nor even fundamentally limited. The Gregorian world-revolution had failed to alter the church-state system of the Conqueror and his sons.

Anselm had attacked this system from the early years of

5. Summary and Conclusion

his pontificate, but in view of the bitter opposition of William II and nearly all the bishops and greater abbots, and the refusal of Urban II to support him against the King, the Primate was unable to reform the English Church along Gregorian lines.

It was not until the pontificate of Paschal II, a fanatical high Gregorian, in the first decade of Henry I's reign, that a concerted attempt was made by the papacy to overthrow William I's church-state system. Paschal adopted the same intransigent attitude towards Henry I that Gregory VII had taken in the German investiture controversy with Henry IV. Because of Henry I's piety and friendly attitude towards him, Anselm did not give Paschal complete support in the English investiture controversy until 1103. Then the Archbishop discovered that the King's opposition to the more fundamental of the Gregorian doctrines was as complete and inflexible as his predecessors' attitude.

Only in the realm of theory was Henry finally willing to make concessions. He proposed to give up lay investiture, with its implications of theocratic monarchy, if he could maintain his real authority over the bishops and abbots through retention of ecclesiastical homage. Paschal eventually accepted this solution and gave up his struggle to overthrow the Anglo-Norman church-state system partly because of the violent opposition to Gregorian doctrines in England, partly because of the pressure of other aspects of papal policy. After Anselm's death, the King completely restored his authority over the English Church, with the constant support of the English primates, and with the steady diminution of interference from Rome, where Gregorian ideals rapidly lost their hold.

Although Anselm failed to achieve his major aims, his pontificate did have a strong effect on the subsequent development of the English Church, especially by bringing the Anglo-Norman ecclesiastics, for the first time, into close contact with the papal court. This tendency was to continue and expand during the twelfth century, aided by temporary weakening of royal authority during Stephen's reign, and by the concession of freedom of appeals to Rome, which the papacy won from Henry II after Becket's martyrdom.

The Gregorian ideal of freedom of the church, however, was never to be realized in England. It was for this ideal that Becket struggled against Henry II, who attempted in the Constitutions of Clarendon of 1164 to reassert royal authority over the English Church after the laxity of Stephen's reign. By Becket's day, however, the Gregorian doctrines had long since become archaic, and not even the papacy supported him in his bitter controversy with the King and his episcopal colleagues. The papacy used Becket's martyrdom to expand its own jurisdiction over the English Church, but it was willing to leave most of the provisions of the Constitutions of Clarendon unchallenged. By the end of Henry II's reign the pattern of church-state relations in medieval England was fully established. Royal authority over the English Church was only limited by papal jurisdiction in certain spheres, while the ideal of *libertas ecclesiae* became a meaningless platitude. This pattern of church-state relations had already been evident in the latter part of Henry I's reign. Henry II was right in claiming that he was only attempting to restore the church-state system of his grandfather's time.

The failure of Anselm and Paschal II to overthrow the church-state system of William I and Lanfranc was thus decisive for the subsequent history of the English Church. In the long-range perspective, therefore, the controversies over church-state relations between 1089 and 1135 were far more important than the famous struggle between Henry II and Thomas Becket. By 1135 the die was cast, and Becket, the last Gregorian, was doomed to inevitable failure.

SELECT BIBLIOGRAPHY

PRIMARY SOURCES
Manuscripts

British Museum
    Add. 28. 188
    Add. 8166
    Cotton Claudius A. I
    Cotton Claudius A. III
    Cotton Claudius E. V
    Cotton Cleopatra E. I
    Cotton Domitian A. V
    Cotton Tiberius A. IX
    Cotton Titus A. IX
    Cotton Titus A. XIX
    Cotton Titus D. XXIV
    Cotton Vitellius A. III
    Cotton Vitellius A. XII
    Harl. 633
    Harl. 692
    Harl. 1005
    Royal 11.D. VIII

Bodleian Library, Oxford
    Arch. Selden B. 16
    Bodley 271
    Bodley 561
    Bodley 810
    Digby 65
    Digby 96
    D'Orville 46
    Laud Misc. 363
    Laud Misc. 547

University Library, Cambridge
    Kl. IV. 6 (2021)

Corpus Christi College, Cambridge
    C.C.C. 146
    C.C.C. 415

Public Library, Rouen
    Rouen Y. 7

Select Bibliography

PRINTED SOURCES

R. Anstruther, ed., *Epistolae Herberti de Losinga, Osberti de Clare, et Edmeri* (Brussels, 1846)

T. Arnold, ed., *Historia Anglorum* by Henry of Huntingdon (*R.S.*, London, 1879)

———, *Symeonis Monachi Opera Omnia*, 2 vols. (*R.S.*, London, 1882)

A. Bernard and A. Bruel, eds., *Recueil des chartes de Cluny*, 6 vols. (Paris, 1876-1903)

E. Bernheim et al., eds., *MGH, Libelli de Lite Imperatorum et Pontificium*, 3 vols. (Berlin, 1892-1897)

G. Bessin, ed., *Concilia Rotomagensis Provinciae* (Rouen, 1727)

M. Bloch, ed., *Vita Sancti Edwardi, Analecta Bollandiana* 41 (Paris, 1923)

M. Bouquet, ed., *Recueil des Historiens des Gaules et de la France*, 24 vols. (Paris, 1840-1904)

E. Caspar, ed., *Register Gregors VII, MGH Epistolae*, vol. 2, fasc. 1 (Berlin, 1920)

Congregation of St. Maur, eds., *Gallia Christiana in provincias ecclesiasticas distributa*, 16 vols. (Paris, 1856-1899)

H.H.E. Craster, ed., "A Contemporary Record of the Pontificate of Ranulph Flambard," *Archaeologia Aeliana*, 4th ser., vol. VII (1930)

L. d'Achery, ed., *Veterum Scriptorum Spicilegium*, 3 vols. (Paris, 1723)

———, and J. Mabillon, eds., *Acta Sanctorum Ordinis S. Benedicti*, 9 vols. (Paris, 1668-1701)

R. R. Darlington, ed., *Vita Wulfstani* (*Camden Soc.*, 3rd ser., vol. 40. London, 1928)

C. W. David, ed., *De Expurgatione Lyxbonensi* (New York, 1936)

H.W.C. Davis, *Regesta Regum Anglo-Normannorum*, I (Oxford, 1913)

D. C. Douglas, ed., *The Domesday Monachorum of Christ Church Canterbury* (London, 1944)

———, *Feudal Documents from Bury St. Edmund's* (London, 1932)

W. Dugdale, ed., *Monasticon Anglicanum*, new ed., 6 vols. (London, 1846)

E. Edwards, ed., *Liber Monasterii de Hyda* (*R.S.*, London, 1866)

W. Farrer, ed., *Early Yorkshire Charters*, vol. I (Edinburgh, 1941)

Select Bibliography

————, "An Outline Itinerary of King Henry the First," *EHR*, xxxiv (1919)

W. Foster, ed., *Registrum Antiquissimum of Lincoln* (Lincoln Record Society, vol. 27, 1931)

J. A. Giles, ed., *Lanfranci Opera*, 2 vols. (London, 1884)

E. M. Goulburn and H. Symonds, *The Life, Letters and Sermons of Bishop Herbert de Losinga*, 2 vols. (London, 1878)

B. Guérard, ed., *Cartulaire de L'Abbaye de Saint-Bertin* (Paris, 1840)

B. Hagenmeyer, ed., *Die Kreuzugsbriefe aus dem Jahren 1088-1100* (Innsbruck, 1901)

————, *Fulcheri Carnotensis Historia Hierosolymitana* (Innsbruck, 1913)

L. Halphen, ed., *Recueil des Actes de Lothaire et de Louis V* (Paris, 1908)

N.E.S.A. Hamilton, ed., *Willelmi Malmesbiriensis Monachi De Gestis Pontificum Anglorum Libri Quinque* (R.S., London, 1870)

T. Hearne, ed., *Heming's Chartulary* (London, 1720)

W. Henderson, ed., *Liber Pontificalis Christopher Bainridge* (Surtees Soc. 61, Durham, 1875)

W. Holtzmann, ed., *Papsturkunden in England*, in *Abh. d. Ges. d. Wiss. zu Göttingen, Phil.-Hist. Kl.*, I: 1930-1, II: 1935, III: 1952

————, ed., "Der Traktat de Simoniacis des Abtes Gilbert von Westminster," *Neues Archiv* 50 (1933)

———— and E. Kemp, eds., *Papal Decretals of the Twelfth Century* (Lincoln Record Society, 47, 1954)

R. Howlett, ed., *Chronicles of the Reign of Stephen, Henry II, and Richard II*, 4 vols. (vol. III: *Gesta Stephani*) (R.S., London, 1884-1889)

J. Hunter, ed., *Historiala de primordiis episcopatus Somersetensis* (*Camden Soc.*, vol. 8, 1840)

————, *Magnum Rotulum Scacarri de anno tricesimo-primo regni Henrici Primi* (London, 1833)

P. Jaffe, S. Lowenfeld et al., eds., *Regesta Pontificum Romanorum*, I (Leipzig, 1885)

M. R. James, ed., *Walter Map De Nugis Curialium* (Oxford, 1914)

I. H. Jeayes, ed., *Descriptive Catalogue of the Charters and Muniments belonging to the Marquis of Anglesey* (William Salt Society, 1937)

C. Johnson, ed., *Dialogus de Scaccario* (Edinburgh, 1950)

———— and H. Cronne, *Regesta Regum Anglo-Normannorum*, II (Oxford, 1956)

W. H. Rich Jones, ed., *Register of St. Osmund*, 2 vols. (*R.S.*, London, 1883)

———— and W. D. Macray, eds., *Sarum Charters and Documents* (*R.S.*, London, 1891)

J. Lair, ed., *De Moribus et Actis Primorum Normanniae Ducum*, by Dudo of St. Quentin (Paris, 1865)

L. M. Larson, ed. and transl., *The King's Mirror* (New York, 1917)

A. Laveille, ed., *Histoire de la Congrégation de Savigny par Dom Claude Auvry* (*Soc. Hist. Norm*. No. 30, vol. I, Rouen, 1896)

J. Leclercq, ed., *Yves de Chartres. Correspondance*, vol. I (Paris, 1949)

J. W. Legg, ed., *Three Coronation Orders* (London, 1900)

L.G.W. Legg, ed., *English Coronation Records* (London, 1901)

J. Le Patourel, ed., "Reports of the Trial on Pennenden Heath," *Studies Presented to F. M. Powicke* (Oxford, 1948)

A. Le Prevost, ed., *Orderici Vitalis Historiae Ecclesiasticae Libri Tredecim*, 5 vols. (Paris, 1840-1855)

F. Liebermann, ed., *Die Gesetze der Angelsachsen*, 3 vols. (Halle, 1903-1916)

————, *Quadripartitus* (Halle, 1892)

————, *Ungedruckte anglo-normannische Geschichtsquellen* (Strasbourg, 1879)

F. Lot, ed., *Études Critiques sur l'Abbaye de St. Wandrille* (Paris, 1913)

H. R. Luard, ed., *Annales Monastici*, 5 vols. (*R.S.*, London, 1864-1869)

————, *Historia Anglicana, by Bartholomew Cotton* (*R.S.*, London, 1859)

————, *Lives of Edward the Confessor* (*R.S.*, London, 1858)

J. Mabillon, ed., *Vetera Analecta* (Paris, 1733)

J. Mansi, ed., *Sacrorum Conciliorum Nova Collectio*, 31 vols. (Venice, 1757-1798)

J. Marx, ed., *Gesta Normannorum Ducum* (*Soc. Hist. Norm.*, Rouen, 1914)

W. T. Mellowes, ed., *The Peterborough Chronicle of Hugh Candidus* (London, 1941)

L. Merlet, ed., "Lettres d'Yves de Chartres et d'autres personnages de son Temps," *Bib. de l'École des Chartes*, XVI (1885)

Select Bibliography

————, *Saint.Yves, évêque de Chartres. Lettres* (Chartres, 1886)

J. P. Migne, ed., *Patrologiae Latinae Cursus Completus*, 222 vols. (esp. vols. 139, 142, 145, 151, 154, 155, 157, 159, 161, 162, 179) (Paris, 1844-1864)

L. A. Muratori, ed., *Rerum Italicarum Scriptores*, new ed., 32 vols. (1900-1942), vol. V: Gaufredus Malaterra, *De Rebus Gestis Rogerii Comitis*

G. H. Pertz, ed., *MGH, Scriptores*, vol. IX (Berlin, 1851)

J. von Pflugk-Harttung, ed., *Acta Pontificum Romanorum Inedita*, vol. I (Tübingen, 1881)

C. Plummer and J. Earle, eds., *Two of the Saxon Chronicles Parallel*, 2 vols. (Oxford, 1892-1899)

J. Raine, ed., *Historians of the Church of York*, 3 vols. (*R.S.*, London, 1886)

Record Commission, *Domesday Book*, vols. I and II (London, 1783)

H. T. Riley, ed., *Chronica Monasterii Sancti Albani*, 12 vols. (*R.S.*, London, 1863-1876)

J. C. Robertson, ed., *Materials for the History of Thomas Becket*, 5 vols. (*R.S.*, London, 1875-1885)

J. H. Round, ed., *Calendar of Documents Preserved in France*, I (London, 1889)

M. Rule, ed., *Eadmeri Historia Novorum in Anglia* (*R.S.*, London, 1884)

H. Saunders, ed., *First Register of Norwich Cathedral Priory* (Norwich Record Society, XI, 1939)

E. P. Sauvage, ed., "Vitae BB. Vitalis et Gaufridi," *Analecta Bollandiana*, I (Paris, 1882) .

F. S. Schmitt, ed., *S. Anselmi Opera Omnia*, 5 vols. (London, 1946-1951)

J. Shepton, ed. and transl., *The Saga of King Sverri of Norway* (London, 1899)

J. Stevenson, ed., *Chronicon Monasterii de Abingdon*, 2 vols. (*R.S.*, London, 1858)

W. Stubbs, ed., *Opera Historica of Ralph de Diceto*, 2 vols. (London, 1876)

————, *Memorials of St. Dunstan* (*R.S.*, London, 1874)

————, *Willelmi Malmesbiriensis Monachi De Gestis Regum Anglorum* (*R.S.*, London, 1889)

J. Tait, ed., *The Chartulary or Register of St. Werburgh, Chester* (Chetham Society, n.s., vol. 79. Manchester, 1920)

Select Bibliography

A. H. Thompson, ed., *Liber Vitae Ecclesiae Dunelmensis* (Surtees Society, vol. 186. Durham, 1923)

B. Thorpe, ed., *Florentii Wigorniensis Monachi Chronicon*, 2 vols. (London, 1848-1849)

R. Twysden, ed., *Historiae Anglicanae Scriptores*, vol. X (London, 1652)

G. Vigfusson and F. York Powell, eds., *Corpus Poeticum Boreale*, 2 vols. (Oxford, 1883)

J. S. Walbran, ed., *Memorials of Fountains Abbey* (Surtees Society, Durham, 1863)

H. Waquet, ed., *Vie de Louis VI le Gros*, by Suger (Paris, 1929)

J.R.H. Weaver, ed., *The Chronicle of John of Worcester* (Oxford, 1908)

H. Wharton, ed., *Anglia Sacra*, 2 vols. (London, 1691)

D. Wilkins, ed., *Concilia Magnae Britanniae et Hiberniae*, vol. I (London, 1737)

E. Williamson, ed., *Letters of Osbert of Clare* (London, 1929)

H. A. Wilson, ed., *The Benedictional of Archbishop Robert* (London, 1902)

————, *The Pontifical of Magdalen College* (London, 1910)

MODERN WORKS

E. Ammann and A. Dumas, *L'Église au pouvoir des laïques (888-1057)* (Paris, 1940)

M. Andrieu, *Les Ordines Romani du haut Moyen-Age* (Louvain, 1931)

F. Barlow, *Durham Jurisdictional Peculiars* (London, 1950)

A. Becker, *Studien zum Investiturproblem in Frankreich* (Saarbrucken, 1955)

E. Bernheim, *Das Wormser Konkordat und seine Vorurkunden* (Breslau, 1906)

————, *Zur Geschichte des Wormser Konkordats* (Göttingen, 1878)

E. Bishop, *Liturgica Historica* (Oxford, 1918)

M. Bloch, *Les Rois Thaumaturges* (Strasbourg, 1924)

T.S.R. Boase, *English Art 1100-1216* (Oxford, 1953)

H. Böhmer, "Das Eigenkirchentum in England," *Festgabe für F. Liebermann* (Halle, 1921)

————, *Kirche und Staat in England und in der Normandie im XI. und XII. Jahrhundert* (Leipzig, 1899)

C.N.L. Brooke, "The Composition of the Chapter of St. Paul's, 1086-1163," *Cambridge Historical Journal*, X (1951)

326

Select Bibliography

————, "Gregorian Reform in Action: Clerical Marriage in England 1050-1200," *Cambridge Historical Journal,* XII (1956)

————, "Married men among the English higher clergy, 1066-1200," *Cambridge Historical Journal,* XII (1956)

Z. N. Brooke, "Lay Investiture and Its Relation to the Conflict of Empire and Papacy," *Proc. Br. Acad.,* XXV (1939)

————, "Pope Gregory VII's demand for fealty from William the Conqueror," *EHR,* XXVI (1911)

————, *The English Church and the Papacy* (Cambridge, 1931)

J. Buhot, "L'Abbaye normande de Savigny," *Le Moyen Age* 46 (1936)

E. Caspar, "Gregor VII in seinen Briefen," *Historische Zeitschrift* 130 (1924)

F. Chalandon, *Histoire de la première Croisade,* 2 vols. (Paris, 1907)

H. M. Chew, *Ecclesiastical Tenants-in-Chief* (Oxford, 1932)

R. Crozet, "Le Voyage de Urban II (1095-1096)," *Rev. Historique* 179 (1937)

R. R. Darlington, "Ecclesiastical Reform in the Late Old English Period," *EHR,* 51 (1936)

C. W. David, *Robert Curthose* (Cambridge, Mass., 1920)

————, "The Claim of Henry I to Be Called Learned," *Haskins Anniversary Essays* (Cambridge, Mass., 1929)

R.H.C. Davis, "The Monks of St. Edmund, 1021-1148," *History* 40 (1955)

M. de Bouard, "De la Neustrie Carolingienne à la Normandie féodale," *BIHR* 28 (1955)

J. Dhondt, *Étude sur la naissance des principautés territoriales en France* (Ghent, 1948)

J. C. Dickinson, *The Origins of the Austin Canons* (London, 1950)

D. C. Douglas, "The Rise of Normandy," *Proc. Br. Acad.* 33 (1947)

F. Dressler, *Petrus Damiani* (*Studia Anselmiana* 34, Rome, 1954)

M. Dueball, *Der Supremastreit zwischen den Erzdiözesen Canterbury und York, 1070-1126* (*Ebering's Hist. Stud.,* Heft 184. Berlin, 1929)

G. Ellard, *Ordination Anointings in the Western Church* (Cambridge, Mass., 1933)

Select Bibliography

A. Esmein, "La question des investitures dans les lettres d'Yves de Chartres," *Bibl. de l'École des Hautes-Études, Sciences Religieuses*, I (1889)

R. W. Eyton, *The Antiquities of Shropshire*, 12 vols. (London, 1854-1860)

A. Fliche, *La Réforme Grégorienne*, 3 vols. (Louvain, 1924-1927)

————, *La Réforme Grégorienne et La Reconquête Chrétienne* (Paris, 1940)

————, "L'influence de Grégoire VII et des idées grégoriennes sur la pensée de Saint Bernard," *Saint Bernard et son temps* (Dijon, 1924)

————, "Y-a-t-il eu en France et en Angleterre une querelle des investitures?", *Rev. Bénédictine* 46 (1934)

R. Foreville, *L'Église et la Royauté en Angleterre sous Henri II Plantagenet* (Paris, 1943)

P. Fournier and G. le Bras, *Histoire des Collections canoniques en Occident*, 2 vols. (Paris, 1931)

E. A. Freeman, *William Rufus*, 2 vols. (Oxford, 1882)

W. H. Frere, *English Pontificals in Manuscript* (London, 1911)

P. Funk, "Der fragliche Anonymous von York," *Hist. Jahrbuch* 55 (1935)

V. H. Galbraith, "The Literacy of the Medieval English Kings," *Proc. Br. Acad.* 21 (1935)

K. Hallinger, *Gorze-Kluny*, 2 vols. (*Studia Anselmiana*, XXII-XXIII. Rome, 1950)

————, "Zur geistigen Welt der Anfänge Klunys," *Deutsches Archiv* 10 (1954)

C. H. Haskins, *Norman Institutions* (Cambridge, Mass., 1918)

C. J. Hefele and H. Leclercq, *Histoire des Conciles*, vol. V (Paris, 1912-1913)

E. K. Henningham, "The Genuineness of the *Vita Aedwardi Regis*," *Speculum* 21 (1946)

A. Hofmeister, "Das Wormser Konkordat. Zum Streit und seine Bedeutung," *Festschrift Dietrich Schäfer* (Jena, 1915)

K. Hoffman, *Der "Dictatus Papae" Gregors VII* (Paderborn, 1933)

W. Holtzmann, "Bohemund von Antiochen und Alexius I," *Neues Archiv* 50 (1933)

R. S. Hoyt, *The Royal Demesne in English Constitutional History* (Ithaca, 1951)

Select Bibliography

P. Imbart de la Tour, "Les paroisses rurales dans l'ancienne France," *Rev. Historique*, vols. 67 and 68 (1898)

———, *Les Élections Épiscopales dans l'Église de France du IXe au XIIe Siècle* (Paris, 1890)

A. O. Johnsen, "Nicolaus Brekespear and the Norwegian Church Province, 1153," *The Norseman*, XI, no. 4 (1953)

E. Jordan, "La Politique Ecclésiastique de Roger I," *Le Moyen Âge* 34 (1923)

E. H. Kantorowicz, "Deus per Gratiam, Deus per Naturam," *Harvard Theol. Rev.* 45 (1952)

———, *The King's Two Bodies* (Princeton, 1957)

H. W. Klewitz, "Das Ende des Reformpapsttums," *Deutsches Archiv* 3 (1939)

———, "Die Entstehung des Kardinalcollegiums," *ZRG, KA*, 25 (1936)

D. Knowles, *The Monastic Order in England* (Cambridge, 1940)

S. Kuttner, *Repertorium der Kanonistik (Studi e Testi* 71. Rome, 1937)

G. B. Ladner, "The concepts of 'ecclesia' and 'Christianitas' and their relation to the idea of papal 'plenitudo potestatis' from Gregory VII to Boniface VIII," *Miscellanea Historiae Pontificiae*, XVIII (1954)

———, *Theologie und Politik vor dem Investiturstreit* (Baden, 1935)

J. Laporte, "Les origines du monachisme dans la province de Rouen," *Rev. Mabillon*, XXXI (1941)

J. Leclercq, " 'Simoniaca Heresis,' " *Studi Gregoriani* I (1947)

——— and J. P. Bonnes, *Un maître de la vie spirituelle au XIe siècle. Jean de Fécamp* (Paris, 1946)

J. F. Lemarignier, *Étude sur les privilèges d'exemption et de juris-diction écclesiastiques des abbayes normandes depuis les origines jusqu'en 1140* (Paris, 1937)

A. L'Huillier, *Vie de Saint Hughes* (Solesmes, 1888)

F. Liebermann, "Anselm von Canterbury und Hugo von Lyons," *Historische Aufsätze G. Waitz Gewidmet* (Berlin, 1886)

———, "Lanfranc and the Antipope," *EHR*, 16 (1901)

———, "Notes on the Textus Roffensis," *Archael. Cantiana* XXIII (1898)

———, "The Text of Henry I's Coronation Charter," *TRHS*, VIII (1894)

Select Bibliography

F. Liebermann, *Ueber das Englische Rechtsbuch Leges Henrici* (Halle, 1901)

———, *Ueber die Leges Edwardi Confessoris* (Halle, 1896)

F. Lot, *Fideles ou Vassaux?* (Paris, 1904)

S. Lowenfeld, "Der Dictatus Papae Gregors VII," *Neues Archiv* 16 (1891)

W. Lunt, *The Financial Relations of the Papacy with England to 1327* (Cambridge, Mass., 1939)

A. J. Macdonald, *Lanfranc* (Oxford, 1926)

L. Maître, *Les Écoles Épiscopales et Monastiques en Occident avant les Universités* (Paris, 1924)

H. K. Mann, *Lives of the Popes*, vol. 8 (London, 1910)

G. Meyer von Knonau, *Jahrbücher des Deutschen Reiches unter Heinrich IV und Heinrich V*, 7 vols. (Leipzig, 1890-1909)

E. Miller, *The Abbey and Bishopric of Ely* (Cambridge, 1951)

C. Mirbt, *Die Publizistik im Zeitalter Gregors VII* (Leipzig, 1894)

H. Mitteis, *Lehnrecht und Staatsgewalt* (Weimar, 1933)

S. Mochi-Onory, *Fonti Canonistische* (Rome, 1951)

B. Monod, *Essai sur les Rapports de Paschal II avec Philippe I* (Paris, 1907)

M. Morgan, *The English Lands of the Abbey of Bec* (Oxford, 1946)

F. Novati, "Les rapports de l'Italie et de la France au XIe siècle," *Comptes rendus 1910, Académie des Inscriptions et Belles-Lettres*

H. S. Offler, "William of St. Calais," *Trans. of Architect. and Archeol. Soc. of Durham and Northumberland*, X (1950)

———, "The *de injusta vexatione Willelmi Episcopi*," *EHR*, 56 (1951)

W. Page, "Churches of the Domesday Survey," *Archaeologia* 66 (1914-1915)

S. Painter, *Studies in the History of the English Feudal Barony*, *Johns Hopkins Studies*, vol. 61 (Baltimore, 1943)

R. Pfister, *Études sur le règne de Robert le Pieux* (Paris, 1885)

A. L. Poole, *From Domesday Book to Magna Carta* (Oxford, 1951)

E. Porée, *Histoire de L'Abbaye de Bec*, 2 vols. (Evreux, 1901)

H. Prentout, *Essai sur les origines et la fondation du Duché de Normandie* (Caen, 1911)

———, *Études Critiques sur Dudo* (Caen, 1916)

———, *Études sur Richard IIe* (Caen, 1929)

Select Bibliography

J. O. Prestwich, "War and Finance in the Anglo-Norman State," *TRHS*, 5th ser., IV (1954)

J. Raine and W. H. Dixon, *Fasti Eboracenses*, vol. I (London, 1863)

L. Reiss, "The Reissue of Henry I's Coronation Charter," *EHR*, 41 (1926)

R. L. Graeme Ritchie, *The Normans in Scotland* (London, 1954)

J. A. Robinson, *Gilbert Crispin* (Cambridge, 1911)

A. Rorey, "La Légation d'Hugues, Archevêque de Lyon, sous le Pontificat d'Urbain II," *Rev. des Questions Historiques*, 112 (1929)

J. H. Round, *Feudal England* (London, 1895)

M. Rule, "Eadmer's *Historia Novorum*," *Cambridge Antiquarian Soc. Proc.*, VI (1888)

S. Runciman, *The History of the Crusades*, 3 vols. (Cambridge, 1951-1954)

E. Sackur, *Die Cluniacenser*, 2 vols. (Halle, 1892-1894)

———, "Ueber den Tractatus des Hugo von Fleury," *Neues Archiv* (1891)

A. Scharnagl, *Der Begriff der Investitur in den Quellen und der Literatur des Investiturstreites* (Stuttgart, 1908)

H. Scherrinsky, *Untersuchungen zum sogennanten Anonymous von York* (Berlin, 1939)

T. Schieffer, *Die päpstliche Legaten in Frankreich* (Berlin, 1935)

P. Schmid, *Die Begriff der Kanonischen Wahl in den Anfängen des Investiturstreites* (Stuttgart, 1926)

F. S. Schmitt, "Die Unter Anselm Veranstalte Ausgabe seiner Werke und Briefe," *Scriptorium*, IX (1956)

P. Schmitz, "Le Monachisme Bénédictin au XIIᵉ Siècle," *S. Bernardo, Pub. d. Un. Cattolica del S. Cuore*, n.s. 46 (1954)

P. E. Schramm, *A History of the English Coronation* (Oxford, 1937)

———, *Herrschaftzeichen und Staatssymbolik* (*MGH, Schriften* 13, 3 vols. Stuttgart, 1954-1956)

———, "Ordines-Studien III: Die Krönung in England," *Arch. f. Urkundenforschung* 15 (1938)

———, "Sacerdotium und Regnum in Austausch ihrer Vorrechte, *Studi Gregoriani*, II (1947)

W. Schultze, "Gerhard von Brogn," *Forsch. z. deutsch. Geschichte*, XXV (1885)

K. Setton and M. Baldwin, eds., *A History of the Crusades*, I (Philadelphia, 1955)

B. Smalley, "Gilbert the Universal," *Recherches de théologie ancienne et mediévale*, VII (1935-1936)

A. L. Smith, "John of Bath and Wells," *Downside Review*, LXX (1942)

———, "The Place of Gundulph in the Anglo-Norman Church," *EHR*, 58 (1943)

L. M. Smith, *Cluny in the Eleventh and Twelfth Centuries* (Oxford, 1930)

R. W. Southern, "Lanfranc and Berengar of Tours," *Studies presented to F. M. Powicke* (Oxford, 1948)

———, *The Making of the Middle Ages* (New Haven, 1953)

———, "Ranulf Flambard and Early Anglo-Norman Administration," *TRHS*, 4th ser., XVI (1933)

———, "St. Anselm and Gilbert, Abbot of Westminster," *Medieval and Renaissance Studies*, III (1954)

———, "St. Anselm and His English Pupils," *Medieval and Renaissance Studies*, I (1941)

———, "The First Life of Edward the Confessor," *EHR*, 58 (1943)

J.C.H.R. Steenstrup, *Normandiets Historie under de syv fyrste Hertuger 911-1066* (Copenhagen, 1925)

F. M. Stenton, *Anglo-Saxon England* (Oxford, 1947)

———, *The First Century of English Feudalism* (Oxford, 1932)

L. Stephen and S. Lee, eds., *Dictionary of National Biography*, 63 vols. (London, 1885-1900)

U. Stutz, *Die Eigenkirche als Element des mittelalterlich-germanischen Kirchenrechts* (Berlin, 1895)

J. Sydow, "Untersuchungen zur kurialen Verwaltungsgeschichte im Zeitalter des Reformpapsttums," *Deutsches Archiv*, II (1954)

G. Tellenbach, *Church, State, and Christian Society at the Time of the Investiture Contest* (trans. R. F. Bennett, Oxford, 1940)

H. Tillmann, *Die päpstlichen Legaten in England* (Bonn, 1926)

W. Ullmann, *Growth of Papal Government in the Middle Ages* (Cambridge, 1955)

L. Voss, *Heinrich von Blois* (Berlin, 1932)

P. L. Ward, "The Coronation Ceremony in Medieval England," *Speculum* 14 (1939)

G. H. White, "Financial Administration under Henry I," *TRHS*, 4th ser., VIII (1925)

Select Bibliography

————, "The Household of the Norman Kings," *TRHS*, 4th ser., XXX (1941)

A. L. Williams, *Adversus Judaeos* (Cambridge, 1935)

G. H. Williams, *The Norman Anonymous of 1100 A.D.* (*Harvard Theol. Studies* 18, Cambridge, Mass., 1951)

W. Williams, "William of Dijon," *Downside Review* 52 (1934)

R. B. Yewdale, *Bohemond I, Prince of Antioch* (Princeton, 1922)

INDEX

Index

Index

Index

Index

Index

Index

Index

Index

Index